D0575390

United Resources Library
8216 Lexington Dr
Washington Court 47140

EXPLORING LIVING SYSTEMS

LIFE SCIENCE

Carl M. Raab
Assistant Principal, Supervision: Science Department
Fort Hamilton High School
Brooklyn, New York

Project Coordinator
Carl M. Raab

 GLOBE BOOK COMPANY
A Division of Simon & Schuster
Englewood Cliffs, New Jersey

Exploring Living Systems: Life Science Program
Student Text
Teacher's Resource Manual

Other programs in this series
Exploring Earth and Space: Earth Science
Exploring Matter and Energy: Physical Science

Project Coordinator
Carl M. Raab
Assistant Principal, Supervision: Science Department
Fort Hamilton High School
Brooklyn, New York

Reviewers

Donald D. Abramson
Former Assistant Principal,
  Supervisor of High School
  Science
Martin Van Buren High School
Queens, New York

Sue Beers
Former Biology Teacher
Westhill High School
Stanford, Connecticut

William F. Esner
Director of Science
West Hempstead Public Schools
West Hempstead, New York

Theresa Flynn-Nason
Former Science Teacher
Jonas Salk Middle School
Old Bridge, New Jersey

Imelda L. Gallagher
Science Chairperson
Harborfields High School
Greenlawn, New York

John W. Kominski
Assistant Director of Science
New York City Board of
  Education
New York, New York

Warren H. Loeffler, Jr.
Lead Science Teacher
John Marshall High School
Rochester, New York

J. J. Olenchalk
Science Department
  Chairman
Antioch Senior High School
Antioch, California

See page 480 for photo credits.

Developmental assistance by The Mazer Corporation.

Cover photo credits: Upper left (deer), Tom Edwards/Animals, Animals; Upper right (sunflower), Robert Maier/Animals, Animals; Lower left (x-rays), Joseph Nettis/Photo Researchers; Lower right (diver), FourByFive. Cover Photographs researched by Rhoda Sidney.

GLOBE BOOK COMPANY
A Division of Simon & Schuster, Inc.
Englewood Cliffs, New Jersey 07632

Copyright © 1991 by Globe Book Company
All rights reserved. No part of this book may be reproduced in any form or by any means without permission in writing by the publisher.
Printed in the United States of America
10 9 8 7 6 5
ISBN: 1-55675-802-2

CONTENTS

CHAPTER 1

INTRODUCTION TO LIFE SCIENCE

The scientist shown in Figure 1-1 is doing medical research. She is searching for the causes of a life-threatening disease. The information this scientist collects will become part of the medical community's growing understanding of life-threatening diseases. Perhaps the information that the scientist discovers will lead to a cure for the disease.

Scientists constantly seek answers to life's puzzles. These puzzles include such questions as, How does the human brain work? How are living things similar? How are they different? How did the human body develop? Answers to these and similar questions become part of the growing body of knowledge about the natural world.

Through the years, research scientists have made discoveries that have resulted in improved health and longer life for humans. There are still many health problems in existence that are being researched now. Many of these problems will be solved in the future through medical research.

1-1 What Is Life Science?

■ *Objectives*
☐ *Define life science.*
☐ *List four topics studied in life science.*

The existing knowledge of the natural world, and the process of gathering this knowledge, is called **science.** Thanks to scientific research, people know much about their world and themselves. For example, they know how characteristics, also called traits, are passed from parents

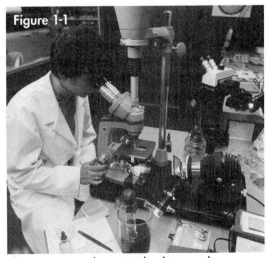

Figure 1-1

This scientist is doing medical research.

Safety in the Science Laboratory

Safety in the laboratory is a very important part of performing science activities. You should always perform activities and dispose of all materials under the direction of your teacher. As you read the activities in this book, you will often see hazard symbols like those in the figure below. Become familiar with the symbols and follow the safety rules for each.

 Poisonous or harmful vapors. Do not breathe vapors.

 Follow animal safety rules.

 Poisonous (toxic). Avoid swallowing. Avoid skin contact. Do not breathe vapors.

 Fragile. Be especially careful.

 Safety goggles must be worn.

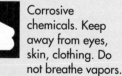 Corrosive chemicals. Keep away from eyes, skin, clothing. Do not breathe vapors.

 Keep hair, clothing, and papers away from flame.

 Lab coat must be worn.

 Electrical shock. Unplug equipment when you are done.

to offspring. They also know what foods make up a healthy diet. Other questions, however, have yet to be answered.

Scientists are working to gather knowledge about all parts of the natural world. This book focuses on **life science,** the study of living things. Scientists who study life science are called **biologists.** Biologists study living things, such as plants and animals. They try to determine what living things are made of, how they work, and how they depend on their surroundings.

Scientists are always adding to the store of scientific information. Often, new discoveries support and expand this information. Sometimes, however, scientists make discoveries that prove that old information is false. In such cases, scientists must change their ideas and search in new directions for solutions to problems.

Section 1-1 Review

Write the definitions for the following terms in your own words.

1. **science**
2. **life science**
3. **biologist**

Answer these questions.

4. In what way is science more than just a collection of knowledge?
5. What are two questions about the natural world that scientists have answered through their discoveries?
6. Suggest two questions that a biologist might try to answer in the future.

1-2 Scientists at Work

■ *Objective*
☐ *Summarize six steps in the scientific method.*

A few years ago, a big bank robbery occurred in New York City. How do you think the detectives found out who did it? They looked at pictures taken by cameras in the bank, questioned witnesses, and collected fingerprints. Then they put together all the information they had gathered. By examining the information carefully, the detectives were able to identify the criminals.

Detectives are not the only people who solve problems by gathering information. Scientists do too. Scientists solve problems by doing research in the laboratory or in the field. A laboratory is a room that is equipped especially for scientific study. Field research takes place outside the laboratory. For example, a scientist who goes to a forest to study tree growth is doing field research. Scientists who collect soil and rock samples for study are also doing field research.

No matter where they conduct their research, scientists follow a process called the **scientific method.** The scientific method is an organized and logical way to solve a problem. The table in Figure 1-2 summarizes the steps in the scientific method. Learning these steps will give you a good idea of how scientists work. Keep in mind that you do not always have to do all the steps. You also may use them in a different order. You will find that the scientific method is an important tool throughout your study of science.

Figure 1-2 The Scientific Method

Steps	Procedure	Example
Identify a problem	Identify a problem that you are interested in studying. State the problem clearly in the form of a question.	You try to grow potted petunia plants in your home, but the plants wilt and die. What caused the petunia plants to die?
State a hypothesis	After stating the problem, suggest a solution. The suggested solution to a problem is called a **hypothesis** (hy-PAHTH-uh-sus).	The petunias died because they did not receive enough light.
Design and conduct an experiment	Test your hypothesis. The procedure scientists use to test a hypothesis is called an **experiment**. Scientists generally design and conduct controlled experiments to test their hypotheses. In a controlled experiment, two or more groups are tested. All of the conditions for each group are the same except for the condition being tested. The condition that differs among the experimental groups is called the **variable** (VER-ee-uh-bul). The group that does not have the experimental condition is called the **control** group. Scientists determine the effect of the variable by comparing the experimental groups to the control group.	Obtain several potted petunia plants of similar size and in the same type of soil. Give each plant the same amount of water. Expose each plant to a different amount of light. Place your control plant in the dark. 

Figure 1-2 The Scientific Method

Steps	Procedure	Example
Gather and record data	Keep careful records of the information you obtain during your experiment. The facts you obtain during an experiment are called **data.** You may organize your data into a diagram, table, or graph.	Each day for two weeks, record in your notebook your descriptions of each plant. Note the color, size, and general health of each plant.
State a conclusion	After you complete your experiment, state a **conclusion** about the results of the experiment. A conclusion is one or more statements that tell whether or not the results of the experiment support your original hypothesis.	After two weeks have passed, review your data. State a conclusion about what amount of light produces the healthiest petunia plant. Write a report in which you explain how you conducted your experiment. State your conclusion in the report.
State new questions	The results of your experiment may identify new problems and lead you to ask new questions. You may need to repeat the steps of the scientific method to answer these questions.	After completing your experiment, ask yourself new questions. Is sunlight better for petunia plants than artificial light? Does the amount of water affect plant growth? Does the type of soil make a difference?

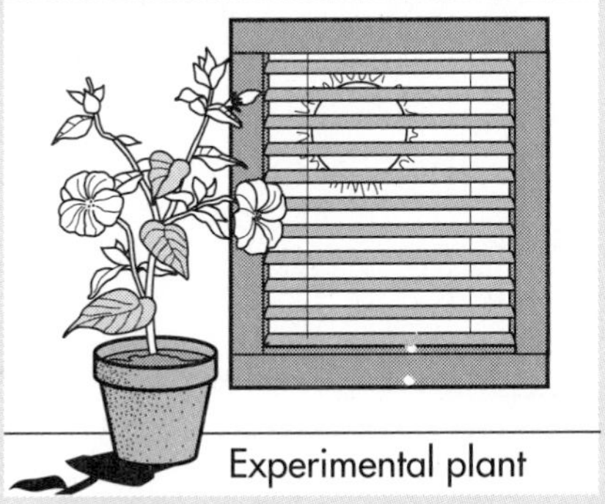

Experimental plant

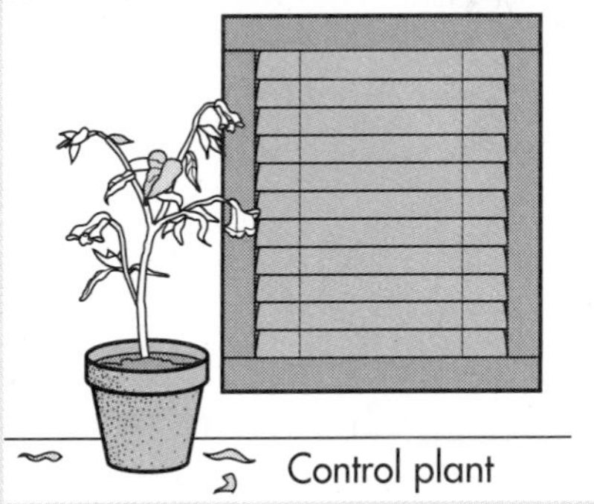

Control plant

Section 1-2 Review

Write the definitions for the following terms in your own words.

1. **scientific method**
2. **hypothesis**
3. **experiment**
4. **data**
5. **conclusion**

Answer these questions.

6. Distinguish between laboratory research and field research.
7. Explain the importance of the control group in a controlled experiment.
8. Most well-designed experiments test only one variable at a time. Why do you think this is so?
9. How might a person organize the data obtained during an experiment?
10. What is the difference between a hypothesis and conclusion?

1-3 Measurement

■ *Objectives*

□ *Use the ruler, graduated cylinder, and the triple beam balance.*

□ *Determine the volume of a solid and a liquid.*

□ *List the metric units of measurement used for length, volume, and mass.*

As you have learned, using the scientific method involves gathering data. One way that scientists obtain data is by measuring.

To **measure** means to use instruments to determine quantities such as distance and temperature. In order to communicate their findings, scientists must make measurements in units that other scientists can understand. For this reason, scientists all over the world use a system of measurement called the metric system.

Length
The distance from one point to another is called **length.** To measure length, scientists sometimes use a ruler. The basic unit of length is the **meter** (m). One meter can be divided into 100 centimeters (cm). One centimeter can be divided into 10 millimeters (mm).

You can see a ruler divided into centimeters and millimeters in Figure 1-3. Find the 2 cm + 4 mm point on the ruler. Since 1 mm equals 0.1 cm, 4 mm equal 0.4 cm. Thus, the reading for this point is 2 cm + 0.4 cm, or 2.4 cm. How many millimeters equal 2.4 cm?

Volume
When you measure length, you measure the distance between two points. When you measure the amount of space an object occupies, you are measuring its **volume.** To see how volume is measured, look at the **cube** in Figure 1-4. A cube is a regularly shaped solid in which the length, width, and height are equal. To determine the volume (v) of a cube, measure the length (l), width (w), and height (h) of the cube and multiply your answers.

You can find the volume of a cube by using the following formula.

$$v = l \times w \times h$$

Figure 1-3 Reading a Metric Ruler

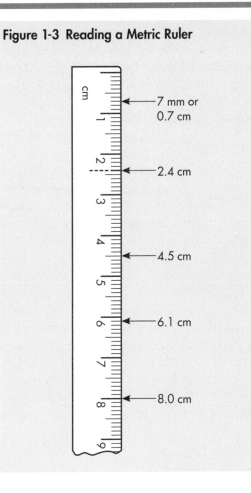

cm

7 mm or
0.7 cm

2.4 cm

4.5 cm

6.1 cm

8.0 cm

Figure 1-4

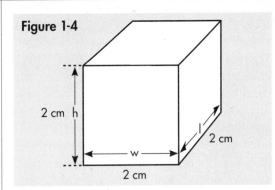

2 cm h

w

2 cm

2 cm

l

2 cm

Use the formula v = l x w x h to determine the volume of a cube.

Figure 1-5 Reading a Graduated Cylinder

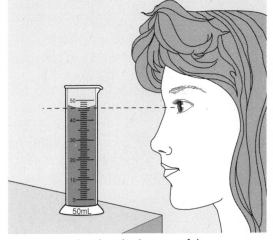

Read at eye level at the bottom of the meniscus.

What is the volume of the cube shown in Figure 1-4? A cube that measures 2.0 cm on each side has a volume of 2.0 cm x 2.0 cm x 2.0 cm, or 8 cubic centimeters (cc).

Suppose you want to measure the volume of a liquid. A liquid has no definite shape. You could fill a hollow cube, whose volume is 1 cubic centimeter, with water. The water inside this cube would have a volume of 1 cubic centimeter. Scientists have decided that 1 cc of water is equal to 1 milliliter (mL). There are 1000 mL in a **liter**. How many cc are in 1 liter?

Scientists, however, do not use hollow cubes to measure the volume of a liquid. They use an instrument called a **graduated cylinder** (SIL-un-dur). Look at the graduated cylinder in Figure 1-5. Notice that it is marked off in milliliters. How many milliliters does this cylinder hold? What part of a liter is this?

Notice that the surface of the liquid in the cylinder in Figure 1-5 forms a curve.

The curved surface of a liquid held in a container is a **meniscus** (muh-NIS-kus). To measure the volume of liquid in a graduated cylinder, first make sure the cylinder rests on a flat surface. Then position yourself so that you can view the meniscus at eye level. The correct reading is the point on the graduated cylinder that matches the bottom of the meniscus. How many milliliters of liquid does the graduated cylinder in Figure 1-5 contain?

Mass

The amount of material an object contains is the object's **mass**. To measure mass, scientists use an instrument called a **triple beam balance**. The basic unit for measuring mass is the **kilogram** (kg). A kilogram can be divided into 1000 **grams** (g).

Look at the triple beam balance in Figure 1-6. Notice that the object to be weighed is placed on the pan. The middle and rear beams contain riders, or weights, that can be moved and positioned in notches along the beams. The rider on the front beam can

be positioned anywhere along that beam. To measure the mass of the object, move the riders along the scales of all three beams until the pointer reaches zero. Then add the readings together to obtain the object's mass. In this example, the mass of the rock is 123.5 grams.

Temperature

In many experiments, you need to measure the temperature of the materials you are working with. For example, some fish will be active only if the water in their tank is at a certain temperature. In the metric system, temperature is measured on the **Celsius** (SEL-see-us) scale. Scientists measure temperature with a thermometer that is marked in Celsius degrees as shown in Figure 1-7. Water freezes at 0°C, read zero degrees Celsius. Water boils at 100°C. Therefore, there are exactly 100 degrees between the temperature at which water freezes and the temperature at which it

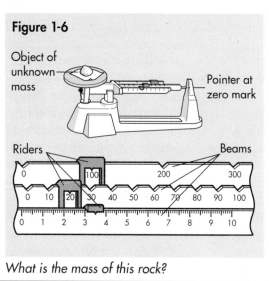

Figure 1-6

Object of unknown mass

Pointer at zero mark

Riders

Beams

What is the mass of this rock?

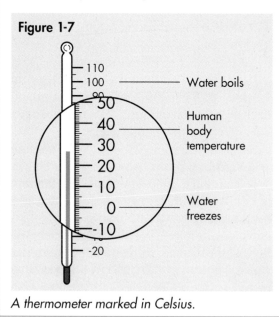

Figure 1-7

110
100 — Water boils
90
50
40 — Human body temperature
30
20
10
0 — Water freezes
-10
-20

A thermometer marked in Celsius.

boils. The normal body temperature of most people is 37°C. A comfortable room temperature is about 21°C.

▬▬ Section 1-3 Review ▬▬

Write the definitions for the following terms in your own words.

1. **meter**
2. **liter**
3. **graduated cylinder**
4. **triple beam balance**
5. **kilogram**

Answer these questions.

6. Why do scientists throughout the world use the same system of measurement?
7. A box measures 10 cm long, 6 cm wide, and 2.5 cm in height. Calculate the volume of the box in cubic centimeters.
8. How much water would the box described in Question 7 hold?
9. Where would you look to find the correct reading when measuring liquid in a graduated cylinder?
10. What is the mass shown in Figure 1-8?

Figure 1-8

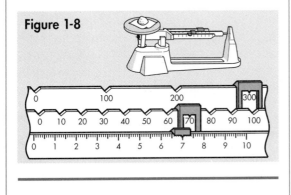

1-4 Science Skills

■ *Objective*
☐ *Describe nine science process skills.*

Scientists use the scientific method to search for solutions to problems. As you read Section 1-2, you probably noticed that scientists must master many skills in order to use the scientific method. A skill involved in using the scientific method is called a **science process skill.**

Learning such skills will make up an important part of your science education. Throughout this book, you will find features called Skill Builders and Activities. Each feature gives you practice in using these science process skills. The following are some of the skills scientists use.

Observing

When you **observe,** you use your five senses to gather information about your surroundings. The five senses include sight, smell, touch, taste, and hearing. Becoming a good observer requires a great deal of practice. Have you ever seen an accident and been asked to describe what happened? Often, two witnesses will give very different descriptions of such an event. People may miss important details or describe something they thought they saw but did not actually see. Skilled observers can accurately describe an experience.

Scientists are skilled observers who use their senses to observe the natural world. From their observations, they ask questions and conduct experiments to find answers. As they experiment, they gather information by making more observations.

What Observations Can You Make About a Goldfish?

Process Skill observing

Materials goldfish in a bowl

Procedure
1. Place a bowl containing a goldfish on your desk or a table.
2. Observe the goldfish for ten minutes.
3. Make a list of everything you observe about the goldfish.
4. Compare your list with the lists of four or five classmates. How are the observations that you made similar to the observations of other students? How are they different?

Conclusions
5. Based on this activity, do most people notice the same or different characteristics when observing a goldfish?
6. What characteristic of a goldfish is usually noticed first?

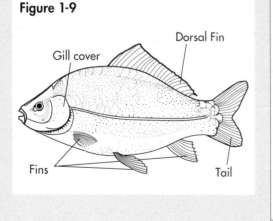

Figure 1-9

Dorsal Fin

Gill cover

Fins

Tail

Measuring
Even the most experienced observers cannot trust their senses to make exact measurements. As you read in Section 1-3, measuring involves using instruments, such as a ruler or thermometer. Look at lines A and B in Figure 1-10. Which line is longer? Although line B appears to be longer than line A, measuring both lines with a ruler shows that the lines are the same length.

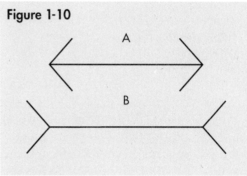

Figure 1-10

A

B

Which line is longer?

Estimating
When an exact measurement is not available, scientists **estimate**, or make an intelligent guess, about a quantity. Suppose you want to estimate the amount of time required to walk to a friend's home eight blocks away. You know that your school is four blocks away, and you can walk to school in eight minutes. Because your friend lives twice as far away as your school, you can estimate that the walk will take twice as long, or sixteen minutes.

Calculating
When you estimated the time required to walk to your friend's house, you obtained your estimate by calculating. To **calculate**

(KAL-kyuh-layt) means to perform a mathematical process to solve a problem. Adding, subtracting, multiplying, and dividing are all examples of mathematical processes.

Suppose you want to calculate the average height of ten students in your class. First, you would measure the height of each student in centimeters. Then you would add the heights of the ten students. Finally, you would divide the total by ten to find the average height.

Organizing

No matter how carefully you observe, measure, and calculate, your efforts will be wasted if you do not organize your work. Scientific study requires careful planning and thought both before and during an experiment. After you have conducted an experiment, you must organize your data so that other people can easily understand the data. For example, suppose you were conducting an experiment on the effect of temperature on how often a goldfish opens its gills. Look at the data table in Figure 1-11. It shows how temperature affects

the number of times in one minute that the gill of a goldfish opens.

Data can also be shown as a line graph. In a graph, a horizontal line and a vertical line are labelled with variables. Then the data are plotted as points and connected with a line. Figure 1-12 shows a graph using the same data as Figure 1-11.

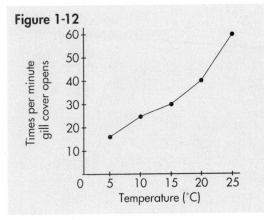

Figure 1-12

Analyzing

After you have gathered and organized your data, you need to **analyze** (AN-eh-lyz) your results. Analyze means to look for patterns and relationships. Scientists analyze data gathered during an experiment to help them form conclusions.

Try to analyze the data in Figures 1-11 and 1-12. Notice that as the temperature increases, the number of times per minute the gill cover opens also increases. Suppose a researcher hypothesizes that for every five-degree increase in temperature, the number of times the gill cover opens doubles. Is this hypothesis correct? Study the data to find out.

Sometimes careful analysis can help a scientist form a conclusion without making

Figure 1-11 How Temperature Affects Goldfish	
Temperature (°C)	Times per minute gill cover opens
5	18
10	25
15	30
20	40
25	60

Analyzing

The data table in Figure 1-13 compares life expectancies in different regions of the world in 1950 and the estimated life expectancies for those regions in the year 2000. The second column shows the number of years a person born in 1950 is expected to live. The third column shows the number of years a person born in 2000 is expected to live.

Use the following questions to help you interpret the data in Figure 1-13. On a separate sheet of paper, write the answer to each question.

1. What general statement about life expectancy can you make based on the information shown in the table?
2. In which region was the life expectancy the shortest in 1950?
3. In which region was life expectancy the longest in 1950?

4. Which region will show the most dramatic increase in life expectancy by 2000?
5. Which region will show the smallest increase in life expectancy by 2000?

Figure 1-13 Life Expectancy

Region	1950	2000
Africa	37	58
Latin America	51	68
United States	69	76
East Asia	48	73
Western Europe	65	75

a direct observation. To make a conclusion without direct observation is to **infer.** For example, suppose you observe goldfish in a pond on a hot day. You do not have a thermometer to take the temperature of the water, yet you see that the gill covers of the goldfish are moving very rapidly. You could infer that the water temperature is warm.

Making a Model

How do scientists communicate their findings if their findings cannot be observed? One way is to construct a **model.** A model is a diagram or an object that helps explain a thing or an event that cannot be observed. For example, although no one has ever seen a dinosaur, scientists have found the bones of dinosaurs. Scientists have used these bones to build models of dinosaurs.

You probably see models every day. For example, you may watch weather reports on television. Weather maps are a type of model that illustrates approaching snowstorms and other forms of weather.

Figure 1-14 is a model that a life scientist might use. It shows how some plants and animals depend on one another for food.

Figure 1-14

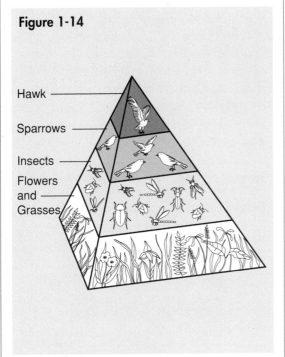

Hawk
Sparrows
Insects
Flowers and Grasses

What does this model show?

You can use this model to answer questions. What would happen to the birds if all the grasses died?

Predicting

Recall from Section 1-2 that scientists design experiments to test a hypothesis.

When testing hypotheses, scientists sometimes have an idea of what results will take place. They **predict,** or state in advance that something will take place.

Look at the data table in Figure 1-15, obtained from an experiment designed to show the length of time needed to digest an egg white. Using these data, a scientist might predict that the amount of digestion

Figure 1-15 Length of Time to Digest an Egg White	
Percentage of egg white digested	**Time (hours)**
5	2
10	4
20	8
50	12
70	16
80	20
85	24

after ten hours would be about 35 percent. Whether or not this prediction is correct can be determined by repeating the experiment, this time measuring the amount of digestion that takes place after ten hours.

Evaluating

After you have performed an experiment and organized and analyzed the data, you

How Does Exercise Affect the Rate of Your Heartbeat?

Process Skills *measuring, organizing*

Materials watch with a second hand, graph paper

Does exercise make your heart beat faster or slower? You can measure changes in your heart rate by taking your pulse. Your pulse is caused by the widening and narrowing of the walls of your blood vessels as blood is pumped out of your heart. Each pulse beat equals one heartbeat.

Procedure
1. Work with a partner for this activity. Use the method shown in Figure 1-16 to find your partner's pulse.
2. Use a watch to count the number of times the pulse beats in 15 seconds. Multiply this number by 4 to find the number of pulse beats per minute.

Figure 1-16 Method for Taking Pulse

To find a person's pulse, lightly place your first two fingers on the person's wrist.

3. Construct a data table like the one shown in Figure 1-17, and record your partner's pulse rate in the table.
4. Have your partner run in place for 3 minutes. **Caution** Students with certain medical conditions should not do this part of the activity. As soon as your partner completes this exercise, take his or her pulse as you did in Step 2. Record this pulse reading in your data table.
5. Repeat Step 2 every 2 minutes for 10 minutes. Record each pulse reading in the data table.

Figure 1-17	
Time recorded	**Pulse**
Before exercise	
Immediately after exercise	
After 2 min.	
After 4 min.	
After 6 min.	
After 8 min.	
After 10 min.	

Conclusion
6. What effect does exercise have on the rate of the heartbeat?

think about the results. What did your experiment accomplish? When you think about the results of your experiment, you are performing a process skill called evaluating. To **evaluate** means to think about the meaning or importance of something. A scientist evaluates an experiment by answering such questions as, Was the design of the experiment good? Should any of the procedures be repeated? Were the observations made accurately? Are the calculations correct? Were the data analyzed carefully? Answers to questions like these help scientists to determine whether their experiment was successful and if they need to investigate a problem further.

■■■ Section 1-4 Review ■■■

Write the definitions for the following terms in your own words.

1. **observe**
2. **estimate**
3. **analyze**
4. **model**
5. **evaluate**

Answer these questions.

6. What are science process skills?
7. Distinguish between measuring and calculating.
8. Give an example of a model.
9. Choose three process skills, and give examples of how you might use these skills in daily life.

1-5 Life Science, Technology, and Society

■ *Objectives*
□ *Discuss how science and technology advance each other.*
□ *Explain how science and technology affect people and their surroundings.*
□ *Explain how science, technology, and society interact.*
□ *Give examples of the global effects of technology.*

Think about the things you have done in the past 24 hours. Have you used a computer or talked on the telephone? Have you cooked food in a microwave oven? Many of the products that you use every day have resulted from applying what scientists have learned. The use of science to develop products and processes that improve the quality of your life is called **technology** (tek-NAL-uh-jee).

How Science and Technology Interact
Technology can improve the quality of life by solving problems and by meeting people's needs. The products of technology are sometimes referred to as technologies. Automobiles, airplanes, VCRs, processed foods, artificial limbs, and medicines are examples of technologies. The table in Figure 1-18 on page 22 presents several examples of scientific discoveries and resulting technological developments.

The table in Figure 1-18 gives examples of how scientific research has advanced technology. However, technology may also

Figure 1-18 Comparing Science and Technology

Scientific discovery	Technological development
Bacteria and viruses cause disease.	Medications and vaccines have been developed that control disease-causing bacteria and viruses.
Acid rain contaminates lakes and ponds and endangers wildlife.	Automakers can install equipment that reduces the production of chemicals that cause acid rain.
A person's body will accept another person's blood if the two people have the same blood type.	Scientists have developed tests to identify blood type; physicians perform blood transfusions on patients who need blood.
People have poor eyesight because their eyes do not bend light rays in the proper way.	Eyeglasses and contact lenses correct vision by bending light rays as they reach the eye.

advance scientific research. The X-ray machine is an example of such a technology. X-ray machines have enabled researchers to increase their knowledge of the human body. In Chapter 3, you will learn about the technological developments that enabled scientists to learn about the materials that make up living things.

How Technology Affects People and Their Surroundings

Researchers develop new technologies in order to improve human lives. Unfortunately, a technology that solves one problem may create another problem. For example, a doctor may prescribe medication to relieve pain, but that medication may also cause drowsiness. Chemicals that destroy harmful pests may also destroy useful birds and insects. These examples show how technology that creates a short-term solution for today's problems also may create a serious long-term consequence for the future.

The helpful and harmful effects of technology are global. In other words, technology issues affect the entire world, not just the area where a technology is being used. For example, you may think that people who live on farms or in the mountains do not need to worry about the pollution caused by factories. However, pollution does not only affect the area in which it is created. Wind and rain can carry pollutants hundreds of miles away.

Making Decisions About Technology

Think of the last time you rode in a car. Did you put on a seat belt? In many states, there are seat belt laws. The laws were passed because scientific studies showed that seat belts save lives. Passing such laws is one way in which people and their government make decisions about technology.

Society, with the help of scientists, must decide if the benefits of a technology outweigh the burden that it places on society. They must decide which technologies should be accepted or rejected. The table in Figure 1-19 compares the benefits and burdens of several technologies. What decisions would you make about each?

Science and technology alone cannot solve all of the problems of the world. However, decisions people make about science and technology will greatly affect the quality of life.

Each chapter in this book contains a Science, Technology, and Society feature. These features present current topics that illustrate how science, technology, and society interact. As you read each Science, Technology, and Society feature, think of how the problems and questions presented might affect your life. Also, think about your future responsibility as a citizen to respond to these issues.

▬ Section 1-5 Review ▬

Write the definition for the following term in your own words.

1. **technology**

Answer these questions.

2. How are science and technology related? Give examples.
3. How do science and technology affect society? Give examples.
4. Most technologies have both advantages and disadvantages. What does this mean? Give examples.
5. Explain the statement that science and technology alone cannot solve the world's problems.

Figure 1-19 Benefits and Burdens of Some Technologies

Technology	Benefits	Burdens
Radiation treatment and chemotherapy	Kills cancer cells	May cause severe side effects
Nuclear energy	Provides cheap and unlimited electricity	Creates risk of exposure to harmful radiation
Food preservatives	Keeps foods fresh for long periods of time	May be harmful to health

SCIENCE, TECHNOLOGY, & SOCIETY

Global Warming

Imagine that you are living in New York in the year 3000. Palm trees and orange trees line the streets of Manhattan. You do not own a winter coat because the temperature never drops below freezing. This description may sound like a scene from a movie, but some scientists predict this future for New York, as shown in Figure 1-20.

Global warming is a permanent rise in the average temperature of the earth. Many scientists think that the temperature is rising because levels of carbon dioxide in the atmosphere are rising. Carbon dioxide warms the earth by trapping heat that would otherwise reflect back into outer space. Scientists call this process the greenhouse effect, because carbon dioxide acts much like the walls of a greenhouse. Greenhouse walls absorb sunlight and thus keep the plants inside warm.

Carbon dioxide comes from many sources. However, technological developments in the past 200 years are mainly responsible for the rising levels of carbon dioxide. For example, factories produce carbon dioxide whenever wood, coal, or oil is burned. Car, bus, and truck engines also give off carbon dioxide.

If carbon dioxide levels continue to increase at the present rate, the average temperature of the earth could rise three or four degrees by the mid-2000s. This increase may seem slight, but it could warm the earth enough to melt the polar ice caps. The result could be severe flooding along coastal areas. Some areas near the equator might become too hot to support life.

Scientists concerned about global warming think the United States government should fund research in this area and pass laws to control carbon dioxide levels. Other scientists do not think that global warming will occur.

Follow-up Activity
Use the library to research the differing opinions on global warming. Then decide how you feel about this issue. Discuss your ideas with several classmates.

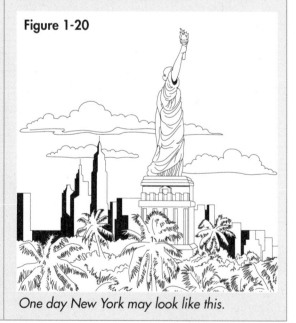

Figure 1-20

One day New York may look like this.

KEEPING TRACK

Section 1-1 What Is Life Science?

1. Science is a collection of knowledge based on the study of the natural world and the processes involved in gathering the knowledge.

Section 1-2 Scientists at Work

1. The scientific method is a logical and organized approach to problem solving.

Section 1-3 Measurement

1. Scientists all over the world use the metric system.

Section 1-4 Science Skills

1. Science process skills include observing, measuring, estimating, calculating, organizing, analyzing, modeling, predicting, and evaluating.

Section 1-5 Life Science, Technology, and Society

1. Technology is the use of science to solve everyday problems.
2. Scientific knowledge often leads to new technologies. These new technologies in turn are used to gather new scientific knowledge.
3. Every technological process or device has advantages and disadvantages.
4. Technology has a global impact.
5. Technological products have improved the standard of living and affect society, business, and industry.

BUILDING VOCABULARY

Write the word from the list that best completes each sentence.

meniscus, process skills, models, mass, grams, measurements, Celsius, predict, graph

Scientists must master many ___1___ to do their work. Scientists may ___2___ the outcome of an experiment, or state what will happen. Often scientists perform ___3___ to obtain data. They may organize their results on either a data table or a ___4___. They use the triple balance beam to measure ___5___. They determine temperature according to the ___6___ scale. When measuring liquid, scientists refer to the curve of a liquid in a container as the liquid's ___7___. When measuring the mass of an object, the results are sometimes expressed in ___8___. Scientists use ___9___ to explain something that cannot be observed.

SUMMARIZING

If the statement is true, write *true*. If the statement is false, change the *italicized* term to make the statement true.

1. Scientists define problems or raise questions by using their *observations*.
2. A possible solution to a problem is called a *conclusion*.
3. In a *controlled* experiment, all conditions are the same except for the condition being tested.
4. The single condition that is changed in an experiment is called the *solution*.
5. A *calculation* is a mathematical process used to obtain data.

6. The science process skill used to obtain the size of an object is called *analyzing*.
7. VCRs, computers, and microwave ovens are examples of products of *technology*.
8. Technologies such as paper manufacturing have a *global* impact.
9. The fact that nuclear energy provides cheap electrical energy is an example of a *disadvantage* of technology.
10. The fact that food preservatives may be harmful to health is an example of an *advantage* of technology.

INTERPRETING INFORMATION

Use the newspaper article shown in Figure 1-21 to answer the following questions on a separate sheet of paper.

Figure 1-21 The Daily Globe

Tough Auto Pollution Standards Voted

A government committee voted today to take steps to pass stricter air pollution standards for automobiles. New cars will have to be equipped with devices that reduce air pollution. The pollution control devices will add about $100 to the cost of every new car. Also, cars will now use more gas because of the new devices. The new standards are set to go into effect in the mid 1990s.

1. What is the benefit of having stricter auto pollution standards?
2. What burdens do these standards pass along to car owners?

3. How can decisions made by the government affect the environment?

THINK AND DISCUSS

Use the section number in parentheses to help you find each answer. Write your answers in complete sentences.
1. In one sentence, describe what science is. (1-1)
2. Design an experiment to prove that a plant needs a certain amount of water to grow. (1-2)
3. Give some examples of instruments that scientists use to obtain measurements. Without such instruments, how might science be different? (1-3)
4. What is the difference between measuring and estimating? (1-4)
5. What are some things that society should consider before deciding to use a technological product? (1-5)

GOING FURTHER

The methods used to solve problems in science can be used to solve many problems in daily life. Think of two daily life problems that someone might have. Apply the scientific method to find a solution to each.

COMPETENCY REVIEW

1. Which of the following statements best describes an observation?
   a. Because the water in the lake is polluted, fish probably do not live there.
   b. Scientists have seen medical wastes floating in the lake.

c. A local hospital must have dumped medical wastes into the lake.

d. Medical wastes may make fish ill.

Questions 2-3 refer to the following experiment.

A student grows bean plants in five pots. Each plant receives a different amount of water. All other conditions are identical. The student records the height of each bean plant three weeks after the start of the experiment.

2. The hypothesis tested is that the
   a. temperature affects the growth of bean plants.
   b. amount of sunlight affects the growth of bean plants.
   c. soil type affects the growth of bean plants.
   d. amount of water affects the growth of bean plants.

3. Which item represents the variable in this experiment?
   a. light
   b. temperature
   c. soil type
   d. water

4. A certain kind of waste from a paper mill causes cancer in mice. This statement is an example of a (an)
   a. scientific measurement.
   b. scientific law.
   c. conclusion.
   d. estimate.

5. A scientist wants to determine the effects of protein on the growth of mice. Which of the following experiments might provide the answer?
   a. Feed 200 mice a protein-free diet.
   b. Feed 100 mice a protein-free diet. Feed the remaining 100 mice a protein-rich diet.
   c. Feed the mice a protein-free diet for 50 days, then feed the same mice a sugar-free diet for 50 days.
   d. Feed half the mice a carbohydrate-free diet. Feed the remaining mice a protein-free diet.

6. *Robots may replace human workers.* What concern about technology is suggested by this statement?
   a. Technology affects people's lives.
   b. Technology affects the environment.
   c. Technology has no advantages.
   d. Technology is dangerous.

7. Which statement about science and technology is not true?
   a. Science advances technology.
   b. Technology advances science.
   c. Science and technology are not related.
   d. Science and technology affect society.

8. Which of the following may be measured in kilograms?
   a. length   b. height
   c. mass   d. temperature

9. Which is a unit of volume?
   a. millimeter
   b. gram
   c. Celsius
   d. cubic centimeter

CHAPTER 2

THE NATURE OF LIVING THINGS

Imagine you are a contestant on a quiz show. Your job is to label things as either *living* or *nonliving*. How would you decide to label something as living? Would you decide by looking? Some things, of course, are easy to label. Birds, for example, are easily labeled *living*. Stones are easily labeled *nonliving*. What about the thing in Figure 2-1? If you labeled it "living," you are correct. The thing shown is coral. Although this coral looks much like stone, it is a living animal found in the sea. Some things, such as coral, cannot be easily labeled by the way they look. Some things are too small to be seen by the unaided eye. If you cannot always tell if something is living or nonliving by looking, how can you decide?

Divide a sheet of paper lengthwise into two columns. Label one column "Living things" and the other "Nonliving things." List ten things in each column that you saw outside today. Do the things in both lists have anything in common? What do the things in your Living Things list have in common with one another?

2-1 Atoms and Molecules

■ *Objective*

☐ *Explain the relationships among atoms, elements, molecules, and compounds.*

Everything is made of **matter.** Matter is anything that has mass and takes up space. Birds, coral, your skin, and trees are living things. They are all made of matter. Stones, oil, and iron are nonliving things. They are also made of matter. Being made of matter is the main thing that all living and nonliving objects have in common.

Figure 2-1

Living or nonliving?

Matter is constantly changing. Living things change matter in order to carry on their activities. For example, they change food to get the energy to move. Understanding how changes in matter happen will help you understand why something is called living, rather than nonliving. It will also help you understand how living things stay alive.

Atoms and Elements

The basic unit of matter is the **atom.** Atoms are so tiny that they cannot be seen even under the most powerful microscope. Recently, scientists have developed instruments and techniques that have helped them learn about atoms.

Study the model of an atom shown in Figure 2-2. This model is called a Bohr model. The center of the atom is the **nucleus** (NYU-klee-us). The nucleus is made up of particles called **protons** and **neutrons.** Protons have a positive electrical charge (+). Neutrons have no electrical charge. Notice that particles with a negative electrical charge (−) surround the nucleus. These particles, called **electrons,** occupy paths called electron clouds. In the model, the paths are shown as orbits. Find the electrons in Figure 2-2. The number of protons

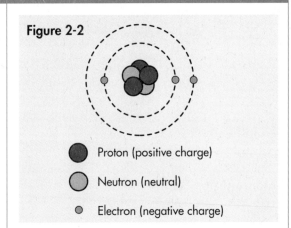

Figure 2-2

- Proton (positive charge)
- Neutron (neutral)
- Electron (negative charge)

in an atom is equal to the number of electrons. How many protons and electrons are in the atom shown in Figure 2-2?

The positive charge of one proton is cancelled by the negative charge of one electron. Because the number of protons is equal to the number of electrons, atoms are neutral. In other words, they do not have an electrical charge. Each positive charge is canceled by a negative charge.

All atoms are not alike. What makes one atom different from another? Different atoms have different numbers of protons, neutrons, and electrons. Use Figure 2-3 to compare atoms of hydrogen, carbon, and oxygen.

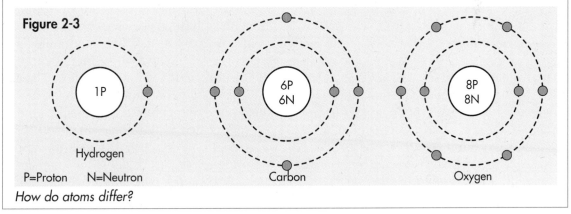

Figure 2-3

1P

Hydrogen

P=Proton   N=Neutron

6P
6N

Carbon

8P
8N

Oxygen

How do atoms differ?

The number of protons, neutrons, and electrons that an atom contains determines the characteristics of that atom. Carbon has six protons, six electrons, and six neutrons. It is very different from oxygen. Oxygen has eight protons, eight electrons, and eight neutrons.

Some substances are made up of only one kind of atom. These substances are called **elements**. So far, scientists have identified 108 different elements. Of these, 88 are natural, and the remaining 20 are made in the laboratory. Each element is made of one of the 108 different kinds of atoms. Tin, for example, is an element. It has only tin atoms. A piece of tin is made up of trillions of tin atoms. Carbon, oxygen, helium, and uranium are other examples of elements.

Molecules and Compounds

Most substances found on Earth are not made of a single element. Most substances are made up of two or more elements and, therefore, two or more kinds of atoms. When atoms of two or more elements combine chemically, they form a **compound.** For example, Figure 2-4 shows that two hydrogen atoms and one oxygen atom have combined chemically to form the compound water.

The building blocks of compounds are **molecules** (MAL-ih-kyuls). A molecule is the smallest possible piece of a substance that has the properties of that substance. The compound water is made up of water molecules. A glass of water contains trillions of water molecules. If you divided a glass of water into drops, each drop would have all of the properties of water. If you

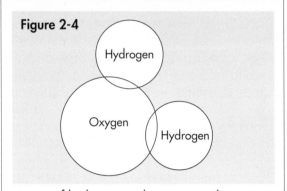

Figure 2-4

Atoms of hydrogen and oxygen combine chemically to form water.

divided one of those drops into molecules, each molecule would have two hydrogen atoms and one oxygen atom. Each molecule would still be water. If you broke the water molecule into its atoms, none of its atoms alone would have the properties of water. You would no longer have water.

Perhaps you have seen the chemical formula for water. Its chemical formula is H_2O. A chemical formula shows the kinds and numbers of atoms that make up a molecule. A chemical formula is written in symbols. The symbol for hydrogen is H, and the symbol for oxygen is O. The formula H_2O tells you that a water molecule is made up of hydrogen and oxygen atoms. The 2 in the formula is called a subscript. The subscript tells you that there are two atoms of hydrogen. If only one atom is present, no subscript is written. In the chemical formula for water, you can see that there are two atoms of hydrogen and one atom of oxygen in the molecule. Find the chemical formula for carbon dioxide in Figure 2-5. What atoms make up one molecule of carbon dioxide? How many of each kind of atom make up the molecule?

bacteria. Bacteria are one-celled organisms. A single bacterial cell can carry out all life processes. Complex organisms like tigers, oak trees, and humans are made up of billions of cells. The cells in these organisms have a variety of shapes. Each shape is suited to a specific job. The human skin cells in Figure 2-9 are one type. Notice that these cells fit together like shingles on a roof. Skin cells form a covering that is used for protection.

Figure 2-9 Human Skin Cells

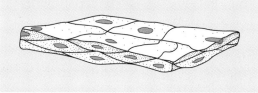

Response

The **environment** (in-VY-run-munt) is everything in an organism's surroundings. Environment includes the amount of sunlight and water, other organisms, and weather conditions. A change in the environment that causes an organism to react, or **respond,** is called a **stimulus** (STIM-yuh-lus). All living things respond to change in the environment. For example, if you accidentally touch a hot object, you will pull your hand away quickly. If dust gets into your nose, you will sneeze. You may react to an unexpected loud noise by jumping. In each case, you react to stimulus.

The ability to respond helps living things escape danger and obtain the things they need to survive. For example, a squirrel responds to an approaching dog by running up a tree trunk. The squirrel responds to colder temperatures and shorter days by gathering food for the winter.

Movement is an important response of living things. If a car approaches as you cross the street, you will move back onto the sidewalk to avoid being hit. You may have watched an earthworm respond to being touched by quickly wriggling away. Can you think of other situations in which an animal responds to a stimulus by moving?

Organisms that do not move from place to place respond to their environment in other ways. For example, even though sponges and barnacles spend most of their lives anchored to one spot, a great deal of movement takes place within their bodies. Look at the barnacles attached to the side of a boat in Figure 2-10. Barnacles capture food by moving little hairs, called cilia, in their bodies.

Even parts of plants move. Plant movements result from uneven growth. For example, the leaves of plants respond to light by growing toward it. This response of plants to light is called **phototropism** (foh-TAH-truh-piz-um). Phototropism takes

Figure 2-10

In what ways is a barnacle dependent on its environment?

Evaluating an Experiment

A scientist wanted to observe how mealworms would respond to light. To do this, the scientist placed some mealworms in a petri dish, as shown in Figure 2-11A. Then the scientist placed a bright light to the right of the petri dish. Twenty-four hours later, the scientist observed the positions of the mealworms as shown in Figure 2-11B.

1. Compare the position of the mealworms at the start of the experiment and 24 hours later. What differences did the scientist observe?

2. In addition to the light, what conditions in the environment might have caused the mealworms to change position?

3. Could the scientist be sure that light was the environmental factor that really caused the mealworms to move?

4. How would you design this experiment to be sure you were observing only the effect of light on mealworms?

5. Suppose that you wanted to observe the effects of temperature on mealworms. How would you design an experiment to observe the effects of temperature?

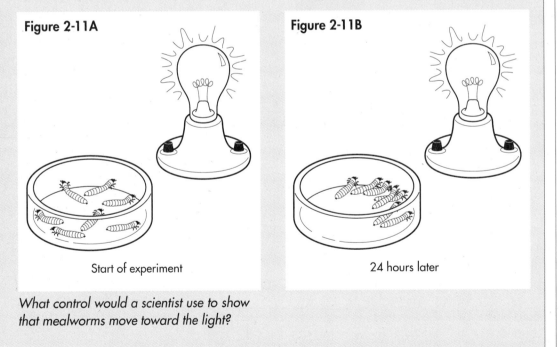

Figure 2-11A

Start of experiment

Figure 2-11B

24 hours later

What control would a scientist use to show that mealworms move toward the light?

place because the cells in the side of the stem facing away from the light grow faster than the cells on the side facing the light. Therefore, the side of the stem in the dark grows slightly longer than the side in the light. As a result, the stem seems to bend in the direction of the light. You can see in Figure 2-12 how uneven growth in the stem causes the leaves to grow toward the light.

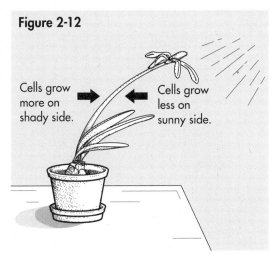

Figure 2-12

Cells grow more on shady side. → ← Cells grow less on sunny side.

How does a plant respond to light?

Adaptation

Living things are adapted, or suited, to conditions in their environment. Only an organism that is well adapted to its environment will survive. Any characteristic of an organism that helps the organism survive and live successfully in its environment is an **adaptation** (ad-ap-TAY-shun). For example, look at the polar bear in Figure 2-13. A polar bear lives in the Arctic Circle. The thickness of its fur protects the bear from the extreme cold of its environment. The white color matches the snow, so that the bear's enemies cannot easily see it. The polar bear's fur is an adaptation for survival in an arctic environment.

You can go to almost any part of the earth and find organisms that are adapted to their environment. A hawk's body, for example, is adapted for flight. It has hollow bones that make it light and feathers that give its wings a large surface area so that the bird can fly. A frog has webs between its toes, making it well suited for swimming in the pond in which it lives.

Figure 2-13

How is this polar bear adapted for survival in the Arctic Circle?

Plants that live in moist areas usually have broad, flat leaves with thousands of tiny openings that release extra water. In what ways is a cactus adapted to the dry desert environment in which it lives? Study Figure 2-14 to learn about some adaptations of several organisms.

Reproduction

Although organisms are adapted for survival, they eventually die. To replace themselves, all organisms produce new generations through the process of **reproduction.** The process of reproduction differs from one type of organism to another. The important point is that all organisms, such as those shown in Figure 2-15, reproduce their own kind.

Figure 2-15

Figure 2-14

Organism	Environment	Adaptations
Goldfish	Water	Gills to take in oxygen dissolved in water Fins for swimming
Duck	Water	Webs of skin between toes for swimming
Frog	Water	Special eyelid for protection when under water
Whale	Water	Flippers for swimming
Oak tree	Soil	Roots to anchor plants in soil and to absorb water Leaves to make food
Seaweed	Water	Water-supported with weaker stems than land plants
Housefly	Air	Light bodies with air tubes and wings for flight

Determining Relationships

To survive, an organism must be adapted, or suited, to the environment in which it lives.

1. Study the four different organisms shown in Figure 2-16.

2. For each organism, name one or two adaptations. Then describe how each adaptation helps the organism survive in its environment.

Figure 2-16

Name at least one adaptation for each of these organisms.

What Are Some Activities Common to Living Things?

Process Skills making observations, drawing conclusions

Materials goldfish in a container of water, grasshopper in a jar, bean seedlings in a small pot

Procedure

1. Observe a goldfish in a container of water for ten minutes. Then observe a grasshopper in a jar for ten minutes.
2. Divide a sheet of paper into three columns. Label the first column "Goldfish" and the second column "Grasshopper." Under the appropriate column, list everything you observe that indicates that the goldfish and the grasshopper are alive.
3. Compare the activities of the goldfish and the grasshopper. How are they similar? How are they different?
4. Observe the bean seedlings for several days. Label the third column of your page "Bean Seedlings." Under this column, record your observations that indicate that the seedling is alive.

Conclusion

5. Compare the observations you have recorded for each of the three organisms. What activities are common to both plants and animals?

Section 2-3 Review

Write the definitions for the following terms in your own words.

1. **cell**
2. **adaptation**
3. **response**
4. **reproduction**
5. **stimulus**

Answer these questions.

6. Why are cells called the building blocks of life?
7. Why must living things be able to respond to stimuli? Give examples of stimuli you responded to on your way to school in the last week. Describe your response to each stimulus.
8. What is an adaptation? Choose five organisms and describe how each is adapted to the environment in which it lives.

2-4 Needs of Living Things

■ *Objective*

☐ *Describe the basic needs of living things.*

Living things exchange materials with their environment. They obtain the things they need to survive from the environment. They pass wastes into the environment. What do living things need to continue living? Think about all the things you do every day that are necessary for survival. You breathe air. You eat food and drink liquids. When outdoors, you wear clothing that keeps your body dry and comfortable.

Different organisms have different ways of obtaining the things they need. However, all organisms have similar basic needs.

Water

Water is a basic need of all living things. Without water, most of the chemical reactions necessary for the life processes cannot take place. Water is a **solvent**, a substance in which chemical dissolve. Water dissolves waste products and carries them away from cells. Water also carries dissolved materials to cells. Water helps keep an organism from becoming too hot or too cold. Water absorbs the heat that is released during cell processes and distributes the heat throughout the body.

Do you ever feel yourself begin to sweat on a hot day? The water that leaves your body as sweat is actually cooling you. When water that leaves your skin evaporates into water vapor, the temperature of your skin is lowered. This makes you feel cooler.

Food and Oxygen

All living things need food. Food provides the raw materials needed for the growth and repair of body parts. Food also provides living things with the energy needed to carry on life processes.

Organisms obtain food in different ways. Green plants make their own food through a process called **photosynthesis** (foht-oh-SINT-thuh-sus). During photosynthesis, plants use sunlight, carbon dioxide, and water from the environment to make food. Unlike plants, animals obtain their food from other animals or plants. For example, a bumblebee might eat nectar, a food produced by flowers. Then a frog might eat the bumblebee.

To release energy from foods, plants and animals need oxygen. Most organisms obtain oxygen from the air or from oxygen dissolved in water. Oxygen combines chemically with the molecules that make up food. Energy is released by a process called **cellular respiration** (SEL-yuh-lur res-puh-RAY-shun). The waste products of cellular respiration are carbon dioxide and water. Both carbon dioxide and water are given off as waste products. They are returned to the environment.

Temperature Range

Most living things can live only in a certain temperature range. Most life activities can occur only at temperatures between 0° Celsius, the freezing point of water, and about 42.8°C. If the temperature in the environment goes outside this range, an organism must adapt in some way or it will die. Humans have a highly developed brain, which helps them adapt. As a result, humans can build shelter and make clothing to protect themselves from extreme temperatures.

Some organisms have adaptations that enable them to withstand extreme temperatures. To survive in very cold climates, bears and many other animals **hibernate** (HY-bur-nayt), or remain inactive, during the winter. Some birds, fish, and mammals **migrate**, or travel long distances, as the seasons change. Some plants survive the cold winter as **dormant**, or inactive, seeds. Dormant seeds will not develop into new plants until spring, when the temperature is warm enough to permit growth.

Write the definitions for the following terms in your own words.

1. **solvent**
2. **hibernate**
3. **photosynthesis**
4. **migrate**
5. **cellular respiration**

Answer these questions.

6. In what ways does an organism depend on its environment?
7. Why do organisms require water?
8. Why do organisms require food?
9. What are three ways organisms deal with severe temperature changes?

2-5 Life Activities

■ *Objective*
☐ *List and define seven life activities.*

Some of the things organisms need to stay alive are water, oxygen, and food. These substances are all needed to carry out life activities. Life processes are those activities necessary for an organism to survive. Each of these processes will be discussed in more detail in later chapters. A brief overview follows.

Nutrition

What did you have for lunch today? Perhaps you ate a sandwich and drank a glass of milk. Whatever you had, you took food into your body. The process of taking in food is called **ingestion** (in-JESH-chun).

Why do you need food? Food provides you with substances called **nutrients** (NYU-tree-unts). Some examples of nutrients are sugar, starch, protein, and fat. Your body receives energy from nutrients. Nutrients also help you to grow. Before your body can use most of the nutrients in foods, it must break down the nutrients through a process called **digestion** (dy-JESH-chun).

Both ingestion and digestion are part of a life process called **nutrition** (nyu-TRISH-un). Nutrition provides the parts of your body with the nutrients required for energy and growth. Nutrition is a life process common to all organisms.

Transport

The food you eat is digested in your digestive tract. The air you breathe enters your lungs. How do the nutrients in food and the oxygen in the air reach all the cells of your body? Nutrients and oxygen are carried throughout your body by a process called **transport**. After food has been completely digested, the nutrients enter the blood. The blood carries, or transports, the nutrients to all parts of the body. When you breathe in air, oxygen enters your lungs. After oxygen enters the lungs, it passes through the lungs into the blood. The blood carries oxygen to all cells of the body.

Respiration and Excretion

Organisms obtain energy from food through the process of **respiration**. Respiration takes place in all the cells and in all organisms. To carry on respiration, most organisms need oxygen. In humans, oxygen enters the lungs and is transported by the bloodstream to the cells. In the cells, oxygen combines with digested food, and energy is released. During respiration, water and carbon dioxide are given off. The body uses much of the water to carry out its life processes. Excess water and carbon dioxide are waste products.

All organisms must remove waste products, which can cause damage. The process of removing wastes from the cells is called **excretion** (ik-SKREE-shun). In humans, some wastes leave the body through the skin during perspiration. Wastes are filtered from the blood as the blood passes through the human kidney.

Regulation

An organism must keep a balance in its internal environment. The ability to maintain a constant internal balance is homeostasis. The process that keeps this balance is a life process called **regulation.**

An organism regulates itself by responding to various stimuli, or signals. A stimulus from one part of the organism receives a response from another part of the organism. An example of this is when you feel a need to breathe deeply. Your cells need a continuous supply of oxygen. Your brain is sensitive to the gases in the blood. It sends a message to the muscles that control your breathing. These muscles respond by taking in more oxygen-rich air.

Growth and Development

The life process called **growth** includes adding new cells and replacing old cells. During growth, cells increase in number. The organism gets larger and gains weight. What is the average weight gain

for a boy and a girl from the ages of 11 to 13? To answer this question use the information found in Figure 2-17.

Every organism undergoes both growth and **development**. The life process called development is those changes that take place in an organism over its lifetime. Look at a picture of yourself when you were an infant. In what ways have you changed?

Figure 2-17 Average Weight in Kilograms

Age	Girls	Boys
11	34.5	33
12	40	37.5
13	47.5	42.5

▬ Section 2-5 Review ▬

Write the definitions for the following terms in your own words.

1. **nutrition**   2. **excretion**
3. **transport**   4. **regulation**
5. **respiration**

Answer these questions.

6. Identify at least five activities a living thing must perform in order to stay alive.
7. Why must organisms carry on respiration?
8. What would happen if organisms could not reproduce?

SCIENCE, TECHNOLOGY, & SOCIETY

Acid Rain Damages Lakes and Forests

The Adirondack Mountains in New York State is a popular spot for camping trips. Today, however, campers are likely to find signs posted warning people not to eat fish or drink water from lakes in the Adirondacks. The reason is that acid rain has damaged many of these lakes.

Acid rain is caused when power plants, industries, and automobiles burn large amounts of fuels such as coal and oil. The burning of these fuels releases chemical wastes, including sulfur and nitrogen oxides, into the air. These chemicals combine with rainwater to form acids.

When acid rain falls on lakes, forests, and farmland, it damages wildlife, trees, and crops. It reduces food supplies and pollutes drinking water.

Controlling acid rain is difficult. One reason is that acid rain often forms in one area and falls in another area as rain clouds drift across the sky. Another reason is that many industries think reducing the amount of harmful chemicals they release would be too costly.

Scientists are urging industries to build equipment that will limit the amount of sulfur dioxide and nitrogen dioxide released into the air. Scientists also want the government to pass laws that will force companies to meet clean air standards. Scientists warn that if people do not control acid rain soon, the lack of clean water will endanger humans as well as fish.

Follow-up Activity

Acid rain affects both individuals and society. Do research in your library to find out about the effects of acid rain on each of the following.

- Human health
- Recreation
- The economy

Write an essay in which you list and describe each effect. Share your essay with your classmates.

Figure 2-18

WARNING
Do not eat fish or drink water from lake

What can you infer about the lake?

KEEPING TRACK

Section 2-1 Atoms and Molecules
1. The atom is the basic unit of matter.
2. An element is a substance made of one kind of atom.
3. A molecule is made of two or more atoms that are combined chemically.

Section 2-2 Compounds and Living Things
1. Living things are made of inorganic and organic compounds. Organic compounds contain both carbon and hydrogen atoms.

Section 2-3 Characteristics of Living Things
1. All living things are made of cells. Cells are the basic units of living things.
2. All living things respond to stimuli in their environment.
3. Each kind of organism is adapted for survival in a particular environment, such as arctic, desert, or ocean environments.
4. Reproduction guarantees that life continues through the production of new individuals.

Section 2-4 Needs of Living Things
1. Living things continually exchange materials with their environment.
2. All living things require water, which is obtained from the environment.
3. All living things require energy and food for growth and repair.
4. Some living things remain dormant or hibernate during severe environmental conditions. Others migrate to avoid very extreme temperatures.

Section 2-5 Life Activities
1. Life processes are the activities an organism must carry on in order to live.
2. All living things obtain energy from food during respiration. During respiration, most organisms take in oxygen and release carbon dioxide.

BUILDING VOCABULARY
Write the term from the list that best matches each statement.

organism, stimulus, environment, reproduction, respiration, adaptation, migrate, respond, protein, carbohydrate

1. Process in which oxygen combines with food to release energy
2. A characteristic that helps an organism survive in its environment
3. Living things do this in order to react to changes in the environment
4. A compound made of amino acids
5. Some animals do this as the seasons change
6. Process of producing more of one's own kind
7. Any change in the environment to which a living thing will react
8. A living thing
9. Organic molecule such as sugar or starch that stores energy
10. The surroundings of an organism.

Explain the difference between the terms in each pair.

11. environment, adaptation

12. hibernate, migrate
13. stimulus, response
14. respiration, photosynthesis
15. ingestion, digestion
16. reproduction, development
17. element, compound
18. sugar, starch
19. organic compound, inorganic compound
20. amino acid, protein

SUMMARIZING

Write the missing word for each sentence.

1. The basic unit of structure and function of living things is the _____.
2. An organism's surroundings make up its _____.
3. Any characteristic of an organism that helps the organism survive is called a(an)_____.
4. Plants make food by a process called _____.
5. To release energy from foods, living things carry on a process called _____.
6. A solvent found in cells is _____.
7. A reaction to a stimulus is called a _____.
8. A compound made of carbon atoms is a (an) _____ compound.
9. Starch is made of a long chain of _____ molecules.
10. Fats, oils, and waxes are examples of a type of compound called a (an) _____.

INTERPRETING INFORMATION

Use Figure 2-19 to answer the following questions.

1. Which are the three most abundant elements found in a human cell?
2. Is the percentage of zinc in the human body greater or less than one percent?

Figure 2-19

Elements found in humans	Approximate % of human body
Carbon	18
Oxygen	65
Hydrogen	10
Nitrogen	3
Calcium	2
Phosphorus	1.4
Potassium	0.4
Other elements	0.2

THINK AND DISCUSS

Use the section number in parentheses to help you find each answer. Write your answers in complete sentences.

1. Compare an element to a compound. (2-1)
2. What is the difference between an organic compound and an inorganic compound? Give three examples of each. (2-2)
3. Select three different kinds of environments and an organism that lives in each kind. Describe how each of the three organisms is adapted for survival. (2-3)

4. Name two basic needs of humans and tell how humans obtain each need. (2-4)
5. Explain the relationship between ingestion and digestion. (2-5)

Think of several different animals that share a similar environment, such as the animals that live in a desert. Use the library to research how each of these animals is adapted for survival. Write a report in which you compare the adaptations for survival for each animal you study.

1. A polar bear lives in the arctic. It has thick white fur. The thick white fur is an example of how the bear
   a. responds to changes in its environment.
   b. adapts to its environment.
   c. moves quickly.
   d. is seen from far away.
2. Living things obtain energy from
   a. oxygen.   b. water.
   c. food.   d. carbon dioxide.
3. Which one of the following sets of statements identifies one difference between plants and animals?
   a. Animals require oxygen. Plants do not require oxygen.
   b. Plants make food. Animals do not.
   c. Animals carry on cellular respiration. Plants do not carry on cellular respiration.

d. Animals release oxygen as a waste product. Plants release carbon dioxide as a waste product.
4. Living things require water because it is a (an)
   a. energy source.   b. solvent.
   c. food source.   d. molecule.
5. To survive the cold winters, some bears
   a. migrate.   b. hibernate.
   c. become more active.
   d. build warmer shelters.
6. A human may jump after hearing a loud noise. This is an example of how a living thing
   a. exchanges materials with its environment.
   b. responds to a stimulus.
   c. uses sound energy to produce food.
   d. saves sound energy.
7. Living things produce new living things as a result of a process called
   a. respiration.   b. regulation.
   c. reproduction.   d. growth.
8. Which organism is correctly matched to an adaptation?
   a. Adult frogs breathe through their gills.
   b. Some birds migrate in the winter.
   c. Whales take in oxygen which is dissolved in water.
   d. Houseflies have webbed feet.
9. Which is not an adaptation possessed by most frogs for survival?
   a. lungs for breathing
   b. sticky tongues for capturing prey
   c. fins for swimming
   d. webbed feet for swimming

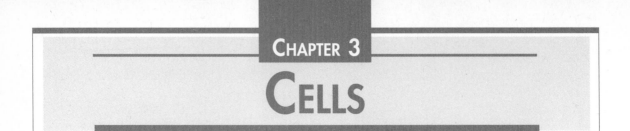

CELLS

Suppose that you had a box filled with 24 compact discs and you removed all 24 discs. What would be left in the box? Did you answer "nothing"? The box would certainly be empty of compact discs, but it would still be full of air. At first glance, *air* might seem to be the same as *nothing*, but air has both living and nonliving things in it. If you are a careful observer, you have probably seen some of the things in the air. You may have seen dust particles bouncing in the sunlight that streams through the windows of a room. Although some things in air, like dust particles, are visible with the unaided eye, most things are not. Air contains many invisible molecules, including hydrogen, oxygen, nitrogen, and carbon dioxide gases. In addition, air often contains organisms, such as bacteria, which are also too small to be seen.

If you allow the particles of soil in water from a stream or river to settle to the bottom of a glass, you might think that the water above the settled particles is clear and empty. However, the water, like air, is filled with organisms and other things that are too small to see.

Figure 3-1 shows living and nonliving things that are visible. In nature, the scene would also be full of many things too small to be seen.

3-1 Cells

■ *Objectives*

☐ *Summarize the events leading to the development of the cell theory.*

☐ *State the cell theory.*

You learned in Chapter 2 that cells, the building blocks of all organisms, are too small to be seen with the unaided eye. How, then, do scientists know cells exist? Cells are visible if viewed through instruments called **microscopes**. When you look at a cell through a microscope,

Figure 3-1

How many living things are in this scene?

you see an image of the cell. The image is larger than the actual cell. You are probably very familiar with the simplest microscope, which is a magnifying glass. A magnifying glass is a lens that has been ground and polished until both its sides are curved. When observed through this kind of lens, an object looks larger than it really is. Look at Figure 3-2, which shows an ant as it appears when viewed through a magnifying glass. Notice that when viewed through the lens, the ant appears larger than its actual size.

The First Microscope
In the mid-1600s, a Dutch merchant and amateur scientist named Anton van Leeuwenhoek (LAY-vun-hook) was one of the first to build a simple microscope. His microscope enlarged objects up to 270

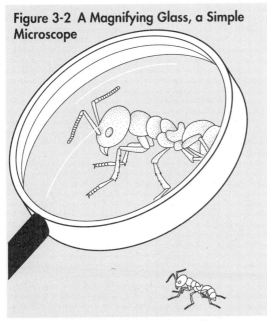

Figure 3-2 A Magnifying Glass, a Simple Microscope

When seen through a magnifying glass, an ant may appear much larger than its actual size.

times. Van Leeuwenhoek used his microscope to look at drops of pond water and rainwater. In these drops, van Leeuwenhoek observed tiny **unicellular** (yu-ni-SEL-yuh-lur) **organisms**. Unicellular organisms are organisms made up entirely of one cell. These organisms include bacteria, amoebas, and some algae. Van Leeuwenhoek was one of the first scientists to observe this hidden world of microscopic organisms, or organisms that are visible only under the microscope. Van Leeuwenhoek also observed the cells of **multicellular organisms**, which are organisms made up of more than one cell. He described in detail and drew accurate diagrams of everything he saw.

Discovering Cells
Robert Hooke was an English scientist who also lived during the 1600s. By 1665, Hooke and other scientists were using a new type of microscope. You can see from Figure 3-3 that Hooke's microscope contained two lenses. A microscope made

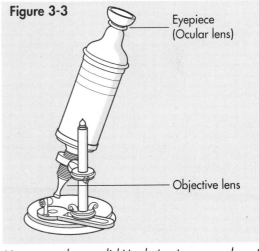

Figure 3-3

Eyepiece (Ocular lens)

Objective lens

How many lenses did Hooke's microscope have?

of two lenses is called a **compound microscope**. The first lens is the objective lens. This lens produces an enlarged image, just as a magnifying glass does. The second lens is the eyepiece, or ocular lens. The eyepiece magnifies, or enlarges, the image produced by the objective lens even more. Many microscopes today have more than one objective lens.

Hooke looked at a very thin slice of cork under his microscope. Cork is the soft bark of a certain kind of oak tree. Hooke was amazed when he looked at the magnified slice of cork. As shown in Figure 3-4, the cork looked like a honeycomb, with many boxes surrounded by thin walls. Hooke called the tiny boxes *cells*, after the small rooms in a monastery where monks lived.

Hooke began to study parts of other plants to see if they too had cells. He studied their roots, leaves, and bark. Every plant part he looked at with his microscope was indeed made of cells. Look at the different types of plant cells in Figure 3-5. After observing dozens of plants, Hooke was ready to form a hypothesis. He suggested that all plants were made of cells.

Figure 3-4

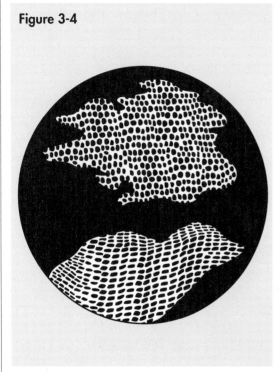

Slice of cork

Figure 3-5

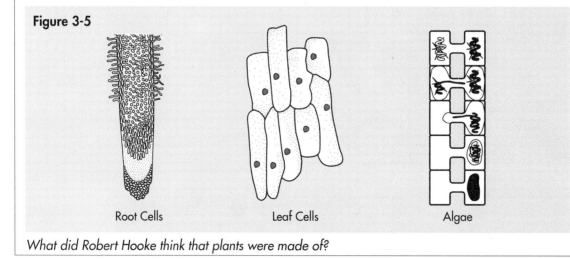

Root Cells   Leaf Cells   Algae

What did Robert Hooke think that plants were made of?

The Cell Theory

Was Hooke's hypothesis correct? Only more observations could provide the answer. However, Hooke alone could not examine every known plant in the world to see if it was made of cells. In addition, his microscope was not powerful enough for him to see cells smaller than cork cells.

Over 100 years passed before scientists could gather enough evidence to show that Hooke's hypothesis was correct. As microscopes of greater power became available, scientists observed more and more cells. They even observed what appeared to be structures within cells. Eventually, a German scientist, Matthias Schleiden (SHLY-dun), concluded that all plants are made of cells.

Meanwhile, other scientists had begun examining animal structures under the microscope. They found that animals too were made of cells. At about the time that Schleiden made his conclusion, German scientist Theodor Schwann (SCWAN) concluded that all animals are made of cells.

Scientists who studied one-celled organisms such a *Paramecium* discovered something very interesting. They observed that these organisms would occasionally divide to form two new organisms. Figure 3-6 shows how *Paramecium* divides in two. Eventually, scientists determined that cells usually reproduced in this way. Onion root cells came from other onion root cells. Human skin cells came from other human skin cells.

The work of Schleiden, Schwann, and other researchers led scientists to develop the **cell theory**. A theory is a hypothesis supported by the results of many different related experiments. The main ideas of the cell theory are listed as follows:

- All living things are made of cells.
- Life processes take place in cells.
- All cells come from other cells of the same type.

Review the life processes you read about in Chapter 2. Notice that the occurrence of life processes in the cell is an important part of the cell theory.

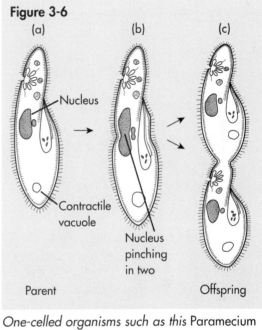

Figure 3-6

(a)　　　(b)　　　(c)

Nucleus

Contractile vacuole

Nucleus pinching in two

Parent　　　Offspring

One-celled organisms such as this Paramecium *reproduce by dividing into two new cells.*

■■ Section 3-1 Review ■■

Write the definitions for the following terms in your own words.

1. **compound microscope**
2. **cell theory**

Answer these questions.

3. What was Anton van Leeuwenhoek's contribution to the discovery of cells?
4. How did the development of the compound microscope contribute to the development of the cell theory?
5. List the three main ideas of cell theory.
6. Explain the following statement. *Cells come from other cells.* Give examples.
7. Explain how the scientific method was used in discovering the cell theory.

3-2 Using Microscopes to Study Cells

■ *Objectives*

☐ *List the procedure to follow when using a compound microscope.*

☐ *Estimate in microns the size of some cells.*

Early microscopes enabled scientists to learn about cells. Today's microscopes are much more powerful. They have helped unlock many secrets of life. Understanding the microscope and its proper use is one of the keys to the successful study of life science.

The Compound Microscope

In the classroom, you will probably use a compound microscope much like the one shown in Figure 3-7. Find the ocular lens, or eyepiece, and the objective lenses. How many objective lenses are there? Many microscopes have three objective lenses,

each with a different **magnification** (mag-nuh-fuh-KAY-shun), or power.

Find the low-power and high-power objective lenses in Figure 3-7. You can use low- or high-power lenses to observe a cell. Figure 3-8 shows human cheek cells as seen under both low and high power. What differences do you observe?

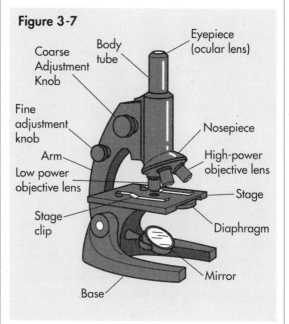

Figure 3-7

Coarse Adjustment Knob — Body tube — Eyepiece (ocular lens) — Fine adjustment knob — Arm — Low power objective lens — Nosepiece — High-power objective lens — Stage — Stage clip — Diaphragm — Stage — Base — Mirror

Magnification

With your teacher's permission, observe a microscope. If you look closely at the eyepiece and objective lenses on your microscope, you will see a number followed by an X. The eyepiece on the microscope you will use in class is probably marked 10X. This number tells you that the power of the eyepiece is ten times. If you look at an object through a 10X lens, the object appears 10 times larger than it is. Now look at the magnification number on the low-power objective lens. The magnification of your low-power objective lens is probably also 10X.

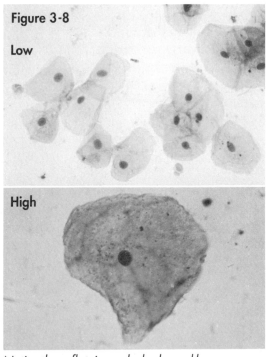

Figure 3-8

Low

High

Notice these flat, irregularly shaped human cheek cells.

To determine the magnification of your microscope using low power, multiply these two numbers. Since $10 \times 10 = 100$, the low-power magnification of your microscope is 100 times. What is the magnification of your microscope when the high-power objective lens is used?

Using the Compound Microscope

Before using your classroom microscope, learn the following rules and procedures.
- Always get permission to use the microscope.
- Use two hands when carrying a microscope. Place one hand on the arm and the other hand under the base.
- Use a piece of lens paper to clean the objective lenses and the eyepiece. Never wipe a lens with your finger, a cloth, or a paper towel.
- Be sure that the low-power objective lens is moved into place.
- While looking through the eyepiece, adjust the mirror so that enough light is passing through the stage. Adjust the diaphragm so a proper amount of light reaches the stage.
- Place a slide on the stage, making sure to position the object to be viewed right over the opening on the stage. The slide may be a prepared slide or one that you prepare yourself.
- Lower the objective lens as far as possible and then, while looking through the eyepiece, raise the objective lens slowly until the object is in focus. Use the coarse adjustment knob first and then the fine adjustment knob for more accurate focusing.

To use the high-power objective lens, do the following.
- While using low power, center the object to be examined.
- Carefully rotate the high-power objective lens into place. If necessary, raise the tube so that it does not hit the slide.
- Adjust the mirror to increase the amount of light being passed through the object.
- The high-power objective lens focuses very close to the object. The objective lens must be raised very slowly, using the fine adjustment knob.

How Do You Use a Compound Microscope to View Onion Cells?

Process Skills using laboratory equipment, observing

Materials compound microscope, onion slice, iodine, 2 glass slides, 2 cover slips, paper towels, forceps

Procedure

1. Use the forceps to peel off two pieces of skin from the inner curved surface of a layer of the onion, as shown in Figure 3-9. Be sure you peel off only one layer.
2. Take two glass slides. Lay a piece of onion skin flat on each glass slide.
3. Cover both pieces of onion skin with a drop of water. Add a drop of iodine to one slide. Place a cover slip over each piece of onion skin. Use a paper towel to soak up any extra water or iodine. You have just prepared two wet mount slides.

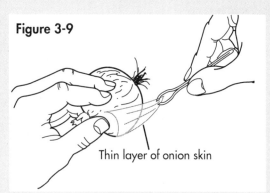

Figure 3-9

Thin layer of onion skin

4. Place the wet mount slide of onion skin without iodine on the microscope stage. Be sure that the specimen covers the opening in the stage.
5. With the low-power objective lens in place, carefully focus your specimen. Draw what you see. Label your drawing.
6. Remove the first slide and replace it with the slide you stained with iodine. Look for the cells. Look for a boundary, or cell membrane, around each cell. What shape does the boundary give the cells?
7. Find the darkly stained dot in the center of a cell. This dot is the nucleus. The area between the boundary of the cell and the nucleus is the cytoplasm. Describe what you see inside the cytoplasm.
8. Draw and label a diagram of the onion skin cell stained with iodine, under low power.
9. Now observe the onion skin under high power. Use the fine adjustment knob to bring the specimen into focus. What you see is an image that is enlarged more than before. Draw what you see and label your drawing.

Conclusions

10. What is the purpose of adding iodine to a wet mount?
11. Which power would you use to see the parts of the onion skin cells in greater detail? Why?

How might you go about measuring something as tiny as an onion skin cell? Scientists use special instruments to make precise measurements, but you can measure cells with a clear metric ruler and a microscope.

The first step is to measure the viewing area, or microscopic field. Look at the section of a metric ruler in Figure 3-10.

Figure 3-10

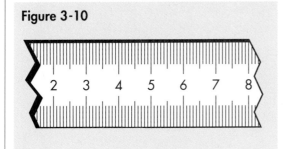

A metric ruler is used to measure length.

How many centimeters are shown? How many millimeters equal 1 centimeter? Turn to page 12 in Chapter 1 if you need help answering these questions.

Figure 3-11 shows how a metric ruler looks under the low-power objective lens

Figure 3-11

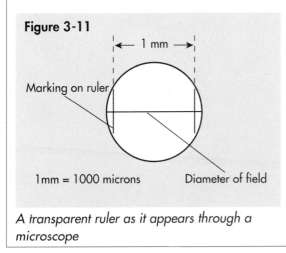

A transparent ruler as it appears through a microscope

(100X) of a microscope. Notice that the diameter, or widest part, of the microscopic field is a little more than 1 millimeter. Now imagine dividing that millimeter into 1000 small sections. Each section measures $\frac{1}{1000}$ mm, or 1 **micron**. Thus, the diameter of the microscopic field is a little more than 1000 microns.

Once you know the size of the microscopic field, you can calculate the size of your specimen. Look at the organism in Figure 3-12. Notice that the organism takes up about one fourth of the field's

Figure 3-12

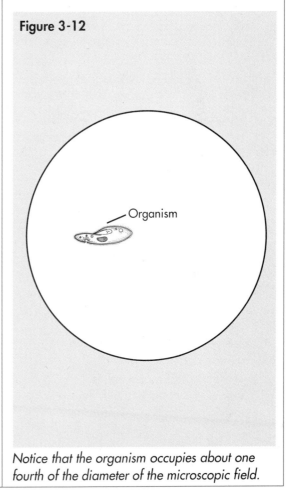

Notice that the organism occupies about one fourth of the diameter of the microscopic field.

diameter. To find out the size of the organism, divide 1,000 microns, the diameter of the field, by 4. The organism is about 250 microns, or ¼ mm in length.

The Electron Microscope

The most powerful microscope used by scientists is the **electron microscope**. The electron microscope can produce magnifications of more than 300,000X. An electron microscope has a camera that makes photographs called **electron micrographs** (MY-kruh-graf). These photographs show not only cells but individual parts of cells that are too small to be seen with a compound microscope.

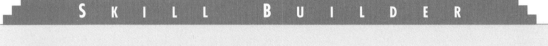

Making Calculations

Study Figure 3-13, which shows the diameter of a microscope field under low power (100X). The onion skin cells shown in the figure look as they would if viewed under low power.

1. Approximately how large in millimeters and in microns is the diameter of the microscopic field?
2. How many onion skin cells fit across the diameter of the field?
3. How long in microns is each onion skin cell? Hint: Divide the length of the diameter in microns by the number of onion cells seen across the diameter.
4. Most people can see objects as small as 100 microns with the unaided eye. Could you see an onion skin cell without the assistance of a microscope?
5. A human red blood cell is 7 microns long. Can you see it with the unaided eye?

Figure 3-13

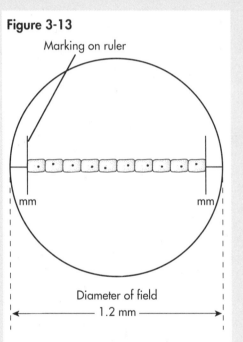

What is the size of one onion skin cell?

Figure 3-14 shows an electron micrograph of just the tip of a cell taken from an animal muscle. The dark structures are microscopic fibers that help muscle cells move. Look back to Figure 3-8 which shows skin cells magnified by a light microscope. Which photograph shows greater details?

Figure 3-14

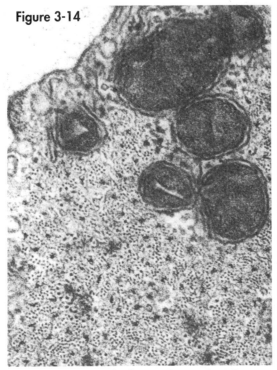

Electron micrograph of smooth muscle cell

▬ Section 3-2 Review ▬

Write the definitions for the following terms in your own words.

1. **magnification**
2. **micron**
3. **electron microscope**

Answer these questions.

4. List and describe the functions of the main parts of the compound microscope.
5. How would you bring more light into your microscope?
6. List the steps involved in preparing a wet mount.
7. What are advantages and disadvantages of observing a cell under the low power objective lens? Under the high power objective lens?
8. Summarize the process of measuring a microscopic object.

3-3 Parts of the Cell

■ *Objectives*
☐ *Identify the major parts of the cell.*
☐ *Distinguish between a plant and an animal cell.*
☐ *List the levels of organization in an organism.*

The cell theory states that all organisms are made of cells and that life processes take place within cells. By now you may be wondering exactly how all this activity can occur within cells. With electron microscopes and other special instruments, scientists have learned that cells contain many important structures. Each of these structures has a specific role, or function, in carrying out life processes.

Animal Cells
Animal cells have a variety of sizes, shapes, and functions. However, most animal cells

have the same basic parts. These parts are called **organelles** (or-guh-NELS). Figure 3-15 shows a typical animal cell and its organelles. As you read about the organelles of an animal cell, use Figure 3-15 to locate the part being discussed.

- Cells are surrounded and protected by the **cell membrane**. The cell membrane consists of a double layer of lipids, in which large protein molecules float. This arrangement makes the cell membrane semipermeable. **Semipermeable** means that only certain substances can permeate, or pass through, a semipermeable membrane. Thus, the cell membrane controls the passage of materials into and out of the cell.

- The fluid that fills the inside of the cell is the **cytoplasm** (SYT-oh-plaz-um). Many life processes take place in the cytoplasm.

- The control center of the cell is the **nucleus**. A membrane called the **nuclear membrane** surrounds the nucleus and separates it from the cytoplasm. Inside the nucleus are threadlike structures called **chromosomes** (KRO-muh-sohms). Each chromosome is made of a great number of units, called **genes**, linked together in a kind of chain made of DNA. Genes control chemical activities in a cell. When a cell divides, chromosomes also divide and are passed on to each new cell. Each kind of living thing has a definite number of chromosomes.

- A round structure called the **nucleolus** (nyoo-KLEE-oh-lus) is found in the nucleus. The nucleolus produces the chemical **ribosomal RNA**. This chemical is used to manufacture parts of cell organelles called **ribosomes** (RY-buh-sohms). Ribosomes combine amino acids to form the proteins necessary for life processes in the cells.

- Recall from Chapter 2 that during cellular respiration, digested food combines with oxygen and energy is released. The sites of cellular respiration are the **mitochondria** (myt-oh-KAN-dree-uh). A chemical called ATP, which is made in the mitochondria, captures and stores this energy. The energy stored in ATP is released when the body needs it to carry out life processes. For this reason, mitochondria are sometimes called the powerhouses of cells.

- Some chemicals are made on a group of membranes called the **endoplasmic reticulum** (en-duh-PLAZ-mik rih-TIK-yuh-lum). In addition to making chemicals, the endoplasmic reticulum stores, sorts, and transports these chemicals to other parts of the cell.

- The **Golgi bodies** are stacks of flattened membranes found in the cytoplasm. The Golgi bodies put together and release special chemicals. These special chemicals are used by the cells of the body.

- Sacklike organelles that carry out various functions, including storage and cell digestion, are the **vacuoles** (VAK-yuh-wohls). Vacuoles are filled with fluid and surrounded by membranes. Unicellular organisms have **food vacuoles** in which digestion takes place. These organisms have **contractile** (kun-TRAK-tul) **vacuoles** that store and pump out extra water.

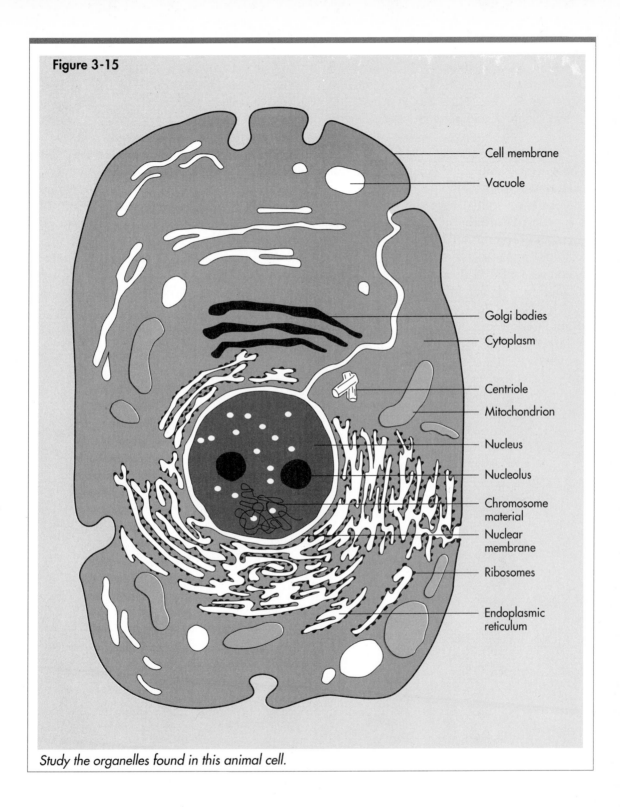

Figure 3-15

Cell membrane

Vacuole

Golgi bodies

Cytoplasm

Centriole

Mitochondrion

Nucleus

Nucleolus

Chromosome material

Nuclear membrane

Ribosomes

Endoplasmic reticulum

Study the organelles found in this animal cell.

- One organelle that animal cells have and that plant cells do not have is a **centriole**. Centrioles play an important role in animal cell reproduction.

Plant Cells

The cells of plants have most of the organelles that animal cells have. By comparing the plant and animal cells shown in Figure 3-16, you can see that plant cells also have parts that animal cells do not have. For example, in plant cells a layer, or covering, called the **cell wall** surrounds the cell membrane. In fact, it is the cell wall of cork cells that formed the boxes Robert Hooke observed.

The cell wall is made of cellulose, a substance that makes the wall tough and stiff. Cellulose is manufactured in the Golgi bodies of plant cells. The cell wall protects and supports the plant cell and gives the cell a regular shape. Plant cells also contain a very large vacuole, which takes up most of the space of the cell. Both the cell wall and the vacuole make the plant stand tall and rigid.

Plant cells are also different from animal cells because they have **chloroplasts** (KLOHR-uh-plasts). Chloroplasts are small green-colored organelles scattered throughout the cytoplasm of a plant cell. Chloroplasts have a green pigment called **chlorophyll** (KLOHR-uh-fil), which gives leaves and stems their green color. Photosynthesis, which you read about in Chapter 2, takes place in the chloroplasts. Because their cells do not contain chloroplasts, animals cannot carry out photosynthesis.

Figure 3-16

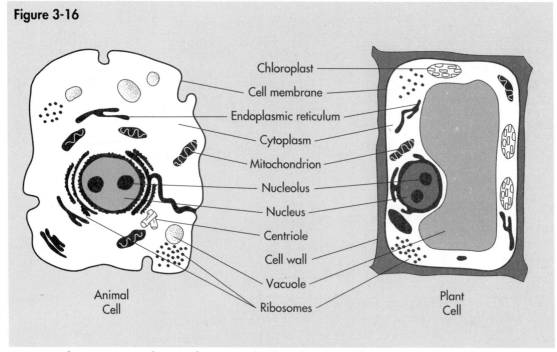

Chloroplast
Cell membrane
Endoplasmic reticulum
Cytoplasm
Mitochondrion
Nucleolus
Nucleus
Centriole
Cell wall
Vacuole
Ribosomes

Animal Cell

Plant Cell

Compare the structure and parts of an animal cell and a plant cell.

Differences Among Cells

Although most kinds of cells have the same basic parts, all cells are not identical. For example, cells in an onion are shaped like rectangles. Some one-celled organisms are oval and have tiny microscopic hairs called cilia. Human skin cells are broad and flat. Differences exist even among the cells found in one kind of living thing. For example, human red blood cells are round and have no nucleus. Human nerve cells are long and thin with many branches. Human muscle cells are thin and flexible. Look closely at Figures 3-17, 3-18, and 3-19 to see different types of human cells.

Multicellular organisms, such as trees, birds, and humans, may contain billions of cells. Among the billions of cells, there are different cells that do different jobs. For example, you have skin cells that cover and protect your body, bone cells that support your body, and muscle cells that help move your body.

Figure 3-17

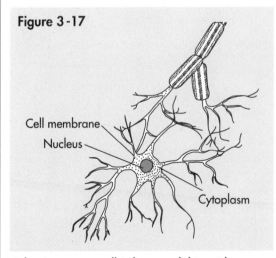

A human nerve cell is long and thin with many branches.

Figure 3-18

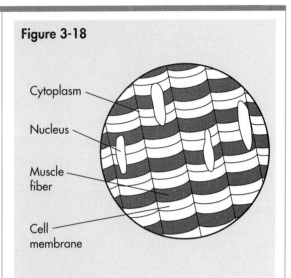

A human muscle cell is thin and flexible.

Figure 3-19

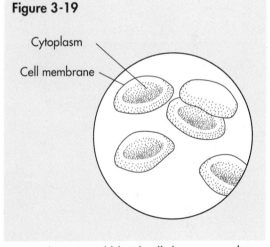

Mature human red blood cells have no nucleus.

No cell in a multicellular organism can live by itself. Each cell depends on other cells around it to survive. Your red blood cells, for example, carry oxygen through the bloodstream to all the other cells in your body. Nerve cells carry messages from one type of cell to another.

Groups of cells that look the same and do the same job are called tissues. Groups of skin cells, for example, make up your skin tissue, and groups of nerve cells make up your nerve tissue.

Tissues that work together to do a certain job form an organ. Your leg is an organ. It is made of many different kinds of tissues, such as skin tissue, bone tissue, and muscle tissue. Your stomach, kidneys, and lungs are also organs.

Finally, groups of organs that work together to do a certain job form organ systems. Your nervous system includes your brain, spinal cord, and all the nerves in your body. Notice the different levels of organization, which are illustrated in Figure 3-20.

There is one kind of cell that does live by itself. It is a unicellular organism, such as bacterium and *Paramecium*. A single cell carries on all the life processes necessary to keep the organism alive.

Figure 3-20

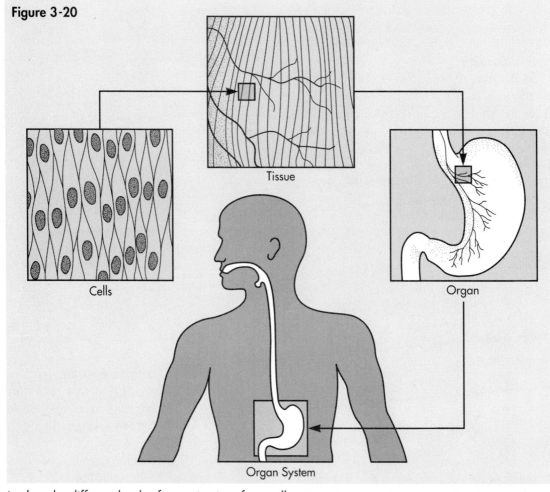

Tissue

Cells

Organ

Organ System

Look at the different levels of organization, from cell to tissue to organ to organ system to organism.

Making Observations

Look at the drop of pond water shown in Figure 3-21 as it appears under a microscope. The drop of water contains a variety of organisms.

1. How many different kinds of organisms are shown?
2. How is each organism different from the other organisms?
3. Carefully draw three different organisms. For each organism, label the organelles that all three have in common.

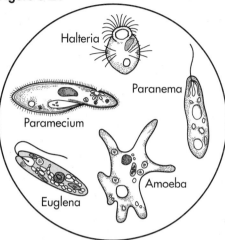

How are these organisms alike? How are they different?

Section 3-3 Review

Write the definitions for the following terms in your own words.

1. **cell membrane**
2. **cytoplasm**
3. **nucleus**
4. **ribosomes**
5. **mitochondria**

Answer these questions.

6. Which organelle controls the passage of materials into and out of the cell?

7. Describe three important structures found in the nucleus.
8. How does a plant cell differ from an animal cell? How are plant and animal cells similar?
9. Suppose you find two sets of incomplete notes on cell experiments. Set A gives data about mitochondria, cytoplasm, and ribosomes. Set B discusses nucleolus, nucleus, and cell wall. Can you tell from the notes if Set A is about a plant or an animal? How do you know? Is Set B about a plant or an animal? How do you know?

SCIENCE, TECHNOLOGY, & SOCIETY

Surgery on Cells

Advanced technologies like the electron microscope and microdissection tools enable scientists to perform surgery on cells. When this kind of surgery is performed, the character of the cell may change.

In one recent surgery, scientists removed the nucleus from one cell and transplanted it into a cell with no nucleus. As a result, the cell that received the nucleus took on the character of the cell from which the nucleus was removed.

In an earlier experiment, a scientist successfully removed the gene holding the instructions for making insulin from a human cell. Then the scientist transferred this gene into a bacterium cell. The bacterium cell, with its new gene, became able to make human insulin. Insulin is the chemical in humans that helps the body use sugar properly. Individuals who cannot manufacture enough insulin suffer from the disease diabetes. As a result of this gene transplant, diabetics can now depend upon bacteria to make the insulin they must take.

Scientists may one day be able to transplant any human gene they wish from one organism to another. They may, for example, be able to transfer human genes from individual to individual. There have been many discussions about whether scientists should be permitted to alter the character of a human life by transplanting genes. The question of whether genes should be transplanted is a question that you may someday have to answer.

Follow-up Activity

Your teacher will divide your class into discussion teams. Meet with your team to discuss the issue. Should society permit biologists to develop microsurgical techniques like gene transplants to alter the character of human life?

Figure 3-22

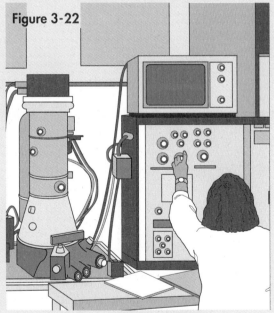

A scientist uses an electron microscope to examine cells.

Section 3-1 Cells

1. The development of the microscope led to the discovery of cells.
2. The cell theory states that the cell is the basic unit of all living things. Every living thing is made of cells, which carry on the basic life processes of the organism.

Section 3-2 Using Microscopes to Study Cells

1. Cells can be observed under the compound microscope, using either low or high power.
2. You can measure microscopic specimens in microns. First, you measure the diameter of the microscopic field. Then you estimate the portion of the diameter taken up by the cell.

Section 3-3 Parts of the Cell

1. A cell contains many cell structures, called organelles, that carry on life activities. These organelles include the mitochondria, ribosomes, Golgi bodies, and the endoplasmic reticulum.
2. Plant cells differ from animal cells in that they have a cell wall and chloroplasts.
3. Organisms made of one cell are called unicellular organisms. Those made of many cells are called multicellular organisms.

Write the terms from the list that complete the sentences.

magnification, organelles, cell membrane, chromosomes, nucleus, mitochondria, microscope, ribosomes, cell theory, electron

An instrument called the ___1___ enables biologists to see the cell. According to the ___2___, every living thing is made of cells. Each cell contains structures called ___3___, which carry on the life processes of the organism. For example, the ___4___ carry on cellular respiration. The ___5___ manufacture proteins. The ___6___ surrounds and protects the cell. The control center of the cell is the ___7___. Inside the control center are threadlike structures called ___8___. In recent years, scientists have used a very powerful microscope called the ___9___ microscope to observe cells. It has enabled biologists to observe cells with increased ___10___.

If the statement is true, write *true*. If the statement is false, change the *italicized* term to make the statement true.

1. A *cell* is the basic unit of all living things.
2. Bacteria are an example of *multicellular organisms*.
3. To increase the amount of light entering the microscope, use the *coarse adjustment knob*.
4. Structures on chromosomes called *nucleoli* determine the appearance of the organism.
5. The *cytoplasm* is the part of the cell containing all the organelles.

CHAPTER REVIEW

6. Digestion in one-celled organisms takes place in the *contractile* vacuole.
7. Plant cells have green-colored organelles called *Golgi bodies*.

Refer to Figure 3-23, Characteristics of Some Living Cells, to answer the following questions.

1. Which cell cannot be seen with the human eye?
2. Which cell has no chromosomes?
3. How many times larger than a human egg cell is a *Paramecium*?
4. Which cell represents a unicellular organism?

Use the section number in parentheses to help you find each answer. Write your answers in complete sentences.

1. Discuss how the scientific method was used to develop the cell theory. (3-1)
2. What is the advantage of applying a stain before looking at a cell? (3-2)
3. A biologist wants to study in detail the structure of the mitochondria. What kind of microscope should the biologist use? Why? (3-2)
4. What would happen if all the mitochondria in a person's cells were suddenly destroyed? (3-3)
5. A scientist discovered a new marine organism. How could the scientist determine whether this new organism was a plant or an animal? (3-3)

1. Visit a local hospital, university, or science research center. Find out what research on cells is being done there. Write a report summarizing your findings.
2. Do you enjoy using the microscope in your science class? Ask your teacher to provide additional opportunities for you to use the microscope.

Figure 3-23 Characteristics of Some Living Cells

Cell Type	Approximate Size	Distinguishing Characteristics
Paramecium	220 microns	Has cilia to move
Red blood cell	7 microns	Has no nucleus
Human egg cell	110 microns	Contains stored food

CHAPTER THREE

1. While looking at a drop of pond water under the microscope, a scientist observed some things she had never seen before. Which one of the following observations convinced the scientist that these things were alive?
   a. They had a regular oval shape.
   b. They increased in their numbers.
   c. They were clear in color.
   d. They never grew in size.
2. A microscope has an eyepiece marked 10X and a low-power objective lens marked 10X. The magnification of this microscope under low power is
   a. 10X
   b. 20X
   c. 100X
   d. 1,000X
3. A Paramecium is 0.25 millimeters in length. How long is this Paramecium in microns?
   a. 125 microns   b. 250 microns
   c. 500 microns   d. 750 microns
4. A student studied a cell under the microscope. The cell had a cell wall and chloroplasts. The cell could have come from a (an)
   a. piece of cork.   b. lettuce leaf.
   c. grasshopper.   d. organelle.

Questions 5 and 6 are based on the picture of the cell shown in Figure 3-24.

5. The part of the cell where cellular respiration takes place is shown by letter
   a. A   b. B
   c. C   d. D

6. The part of the cell that controls which materials enter the cell is shown by letter
   a. A   b. B
   c. C   d. D

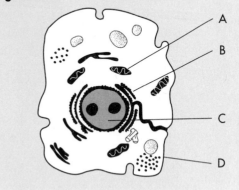

Figure 3-24

7. Structures inside the cell that carry on life functions are called
   a. tissues.
   b. organs.
   c. systems.
   d. organelles.
8. The cell theory states that
   a. different cells have different colors.
   b. all cells are exactly alike.
   c. all living things are made of cells.
   d. all cells have chloroplasts.
9. To study the structure of mitochondria, a scientist would use which of the following instruments?
   a. simple microscope
   b. compound microscope
   c. electron microscope
   d. any one of the above

CHAPTER 4

REPRODUCTION

Living things grow older and eventually die. However, they also produce new organisms to replace them as shown in Figure 4-1. The life process by which living things produce more of their kind is reproduction. You can see evidence of this life process all around you. You can see new plants sprouting from the ground in the spring. You can see robins' nests filled with newly hatched chicks and ponds filled with tadpoles. If your refrigerator contains old bread or cheese, you might even see evidence of reproduction in the mold that has grown there. If you were to visit a park or zoo, what are some other examples of reproduction you might see?

You learned in Chapter 2 that organisms reproduce more of their own kind. Frogs produce new frogs, maple trees produce new maple trees, and humans produce more humans. Even microscopic organisms reproduce their own kind. In this chapter, you will learn about the activities that take place within cells as living things grow, develop, and reproduce. You will also learn about several types of reproduction and how these types of reproduction adapt organisms for survival.

4-1 Life from Life

■ *Objectives*

☐ *Explain why people once believed in spontaneous generation.*

☐ *Explain how Redi's experiment proved that living things only come from other living things.*

The idea that living things come from other living things may not strike you as very exciting. For thousands of years, however, people believed that living things came from nonliving things. For example, people

Figure 4-1

Living things reproduce their own kind.

observed flies on rotting meat and concluded that flies came from the meat. They saw young frogs burrowing in the mud near ponds and believed that frogs were formed from the mud. This idea of life from nonlife is called **spontaneous** (span-TAY-nee-us) **generation**. As you know, scientific knowledge does not come from observations alone. Scientists gain knowledge about the natural world by conducting experiments.

One person who did not believe in spontaneous generation was Francesco Redi, an Italian scientist who lived in the seventeenth century. Redi hypothesized that flies did not come from rotting meat. He conducted an experiment to test his hypothesis.

Figure 4-2 shows how Redi set up his experiment. He placed pieces of raw meat in each of three jars. He left one experimental jar open. He covered another jar with a piece of fine screen. The last jar was the control jar. It was tightly sealed with a lid.

Then Redi set the jars out where the odor of the meat would attract flies. A few days later, Redi observed fly eggs and maggots, or newly hatched flies, on the meat in the uncovered jar. He also found eggs and maggots on the screen that covered the second jar. However, he observed no eggs or maggots in or around the tightly sealed jar. You can see Redi's results in Figure 4-2.

Redi's experiment proved that his hypothesis was correct. If maggots came from the meat alone, they would have appeared in all three jars. However, the maggots appeared only on the meat that was exposed to the surroundings. Therefore, something other than the meat must have produced the flies. Noting the fly eggs and maggots on the screen that covered the second jar, and on the meat in the first jar, Redi concluded that flies came from eggs produced by other flies. The eggs developed into maggots, which in turn developed into flies.

Even though Redi proved that flies did not come from rotting meat, the theory of spontaneous generation was not discarded completely until the middle of the nineteenth century. By this time, improvements in scientific instruments, such as microscopes, allowed scientists to see the actual means of reproduction.

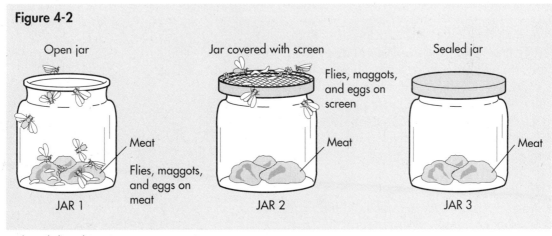

Figure 4-2

Open jar — JAR 1 — Meat — Flies, maggots, and eggs on meat

Jar covered with screen — JAR 2 — Flies, maggots, and eggs on screen — Meat

Sealed jar — JAR 3 — Meat

What did Redi's experiment prove?

Section 4-1 Review

Write the definition for the following term in your own words.

1. spontaneous generation

Answer these questions.

2. What led some people to believe that life could come from nonlife?
3. Describe the experiment Redi conducted to disprove spontaneous generation.
4. Why did Redi need a control jar in his experiment?

4-2 Cell Reproduction

■ *Objectives*

☐ *List and describe the stages of mitosis.*

☐ *Explain the importance of cell division for the continuation of life.*

☐ *Describe the role of mitosis in unicellular and multicellular organisms.*

☐ *Explain why reproduction is necessary for the continuation of the species and not the individual.*

The cell theory states that cells come from other preexisting cells. Cells produce new cells through the process of **cell division.** Unicellular, or one-celled, organisms reproduce by cell division. Multicellular, or many-celled, organisms, which begin life as a single cell, grow and develop into mature organisms by cell division.

Cell Division

Figure 4-3 shows an amoeba, which is a unicellular organism. In Figure 4-3, the amoeba is reproducing. The two new amoebas, called **daughter cells,** will grow to be identical to the parent amoeba.

The chromosomes carry the instructions that determine what an organism will look like and how it will function. These chromosomes and, as a result, traits are passed on from one generation to the next. Before an amoeba or any cell reproduces, each of its chromosomes must first double, or **replicate** (REP-luh-kayt). Then when the cell divides, each daughter cell receives one chromosome from each pair. In this way, each daughter cell receives a complete set of chromosomes that is identical to that of the parent cell. The duplication of the chromosomes takes place during a process called **mitosis** (my-TOH-sus).

Mitosis

Two important events take place during cell division. First, the chromosomes in the nucleus replicate themselves, forming two identical sets. This is the nuclear division called mitosis. Second, the cytoplasm of the cell divides to form two complete new daughter cells.

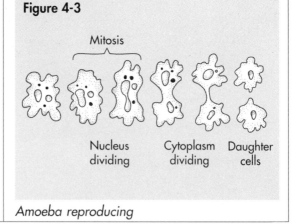

Figure 4-3

Mitosis

Nucleus dividing   Cytoplasm dividing   Daughter cells

Amoeba reproducing

Mitosis is a continuous process. However, to help you understand it, mitosis can be divided into five stages. Find each stage in Figure 4-4 as you read.

When a cell is not undergoing mitosis, the chromosomes exist in a loose, uncoiled state. The chromosome material in this state is known as **chromatin** (KROH-mut-in). In stage 1 of mitosis, the chromatin replicates.

During stage 2, the chromatin shortens and thickens to form the chromosomes. The cell now contains doubled chromosomes, consisting of the original chromosome and its replica, or double. Protein fibers begin to appear during stage 2. After the chromosomes form, the nuclear membrane begins to disappear.

During stage 3, each doubled chromosome lines up at the center of the cell and attaches to a fiber.

During stage 4, the fibers pull the doubled chromosomes apart toward opposite ends of the cell. As a result, two new and identical sets of chromosomes lie at opposite ends of the cell.

During stage 5, the cytoplasm begins to divide. A new nuclear membrane forms around each set of chromosomes, and the cell divides into two daughter cells. The cell membrane encloses each new cell.

As a result, two daughter cells are formed. Because each daughter cell has an identical set of chromosomes, the instructions for life are passed on from one cell

Figure 4-4

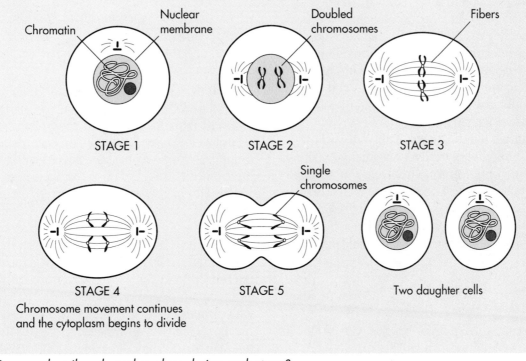

STAGE 1
STAGE 2
STAGE 3
STAGE 4
Chromosome movement continues
and the cytoplasm begins to divide
STAGE 5
Two daughter cells

Can you describe what takes place during each stage?

to another. The process of cell division is similar for both plant cells and animal cells.

Cell Division in Multicellular Organisms

You may know that multicellular organisms begin life as a single cell. This single cell divides into two cells, these two cells divide into four cells, and so on. At this moment, cells within your body are reproducing, causing your body to grow and develop. Each of these cells contains the same number and kind of chromosomes.

You might wonder, then, why the cells of a mature organism look so different from one another. How could the cells of your skin, eyes, and muscles have developed from the same cell? The answer is that your chromosomes contain instructions that direct the cells of your body to grow and function in a certain way. In each kind of cell, only certain chromosomes are working. For example, in the cells of your eye, chromosomes with instructions about how eye cells grow would be working, but chromosomes that control muscle cell growth would not. Although each kind of cell develops differently, all the cells in your body contain identical sets of chromosomes.

Even in fully grown organisms, cell division continues to take place. For example, if you cut your knee, skin cells divide to replace the injured cells and heal the wound. If you break the bones in your wrist, bone cells divide to make new cells to repair the break.

▰▰▰ Section 4-2 Review ▰▰▰

Write the definitions for the following terms in your own words.

1. **cell division**   2. **mitosis**
3. **daughter cell**   4. **chromatin**

Answer these questions.

5. How are mitosis and cell division related to each other?
6. Describe what happens during mitosis to prevent daughter cells from having half the number of chromosomes as their parent cells.
7. How does the role of cell division differ in unicellular and multicellular organisms?

4-3 Types of Asexual Reproduction

■ *Objectives*

☐ *List five types of asexual reproduction.*

☐ *Compare the different types of asexual reproduction.*

The process by which a one-parent organism produces a new organism is called **asexual reproduction**. An example is the amoeba. Like most unicellular organisms, amoebas come from one parent cell. In addition to unicellular organisms, many multicellular organisms can reproduce asexually.

Binary Fission

You already learned about one type of asexual reproduction in Section 4-2. Amoebas reproduce when a parent cell divides in two. This process is called binary (BY-nuh-ree) fission. Bacteria, *Paramecia*, and other unicellular organisms reproduce by binary fission. In this section, you will learn about additional types of asexual reproduction.

Budding

When binary fission takes place, each daughter cell receives an equal amount of both nuclear material and cytoplasm. In another type of asexual reproduction, called **budding,** the division of the nuclear material is equal, but the division of the cytoplasm is unequal. As a result, only one daughter cell forms, while the parent cell remains intact. Sometimes, the daughter cell remains attached to the parent by the cell membrane, as shown in Figure 4-5. In other cases, the daughter cell breaks completely away from the parent cell and develops into a mature organism.

Some simple multicellular organisms also reproduce by budding. Figure 4-6 illustrates the process of budding in a small pond-dwelling organism called hydra. The bud of a hydra consists of many cells, all of which arise by cell division from one parent hydra.

Figure 4-6

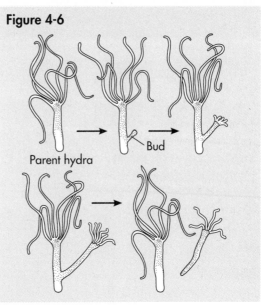

Parent hydra

Bud

Budding in the hydra

Spore Formation

Some organisms reproduce by forming **spores,** which are tiny structures that can grow into a new organism. Many one-celled organisms and molds reproduce by spores.

Figure 4-5

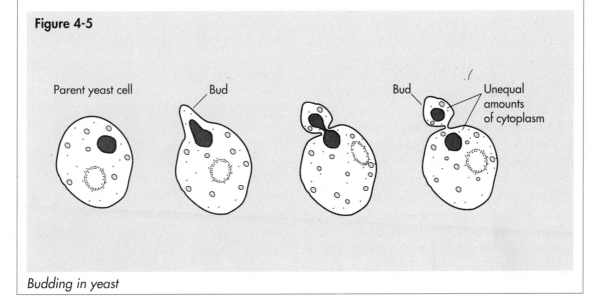

Parent yeast cell

Bud

Bud

Unequal amounts of cytoplasm

Budding in yeast

Interpreting a Graph

Yeast are one-celled organisms that reproduce by budding. A scientist studied the rate of budding of yeast placed in a sugar solution. Study the graph in Figure 4-7, which shows the pattern of reproduction of yeast in a sugar solution.

1. Between which two time periods did the reproduction of yeast increase?

2. Do you think the yeast stopped reproducing completely during the time period between 2 and 3? Why or why not?

3. Only a small amount of sugar was placed in the solution. How can this fact explain what happened to the rate of reproduction in the time period between 3 and 4?

Figure 4-7

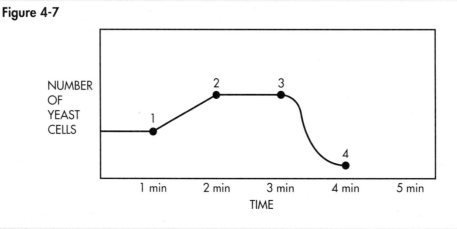

Reproduction of yeast in a sugar solution

Figure 4-8 shows mold growing on bread. Figure 4-9 shows what bread mold looks like under a microscope. Notice the balloon-like structures on top of each stalk in the mold in Figure 4-9. Each round structure is a **spore case**. Each spore case contains thousands of spores. Because spores are produced by mitosis, each spore has the same chromosomes as the parent organism.

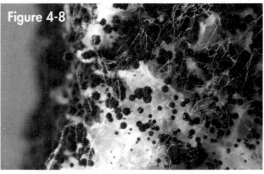

Figure 4-8

Bread mold on bread

Figure 4-9

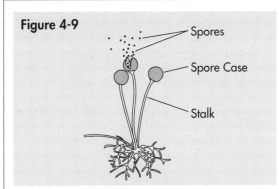

Spores

Spore Case

Stalk

Microscopic view of a stalk and spore case

When a spore case bursts, thousands of spores are released. Some of the spores will land on the bread. They will then undergo cell division and eventually form a new bread mold.

Regeneration

Many simple multicellular organisms can reproduce asexually from just a part of an existing organism. For example, if you cut a flatworm in two, each half can grow into

How Do Molds Reproduce by Means of Spores?

Process Skills *developing skills using laboratory equipment, making observations*

Materials jar with lid, slice of preservative-free bread, dust, microscope, magnifying glass, slides and cover slips, medicine dropper, forceps

Procedure

1. Thoroughly moisten a slice of bread and then sprinkle it with dust.
2. Place the bread in a jar. Tightly screw the lid on the jar. Set the jar aside in a warm place.
3. After several days, mold should begin to appear. Use a magnifying glass to look for black spots on the mold. These black spots are spore cases.
4. Use a medicine dropper to place a drop of water in the center of a microscope slide.
5. With forceps, place a tiny bit of the mold into the drop of water.
   Caution Keep face away from the mold. Do not do this part of the activity if you are allergic to mold.
6. Place a cover slip on the glass slide over the preparation.
7. Observe the specimen using both low power and high power on your microscope.
8. Draw and label what you see.

Conclusions

9. Where did the bread mold come from?
10. Why was it necessary to moisten the bread before placing it in the jar?
11. Preservatives are chemicals that slow the growth of mold. What would happen if you performed this activity using bread with preservatives?

a complete flatworm. The process by which body parts of animals grow into new organisms is called **regeneration.**

During regeneration, the cells of a detached body part undergo cell division and develop into a complete organism. Look at the starfish in Figure 4-10. The arm that has broken from this starfish will regenerate into a completely new starfish. Notice that the parent starfish in the figure will also regrow its lost arm. How will the two starfish compare?

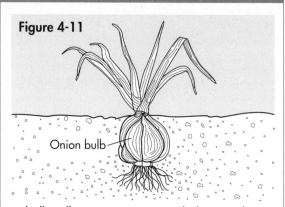

Figure 4-11

Onion bulb

A bulb will regenerate into a whole new plant.

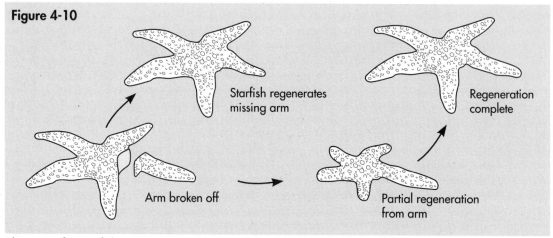

Figure 4-10

Starfish regenerates missing arm

Regeneration complete

Arm broken off

Partial regeneration from arm

The arm of a starfish regenerates.

Vegetative Propagation

Like earthworms and starfish, plants can also develop into a complete organism from a part of an organism. In plants, this process is called **vegetative propagation** (VEJ-uh-tayt-iv prap-uh-GAY-shun). Parts of plants such as roots, stems, and leaves can grow into new plants by vegetative propagation.

An onion plant may come from a **bulb,** an underground stem surrounded by fleshy leaves. Figure 4-11 shows an onion bulb growing into a new onion plant. Figure 4-12

shows a potato plant, which produces a thick underground stem called a **tuber.** The potatoes you eat are actually mature tubers. Find the **buds** on the potato shown in Figure 4-12. Each bud contains the start of a new stem and leaves. If the tuber is planted, each bud can grow into a new potato plant.

Some plants, such as the strawberry, have a **runner**, or horizontal stem. Runners grow close to the ground. They produce new plants whose roots grow into the soil. Find the new plants growing from the runners

Figure 4-12

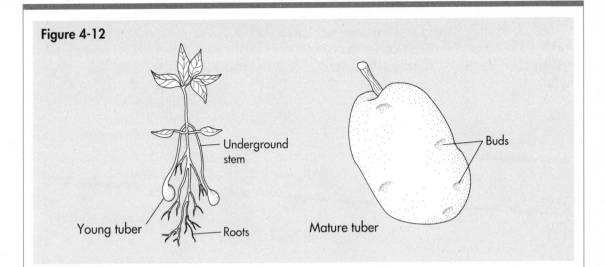

Underground stem

Buds

Young tuber

Roots

Mature tuber

of the strawberry plant shown in Figure 4-13. Why is reproduction through runners a type of asexual reproduction?

Figure 4-13

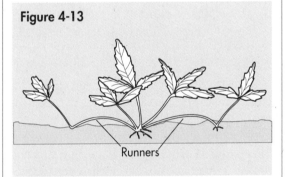

Runners

Runners of a strawberry plant

People have developed artificial methods of vegetative propagation. Such techniques enable people to reproduce desirable plants quickly. Some of these techniques are described here.

Cutting   Suppose your friend has a geranium plant. You would like to have one just like it. Ask your friend for a **cutting**. A cutting is a piece of the stem and leaves of a plant. When placed in water or soil, the cutting will grow roots and develop into a new plant. The new plant will look exactly like your friend's plant. Can you explain why?

Layering   Growers also propagate plants such as raspberries and climbing roses by **layering**. In layering, a stem cutting that remains attached to the parent plant is placed in the ground. A mature plant can then grow from this cutting.

Grafting   Have you ever eaten a seedless orange? Because many people do not like seeds in their fruit, scientists have performed experiments to develop seedless fruits. To reproduce these fruits, growers use a technique called **grafting.** In grafting, a branch from one tree is attached to the trunk or branch of another tree.

Gardeners and farmers use grafting to propagate special varieties of flowering shrubs and seedless fruit. A branch from a seedless orange tree is grafted onto the trunk of the other tree. The grafted branch will produce seedless oranges as shown in Figure 4-14.

Figure 4-14

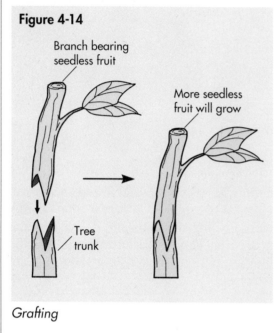

Branch bearing seedless fruit

More seedless fruit will grow

Tree trunk

Grafting

▬▬ Section 4-3 Review ▬▬

Write the definitions for the following terms in your own words.

1. **binary fission**
2. **budding**
3. **spore**
4. **regeneration**
5. **vegetative propagation**

Answer these questions.

6. Define asexual reproduction.
7. How are binary fission and budding similar? How are they different?

8. Explain why spore formation in bread mold is considered to be a type of asexual reproduction.
9. How are regeneration and vegetative propagation similar?
10. What are the advantages of growing plants by artificial propagation rather than from seed?

4-4 Sexual Reproduction

■ *Objectives*

☐ *Distinguish between sexual and asexual reproduction.*

☐ *Explain the significance of meiosis in sexual reproduction.*

☐ *Describe the process of meiosis.*

☐ *Describe with the help of diagrams how sexual reproduction results in variation among offspring.*

Not all organisms reproduce asexually. In fact, most complex plants and animals arise from **sexual reproduction**. Two parents, a male and a female, are required for sexual reproduction. Each parent produces a specialized sex cell, or **gamete** (GAM-eet).

Gametes

The male gamete is called the **sperm** cell. The female gamete is called the **egg** cell. You can see the structure of these cells in Figure 4-15. During sexual reproduction, a sperm unites with an egg cell in a process known as **fertilization**. The fertilized egg, or **zygote** (ZY-goht), is the first cell of the next generation. The zygote receives one

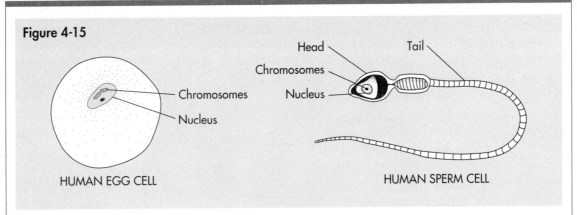

Figure 4-15

Chromosomes

Nucleus

HUMAN EGG CELL

Head　　　　Tail

Chromosomes

Nucleus

HUMAN SPERM CELL

Human gametes

set of chromosomes from both the sperm and the egg. After fertilization takes place, the zygote undergoes rapid cell division to develop into a new organism.

Since a zygote has two sets of chromosomes, one from the mother and one from the father, you might expect it to have twice as many chromosomes as its parent. However, the number of chromosomes remains the same from generation to generation. The chromosome number stays the same because gametes are formed as a part of a special kind of cell division called **meiosis** (my-OH-sus).

Meiosis

Meiosis results in the production of gametes that have only half the chromosome number found in the body cells of that organism. For example, human body cells contain 23 pairs, or 46 chromosomes. However, human sperm and eggs contain only one of each chromosome pair, or 23 chromosomes in all.

When a sperm and egg cell unite during fertilization, the zygote receives 23 chromosomes from the male and 23 from the female. Thus, the zygote has a total of 46 chromosomes, the same number found in the body cells of the parents.

The chromosomes double early in the process of meiosis, just as in mitosis. During meiosis I, chromosomes line up in pairs in the center of the cell. Remember that each chromosome has doubled. At the end of meiosis I, one member of each pair of doubled chromosomes moves to one end of the cell. The cell divides, forming two cells. Notice that each cell now contains one set of doubled chromosomes.

In meiosis II, the chromosomes in each daughter cell line up in the center of the cell. This time, however, the doubled chromosomes separate and move to opposite ends of the cell. Cell division takes place again, producing a total of four daughter cells, or gametes. Each gamete now contains one member of each chromosome pair, or half the total number of chromosomes.

When one of these gametes unites with a gamete from another parent, the zygote will have a complete set of chromosome pairs. The new organism inherits one chromosome of each pair from its father and one from its mother. Look at figure 4-16, which shows the stages of meiosis.

You know that one result of meiosis is the production of gametes with half the normal chromosome number. Another result of meiosis is the variation produced in the next generation of offspring. Figure 4-17 shows a sperm-producing cell of a male organism that has not yet undergone meiosis. The cell contains four pairs of chromosomes. Notice that the chromosomes contributed by the organism's father are shown in gray; the chromosomes contributed by its mother are shown in white. When this cell undergoes meiosis, each gamete will receive a chromosome from each pair that came from either the organism's male or female parent. The figure shows the many different combinations of chromosomes that may then appear in a gamete. How many different kinds of gametes can be

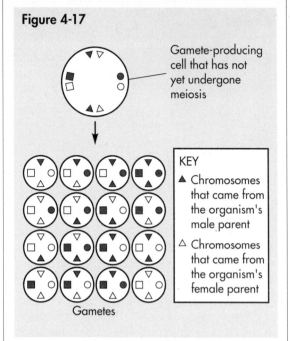

Figure 4-17

Gamete-producing cell that has not yet undergone meiosis

KEY
▲ Chromosomes that came from the organism's male parent
△ Chromosomes that came from the organism's female parent

Gametes

Meiosis produces a variety of gametes with different chromosome combinations.

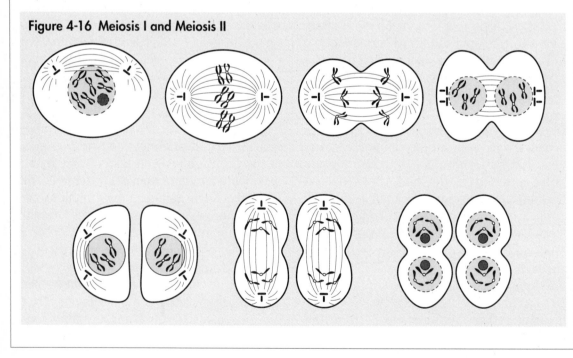

Figure 4-16 Meiosis I and Meiosis II

produced by meiosis in an organism that contains four pairs of chromosomes? Meiosis produces gametes with a vast number of chromosome combinations. The traits an organism inherits from its parents depend on which gametes unite during fertilization.

▬▬ Section 4-4 Review ▬▬

Write the definitions for the following terms in your own words.

1. **gamete**
2. **zygote**
3. **sperm**
4. **meiosis**
5. **egg**

Answer these questions.

6. What is the difference between asexual reproduction and sexual reproduction?
7. How does the number of chromosomes in gametes differ from other cells of the body?
8. How does meiosis ensure that offspring have the same number of chromosomes as their parents?
9. How does meiosis provide for variation in the traits of organisms?
10. Why is the variation produced by meiosis an advantage for an organism's survival?

4-5 Reproduction in Animals

■ *Objectives*

☐ *Compare sexual reproduction in earthworms, fish, frogs, and mice.*

☐ *Describe how the embryos of earthworms, fish, frogs, and mice are adapted for survival.*

Most complex animals reproduce sexually. That is, new generations of most animals develop from the union of a female egg and a male sperm. Animals reproduce in a variety of ways. In this section, you will learn about sexual reproduction in earthworms, fish, frogs, and mice.

Reproduction in the Earthworm

In most sexually reproducing animals, males have structures that produce sperm, and females have structures that produce eggs. However, an earthworm has both male and female reproductive structures. Therefore, a single earthworm produces both eggs and sperm. Organisms that produce both sperm and eggs are called **hermaphrodites** (hur-MAF-ruh-dyts).

Although the earthworm produces both sperm and egg cells, eggs from one earthworm must be fertilized by sperm from another earthworm. Therefore, earthworms must mate in order to reproduce. One earthworm cannot reproduce on its own.

Each earthworm produces sperm in structures called **testes.** When two earthworms mate, they exchange sperm. After sperm have been deposited into another worm, they are stored in structures called **seminal** (SEM-un-ul) **receptacles.** From there, sperm travel through a tube called a **sperm duct** to the outside of the worm's body. Eggs are produced in structures called **ovaries** (OHV-uh-reez). They travel from the ovaries to the outside of the body through tubes called **oviducts** (OH-vuh-dukts).

Use Figure 4-18 to locate the ducts that carry sperm and eggs. After two earthworms exchange sperm, the **clitellum** (kly-TEL-um), a smooth band around the earthworm, secretes a mucus covering that slips forward along the worm. The clitellum is shown in Figure 4-19. Sperm and eggs are released into the mucus covering, where fertilization takes place. After fertilization, the mucus covering slips off, forming a protective **cocoon**, or covering. The earthworm **embryos** (EM-bree-ohz), or developing zygotes, form in the cocoon. Eventually, the offspring break out of the cocoon and crawl away.

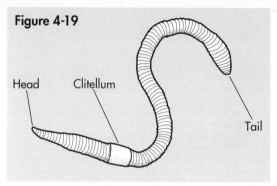

Figure 4-19

Head Clitellum Tail

An earthworm with its clitellum

Reproduction in Fish

Unlike the earthworm, fish are either male or female. Many fish reproduce by external fertilization. This means that fertilization takes place outside the female's body. The female fish produces eggs in her ovaries and lays them in water. The male produces sperm in his testes and deposits sperm in the water near the eggs. Sperm swim through the water and fertilize many of the eggs. After fertilization, an embryo develops. The egg contains enough stored food to nourish the embryo until it is ready to feed on its own.

In other fish, the male places sperm into the female's body. Fertilization that takes place inside the female's body is called internal fertilization. After fertilization, the eggs develop within the body of the female fish. The eggs eventually hatch within her body, and she gives birth to live young.

Reproduction in Frogs

Frogs belong to a group of animals that live most of their life on land but must reproduce in water. These animals are called **amphibians** (am-FIB-ee-unz). Amphibians reproduce in water because fertilization takes place externally. Sperm must swim

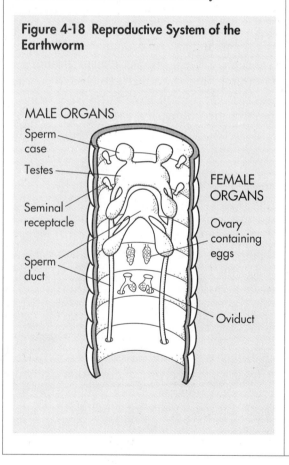

Figure 4-18 Reproductive System of the Earthworm

MALE ORGANS

Sperm case

Testes

Seminal receptacle

Sperm duct

FEMALE ORGANS

Ovary containing eggs

Oviduct

What Happens to Frog Eggs after Fertilization?

Process Skills using *laboratory equipment, making observations*

Materials fertilized frog eggs, *Elodea*, boiled lettuce leaves, microscope, pond or aquarium water, forceps, scissors, depression slide, medicine dropper, large-mouthed jar

Procedure

1. Use scissors and forceps to cut a clump of about 50 frog eggs. Eggs whose black side faces up are fertilized. Eggs whose white side faces up are unfertilized. Use the forceps to remove all the unfertilized eggs from the clump and discard them.

2. Put the clump of fertilized eggs into a large-mouthed jar about three-fourths full of pond or aquarium water. Add a few water plants such as *Elodea* to the water in the jar. Why are the plants necessary?

3. With scissors and forceps, carefully cut out a developing embryo from one of the eggs. Put this embryo into a depression slide containing pond or aquarium water.

4. Use a microscope to examine the embryo. Write a paragraph in your notebook describing what you see.

5. Make a drawing of your embryo.

6. Look at Figure 4-20. Select the stage of frog development of the embryo you are observing.

7. Each day for two weeks, select another embryo. Repeat steps 3 through 6. Keep a daily record.

8. During the two-week period, some eggs will probably hatch into tadpoles. Feed your tadpoles bits of a boiled lettuce leaf. Be sure to remove any uneaten food daily.

Conclusions

9. Why did you have to feed the tadpoles but not the embryos?

10. Why were cells in the early stages of the frog's development so alike?

Figure 4-20

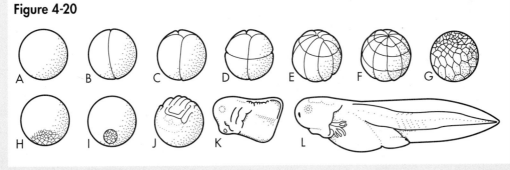

Stages in the development of a frog embryo

through water to reach the eggs that have been deposited by females.

Find the frog's ovaries and testes in Figure 4-21. Frog eggs pass from the ovaries through the oviducts. The eggs are covered by a jellylike material and then deposited into the water. In some cases the male frog helps the female deposit eggs. He mounts the female from the back, thereby creating pressure that squeezes the eggs out of her body. The male frog produces sperm in the testes. The sperm move through sperm ducts and from there are deposited in the water near the eggs. As with many fish, fertilization and embryo development take place in the water. You will learn more about the development of frogs in the next section.

Reproduction in the Mouse

You have seen that fish and amphibian eggs usually develop outside the female's body. After the eggs hatch, the young must obtain their own food. However, the embryos of other animals, such as the mouse, develop within the female's body. The mouse belongs to a group of animals called **mammals.** Mammals are animals whose females feed milk to their offspring. This milk is produced in **mammary glands.**

Look at the reproductive system of the female mouse shown in Figure 4-22. The eggs produced inside the ovaries are very tiny, about 0.15 mm across, and contain little stored food. From the ovaries, eggs pass into one of the two oviducts. The male deposits sperm into the female's vagina, an internal reproductive structure. The

Figure 4-21 Reproductive Systems of the Male and Female Frog

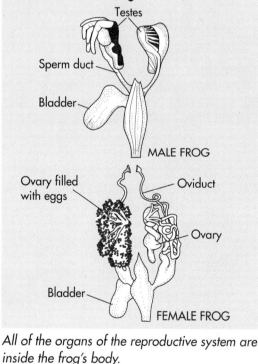

All of the organs of the reproductive system are inside the frog's body.

Figure 4-22

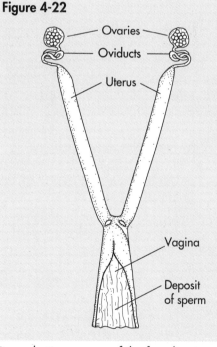

Reproductive organs of the female mouse

sperm swim to the oviduct, where fertilization takes place.

After fertilization, the zygote passes down through the oviduct to a large, muscular structure called the **uterus.** The wall of the uterus is thick and filled with blood vessels. The mouse embryos develop in the uterus.

Since mouse eggs contain little food, embryos receive nourishment from the bloodstream of the mother. Figure 4-23 shows a mouse developing in the uterus.

Figure 4-23

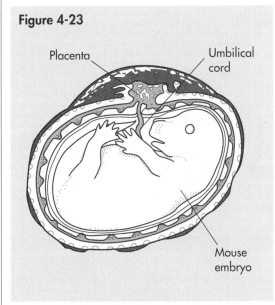

Placenta

Umbilical cord

Mouse embryo

A mouse embryo developing inside the uterus

Find a structure called the **placenta.** The placenta provides the developing mouse with nourishment. Dissolved food and oxygen in the mother's bloodstream pass from the placenta to the **umbilical** (um-BIL-i-kul) **cord.** The umbilical cord is a structure that connects the embryo and the placenta. Blood vessels in the umbilical cord carry food and oxygen from the placenta to the embryo. Blood vessels in the umbilical cord also carry wastes from the embryo to the placenta. At the placenta, the wastes pass from the embryo's bloodstream to the mother's bloodstream. These wastes are excreted from the mother's body along with her own wastes.

About 20 days after fertilization, mouse embryos are ready for birth. At that time, the uterus contracts and the offspring leave the mother's body through the vagina. The newborn mice receive milk from the mother's mammary glands until they are ready to find their own food.

Section 4-5 Review

Write the definitions for the following terms in your own words.

1. **ovaries**
2. **uterus**
3. **umbilical cord**

Answer these questions.

4. Why is the earthworm considered a hermaphrodite?
5. How are reproduction in fish and reproduction in frogs similar?
6. How does the developing mouse embryo obtain nourishment while it is developing inside the mother?
7. Most mammals live on land. However, sperm must be able to swim. How do the reproductive structures of mammals help sperm reach the eggs?

4-6 Life Cycles

Your body looks very different today from the way it looked when you were a newborn. The difference will be even greater ten years from now. A developing organism passes through a series of changes before it becomes an adult. This series of changes, or stages, is called its **life cycle.**

Life Cycle of a Moth

A moth is an insect, a group of animals that also includes grasshoppers, ants, bees, and fruit flies. A moth passes through four major stages throughout its life cycle. Find these stages in Figure 4-24 as you read.

The zygote is the first stage of the moth's development. Fertilization takes place internally. Then, the female lays the fertilized eggs, or zygotes, on the surface of leaves. After a few days, the second stage of development begins. The eggs hatch into wormlike **larvae,** which feed on the leaves and its juices. The larva of a moth is called a caterpillar. During the third stage of development, the larva changes into a **pupa.** An insect may form a covering around itself during this stage. For example, the caterpillar covers itself with threads of silk, forming a cocoon. Many changes take place inside the cocoon, including the formation of wings. In the fourth stage of development, the adult moth emerges from its cocoon.

Figure 4-24

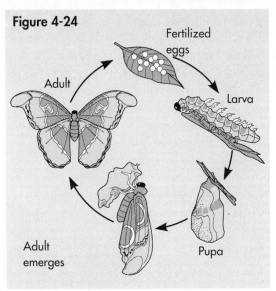

Find the four stages in a moth's development.

Life Cycle of a Frog

Like the moth, the frog begins its life cycle as a zygote. Mating takes place in early spring in ponds and other shallow waters. Fertilized eggs develop in the water. About 12 days after fertilization, the eggs hatch into **tadpoles.** Tadpoles are the larva stage. A tadpole has gills that enable it to breathe under water. Its tail enables it to swim.

After a time, the tadpole begins to change. The gills close and lungs begin to form. The tail disappears and legs form. Figure 4-25 shows the stages in the life cycle of a frog.

The change from tadpole to adult frog takes about 90 days to complete. The mature frog is adapted for life on land. It will return to water, however, when the next mating season arrives.

New generations of living things develop as a result of life cycles. These life cycles continue as a result of activities within the

Designing a Controlled Experiment

A hormone is a chemical that regulates or controls life processes. The following experiment tests the effects of a hormone on the rate of tadpole development.

Two groups of tadpoles are tested, group A and group B. Group A is treated with a hormone called thyroxin. Group B is not treated with thyroxin. Keep in mind that tadpoles produce their own thyroxin. Therefore, tadpoles treated with thyroxin have more than the normal amount of this substance. At the end of the experiment, the group A tadpoles had developed into frogs at a faster rate than the group B tadpoles.

1. Which is the control group and which is the experimental group? What is the variable in this experiment?
2. Why is a control group needed in this investigation?
3. Based on the results of this experiment, what conclusions can you draw about the effects of thyroxin on a frog's life cycle?

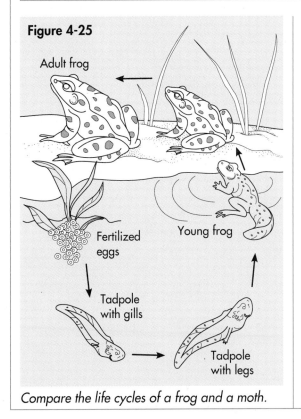

Figure 4-25

Adult frog

Fertilized eggs

Young frog

Tadpole with gills

Tadpole with legs

Compare the life cycles of a frog and a moth.

cells. The processes of fertilization, mitosis, and meiosis cause the continuing cycles of reproduction, growth, and development.

Section 4-6 Review

Write the definitions for the following terms in your own words.

1. **life cycle**   2. **pupa**
3. **larva**   4. **tadpole**

Answer these questions.

5. List the four stages of a moth's life cycle.
6. What changes take place as a tadpole develops into an adult frog?
7. How are fertilization, mitosis, and meiosis related to the life cycle of an organism?

SCIENCE, TECHNOLOGY, & SOCIETY

Toxic Wastes in the Great Lakes

The Great Lakes make up the world's largest source of fresh water. The water in these lakes, however, is not really so fresh. Nearby factories spill poisonous, or toxic, wastes into the lakes. These toxic wastes include pesticides and other chemicals.

These toxic wastes are affecting the reproduction of wildlife living in and around the Great Lakes. For instance, the regional population of bald eagles is declining. Female eagles that have eaten fish contaminated with toxic chemicals lay eggs with thinner shells. The embryos that develop inside these eggs are not well protected and are less likely to survive. Figure 4-26 shows some of the dangers to wildlife in the Great Lakes.

The toxic wastes in the Great Lakes also affect humans. Scientists have warned women of childbearing age to limit their intake of Great Lakes fish to one meal per month. Eating greater amounts could increase the toxins in their bodies and thus increase the chance of their children having birth defects.

To clean up the Great Lakes, politicians, scientists, and other concerned citizens have suggested an agency to protect the health of humans and wildlife and to provide funds to clean up the lakes. They also suggest passing laws that require industries to reduce the amount of pollution in the lakes.

Follow-up Activity

How has water pollution affected the reproduction of wildlife in your area? To find out, contact your local Environmental Protection Agency office and request information. Present your findings to the class.

Figure 4-26 Dangers to Wildlife in the Great Lakes

Danger	Bald eagle	Herring gull	Lake trout	Snapping turtle
Reduced population	✓	✓	✓	✓
Fewer offspring	✓	✓	✓	✓
Eggshell thinning	✓	✓		

Section 4-1 Life from Life

1. In the seventeenth century, Francesco Redi disproved spontaneous generation.
2. Scientists believe that living things come from other living things.

Section 4-2 Cell Reproduction

1. Mitosis is a kind of nuclear division that results in the production of new cells.
2. Mitosis keeps the chromosome number constant in the body cells of an organism.

Section 4-3 Types of Asexual Reproduction

1. During asexual reproduction, offspring arise by mitosis from a single parent.
2. Some unicellular organisms reproduce by binary fission or budding.
3. Molds reproduce by spore formation.
4. Many simple animals reproduce by regeneration.
5. Many plants reproduce by vegetative propagation.

Section 4-4 Sexual Reproduction

1. Most animals reproduce sexually.
2. Sperm and eggs are produced by a kind of nuclear division called meiosis.
3. Meiosis results in the production of gametes with half the chromosome number characteristic of the organism.

Section 4-5 Reproduction in Animals

1. In some fish and amphibians, fertilization and development take place externally.

2. In mammals, fertilization and development take place internally.

Section 4-6 Life Cycles

1. The life cycle of an organism is the series of changes it goes through in its development and the reproduction of its own kind.

Write the term from the list that best matches each statement.

fertilization, spore case, mammary gland, tadpole, cutting, embryo, seminal receptacle, hermaphrodite

1. a stage in early development
2. section of a plant that can grow into a new plant
3. joining of sperm and egg to form a zygote
4. organism that produces both male and female gametes
5. milk-producing structure in female mammals
6. water-dwelling form of a frog
7. reproductive structure in molds
8. structure in which sperm are stored

Explain the difference between the words in each pair.

9. asexual reproduction, sexual reproduction
10. runner, bulb
11. grafting, layering
12. tuber, bud
13. placenta, umbilical cord
14. clitellum, cocoon

15. oviduct, sperm duct
16. amphibian, mammal

SUMMARIZING

Write the missing term for each sentence.

1. The belief that life arises from nonlife is known as _____.
2. The instructions for life are found in structures in the cell's nucleus called _____.
3. The type of nuclear division in which the daughter cells receive the same number of chromosomes as the parent cell is called _____.
4. Amoebas reproduce asexually by a process called _____.
5. Bread molds reproduce by means of special structures called _____.
6. A piece of a stem and leaves from a plant that can produce a whole new plant is called a _____.
7. A human body cell contains 46 chromosomes, but a human egg cell contains only _____.
8. The union of a sperm and an egg occurs during a process called _____.
9. Eggs are produced in the _____.
10. Developing mammals receive nourishment from a structure called the _____.

INTERPRETING INFORMATION

Use the data table in Figure 4-27 to help you answer the following questions.

Figure 4-27

Organism	Number of eggs produced
Salmon	Thousands in a mating season
Frog	Hundreds in a mating season
Chicken	As many as one per day throughout the year
Dog	Eight to ten about twice a year
Human	One each month throughout the year

1. Which organism produces the most eggs? Which organism produces the fewest?
2. Which organisms reproduce only during a particular mating season?
3. Why do you think that the number of eggs produced by these organisms varies?

THINK AND DISCUSS

Use the section number in parentheses to help you find each answer. Write your answers in complete sentences.

1. Explain how Redi used the results of his experiment to disprove the theory of spontaneous generation. (4-1)

2. Why is chromosome replication important in the process of mitosis? (4-2)
3. Fishermen used to try to kill starfish by breaking off their arms and then throwing them back into the water. Was this a good idea? Why or why not? (4-3)
4. Compare mitosis and meiosis. What are the outcomes of each? (4-4)
5. Some frogs live in the desert. Why must desert frogs wait for a rainstorm before they can reproduce? (4-5)
6. When do the processes of meiosis, fertilization, and mitosis take place in the life cycle of a frog? (4-6)

GOING FURTHER

Scientists have successfully fertilized mammal eggs in a test tube. This process is called *in vitro* fertilization. Scientists can implant one of these fertilized eggs into a female's uterus, where it will develop into an embryo. Ask your school librarian to help you research *in vitro* fertilization in humans. How successful have scientists been in performing *in vitro* fertilization?

COMPETENCY REVIEW

1. The formation of a new bread mold from a spore results from
   a. respiration.   b. replication.
   c. regulation.   d. reproduction.
2. Which statement concerning the origin of all living things is correct?
   a. All living things come from other living things.
   b. All living things come from nonliving things.
   c. All living things originate as a result of asexual reproduction.
   d. All living things originate as a result of sexual reproduction.
3. Which one of the following statements concerning sexual reproduction is true?
   a. Sexual reproduction leads to variation in the next generation.
   b. Sexual reproduction does not lead to variation in the next generation.
   c. Sex cells are produced by mitosis.
   d. Sexual reproduction involves only one parent.
4. If a starfish loses an arm it may produce a new one through the process of
   a. regeneration.
   b. sexual reproduction.
   c. spontaneous generation.
   d. meiosis.
5. If an organism has 24 chromosomes in its body cells, how many chromosomes will be found in the sperm or in the eggs of the organism?
   a. 24   b. 48
   c. 12   d. 23
6. The structure that forms as a result of fertilization is called a(n)
   a. gamete   b. chromatin
   c. zygote   d. embryo
7. The series of stages a developing organism passes through is called a
   a. menstrual cycle. b. reproductive cycle.
   c. life cycle   d. chemical cycle.

CHAPTER 5

THE CLASSIFICATION OF LIFE

Have you ever collected baseball cards? If so, you probably organized your collection in some way. First, you might have divided your collection into American and National Leagues, then into East and West Divisions. Then you would have grouped together all the cards for each team. Finally, you might have placed together all the pitchers on the team, all the catchers, and so on. Later, if a friend had wanted to trade for a certain card, you would have been able to tell immediately if that card was part of your collection.

Biologists organize living things in much the same way. Over 3 million kinds of organisms have been identified, and perhaps millions more have yet to be discovered. Imagine trying to keep track of these millions of organisms. Biologists simplify their work by grouping together organisms that have similar characteristics. In this chapter, you will learn how biologists identify these characteristics and use them to determine relationships among organisms.

5-1 Basis of Classification

■ *Objectives*

☐ *Explain the purpose for the classification of organisms.*

☐ *List the seven major classification groups.*

☐ *Describe the characteristics of each of the five kingdoms.*

Biologists group all living things into an orderly system. The organization of living things according to their similarities is

Figure 5-1

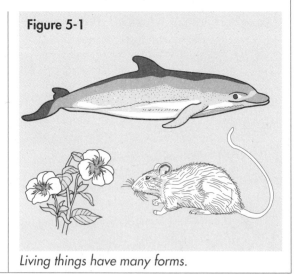

Living things have many forms.

called **classification.** A classification system helps biologists study groups of organisms, rather than each individual organism. It also helps biologists determine whether an unfamiliar organism has already been identified by other scientists.

Early Classification System

The practice of classifying living things began in the 1700s with a biologist named Carolus Linnaeus. Linnaeus first classified an organism as either a plant or an animal. He called these two largest groups of organisms **kingdoms.** Linnaeus then divided each kingdom into smaller groups of similar organisms. He called each of these smaller groups a **phylum** (FY-lum)**.** Each phylum was further divided into smaller and smaller groups. The smallest groups, **species,** contain only one kind of organism. All members of a species look alike and reproduce among themselves.

Figure 5-2 shows how a human, a tiger, and a lion are classified. Note the names of each classification group. Which of these animals belong to the same class? Which

belong to the same family? Notice that the further you go into classification groups, the more similar in appearance the organisms become.

Linnaeus also developed a system of naming organisms. He gave each organism a two-part scientific name consisting of its genus and species. For example, the name of the genus that includes all catlike animals is *Felis*. The species name for the lion is *leo*. Thus, the scientific name for the lion is *Felis leo*.

Biologists all over the world use this system of naming organisms. Biologists from different countries may have different names for the common dog. However, all biologists recognize its scientific name, *Canis familiaris*.

Modern Classification System

The basic classification system Linnaeus developed is still used by biologists today. However, as biologists gather new knowledge about organisms, they may change the manner in which organisms are grouped. The classification system is an artificial

Figure 5-2 Classification of the Human, Tiger, and Lion

Group	Kingdom	Phylum	Class	Order	Family	Genus	Species
Human	Animal	Chordata	Mammal	Primate	Hominidae	Homo	sapiens
Tiger	Animal	Chordata	Mammal	Carnivore	Felidae	Felis	tigris
Lion	Animal	Chordata	Mammal	Carnivore	Felidae	Felis	leo

system designed by scientists for their own use. Thus, the system may be changed as new information becomes available.

Since Linnaeus's time, biologists have discovered many organisms that do not fit into a two-kingdom system. Most scientists today use a five-kingdom system, which includes monerans, protists, fungi, animals, and plants. Figure 5-3 shows some organisms from each kingdom.

Figure 5-3

How Can Different Objects Be Classified?

Process Skills *making observations, classifying*

Materials pencil, paper

Scientists classify many objects according to their similarities. For example, they organize elements into groups with similar chemical properties. They classify organisms into groups with similar structures. Scientists classify objects so that they can study them in groups, rather than studying each one individually.

Procedure

1. Study the objects in Figure 5-4. Note similarities and differences.
2. Divide the figures into two groups, A and B. On a separate sheet of paper, record the numbers of the objects you have placed in group A and group B.
3. Now divide the objects in group A into two smaller groups, C and D, with each group having similar characteristics. Likewise, divide group B into two groups, E and F. Record the numbers of the objects you have placed into each of these groups. On what did you base your classification of the objects?

Conclusions

4. Compare your classifications with those of your classmates. Did you classify the objects in the same way? If not, describe the differences in classifications.
5. Which method of classification is correct? Explain why the classification of objects is an artificial process.

Figure 5-4

Section 5-1 Review

Write the definitions for the following terms in your own words.

1. **classification**   2. **kingdom**
3. **phylum**   4. **species**

Answer these questions.

5. Why do biologists classify living things?
6. Name the seven major classification groups.
7. Why is it helpful to give organisms a scientific name?
8. Classify a human using the seven major classification groups. What is the scientific name for humans?
9. Give examples of an organism from each of the five kingdoms.

5-2 Viruses and Monerans

■ *Objectives*

☐ *Explain why scientists find it difficult to classify viruses.*

☐ *Describe the life cycle of a virus.*

☐ *Explain why bacteria and blue-green bacteria are classified in the moneran kingdom.*

At one time or another, you have probably suffered from a cold or the flu. Do you know what causes these illnesses? They are caused by objects so small that they can be seen only under the most powerful microscopes.

Viruses

Colds and the flu are caused by **viruses.** Viruses have characteristics of both living and nonliving things. They are visible only under the electron microscope. For this reason, biologists have only recently been able to study viruses in detail. Viruses are so different in their characteristics that they do not belong to any of the five kingdoms.

Unlike living things, viruses are not made of cells. Viruses have two parts, a head and a tail. The head may consist of DNA surrounded by a protein coat. You can see the structure of a virus in Figure 5-5.

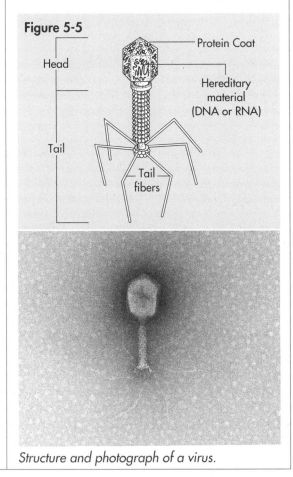

Figure 5-5

Head
Tail
Protein Coat
Hereditary material (DNA or RNA)
Tail fibers

Structure and photograph of a virus.

Viruses are like living things in that they reproduce their own kind. However, to reproduce, the virus must enter the cell of a living organism. The virus injects its DNA into the cell. The DNA of the virus instructs the cell to produce more viruses. As new viruses are produced, that cell is destroyed. You will learn more about the reproduction of viruses in Chapter 23.

Different kinds of viruses attack different kinds of cells. The virus shown in Figure 5-5 is a **bacteriophage** (bak-TIR-ee-uh-fayj), a virus that attacks bacteria. Other viruses attack plant cells or animal cells.

Monerans

The simplest organisms belong to the moneran kingdom. **Monerans** are one-celled organisms that have both a cell membrane and a cell wall. However, these cells lack a nuclear membrane to separate the nuclear material from the rest of the cell. Monerans also lack other organelles such as mitochondria and chloroplasts. Monerans include bacteria and blue-green bacteria.

Bacteria A typical bacterial cell is about 50 times smaller than most of the cells found in the human body. Although you can see them only with the aid of a microscope, bacteria exist almost everywhere. They live in air, water, and soil. They live on your skin and inside your body.

A few types of bacteria contain chlorophyll. Bacteria that contain chlorophyll can make their own food by photosynthesis. Most bacteria do not contain chlorophyll. These bacteria depend on their environment for food.

Biologists group bacteria according to their shape as shown in Figure 5-3. Some bacteria are round, some are shaped like rods, and others are shaped like a spiral. They are often found grouped together in clusters or in chains. Bacteria reproduce by binary fission.

Blue-green Bacteria Although they are unicellular, some blue-green bacteria cells join together to form very long chains. These chains are visible in the ponds and damp rocks where blue-green bacteria grow. These organisms look blue-green because they contain a blue protein and, like plants, they contain chlorophyll. They use chlorophyll to make food.

▬▬ Section 5-2 Review ▬▬

Write the definitions for the following terms in your own words.

1. **virus**
2. **bacteriophage**
3. **moneran**

Answer these questions.

4. Explain how the structure of a virus differs from the structure of a cell.
5. Name the two major groups of organisms found in the moneran kingdom.
6. List two characteristics that all monerans share.
7. How would you classify a moneran that has a cell membrane and cell wall but no nucleus or chlorophyll?

5-3 Protist Kingdom

■ *Objectives*

☐ *Compare the characteristics of a moneran cell with those of a protist cell.*

☐ *List the properties of each of the four main groups of protists.*

☐ *Explain why protozoa, algae, Euglena, and the slime mold are placed in the protist kingdom.*

The **protist** kingdom includes both unicellular and multicellular organisms. However, protist cells differ from moneran cells. First of all, protist cells are larger than moneran cells. Unlike moneran cells, protist cells have a true nucleus surrounded by a nuclear membrane. Protist cells also contain cell structures that monerans lack, such as mitochondria.

Protozoa

Members of one large group of protists have some characteristics of animals. These animal-like protists are called **protozoa** (proht-uh-ZOH-uh). Most protozoa are unicellular. Some live together in colonies. Protozoan cells have a cell membrane but not a cell wall. Many protozoa reproduce asexually by binary fission.

Protozoa such as *Paramecium* and amoebas live in lake and pond water. Look at the *Paramecium* in Figure 5-6. Find the short hairlike structures called **cilia.** Cilia beat back and forth, propelling the *Paramecium* through the water.

The *Paramecium* takes in food through a mouthlike opening that leads into the **oral groove.** Food is digested in the food

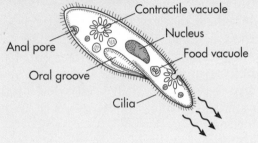

Figure 5-6 Paramecium

Contractile vacuole
Nucleus
Food vacuole
Anal pore
Oral groove
Cilia

vacuole. Solid wastes leave the cell through a structure called the **anal pore.** Liquid wastes are pumped out of the cell by the contractile vacuole.

Compare the *Paramecium* with the amoeba in Figure 5-7. Find the false feet, or **pseudopods** (SOOD-uh-pad), of the amoeba. The amoeba moves as cytoplasm flows into the pseudopods. When an amoeba finds food, the pseudopods wrap completely around it. The food then becomes trapped in a food vacuole, where it is digested. Liquid wastes are removed by the contractile vacuole.

Algae

Protists also include the large group of organisms known as **algae.** Algae are

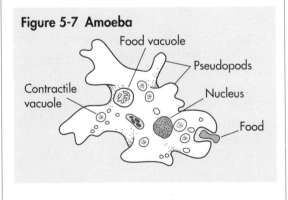

Figure 5-7 Amoeba

Food vacuole
Pseudopods
Contractile vacuole
Nucleus
Food

plant-like protists. Many algae are unicellular, but others are multicellular and quite large. Most algae live in lakes and oceans. Many water animals rely on algae for food.

Like plants, the cells of algae contain chloroplasts and a cell wall. Although all algae cells contain chlorophyll, not all algae look green. Some algae have other proteins that make them look red, yellow, or brown.

Figure 5-8 shows two multicellular species of algae, kelp and rockweed. These algae are plant-like in appearance. However, algae lack specialized plant structures such as leaves, stems, and roots. For this reason, biologists classify multicellular algae as protists.

Euglena

A *Euglena* is a protist that has characteristics of both plants and animals. Look at the *Euglena* in Figure 5-9. Like animals, the *Euglena* has a cell membrane but no cell wall. The *Euglena* can also move. The back and forth movement of the whiplike **flagellum** propels the *Euglena* through water.

Euglena can also take in and digest food from the environment. However, like plants, *Euglena* also have chloroplasts with which they make their own food.

Figure 5-9 Euglena – A Protist

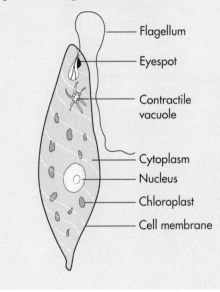

- Flagellum
- Eyespot
- Contractile vacuole
- Cytoplasm
- Nucleus
- Chloroplast
- Cell membrane

What plantlike qualities does the Euglena have? What animal-like qualities does it have?

Figure 5-8

Kelp

Rockweed
(also known as fucus)

Have you seen these two kinds of algae at the seashore? They may look like plants to you, but they are classified in the protist kingdom. Do you know why?

Slime Molds

The last major group of protists are the **slime molds.** Slime molds are fungus-like protists. Slime molds grow in damp places like the forest floor or on the surface of a decaying log. Use Figure 5-10 to trace the three stages of a slime mold's life cycle.

During the first stage, the slime mold exists as a slimy mass and functions like an amoeba. It forms pseudopods that move the organism and trap food.

During the second stage of its life cycle, the slime mold stops moving and reproduces asexually with spores. During the third stage, the spores grow and develop into new individuals. The young slime mold has a flagellum, like that of the *Euglena*. As the slime mold matures, its cells lose their flagella and enter the slimy mass, or first stage in the life cycle.

Figure 5-10

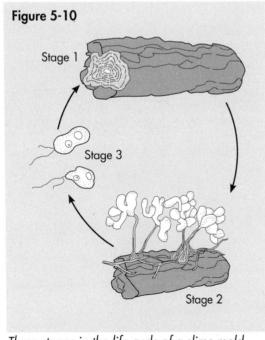

Stage 1

Stage 3

Stage 2

Three stages in the life cycle of a slime mold

Section 5-3 Review

Write the definitions for the following terms in your own words.

1. **protist**
2. *Euglena*
3. **protozoa**
4. **slime mold**
5. **algae**

Answer these questions.

6. How does a protist cell differ from a moneran cell?
7. Why are protozoa and algae classified in the same kingdom?
8. Compare a *Paramecium* to an amoeba.
9. Why is the *Euglena* considered both an animal-like protist and a plantlike protist?

5-4 Fungi Kingdom

■ *Objectives*

☐ *List the characteristics of each of the three groups of organisms in the fungi kingdom.*

☐ *Identify the characteristics shared by the three groups of organisms in the fungi kingdom.*

In the past, scientists classified **fungi** (FUN-jy) as plants. Fungi are organisms that are mostly multicellular. Like plants, fungi do not move, and their cells are surrounded by cell walls. However, unlike plants, fungi do not have chloroplasts or chlorophyll. For this reason, scientists now place fungi in their own kingdom.

Since fungi can use many types of food, fungi live in many different places. You may have seen fungi on rotting logs, clothing, and food, as well as in many other places.

Yeast

A **yeast** is a one-celled fungus. Yeast cells usually reproduce asexually by budding. However, when conditions are not right for budding, yeast cells reproduce asexually by spores. You may know that yeast is used to bake bread. These live yeast cells break down the sugar in the dough to get energy. Bubbles of carbon dioxide released during the process make the dough rise.

Molds

The fungi known as **molds** consist of masses of tiny threadlike structures. Each tiny thread contains cytoplasm within which many nuclei are found. Recall from Chapter 4 that molds, including bread mold, reproduce asexually by forming spores.

Bread molds obtain food by releasing chemicals into bread. These chemicals break down starch in the bread into sugar. The mold then absorbs the sugar.

Although molds may cause bread and other foods to spoil, many molds benefit humans. For example, molds are used to make cheese. *Penicillium* mold is used to make the drug penicillin. Molds also enrich the soil by breaking down the bodies of dead organisms.

Mushrooms

The largest fungi are mushrooms. Figure 5-11 shows a typical mushroom. Find the thick stalk and the umbrella-shaped cap. The mushroom cap is made of many closely arranged fine threads.

The cap is the reproductive part of the mushroom. Thousands of spores are produced there. The spores drop from the mushroom cap onto the ground. If a spore lands in a moist place with a source of food, it may grow and develop into a new mushroom. As you can see in Figure 5-11, part of the mushroom grows underground.

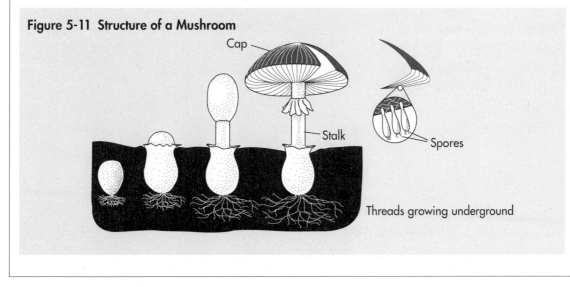

Figure 5-11 Structure of a Mushroom

Cap

Stalk

Spores

Threads growing underground

Write the definitions for the following terms in your own words.

1. **fungus**
2. **yeast**
3. **mold**

Answer these questions.

4. Name the three major groups of organisms in the fungi kingdom.
5. Why is yeast classified as a fungus?
6. Give examples of how molds are both harmful and helpful to humans.
7. What characteristics do molds and mushrooms share?

5-5 Plant Kingdom

■ *Objectives*

☐ *Describe the characteristics of the organisms in the plant kingdom.*

☐ *Distinguish between a bryophyte and a tracheophyte.*

☐ *List the characteristics shared by ferns, conifers, and flowering plants.*

☐ *Distinguish between conifers and flowering plants.*

The plant kingdom includes over 275,000 species. All plants are multicellular organisms. Plant cells contain cell walls and chloroplasts. Plants use the chlorophyll in chloroplasts to make their own food. However, unlike other organisms that have cell walls and chlorophyll, plants are complex organisms with many specialized structures.

Biologists classify plants into two major groups. Members of one group have a system of tubes called **vascular tissue.** Vascular tissue conducts food and water to all parts of the plant. Members of the other phylum lack vascular tissue.

Bryophytes

Plants that do not have vascular tissue are called **bryophytes** (BRY-uh-fyts). Because bryophytes lack vascular tissue, they are referred to as nonvascular plants. You may have noticed velvety green plants growing on a damp forest floor or on bare rocks. These tiny bryophytes are called mosses.

Mosses rarely grow more than a few centimeters tall. The lack of vascular tissue limits the size of bryophytes. Study the structure of the moss plant in Figure 5-12. Find the tiny leaflike parts. The cells of these leaflike parts contain the chloroplasts that manufacture food. The moss also has tiny rootlike structures that anchor the

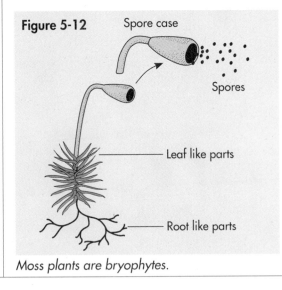

Figure 5-12

Spore case

Spores

Leaf like parts

Root like parts

Moss plants are bryophytes.

moss in the soil. However, these rootlike parts are simpler in structure than true roots. Materials must move from cell to cell because there are no transport tubes.

A long stalk grows out from the moss. At the top of this stalk you can find a spore case that contains hundreds of spores. When the spore case bursts, the spores are released. If these spores fall in a moist place, they may grow into new moss plants.

Tracheophytes

Plants that have vascular tissue are called **tracheophytes** (TRAY-kee-uh-fyts). Tracheophytes have true roots, stems, and leaves. Because tracheophytes have vascular tissue to transport food and water throughout the plant, they can grow much taller than bryophytes. The veins in a leaf or the "strings" in celery are examples of vascular tissue.

Ferns   The fern shown in Figure 5-13 is one kind of tracheophyte. Ferns grow in wet,

shady areas, such as the forest floor. Each leaf of a fern is called a frond. Notice that each frond consists of a series of leaflets. Spore cases are found on the underside of each leaflet. If a spore lands on moist soil, it may develop into a small heart-shaped plant. Eventually, a mature fern plant will develop.

Conifers   Pine, hemlock, spruce, and cedar trees are examples of tracheophytes called **conifers**. Most conifers are evergreens, such as the white pine shown in Figure 5-14. Evergreens have needlelike leaves that stay on the tree year-round. Conifers develop from seeds instead of from spores.

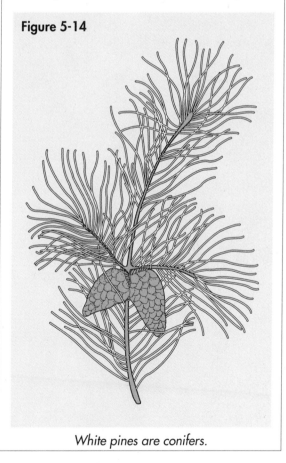

Figure 5-14

White pines are conifers.

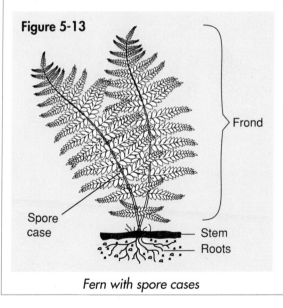

Figure 5-13

Spore case

Frond

Stem

Roots

Fern with spore cases

All conifers have reproductive structures called **cones.** Study the pinecone in Figure 5-14. Notice that the cone is made up of flat, woody sections. Seeds lie uncovered on these sections. When the cone opens, the ripened seeds fall to the ground. If conditions are right, the seeds grow into plants.

Flowering Plants The largest group of plants are the flowering plants. More than half of the known species of plants have **flowers** as reproductive structures. Most of the plants that you are familiar with are flowering plants. Figure 5-15 gives an idea of the variety of flowering plants. In addition to tulips, geraniums, begonias, and roses, grasses, maple trees, corn, and wheat are flowering plants.

How do the seeds of flowering plants differ from the seeds of conifers? The seeds of conifers are uncovered and thus exposed to the environment. The seeds of flowering plants are covered and protected by the **fruit.** The fruit forms when the ovary of the flower enlarges and ripens. This protection makes the seeds of flowering plants more likely to develop into mature plants.

Biologists classify flowering plants into two groups based on the structure of their seeds. All seeds have a food supply called a **cotyledon** (kat-l-EED-n). Flowering plants whose seeds have two cotyledons are called **dicots.** Bean and pea plants are dicots. Dicot seeds easily split in two. Flowering plants whose seeds have only one cotyledon are called **monocots.** Corn

Figure 5-15

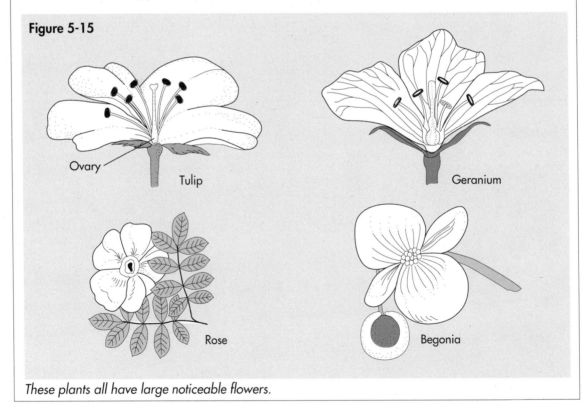

Ovary

Tulip

Geranium

Rose

Begonia

These plants all have large noticeable flowers.

and grass plants are monocots. Look at the dicot and monocot seeds in Figure 5-16. What differences can you observe?

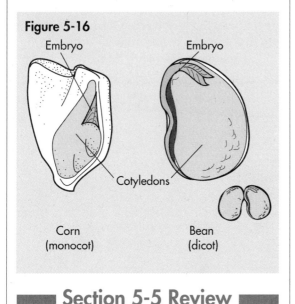

Figure 5-16

Embryo

Embryo

Cotyledons

Corn
(monocot)

Bean
(dicot)

Section 5-5 Review

Write the definitions for the following terms in your own words.

1. **vascular tissue**   2. **conifer**
3. **bryophyte**   4. **flower**
5. **tracheophyte**

Answer these questions.

6. How are all organisms in the plant kingdom alike?
7. What is the difference between a bryophyte and a tracheophyte?
8. What characteristics do ferns, conifers, and flowering plants share?
9. List three differences between conifers and flowering plants.

5-6 Animal Kingdom

■ *Objectives*
☐ *Distinguish between an invertebrate and a vertebrate.*
☐ *Identify the main characteristics of the invertebrate phyla.*
☐ *Identify the main characteristics of the five classes of the arthropod phylum.*

Of all the kingdoms of living things, the animal kingdom contains the greatest variety. This kingdom includes such familiar species as sparrows, rabbits, ants, and goldfish. Humans belong to the animal kingdom as well.

All of these animals share important characteristics. Animal cells have no cell wall and no chloroplasts. Because animals have no chloroplasts, they cannot make their own food. Animals obtain food from plants or other animals. The lack of a cell wall makes it easier for animals to move about to find food and avoid danger. The cells of animals are specialized for doing a certain job. These different types of cells work together to keep the animal alive.

Classifying Animals

Biologists classify the animal kingdom into two major groups, those with backbones and those without backbones. Animals without a backbone are called **invertebrates.** Invertebrates include jellyfish, earthworms, cockroaches, crayfish, and starfish. In fact, about 95 percent of all animals are invertebrates. Animals that have a backbone are called **vertebrates.** Vertebrates include fish, frogs, lizards, chickens, and humans.

Invertebrates

Biologists divide invertebrates into several different phyla. Figure 5-17 lists some of these phyla, their characteristics, and examples of species in each phylum. Another phylum, the Arthropoda phylum, includes more animals than any other group.

Characteristics of Arthropods

Arthropods include crabs, lobsters, grasshoppers, spiders, bees, ants, and other species. One characteristic common to all arthropods is the **exoskeleton** (ek-soh-SKEL-ut-n), a supporting frame on the outside of the body. The exoskeleton is divided into sections as

Figure 5-17 Phyla of Invertebrates

Phylum	Characteristics	Examples
Porifera	Body contains pores. Cells remove water and food from the ocean as water flows through pores. Remains attached to one spot on the ocean floor.	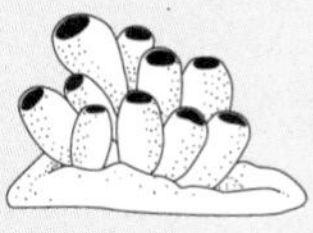 Sponge
Coelenterata	Contains a central cavity with one opening Uses tentacles for capturing food Has stinging cells on the tentacles for paralyzing prey	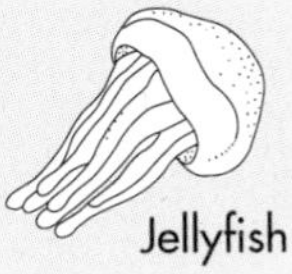 Jellyfish
Platyhelminthes	Flat body Lives in ponds and streams Reproduces by regeneration	 Planaria
Annelida	Segmented body Divided digestive system	 Earthworm
Mollusca	Mantle with a shell Soft body protected by the shell Muscular foot for movement	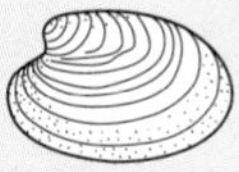 Clam
Echinodermata	Spiny skin Tiny tube feet for movement	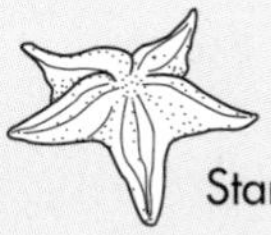 Starfish

shown in the diagram of the grasshopper in Figure 5-18. Arthropods also have several **joints**. The joints enable the arthropod to bend and move its legs and other body parts. In addition to providing for movement, the exoskeleton covers and protects the soft inside parts of the body.

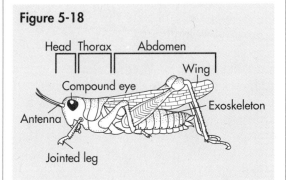

Figure 5-18

Head Thorax   Abdomen

Wing

Compound eye

Exoskeleton

Antenna

Jointed leg

How is the body of a grasshopper divided?

The exoskeleton does not grow. Thus, as the inside of an arthropod grows, it becomes too big for its exoskeleton. When this happens, the arthropod sheds, or **molts,** its exoskeleton. After molting, a new and larger exoskeleton grows.

Notice that the grasshopper's body is divided into three sections, the head, thorax, and abdomen. The bodies of many different types of arthropods are divided into these three sections. What structures are attached to each of these sections?

Classes of Arthropods The Arthropoda phylum can be further divided into five main classes. One of the ways biologists classify arthropods is by the number of legs each of its body sections has. Study the characteristics of the arthropod classes listed in Figure 5-19.

Figure 5-19 Classes of Arthropods

Class	Characteristics	Examples
Chilopoda	One pair of legs per body section, Flat body	Centipede
Diplopoda	Two pairs of legs per body section, Round body	Millipede
Crustacea	Five pairs of legs, Hard exoskeleton, Two pairs of antennae	Lobster
Insecta	Three body sections, Three pairs of legs, One pair of antennae	Cockroach Bee
Arachnida	Two body sections, Four pairs of legs, No antennae	Spider

Section 5-6 Review

Write the definitions for the following terms in your own words.

1. **invertebrate**   2. **exoskeleton**
3. **vertebrate**   4. **molt**
5. **arthropod**

Answer these questions.

6. What is the difference between a vertebrate and an invertebrate? Give three examples of each.
7. List seven phyla of invertebrates. Use Figures 5-17 and 5-18 to briefly discuss the characteristics of each phylum.
8. How do the organisms in the five classes of arthropods differ from each other?

5-7 Vertebrates

■ *Objectives*

□ *List the characteristics of chordates.*
□ *List the five main classes of vertebrates.*
□ *Describe the characteristics of each of the five main classes of vertebrates.*

Characteristics of Chordates

All vertebrates, as well as a few invertebrates, belong to the Chordata phylum. All **chordates** have several characteristics in common. At some time in their development, all chordates have a solid rod of bonelike material that runs along their back. In invertebrates, this rod remains in the organism throughout its lifetime. In vertebrates, this rod develops into the backbone during embryo development. Chordates also have a hollow **nerve cord** along their back. The front part of the nerve cord enlarges to form the brain.

Some time in its development, every chordate has a pair of **gill slits**. In fish, the gill slits develop into gills. Fish use gills to absorb oxygen from the water. In other chordates, the gill slits disappear during embryo development.

Characteristics of Vertebrates

Almost all chordates are vertebrates. All vertebrates have an **endoskeleton,** a skeleton inside the body. A major part of the endoskeleton is the backbone that surrounds the nerve cord. The backbone is jointed for flexibility and for movement. An enlargement of the front part of the nerve cord forms the brain.

Vertebrates are adapted for life in water, in air, or on land. A wide variety of characteristics enable different vertebrates to live in one of these environments. By studying these characteristics, biologists have classified vertebrates into five main groups called classes.

Fish

Fish are aquatic, or water-dwelling, vertebrates. Like most aquatic organisms, fish use oxygen that is dissolved in the water. Fish have **gills**, which filter dissolved oxygen from water. Gills are thin flaps of tissue that are rich in blood vessels. As water passes through the gills, oxygen is absorbed into the blood vessels.

Look at the bony fish in Figure 5-20. Notice its streamlined body. Find the fins and the tail. The streamlined shape and fins and

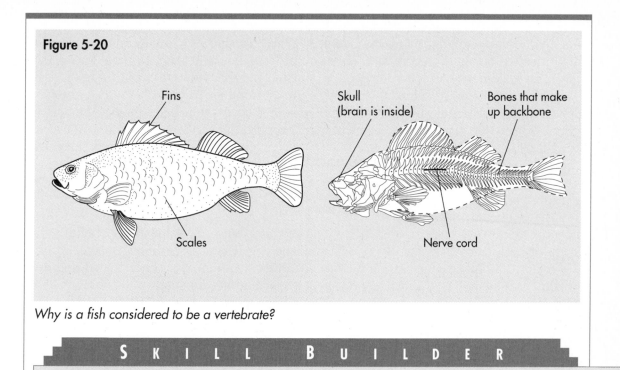

Figure 5-20

Fins

Scales

Skull
(brain is inside)

Bones that make
up backbone

Nerve cord

Why is a fish considered to be a vertebrate?

Interpreting Information from a Graph

People have long valued ivory for its beauty. Ivory has been used to make jewelry and other decorative objects, billiard balls, and piano keys. Ivory comes from the tusks of elephants. Over the years, the African elephant has been hunted excessively for its tusks. Today, the African elephant is considered an endangered species. Carefully study Figure 5-21. Then answer the following questions.

1. What is happening to the elephant population in each of these African countries? Why?
2. From the information in this graph, what can you infer about the future of the African elephant? What can be done to help it?

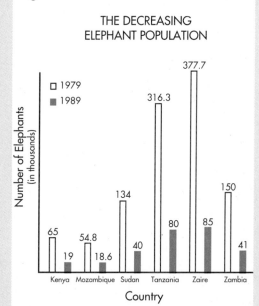

Figure 5-21

THE DECREASING
ELEPHANT POPULATION

□ 1979
■ 1989

Number of Elephants (in thousands)

Kenya 65 / 19
Mozambique 54.8 / 18.6
Sudan 134 / 40
Tanzania 316.3 / 80
Zaire 377.7 / 85
Zambia 150 / 41

Country

tail help fish swim through water. Look at the scales on the outer surface of the fish. The scales cover and protect the skin.

Fish are cold-blooded animals. The body temperature of a cold-blooded animal changes with the temperature of its surroundings. If the water temperature rises, the body temperature of the fish rises also. Often fish and other cold-blooded animals are more active in warm temperatures and less active in cold temperatures.

Amphibians

Like fish, amphibians are cold-blooded. Amphibians include frogs, toads, and salamanders. As you learned in Chapter 4, amphibians spend part of their life in water and part of their life on land. Most amphibians have a smooth, slimy skin. The moist skin allows oxygen to pass through it. An amphibian breathes with both its skin and its lungs.

Reptiles

Reptiles are cold-blooded vertebrates that may live either on land or in water. The major groups of reptiles are snakes, lizards, turtles, and alligators and crocodiles. Figure 5-22 shows a garter snake, the most common reptile in North America. Scales cover the snake's body. The scales help prevent the reptile from losing water. A reptile uses its lungs to breathe oxygen from the air.

Unlike amphibians, all reptiles reproduce on land. The egg is fertilized inside the female's body. Then the female lays her eggs on land. A hard leathery shell covers the egg. The shell prevents water loss and protects the embryo. The fertilized eggs develop and hatch on land.

Snakes move by wiggling their muscular bodies. Their scales grip the ground, enabling the snake to move forward.

Unlike snakes, most lizards walk on four legs. Most lizards are small and eat insects. They are most often found in tropical areas. Some lizards, such as the chameleon, can change color to match their surroundings. In this way, they can hide from enemies.

Turtles are reptiles that have two bony shells which protect and support their

Figure 5-22

How do the scales covering this garter snake help it to survive?

bodies. Although turtles lay eggs on land, some types spend most of their life in water. They use their legs as flippers when they swim. Turtles often keep the tip of their head above the water as they swim. They can then use their nostrils to take in air.

Alligators and crocodiles are the largest of all the reptiles. Alligators and crocodiles are similar in size and shape. Both spend most of their time in the water. Like turtles, alligators and crocodiles keep their nostrils above the water so that they can breathe air. They eat fish, water birds, and other animals.

Birds

The vertebrates also include birds, animals with wings and feathers. Most birds use their wings to fly. The bird's body shows many adaptations for flight. Birds have hollow, air-filled bones that make them light in weight. Their wings contain large feathers that provide lift so that the bird can stay in the air. In addition to aiding flight, the feathers trap heat and keep the bird warm.

Birds are warm-blooded. The body temperature of warm-blooded animals remains constant, regardless of the outside temperature.

Birds eat large amounts of food. This food provides the energy needed for flight and for maintaining a constant body temperature. The type of food birds eat depends on the environment in which they live.

Studying the feet of birds gives an idea of the differences among birds. Figure 5-23 shows the feet of several bird species. Each foot is an adaptation for a different environment. Aquatic birds, such as ducks, have webbed feet for swimming. Ospreys

have sharp claws for capturing their prey. What other adaptations do you see in Figure 5-23?

Mammals

Mammals, like birds, are warm-blooded. However, the bodies of all mammals are covered with hair or fur, instead of feathers. The hair or fur keeps the mammal's body warm. Mammals have the most highly developed brains of all vertebrates. Mammals also give greater care and protection to their young than do most other animals. For example, young mammals feed on milk produced in the mammary glands of females.

Mammals are adapted for life in many different environments. Bats have wings and lightweight bones that adapt them for flight. Camels and some species of rats

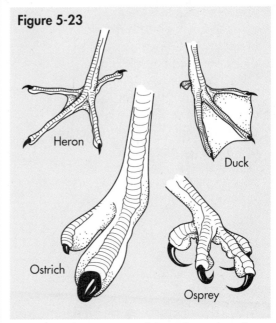

Figure 5-23

Heron

Duck

Ostrich

Osprey

How does the structure of these feet adapt these different birds for survival?

What Are Some Similarities and Differences among Vertebrates?

Process Skills observing, determining relationships

Materials goldfish in a bowl, frog in a terrarium, mouse in a cage

Vertebrates have many structures in common. They also have many differences. In this activity, you will observe similarities and differences in three types of vertebrates.

Procedure

1. Observe and describe the activities of a goldfish, a frog, and a mouse.
2. Sprinkle some fish food into the goldfish bowl. Place a mealworm or insect into the terrarium. Drop a piece of bread into the mouse's cage. Describe how each organism approaches and eats its food.
3. Observe the movements of each organism. What structures adapt each organism for movement?
4. How does each organism breathe?
5. Describe the outer covering of each organism.

Conclusions

6. Make a list of the characteristics of each organism.
7. Why are all three organisms classified as vertebrates?
8. Why is each organism classified into a different vertebrate group?

store water in their body tissues, an adaptation for life in the desert. Whales, sea lions, and porpoises are adapted for life in water. They have streamlined bodies, with flippers and a tail to help them swim. What other adaptations can you find in the mammals shown in Figure 5-24?

Biologists classify mammals according to the way they reproduce. Fertilization always takes place inside the female's body. However, development after fertilization is unusual for some types of mammals. A few mammals, such as the duckbill platypus, are egg-laying mammals. After the egg is laid, the embryo within the leathery egg develops outside the female's body.

Other unusual mammals, such as the female kangaroo, have a pouch in which the embryo develops. Fertilized eggs undergo early development within the female's body. A supply of yolk inside the egg nourishes the embryo during this time. Midway through development, the embryo is born. It crawls into the pouch located on the mother's belly. Development is completed within the pouch.

Most mammals, including humans, dogs, cats, mice, whales, and bats, are **placental mammals.** The entire process of embryo development in placental mammals takes place inside the female's body. As you learned in Chapter 4, food, oxygen, and wastes are exchanged between mother and embryo through the placenta.

Section 5-7 Review

Write the definitions for the following terms in your own words.

Figure 5-24

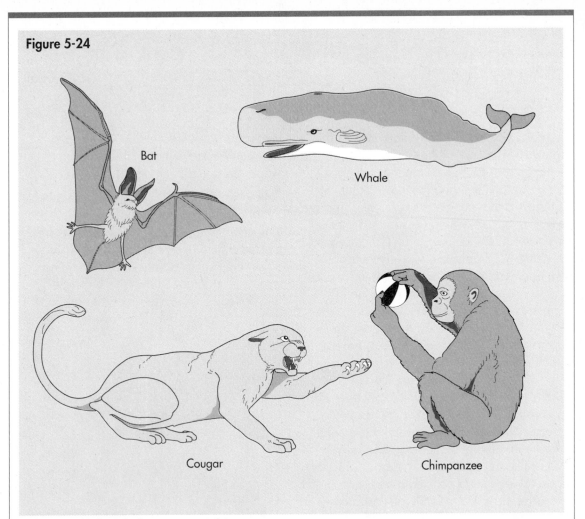

Bat

Whale

Cougar

Chimpanzee

Why is each classified as a mammal?

1. **chordate**
2. **endoskeleton**
3. **nerve cord**
4. **gill**
5. **gill slits**

Answer these questions.

6. What characteristics do all chordates have in common?
7. Describe the characteristics of each of the five main classes of vertebrates.
8. Give three examples of organisms in each of the five main classes of vertebrates.
9. What is the difference between a cold-blooded and a warm-blooded animal?
10. Choose three mammals and describe how each is adapted to its environment.

SCIENCE, TECHNOLOGY, & SOCIETY

Endangered Species

Humans rely on countless plant and animal species for food, clothing, medicines, building materials, and other products. However, our demand for these plants and animals is threatening the survival of many species. We are killing off some species faster than they can reproduce themselves. If we do not take steps to preserve the environment, we could destroy hundreds of thousands of species, even some that scientists have not yet classified.

The human population may increase dramatically in the next 20 years. Forests will be cut down and converted to farm-land to feed the growing population. The lumber will be used for building shelter and burning fuel. As a result, many forest species will lose their homes and die out.

Careless use of technology has killed thousands of organisms. Huge oil spills from tankers have polluted the earth's oceans. The 1989 oil spill in Alaska covered many aquatic organisms with oil like the bird shown in Figure 5-25. Within six months after the spill, almost 1,000 otters and over 33,000 birds had died.

Excessive hunting has endangered many species. In Africa, for example, elephants are being hunted for the ivory in their tusks. Many other species are also over-hunted. Whales are sought for their oil, snakes for their skin, and foxes for their fur.

Humans can take measures to help ensure the survival of animal and plant species. Governments can establish more protected areas for wildlife, called pre-serves. Wildlife living in these preserves would be saved from destruction.

Follow-up Activity

What can you do to help prevent the extinction of species? Write a letter to an elected official expressing your concerns about the protection of plant and animal species. Ask other students to help you think of some other activities that might help save the species. Share your concerns with others.

Figure 5-25

This oily sea bird was cleaned in order to save its life.

KEEPING TRACK

Section 5-1 Basis of Classification

1. Kingdoms are subdivided into six smaller groups, phylum, class, order, family, genus, and species.
2. The five kingdoms of organisms are monerans, protists, fungi, plants, and animals.

Section 5-2 Viruses and Monerans

1. A virus has the properties of both living and nonliving things.
2. All organisms in the moneran kingdom are unicellular. A moneran cell has no separate nucleus.
3. Bacteria and blue-green bacteria are classified as monerans.

Section 5-3 Protist Kingdom

1. Protists include protozoa, algae, *Euglena*, and slime molds.
2. Protists with animal-like characteristics, such as *Paramecium* and amoebas, are called protozoa.
3. Protists with plant-like characteristics are called algae.
4. Protists with fungus-like characteristics are called slime molds.

Section 5-4 Fungi Kingdom

1. Fungi do not have conducting tissue and lack true stems, roots, and leaves.
2. Fungi do not contain chlorophyll and therefore cannot make their own food.
3. Fungi include yeasts, molds, and mushrooms.

Section 5-5 Plant Kingdom

1. Bryophytes are small, nonvascular plants that grow in moist areas. Mosses are bryophytes.
2. Tracheophytes have vascular tissue and true roots, stems, and leaves. Ferns, conifers, and flowering plants are tracheophytes.
3. Ferns reproduce by spores. Conifers and flowering plants produce seeds.

Section 5-6 Animal Kingdom

1. Animals with backbones are vertebrates. Animals without backbones are invertebrates.
2. The largest group of invertebrates are the arthropods. Arthropods have exoskeletons and jointed bodies and legs.

Section 5-7 Vertebrates

1. All vertebrates have an endoskeleton with a backbone and a hollow nerve cord.
2. The five main classes of vertebrates are fish, amphibians, reptiles, birds, and mammals.

BUILDING VOCABULARY

Write the word from the list that best completes each sentence.

vertebrates, conifers, moneran, invertebrates, bryophytes, vascular, protist, species, classification, fungi

The great number of different kinds of living things makes a ___1___ system necessary. Each kind of organism is given a scientific name, which is made up of its genus and ___2___. The simplest organisms like bacteria and blue-green bacteria are placed in the ___3___ kingdom. Protozoa and algae are grouped in the ___4___ kingdom. The three main groups of organisms placed in the ___5___ kingdom include yeast, molds, and mushrooms. Two major groups in the plant kingdom include the ___6___ and the tracheophytes. Tracheophytes are plants with ___7___ tissue. Ferns, ___8___, and flowering plants are examples of tracheophytes. ___9___ are animals without backbones. Animals with backbones are called ___10___ and are placed in the Chordata phylum.

SUMMARIZING

Write true if the statement is *true*. If the statement is false, change the *italicized* term to make the statement true.

1. The scientific name of an organism consists of its genus and *species*.
2. Bacteria and *green* bacteria are classified as monerans.
3. Protists with fungus-like characteristics are called *bread molds*.
4. Tracheophytes are *nonvascular* plants.
5. Ferns reproduce by means of *spores*.
6. Conifers produce seeds in *flowers*.
7. Insects belong to the *Chordata* phylum.
8. An *invertebrate* is an animal with a backbone.
9. Fish are *warm*-blooded animals.
10. Lizards belong to the *amphibian* class.

INTERPRETING INFORMATION

Figure 5-26 lists some of the organisms that live on or inside a deer. Use Figure 5-26 and the information in this chapter to answer the following questions.

Figure 5-26 Organisms That Live on Deer

Organisms	Phylum
Tapeworm	Platyhelminthes
Tick	Arthropoda
Mite	Arthropoda
Flea	Arthropoda

1. In what phylum are the mite, tick, and flea placed? What characteristics do all three have in common?
2. Which large group of animals does a deer belong to? Which class does a deer belong to?
3. The organisms that live on deer can be transmitted to other animals, including humans. How, do you think, are these organisms transmitted from the deer to other animals? Do you think these organisms are helpful or harmful? Explain your answer.

CHAPTER REVIEW

THINK AND DISCUSS

Use the section number in parentheses to help you find each answer. Write your answers in complete sentences.

1. What are some differences among monerans, protists, fungi, plants, and animals? (5-1)
2. In what ways are bacteria and blue-green bacteria similar? (5-2)
3. Some scientists classify slime molds as protists. Others classify them as fungi. Explain why. (5-3)
4. How are algae different from bread molds? (5-4)
5. Why can ferns and flowering plants grow larger than mosses? (5-5)
6. What characteristics do all arthropods share? (5-6)
7. Why are all vertebrates classified in the Chordata phylum? (5-7)

GOING FURTHER

Select ten organisms that live in your area. Include both plants and animals. Classify these organisms from kingdom to species. Use reference books from the library to help you. Which organisms in your group are most closely related to each other? Explain your answer.

COMPETENCY REVIEW

1. In which group should yeast and mushrooms be placed?
   a. moneran   b. fungus
   c. protozoa   d. slime mold

2. An organism that lives in water, is covered with scales, has lungs, and lays eggs on land is a
   a. fish.   b. amphibian.
   c. reptile.   d. mammal.
3. The smallest classification group is the
   a. kingdom.   b. family.
   c. genus.   d. species.
4. The scientific name of an organism consists of its
   a. kingdom and phylum.
   b. genus and species.
   c. kingdom and species.
   d. phylum and class.
5. Molds and mushrooms are classified as fungi and not plants because they
   a. produce seeds.
   b. do not have chlorophyll.
   c. carry on photosynthesis.
   d. provide food for humans.
6. Lobsters, cockroaches, and centipedes are classified as arthropods because all three have
   a. three pairs of antennae.
   b. an exoskeleton.
   c. legs.
   d. a pair of eyes.
7. A cold-blooded vertebrate that has gills and lives in water might be a
   a. turtle.   b. snake.
   c. codfish.   d. clam.
8. Which statement is true?
   a. All chordates are vertebrates.
   b. All vertebrates are chordates.
   c. All organisms that fly are birds.
   d. All birds can fly.

CHAPTER 6

EVOLUTION

When visiting a zoo, have you noticed how much tigers, lions, and jaguars resemble each other? Each of these organisms represents a different species. A species is a group of organisms that look alike and can reproduce among themselves. All members of a species have similar characteristics and similar adaptations for survival. For example, look at the lion in Figure 6-1. Lions have sharp claws and teeth for capturing other animals for food.

How did these different species come to exist? According to scientific evidence, lions, tigers, and jaguars are related. They came from common ancestors. These common ancestors were animals that lived long ago. They resembled modern lions, tigers, and jaguars but were of separate species. The process by which species change over time, giving rise to new species, is called **evolution.**

Scientists classify organisms on the basis of similarities. Organisms that have a similar structure are usually classified in the same group. Biologists think that organisms that belong to the same group evolved from common ancestors.

6-1 Evidence of Evolution

■ *Objectives*

☐ *List and describe five types of evidence of evolution.*

☐ *Identify the eras, periods, and epochs in the geologic time scale.*

The evolution of life has taken place over hundreds of millions of years. Evidence of evolution comes both from organisms that lived long ago and organisms that exist today.

Figure 6-1

The lion is related to other big cats.

Fossil Evidence

Scientists obtain much evidence of evolution from **fossils.** A fossil is an imprint or the remains of an organism that lived in the past. Scientists have found most fossils in **sedimentary** (sed-uh-MENT-uh-ree) **rock.** Sedimentary rock forms under water from small particles of sand, silt, and clay. These particles are carried from the land by streams and rivers and are deposited in layers at the bottom of lakes and oceans. The heavy top layers of sediment push down on the bottom layers with great pressure. This pressure causes the bottom layers to harden and change to layered or sedimentary rock.

Look at the sedimentary rock shown in Figure 6-2. Which rock layer is the oldest? The bottom layer is the oldest because it was the first to be deposited.

Figure 6-2

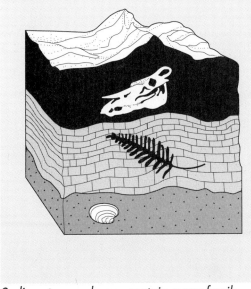

Sedimentary rock may contain many fossils.

Figure 6-3 shows a fossil of a fish that lived several million years ago. When the fish died, its body dropped into the sediment on the ocean bottom. There, the soft parts of the body decayed, or broke down, into simpler substances. Only the hard bones remained. These became sandwiched between the layers of sediment. The sediment eventually hardened into rock and preserved the fossil of the fish.

Figure 6-3

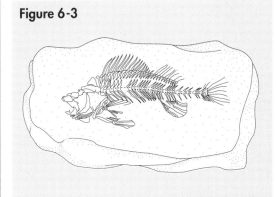

How do you think this fossil of a fish formed?

Kinds of Fossils Most fossils form from the hard parts of organisms. Figure 6-4 shows a seashell fossil called a **mold.** This fossil formed as the sand surrounding the shell

Figure 6-4

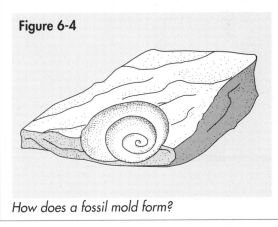

How does a fossil mold form?

slowly turned to rock. Water dissolved the shell, leaving an empty space in the shape of the shell. Sometimes a mold may fill with minerals from the water, forming a fossil called a **cast**. A cast is shown in Figure 6-5.

Figure 6-5

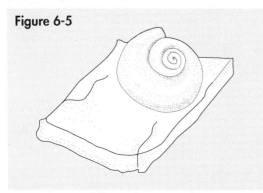

How is a cast different from a mold?

Figure 6-6 shows a third type of fossil, a preserved footprint of a dinosaur. This type of fossil is called an **imprint**. How do you think an imprint forms?

Figure 6-6

How do you think this imprint fossil formed?

Learning from the Fossil Record By studying fossils, scientists learn how the earth and its organisms have changed throughout its history. For example, the presence of seashells in sedimentary rock in the Grand Canyon suggests that a large body of water once covered this area.

Scientists can also learn about species of organisms that existed during earlier periods in the earth's history but that no longer exist today. A species that no longer exists is said to be **extinct.** Figure 6-7 shows an extinct sea animal called the trilobite. Trilobites lived 500 to 600 million years ago.

Figure 6-7

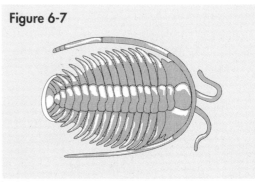

Trilobites are now extinct.

Scientists have also discovered species called **living fossils.** A living fossil has undergone very little change over hundreds or millions of years. A fish called a coelacanth, shown in Figure 6-8, is an

Figure 6-8

This coelacanth is a living fossil.

example of a living fossil. It exists today, yet is also found in the fossil record. Species that have changed very little in the millions of years they have existed on earth include some algae, insects like the cockroach, and the horseshoe crab, shown in Figure 6-9.

Most species that exist today have evolved and changed over time, however. Figure 6-10 shows the changes that have taken place in the horse. Scientists have studied the fossil record to obtain evidence of this evolution.

Figure 6-9

The horseshoe crab has not changed much over the course of evolution.

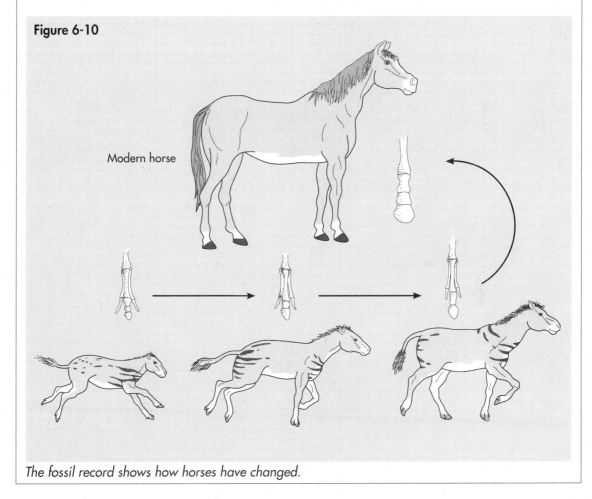

Figure 6-10

Modern horse

The fossil record shows how horses have changed.

The fossil record also provides evidence that some groups of organisms have evolved from other groups. Figure 6-11 shows a fossil of *Archaeopteryx,* an animal that lived 180 million years ago. Fossils of *Archaeopteryx* show that this organism had a jaw with teeth and claws on its front limbs like a reptile, and wings and feathers like a bird. *Archaeopteryx* provides evidence that birds may have evolved from reptiles.

Geological Evidence

Geology is the study of the earth. Geology also provides evidence of evolution. Geologists study the surface of the earth and how it has changed over time. Geologists estimate the earth to be 4 to 5 billion years old. Since scientists consider evolution to be a very slow process, 4 to 5 billion years would provide enough time for the process to have taken place.

Scientists can also calculate the age of a rock or fossil by using a technique called **radioactive dating.** Some rocks contain a radioactive element called uranium 238. Fossils that come from organic material contain a radioactive element called carbon 14. Uranium 238 decays into lead, and carbon 14 decays into nitrogen.

Radioactive elements such as carbon 14 decay at a constant rate. The time required for half of the amount of carbon 14 in an object to decay into nitrogen is its **half-life.** The half-life of carbon 14 is 5730

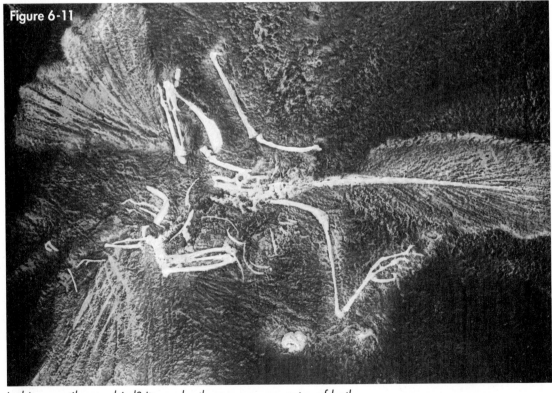

Figure 6-11

Is this a reptile or a bird? It may be the common ancestor of both.

Calculating

A scientist found a fossil containing 25 grams of carbon 14. Further study showed that this amount represented one fourth the original amount of carbon 14. The fossil contained 100 grams of carbon 14 when it first formed. Three fourths of the original amount, or 75 grams, has decayed to form nitrogen. How old is this fossil?

Original amount of Carbon 14:
100 grams

Present amount of Carbon 14:
25 grams

1. Use the concept of half-life to determine the age of this fossil. Keep in mind that the half-life of carbon 14 is 5730 years.
2. Explain how you got your answer.

years. In other words, it takes 5730 years for one half of the amount of carbon 14 in a fossil to decay into nitrogen. The half-life of uranium is 4.5 billion years. It takes 4.5 billion years for one half of the amount of uranium in a rock to decay into lead.

The ability to estimate the age of a fossil enables scientists to organize fossil evidence in a logical way. They assemble bits and pieces of evidence to answer questions about evolution. For example, the fossils of the earliest reptiles are much older than those of birds. Scientists have used this information, along with observations of fossils like *Archaeopteryx,* to conclude that birds evolved from reptiles.

Suppose scientists determine that a certain fossil organism lived on the earth for only a short time. They may find a similar organism embedded in rock in several parts of the world. Since scientists know how old the fossil is, they can use this information to determine the age of the rocks in which the fossils were found. An organism that once lived in large numbers throughout the earth for a short period of time is called an **index fossil.**

The trilobite fossil shown in Figure 6-7 is an example of an index fossil. Scientists know that certain trilobites lived 500 to 600 million years ago in large numbers all over the earth. The widespread presence of these trilobite fossils in rock layers shows that the layers, no matter where they are found, are about the same age.

Scientists have used knowledge of the age of rock layers and fossils to construct a time scale. This scale divides the history of the earth, or geological time, into **eras.** An era is a span of time millions of years in length.

Each era of the time scale is made up of smaller divisions called **periods.** Each period is divided into still smaller segments called **epochs** (EP-uks). Figure 6-12 shows that the first life-forms appeared in the Pre-cambrian period, about 4.5 billion years ago. Scientists think the first life-forms included bacteria and blue-green bacteria. More complex life-forms, such as fish, plants, and land animals, evolved from these first organisms.

Figure 6-12 Geologic Time

Era	Period	Epoch	Years	Characteristics
Cenozoic	Quaternary	Recent Pleistocene	11,000 .5-3 million	Modern man Early man
		Pliocene Miocene	13 million 25 million	Large carnivores First grazing mammals
	Tertiary	Oligocene	38 million	Early apes
		Eocene	60 million	Early horses
		Paleocene	65 million	First placental animals
Mesozoic	Cretaceous		135 million	Flowering plants
	Jurassic		180 million	Age of dinosaurs; first birds
	Triassic		230 million	First dinosaurs
Paleozoic	Permian		280 million	Extinction of trilobites
	Carboniferous		345 million	Great coal forests; first reptiles
	Devonian		410 million	First amphibians
	Silurian		425 million	First land animals and plants
	Ordovician		500 million	First fish
	Cambrian		600 million	Abundant marine invertebrates
	Precambrian		4.5 billion	First forms of life, or monerans

How Much Time Does the Geologic Time Scale Represent?

Process Skills *making a model, performing numeric calculations*

Materials metric tape measure, roll of adding machine paper, pencil, scissors

In this activity you will make a model of the geologic time scale.

Procedure

1. Study the list of events found in Figure 6-13. Notice that the earliest events are at the bottom of the chart.
2. Use a metric tape measure to measure 15 meters of adding machine paper. Use scissors to cut 15 meters of paper from the roll. If 1 meter equals 1 billion years, how many billions of years does this length of paper represent? What significant event occurred 15 billion years ago? Label this event at the end of the tape.
3. Place a mark 4.5 meters from the end of the tape. How many billions of years does 4.5 meters represent? Refer to Figure 6-13 to see what event occurred at this time. Indicate this event on the tape.
4. Place the rest of the events included in Figure 6-13 in their proper position on the time scale. Use the scale 1 mm = 1 million years.

Conclusion

5. How many millimeters on your time scale show the appearance of humans? Compare this length to the rest of your model by making a fraction.

Figure 6-13

Event	Years Ago
Today	The present
Last Ice Age	10,000
Beginning of Pleistocene epoch, age of appearance of early humans	3 million
Beginning of the Paleocene epoch, first placental mammals	65 million
Beginning of Jurassic period, age of dinosaurs	180 million
Beginning of Devonian period, first amphibians appear	410 million
Beginning of Ordovician period, first fish appear	500 million
Beginning of Cambrian period, abundance of invertebrate fossils	600 million
Age of the oldest rocks	3.5 billion
Formation of the earth	4.5 billion
Beginning of the universe	15 billion

Inferring

From studying fossils found in sedimentary rocks, scientists make inferences about the history of life on Earth. An inference is a conclusion based on facts, not direct observation. Read the following descriptions of the discoveries made by scientists. Then answer the questions that follow each description.

1. Fossils of seashells are found in sedimentary rocks in the Rocky Mountains. What might scientists infer about where these rocks formed?

2. The fossil of an extinct mammal was found in a layer of sedimentary rock. In this same layer, fossils of ferns and palm trees were abundant. What would scientists think the climate was like at the time these extinct mammals lived?

Evidence from Anatomy Scientists use fossil evidence to trace evolutionary history. They also obtain evidence of evolution from similarities in the anatomy, or structure, of existing organisms. If the anatomy of two species shows similarities, the species probably share a common ancestor.

Figure 6-14 shows the bones of three mammals. These bones are the flipper of a whale, the wing of a bat, and the arm of a human. Notice that the bones are similar in structure. Body parts with similar bone structures are called **homologous** (hoh-MAHL-uh-gus) **structures.** The presence of homologous structures in different species suggests that these species evolved from a common ancestor. Thus, homologous structures in the whale, bat, and human suggest that these species evolved from one mammal-like ancestor.

Scientists also study **vestigial** (ve-STIJ-ee-ul) **structures** to determine evolutionary relationships. A vestigial structure is a structure that is reduced in size and has

Figure 6-14

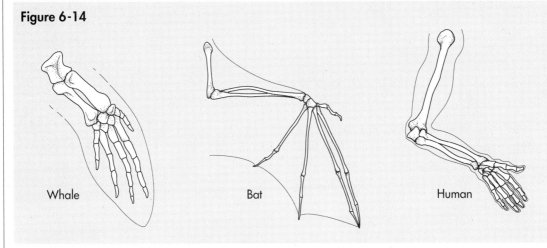

Whale   Bat   Human

Compare the bone structure in the whale's flipper, the bat's wing, and the human's arm.

no function. The human appendix is an example of a vestigial structure.

You may wonder why vestigial organs exist if they have no function. Scientists think these structures did have a function in the ancestors of the organisms that now have them.

Evidence from Embryo Development You learned in Chapter 4 that the cells of a growing embryo multiply and eventually develop into specific body parts. Embryo development takes place in a certain order. In other words, every organism within a species develops in the same way. Scientists often identify evolutionary relationships between species by comparing embryo development.

Look at the fish, bird, and human embryos in Figure 6-15. Notice the similarities in the embryos, such as the presence of gill slits and a tail. The similarities are so strong in these early stages that it is difficult to tell these organisms apart. Similarities in the way these early embryos develop suggest that these organisms evolved from a common ancestor.

Evidence from Biochemistry More evidence for evolution is found in the study of **biochemistry**. Biochemistry is the study of the atoms and molecules found in the cells of organisms. Although some molecules are found in all organisms, many are found only in certain groups of organisms.

For example, a blood protein called hemoglobin is identical in humans and chimpanzees. A similar type of hemoglobin is also found in gorillas and monkeys. This similarity of hemoglobin structure suggests that these species evolved from a common ancestor.

Figure 6-15

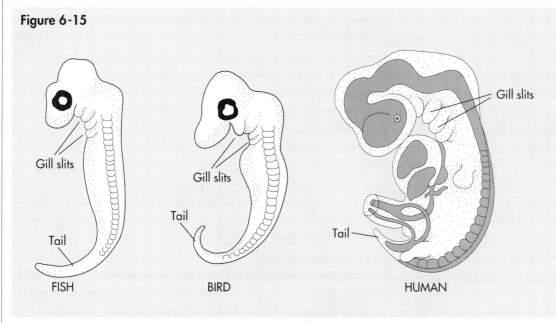

In these early stages of development, it is difficult to tell the organisms apart.

▰▰ Section 6-1 Review ▰▰

Write the definitions for the following terms in your own words.

1. **evolution**
2. **fossil**
3. **radioactive dating**
4. **half-life**
5. **homologous structures**

Answer these questions.

6. What information about life in the past do scientists learn from the study of fossils?
7. How do fossils form?
8. What is radioactive dating? How is it used to determine the age of a fossil?
9. What is the difference between a homologous structure and a vestigial structure? Explain how each is used as evidence of evolution.
10. What observations from embryo development are used as evidence of evolution?

6-2 Theories of Evolution

■ *Objectives*
☐ *Distinguish between Lamarck's and Darwin's theories of evolution.*
☐ *Explain the role of natural selection in the origin of new species.*

Evidence from the fossil record supports the theory of evolution. The fossil record shows that most species change over geologic time. New species come about as others become extinct. What causes a species to change? How does a new species form? How does evolution take place?

In the early 1800s, two scientists developed theories to explain how evolution takes place. The first theory was proposed by a French biologist named Jean Baptiste Lamarck. The theory that is accepted today was developed by a British scientist named Charles Darwin.

Lamarck's Theory

Lamarck proposed his theory in 1809. He called the first part of his theory use and disuse. Lamarck stated that living things change to meet the demands of their environment. New **traits,** or characteristics, of an organism may appear, or existing traits may change in structure or function. In addition, traits that a living thing no longer uses will become reduced in size or disappear.

Lamarck also suggested the inheritance of **acquired characteristics**. These are traits that develop in an organism for survival. Lamarck stated that acquired characteristics would be passed on to future generations. In this way, future generations benefit from traits acquired by their ancestors.

Figure 6-16 shows an example of Lamarck's idea, the evolution of the giraffe's neck. The earliest giraffes were grass-eating animals and, according to Lamarck, had short necks. They had to compete with other grass-eating animals for food. Eventually the supply of grass became scarce. Some giraffes began to stretch their necks to reach for leaves growing on trees.

Figure 6-16

Three giraffes with short necks

Giraffes stretching their necks to reach leaves on tall trees

Three giraffes with long necks

How did Lamarck explain the origin of giraffes with long necks?

Lamarck believed that these first giraffes were not born with long necks. They acquired a long neck as an adaptation to the environment. He thought that the newly acquired trait was passed on to the next generation. Over many generations, long necks evolved in all giraffes.

Scientists tested Lamarck's theory by changing an organism in some way and looking for the new trait in later generations. They found that organisms did not inherit acquired characteristics. Lamarck's theory was incorrect. Soon a new theory of evolution was to be introduced.

Darwin's Voyage

Charles Darwin was a young scientist traveling through the Galapagos Islands, a group of islands off the west coast of Ecuador. Darwin noticed that some island organisms differed from those found on the South American mainland. For example, Darwin identified 13 different species of finches on the islands. Notice the different beak sizes and shapes of the finch species shown in Figure 6-17. Each kind of beak is adapted for obtaining a certain kind of food.

Besides these differences, Darwin observed similarities among the 13 species.

Figure 6-17

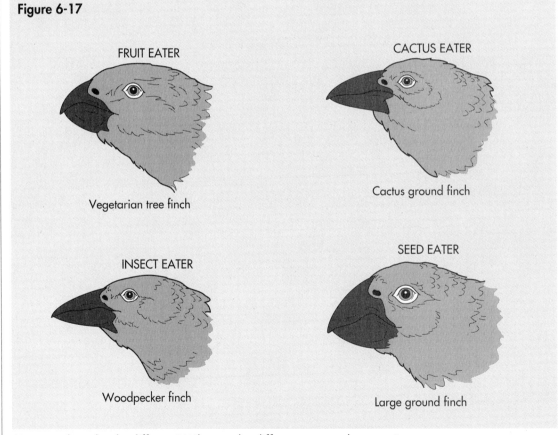

FRUIT EATER

Vegetarian tree finch

CACTUS EATER

Cactus ground finch

INSECT EATER

Woodpecker finch

SEED EATER

Large ground finch

How are these beaks different? Why are the differences an advantage?

These species were also similar to the single species of finch that lived on the mainland. From these observations, Darwin concluded that at one time only the mainland species of finch existed. Some of these finches flew to the islands in search of food. Each island contained different food sources. There was not enough of one kind of food on each island for the birds to eat. Some finches adapted by eating new foods. They survived and reproduced. Eventually, several new species of finch arose that were adapted to eating the different foods of each island. Each of these species evolved from the species living on the mainland.

Charles Darwin presented his theory of evolution in a book called *The Origin of Species,* published in 1859. Since then, other scientists have changed Darwin's theory to reflect new scientific knowledge. Darwin's basic theory, however, remains widely accepted today.

Darwin's Theory

According to Darwin, changes in species occur slowly and are affected by the environment. Darwin based this idea on observations of living things. Darwin observed that each species produces more offspring than will survive long enough to mature and reproduce. For example, the green frog lays thousands of eggs during each mating season. Only a few eggs develop into frogs. Individual frogs compete for food, water, and living space. What determines which frogs survive and reproduce?

Darwin also observed variation among members of a species. He did not know what caused this variation. He hypothesized, however, that individuals have different traits, and some traits are better suited to the environment than others. For example, a fast horse is more likely to survive than a slow horse.

Those members of a species that have traits that are suited to the environment are best fit for survival. Organisms that are well adapted to the environment produce offspring, so the traits of these organisms are passed on to future generations. Organisms that do not have these traits will probably not reproduce. As a result, their traits are not passed on to future generations. Thus, evolution occurs as those organisms best suited to their environment pass their traits on to their offspring. Darwin called this process of survival by those organisms best suited to the environment **natural selection.**

Think about the example of how giraffes got their long necks. According to Darwin's theory, necks of early giraffes ranged in length from short to long. Most giraffes had short necks. They were well suited for eating grass. Since short-necked giraffes were best adapted to their environment, they were more likely to pass this trait on to future generations. As grasses became scarce, however, giraffes had to look elsewhere for food. Now long-necked giraffes had an advantage over short-necked giraffes. They could reach leaves on tree branches. The natural environment selected long-necked giraffes for survival. The longer-necked giraffes survived and reproduced. Unable to get enough food, the short-necked giraffes died and their traits died with them.

Section 6-2 Review

Write the definitions for the following terms in your own words.

1. **acquired characteristics**
2. **natural selection**
3. **trait**

Answer these questions.

4. Summarize the major ideas in Lamarck's theory of evolution.
5. Summarize the major ideas in Darwin's theory of evolution.
6. Why can natural selection take place only if variation exists?
7. Many years ago a scientist wanted to test Lamarck's theory. In an experiment, he cut off the tails of mice and then mated the mice. All of the young were born with tails. Did his results support Lamarck's theory? Explain.

6-3 Variation and Adaptation

■ *Objectives*
☐ *Explain the causes of variation in organisms.*
☐ *Explain the role of adaptations in species survival.*

Darwin explained how species gradually change over time. He explained that traits vary among members of the same species. He further explained that as a result of natural selection, individuals having traits best suited to the environment survive and reproduce.

Causes of Variation

Although Darwin could not explain the cause of variation, today scientists can. Recall from Chapter 4 that sexual reproduction is an important source of variation. The process of meiosis produces many different combinations of chromosomes in the gametes. Any one of these gametes may be involved in the fertilization process.

In addition, an organism receives chromosomes from two different parents. Since each organism inherits its own set of chromosomes, its traits will differ from those of other members of its species. The resulting variation explains why you look different from your classmates, and even from others in your family.

Variation can also result from a **mutation** (myoo-TAY-shun). A mutation is a sudden change in a gene or chromosome. A mutation may cause changes in color, size, or shape of a body part. It may also cause changes in the way a body part functions. Find the white rat in the litter shown in Figure 6-18. The white rat, called an albino, lacks normal color. An albino is an example of a mutation in the gene or genes that control an organism's color.

Most mutations are harmful. For example, an albino deer is easily seen in a forest. It is more likely to be killed by an enemy. A fruit fly born with stumped wings would be unable to fly. It may be captured and eaten. The cells of a human born with a disease called sickle-cell disease do not receive enough oxygen. This condition causes weakness and even death.

Figure 6-18

Can you find the albino rat?

Some mutations, however, are helpful. A mutation may produce a hawk with unusually keen eyesight. This hawk will be better able to compete with other birds for food. If a mutation improves an organism's ability to survive, the organism will pass the mutation on to its offspring.

Adaptation

Survival of a species depends on its ability to adapt to its environment. Each species represents a collection of adaptations that make it fit for survival in its particular environment. The result of evolution is the existence of living things well adapted to their environment.

No matter where they live, species are adapted to survive in their environment. You learned about several such adaptations in Chapter 2. For example, the ability of cactus plants to store water is an adaptation for a dry environment. The thick fur and layers of fat found in polar bears are adaptations for extreme cold. Adaptations are the results of evolution. As a result of the process of evolution, only those organisms best suited to live in their environments survive.

■■■ Section 6-3 Review ■■■

Write the definition for the following term in your own words.

1. **mutation**

Answer these questions.

2. Describe two sources of variation in a species.
3. How can variation exist in species that reproduce asexually?

Humans Affect the Course of Evolution

The peppered moth is a species commonly found in England. Some of these moths are light colored, and others are dark. If you had lived in England 250 years ago, you would have seen mostly light moths. At that time, natural selection favored light moths. Both light and dark moths would rest on tree trunks covered with light gray, crusty organisms called lichens. The light moths blended in with the color of the lichens. Because dark moths stood out, they were more likely to be seen and eaten by birds.

Beginning in the mid-1700s, however, the moth's environment started to change. The industrial revolution began in England. During this time, there were many factories powered by burning coal. As coal burned, soot from factory chimneys polluted the environment. This soot killed the lichens and left the tree trunks bare and black.

As blackened tree trunks became common, natural selection began to favor dark moths. Dark moths that landed on the dark tree trunks would not be easily seen and eaten by birds. Thus, the dark moths survived and increased in number.

In recent decades, England has reduced the amount of pollution produced by its factories. As the air has become free of soot, lichens once again have begun to grow on tree trunks. As a result, light-colored peppered moths are beginning to thrive throughout England.

Follow-up Activity

Many human activities have affected organisms in the environment. For example, the use of insecticides has increased the rate at which mutations occur in some insects. Other human activity has contributed to the extinction of many organisms. Use the library to research one area of human activity and its effects on the environment. Write a report in which you summarize your findings.

Figure 6-19

Which color moth survives best on dark tree trunks?

██████ KEEPING TRACK ██████

Section 6-1 Evidence of Evolution

1. From the fossil record, scientists have learned about the history of life on Earth.
2. Scientists believe that the earth is about 4.5 billion years old, old enough for evolution to have taken place.
3. Scientists use radioactive dating and index fossils to determine the age of rock layers.
4. Some organisms have changed throughout the course of Earth's history.
5. The existence of similar structures and similar stages in early embryonic development of some organisms suggests that organisms evolved from a common ancestor.

Section 6-2 Theories of Evolution

1. Lamarck thought that species developed traits through use and disuse. He believed that acquired traits are developed during an organism's lifetime and are passed on from generation to generation.
2. Darwin based his theory of evolution on the existence of variation and natural selection.
3. Through natural selection, the environment selects which organisms will survive.

Section 6-3 Variation and Adaptation

1. Variation arises through sexual reproduction and mutation.
2. Mutations are sudden changes in the structure of chromosomes and genes.
3. Each species represents a collection of adaptations that make it fit for survival in its environment.

██████ BUILDING VOCABULARY ██████

Write the term from the list that best matches each phrase.

imprint, adaptation, sedimentary rock, extinct, homologous structures, era, vestigial structures, mutation, biochemistry, half-life

1. study of atoms and molecules found in organisms
2. preserved impression of part of an organism, such as a fish skeleton
3. longest period of geologic time
4. term that refers to an organism that no longer exists on the earth
5. made of hardened layers of sand, silt, or clay
6. change in the structure of a chromosome or gene that results in variation in the members of a species
7. the time it takes for half of the amount of a radioactive element to decay
8. body parts having the same basic structure
9. characteristic in an organism that helps it survive
10. structures that are reduced in size and seem to have no function

Explain the difference between the words in each pair.

11. cast, mold
12. homologous structures, vestigial structures
13. radioactive dating, half-life

14. mutation, adaptation
15. use and disuse, acquired characteristic
16. mutation, natural selection

SUMMARIZING

Write the missing word for each sentence.

1. A ___ is an imprint or remains of an organism that lived in the past.
2. Trilobites and dinosaurs are examples of organisms that have become ___.
3. Fossils may be found in a type of layered rock called ___ rock.
4. A footprint of an animal is a kind of fossil called an ___.
5. The method used by scientists to determine the age of a fossil is called ___.
6. Humans appeared on Earth during the ___ era.
7. Body parts that have the same basic structure are called ___ structures.
8. The scientist who proposed the theory of evolution by natural selection was ___.
9. A change in the structure of a chromosome or gene is called a ___.

INTERPRETING INFORMATION

Use Figure 6-20 to answer questions 1–4.

1. Which organisms shown do you know to be extinct?
2. Which organism was the first to become extinct? During which period shown?
3. Which organisms have continued to increase in number over geologic time?

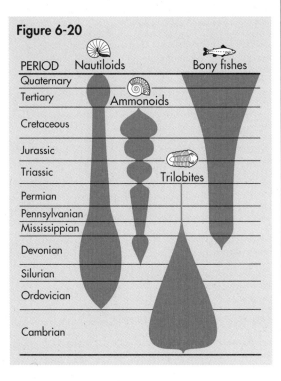

Figure 6-20

4. During what period did bony fish first appear on the earth?

THINK AND DISCUSS

Use the section number to the right of each question to find the answer. Write your answers in complete sentences.

1. What do scientists learn about species from the fossil record? (6-1)
2. Most scientists think that humans and apes evolved from a common ancestor. What evidence supports this idea? (6-1)
3. How do the theories of evolution proposed by Lamarck and Darwin differ? (6-2)

4. How would Darwin explain the evolution of long-necked giraffes? (6-2)
5. How is variation among members of a species related to evolution? (6-3)

GOING FURTHER

Some species, such as the trilobite and dinosaur, have become extinct. Use the library or a natural history museum to research possible reasons for their extinction. Write a summary of your findings in your own words.

COMPETENCY REVIEW

1. Rock layer A is above rock layer B. How would fossils found in rock layer A compare with those found in rock layer B?
   a. The fossils in rock layer A would be older than those found in rock layer B.
   b. The fossils in rock layer A would be younger than those in rock layer B.
   c. The fossils found in both layers would be the same age.
2. Similarities of two organisms in the early stages of development would support the idea that organisms
   a. evolved from a common ancestor.
   b. use their tail to swim in the water.
   c. use their gills to get oxygen.
   d. look alike by chance.
3. The one that is not a type of fossil is a (an)
   a. cast.   b. mutation.
   c. imprint.   d. mold.
4. The bones in the front leg of a cat and in the arm of a human are examples of
   a. vestigial structures.
   b. homologous structures.
   c. embryological structures.
   d. dominant structures.
5. The time needed for half of a sample of carbon 14 to decay is known as its
   a. geologic age.
   b. half-life.
   c. mutation rate.
   d. epoch.
6. The idea that ducks developed webbed feet to be able to swim corresponds to the theory of evolution of
   a. Darwin.
   b. Redi.
   c. Lamarck.
   d. Hooke.
7. Variation among species may result from
   a. asexual reproduction.
   b. environmental conditions.
   c. mutation.
   d. extinction.
8. The environmental selection of organisms with the adaptations needed to survive is called
   a. extinction.   b. use and disuse.
   c. mutation.   d. natural selection.
9. New species arise through
   a. reproduction.   b. use and disuse.
   c. evolution.   d. fossil formation.
10. The theory of evolution by natural selection was proposed by
    a. Lamarck.
    b. Weismann.
    c. Redi.
    d. Darwin.

CHAPTER 7

PLANTS

If you made a list of some places where you have seen plants growing, it would be a long list. Plants grow in many different places and are essential to life on Earth.

You do not have to be a farmer or a gardener for plants to affect your life. The cotton used to make your blue jeans and T-shirts comes from a plant. The wood used to make buildings, furniture, and the pages of this book comes from trees. Many medicines and dyes come from plants as well. Plants add beauty to the world and make life more comfortable. Without plants, there would be no gardens, parks, or forests. You would not be able to climb a tree or pick fresh flowers.

However, plants affect your life in even more important ways. Plants make the food on which all other life-forms depend. Recall from Chapter 2 that through the process of photosynthesis, plants use energy from the sun to make food. The food you eat is manufactured by green plants and by plant-eating animals, such as cows and lambs. Plants also supply the air with the oxygen you breathe. Without oxygen, life could not exist on Earth. Thus, all life-forms, including protists, fungi, and animals, could not live without plants.

7-1 Plant Structure

■ *Objectives*

☐ *Name the three major structures that make up a plant.*

☐ *Identify the functions of the roots, stems, and leaves.*

☐ *Describe the structure and function of the different types of tissues found in the root, stem, and leaf.*

All plants make their own food by carrying on photosynthesis. To carry on

Figure 7-1

The cotton plant, like many others, is useful and beautiful.

photosynthesis and other life processes, plants must obtain carbon dioxide, water, and minerals from the environment. Thus, plant structure is adapted for obtaining these materials and transporting them to the necessary parts of the plant.

Roots

Have you ever tried to pull a plant out of the ground? You may not have been able to. Plants are held firmly in the soil by underground structures called **roots**.

Figure 7-2 shows two main types of plant root systems, the **fibrous root** system and the **taproot** system. Notice that the fibrous root system has many branches. Grass and trees have fibrous root systems. The taproot system contains one long, thick main root from which many thin roots grow. Carrots, radishes, and beets have taproots.

The outermost cells, or surface cells, of roots are adapted for absorbing water and minerals from the soil. Look at the microscopic views of a root in Figure 7-3. Find the **root hairs,** which extend from the outer cells just above the root tip. Root hairs

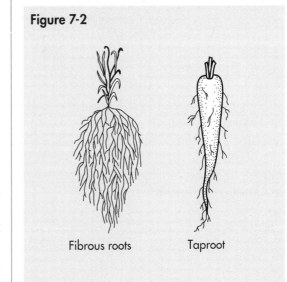

Figure 7-2

Fibrous roots   Taproot

Compare the taproot and fibrous root systems.

increase the surface area of the root, which enables the plant to absorb water and minerals quickly.

Water and minerals pass through the root hairs into the vascular system. The vascular system contains the conducting or transport tissues. Plants have two types of vascular tissue, **xylem** (ZY-lum) and

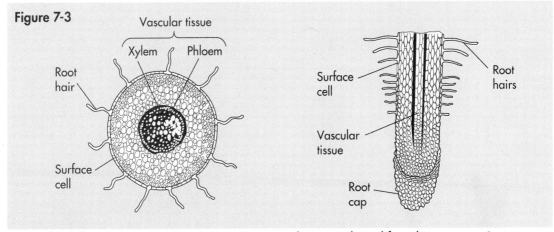

Figure 7-3

Vascular tissue

Xylem   Phloem

Root hair

Surface cell

Surface cell

Vascular tissue

Root hairs

Root cap

Name the different types of tissues in a root. How is the root adapted for taking in water?

phloem (FLOH-em). The xylem carries water and minerals from the roots to all parts of the plant. The phloem carries food produced in the leaves or stored in the roots to all parts of the plant.

Find the **root cap** at the tip of the root. The cap covers and protects the cells of the root tip as the root pushes through the soil. The cells behind the root cap reproduce rapidly and develop into the different cells and tissues of the plant.

Stem

Food, water, and minerals are transported from one part of a plant to another through the stem. The plant stem holds the xylem and phloem, which transport materials throughout the plant. The stem also holds and supports the leaves and flowers. Find the xylem and phloem in Figure 7-4.

Biologists classify stems into two types, herbaceous and woody. Herbaceous stems are usually soft, thin, and green. Beans, peas, and squash have a herbaceous stem. Woody stems are thick, hard, and tough with an outer layer of bark. Woody stems lack the green color and usually grow much taller and thicker than herbaceous stems.

Figure 7-4

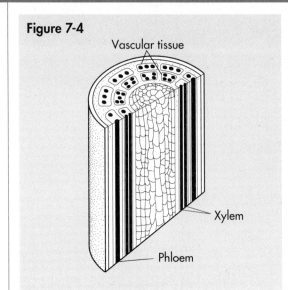

Name the two kinds of vascular tissue. What is the function of each? In what other organ of the plant is vascular tissue found?

Beech, oak, and maple trees have a woody stem.

Leaves

The xylem transports water and minerals to the leaves, where photosynthesis takes place. Leaves come in a variety of shapes and sizes. Notice in Figure 7-5 that each

Figure 7-5

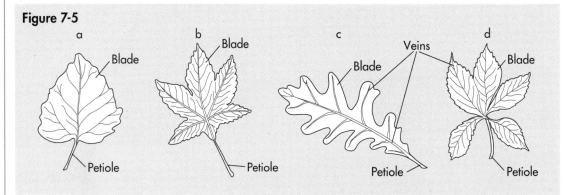

What are the two main parts of a leaf? How do the leaves of plants differ from one another?

leaf has two parts, a **petiole** (PET-ee-ohl) and a **blade**. The petiole attaches the leaf blade to the plant stem. The broad, flat shape of the blade is an adaptation for capturing light, which provides the energy needed for photosynthesis to take place.

Locate the uppermost layer, or **upper epidermis** (ep-uh-DUR-mus), of the leaf in Figure 7-6. The cells of the upper epidermis protect the inner cells of the leaf and prevent water loss. In many plants, a waxy layer covers the upper epidermis and further protects the plant from water loss.

Find the lowest layer of plant tissue, called the **lower epidermis.** Notice the tiny openings, or **stomates** (STOH-mayts), scattered throughout the lower epidermis. A pair of bean-shaped **guard cells** surround each stomate and control the opening and

closing of the stomates. When the guard cells are open, gases and water can pass through the stomates. When the guard cells are closed, no materials can pass through.

Photosynthesis takes place in the two layers of cells which lie just below the upper epidermis. The top layer of cells called the **palisade layer,** consists of closely packed cells. The lower layer, or **spongy layer,** is located beneath the palisade layer. The spongy layer consists of loosely arranged cells with large, moist air spaces between them. These air spaces increase the surface area for the passage of carbon dioxide and oxygen through the cell membrane.

The cells of the palisade and spongy layers contain chloroplasts, the organelles that carry out photosynthesis. The water and

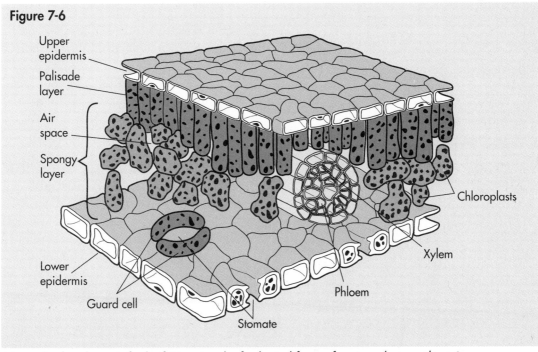

Figure 7-6

Upper epidermis
Palisade layer
Air space
Spongy layer
Chloroplasts
Lower epidermis
Guard cell
Stomate
Phloem
Xylem

Name the four layers of a leaf. How is a leaf adapted for performing photosynthesis?

minerals needed for photosynthesis and other life processes reach the cell layers through vascular tissues called **veins.** Veins contain xylem and phloem. Notice in Figure 7-5 that the veins branch from the petiole throughout the leaf.

▬▬ Section 7-1 Review ▬▬

Write the definitions for the following terms in your own words.

1. **root**
2. **xylem**
3. **phloem**
4. **stomate**
5. **vein**

Answer these questions.

6. What are four important functions of the roots?
7. What are two important functions of the stem?
8. Name the four layers of leaf tissue and describe the function of each.
9. More chloroplasts are found in the palisade layer than in the spongy layer. How is this an adaptation for survival?

7-2 Photosynthesis

■ *Objectives*
☐ *Explain the function of photosynthesis.*
☐ *Write the summary equation for photosynthesis.*

☐ *Explain how the water and carbon dioxide needed for photosynthesis reach the cells of the leaves.*

How do plants actually make their food? The word photosynthesis provides a clue. Photo means light, and synthesis means to put together. Thus, during photosynthesis, plants use light energy to put together, or make, food.

Getting the Raw Materials to the Cells

As you know, photosynthesis takes place in the chloroplasts. Each chloroplast contains the green pigment **chlorophyll** (KLOHR-uh-fil). Chlorophyll traps the light energy needed for photosynthesis.

In addition to light, the plants must obtain carbon dioxide and water from the environment. Carbon dioxide enters the leaf through the stomates. From the stomates, it passes into the moist air spaces and then into the cells in both the spongy and the palisade layers.

Water from the soil enters the root hairs. From there, water passes through the xylem to the veins in the leaf. Finally, water passes into the air spaces and into the spongy and palisade layers.

Photosynthesis takes place when light energy, carbon dioxide, and water are present in the chloroplasts. The plant uses trapped light energy to combine water and carbon dioxide to form the simple sugar glucose, oxygen, and water. The following equation summarizes the process of photosynthesis.

$$\text{carbon dioxide} + \text{water} \xrightarrow[\text{chlorophyll}]{\text{light}} \text{glucose} + \text{oxygen} + \text{water}$$

Analyzing Data from an Experiment

A plant was placed in a test tube and a light was placed at different distances from the plant. Bubbles of oxygen given off by the plant each minute were counted. Figure 7-7 shows the data collected.

1. What is the variable in this experiment?
2. What is the relationship between distance from light source and amount of oxygen released? Suggest a reason for this relationship.
3. How many oxygen bubbles would be released if the plant were placed in a darkened room? Explain.

Figure 7-7

Distance of light from the plant (cm)	Number of bubbles per minute
10	60
20	25
30	10
40	5

Many complex reactions take place in the process of converting carbon dioxide and water to glucose, oxygen, and water. These reactions occur in two stages, the **light reaction** and the **dark reaction**. The light reaction can only take place in the presence of light. During the light reaction, chlorophyll traps light energy from the sun. This trapped light energy is used to split water into molecules of hydrogen and oxygen. Oxygen passes into the air spaces and is released into the atmosphere through the stomates. Hydrogen remains inside the chloroplasts, where it functions in the dark reaction.

The dark reaction can take place whether or not light is present. During the dark reaction, the hydrogen produced from the split water molecules combines with carbon dioxide to form glucose. As a result of the two phases of photosynthesis, glucose and oxygen are produced.

Photosynthesis is an essential process because all animals depend on plants for food. Human beings depend on both animals and plants for food. Life as we know it would be impossible without plants. Yet, the plant's job of making food is not over after the complicated steps of photosynthesis are complete. Using the glucose produced through photosynthesis, the plants must then make still more-complicated materials such as starches, fats, and vitamins.

Do Plants Use Carbon Dioxide in Sunlight?

Process Skills *observing, experimenting*

Materials test tubes, bromthymol blue, drinking straws, *Elodea*

Procedure

1. Pour bromthymol blue into two test tubes. Bromthymol blue turns yellow when carbon dioxide is present.
2. Place a drinking straw into each test tube. Referring to Figure 7-8, use the drinking straws to blow bubbles into each test tube.
   Caution Be careful not to get bromthymol blue in your mouth. The carbon dioxide from your breath will cause the bromthymol blue to turn yellow.
3. Place a sprig of *Elodea*, into each test tube. Stopper both test tubes.
4. Place one test tube in a dark place. Place the other test tube in sunlight.
5. Observe the test tubes each day for three or four days. Record any change.

Conclusions

6. What changes did you observe in the color of the water?
7. Suggest an explanation for the changes you observed.
8. Why was the test tube in the darkened area an important part of this experiment?

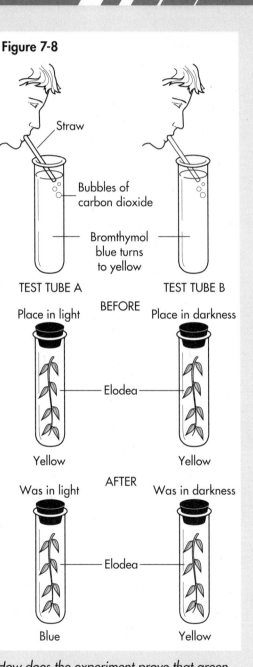

Figure 7-8

Straw

Bubbles of carbon dioxide

Bromthymol blue turns to yellow

TEST TUBE A   TEST TUBE B

BEFORE

Place in light   Place in darkness

Elodea

Yellow   Yellow

AFTER

Was in light   Was in darkness

Elodea

Blue   Yellow

How does the experiment prove that green plants use carbon dioxide in sunlight?

Section 7-2 Review

Write the definitions for the following terms in your own words.

1. **light reaction**
2. **dark reaction**

Answer these questions.

3. How do plants get the water needed for photosynthesis?
4. How does the carbon dioxide needed for photosynthesis reach the leaves?
5. What takes place during the light and dark reactions of photosynthesis?

7-3 Using the Products of Photosynthesis

■ *Objectives*
☐ *Explain how plants use the products of photosynthesis.*

☐ *Compare cellular respiration and photosynthesis.*
☐ *Distinguish between a producer and a consumer.*

How do plants use the products of photosynthesis, glucose, and oxygen? Like all living things, plants need energy to carry on life processes. Plants get this energy through cellular respiration. During cellular respiration, glucose combines with oxygen to produce carbon dioxide, water, and energy.

Cellular Respiration

Figure 7-9 compares the processes of cellular respiration and photosynthesis. Notice that cellular respiration is the opposite of photosynthesis. In photosynthesis, energy from light is used to combine carbon dioxide and water to form glucose and oxygen. In cellular respiration, glucose combines with oxygen to produce carbon dioxide, water, and energy. Photosynthesis occurs only in cells that contain chlorophyll. Respiration occurs in all cells of all organisms.

Figure 7-9

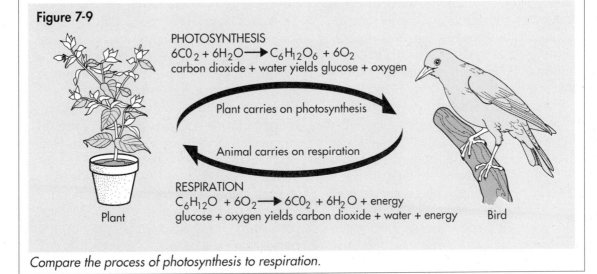

PHOTOSYNTHESIS
$$6CO_2 + 6H_2O \longrightarrow C_6H_{12}O_6 + 6O_2$$
carbon dioxide + water yields glucose + oxygen

Plant carries on photosynthesis

Animal carries on respiration

RESPIRATION
$$C_6H_{12}O + 6O_2 \longrightarrow 6CO_2 + 6H_2O + energy$$
glucose + oxygen yields carbon dioxide + water + energy

Plant

Bird

Compare the process of photosynthesis to respiration.

Hypothesizing

A student placed some fresh sprigs of *Elodea* in a glass funnel, as shown in Figure 7-10. The student plunged the wide mouth of the funnel into a battery jar filled with water. Then the student covered the funnel stem with a test tube, which completely filled with water. The entire preparation was exposed to bright sunlight. After several hours, bubbles of gas had gathered at the top of the test tube.

1. What gas had gathered at the top of the test tube?
2. Explain where the gas came from.

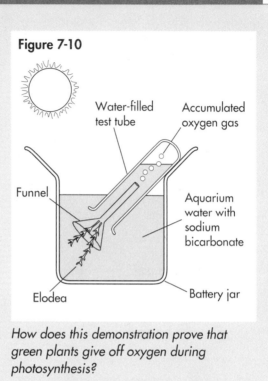

Figure 7-10

Water-filled test tube

Accumulated oxygen gas

Funnel

Aquarium water with sodium bicarbonate

Elodea

Battery jar

How does this demonstration prove that green plants give off oxygen during photosynthesis?

Plants get the raw materials for cellular respiration through photosynthesis. However, animals cannot make their own glucose and oxygen. Animals get the raw materials required to carry on cellular respiration from plants, either directly or indirectly.

Animals take in oxygen that has been released by plants into the environment. They obtain glucose by eating either plants or other animals that have eaten plants. Plants and animals use glucose in the same way. Both plants and animals obtain energy from glucose during cellular respiration. However, plants produce glucose during photosynthesis while animals get glucose from their food.

Forming Starch and Other Nutrients

Most plants produce more glucose than they use. In many plants, these extra glucose molecules are combined to form starch, a complex carbohydrate. Starch is stored in the roots, stems, and leaves. Potatoes and rice are rich sources of starch. Other plants change glucose into fats and oils. Corn oil and peanut oil are two common plant oils.

Plants may also change glucose into proteins and vitamins. To make proteins and vitamins, plants combine glucose with minerals such as nitrogen, phosphorus, and potassium. Peas, beans, and peanuts are rich in plant proteins and vitamins.

Food for All Organisms

Because plants make their own food, they are known as **producers.** Plants provide food not only for themselves but for other organisms. Protists, fungi, and animals depend on plants for food.

Animals are called **consumers** because they consume, or use, food produced by plants. You consume plants when you eat fruits and vegetables. You also eat beef from cows. Cows eat grass and store the excess nutrients in their body. Thus, when you eat beef, you are indirectly obtaining nutrients from plants.

▬ Section 7-3 Review ▬

Write the definitions for the following terms in your own words.

1. **producer** 2. **consumer**

Answer these questions.

3. What gas do plants release to the environment?
4. What other products besides glucose are produced by plants?
5. Why do all life-forms depend on plants?

7-4 Sexual Reproduction in Flowering Plants

■ *Objectives*
☐ *Identify the parts of a flower and their functions.*
☐ *Explain how different flowers are adapted for sexual reproduction.*

☐ *Distinguish between pollination and fertilization.*
☐ *Explain how seeds and fruits form.*

Have you ever visited an apple orchard in the spring? If so, you have seen apple trees dotted with sweet-smelling pink and white **flowers,** the plant's reproduction system. If you revisited the orchard in the fall, you would see a very different sight. Instead of flowers, the branches of the trees would be bent with the weight of apples. Inside these apples are the seeds that form the next generation. Where do apples and seeds come from? To find out, it is necessary to study the parts of the flower.

Parts of the Flower

Look at the flower in Figure 7-11. Find the **sepals,** the outermost leaves in the flower. Sepals are usually green and protect the flower bud before it opens.

Figure 7-11

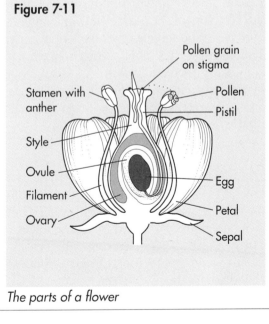

The parts of a flower

Now find the **petals.** The petals of some flowers have a bright color or a pleasant odor that attracts insects and small birds. This attraction plays an important role in plant reproduction.

Since plants reproduce sexually, they have male and female reproductive structures. The **stamen** is the male reproductive organ. It includes the **anther** and the **filament.** The anther, also called the pollen box, contains tiny thick-walled particles called pollen grains. Each pollen grain contains a male gamete, or sperm cell. The filament is a thin stalk that supports the anther.

The **pistil** is the female reproductive organ. Most flowers have only one pistil. The pistil includes three parts. The **stigma** has a sticky or hairy surface that captures pollen grains. The **style** is the thin stalk below the stigma. The style swells at the bottom to form the ovary. Each ovary contains a female gamete, or egg cell.

The flower shown in Figure 7-11 is a **perfect flower.** A perfect flower contains both male and female reproductive organs. Tulips, roses, and apple blossoms are examples of perfect flowers. An **imperfect flower** has either a male or a female reproductive organ. Corn, willow, and oak flowers are imperfect flowers.

Pollination

You have probably seen bees flying from flower to flower. They are feeding on nectar, a sugary liquid produced by many flowers. The bees are also transferring pollen grains from the anther to the stigma, a process called **pollination**.

The transfer of pollen from the anther of a plant to the stigma of the same plant is called **self-pollination.** The garden pea plant in Figure 7-12 self-pollinates. Its petals enclose the reproductive organs, keeping the pollen from leaving the flower.

Figure 7-12

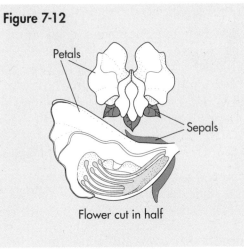

Petals

Sepals

Flower cut in half

The pea plant is self-pollinating.

The transfer of pollen from the anther of one plant to the stigma of another plant is called **cross-pollination**. Cross-pollination results in greater variation among offspring than does self-pollination.

Some flowers are pollinated by the wind. Wind-pollinated flowers are usually small and odorless. In fact, some have no petals at all, leaving the pollen grains exposed to the wind.

Look at the tall tassels of the corn plant in Figure 7-13. Each tassel is a stamen. Wind blows the pollen grains from the tassels to the corn silks that stick out from the corn husk. Each silk is a pistil. Pollen grains, carried by the wind, fall on the stigma at the top of the corn silk.

Figure 7-13

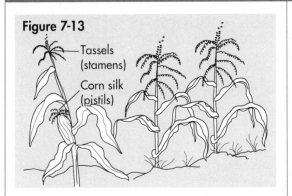

Tassels (stamens)

Corn silk (pistils)

Fertilization

The next step in the reproductive process is fertilization. For fertilization to occur, the sperm in the pollen grain must reach the egg inside the ovule.

After a pollen grain lands on the stigma, it grows a **pollen tube**, which is long and thin and grows down the style into the ovary. Notice from Figure 7-14 that the pollen tube enters an ovule inside the ovary. The ovule contains an egg cell. The sperm travels down the pollen tube into the ovule, where it fertilizes the egg.

After fertilization, the ovule develops into a **seed.** Look at the seed in Figure 7-15. Notice that it consists of an embryo surrounded by food. A **seed coat** surrounds and protects the seed. A seed may remain in

a resting state for months or years until environmental conditions are right. When the temperature is warm and enough oxygen and water are present, the seed coat splits open and the embryo begins to **germinate** (JUR-muh-nayt), or grow.

The seeds of flowering plants are contained in a **fruit.** A fruit forms when an ovary enlarges and ripens after fertilization. Apples, squash, and pea pods are all fruits.

Figure 7-15

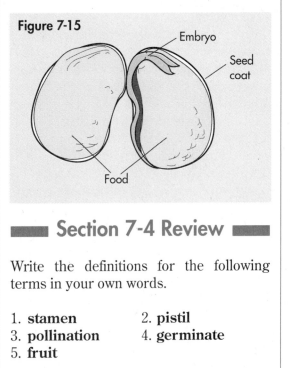

Embryo

Seed coat

Food

Section 7-4 Review

Write the definitions for the following terms in your own words.

1. **stamen**   2. **pistil**
3. **pollination**   4. **germinate**
5. **fruit**

Answer these questions.

6. Draw and label the parts of a flower.
7. Describe the functions of the parts of a flower.
8. What is the difference between cross-pollination and self-pollination?

Figure 7-14

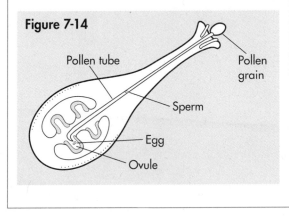

Pollen tube

Pollen grain

Sperm

Egg

Ovule

Science, Technology, & Society

New Hope for the American Elm Tree

Over 77 million American elm trees once occupied forests and lined streets throughout the United States. Today, only a few million remain. A disease called Dutch elm disease has killed most of the American elms.

The fungus that causes the disease had spread among European trees in the 1920s. Logs that were infected with the disease were brought to the United States from Holland in the 1930s.

The fungus lives and reproduces in the xylem of the elm. It blocks the transport of water and nutrients, eventually killing the tree. With no way to stop the spread of Dutch elm disease, scientists once feared the American elm would become extinct.

Today, however, there is new hope. Some American elms are resistant to Dutch elm disease. Researchers may produce more disease-resistant trees by cloning. To clone an organism, scientists remove tissue from the organism and grow the tissue in the laboratory. If the procedure is successful, a new organism exactly like the original will develop.

Scientists have also cross-pollinated the American elm and the Chinese elm. The Chinese elm is resistant to Dutch elm disease. It is hoped that the mixed variety of elm will resist the disease better than the purebred American elm. If these experiments succeed, perhaps the American elm tree will flourish once again in the United States.

Follow-up Activity
Disease is threatening many other plant and animal species with extinction. Do some library research to identify these species and the diseases that are destroying them. Which of these diseases originated in other countries? What efforts are scientists making to save these species?

Figure 7-16

The American elm

KEEPING TRACK

Section 7-1 Plant Structure
1. The three main organs in the plant are the roots, stems, and leaves.
2. Roots anchor the plant in the soil.
3. The vascular system, consisting of xylem and phloem, transports water, minerals, and food throughout the plant.
4. Many leaf cells have chloroplasts, organelles where photosynthesis takes place.

Section 7-2 Photosynthesis
1. Chloroplasts contain the green pigment chlorophyll. Chlorophyll traps the light energy needed for photosynthesis.

Section 7-3 Using the Products of Photosynthesis
1. Plants use glucose and oxygen to carry on cellular respiration.
2. Plant cells use glucose to make other nutrients, including starch, fats, oils, vitamins, and proteins.

Section 7-4 Sexual Reproduction in Flowering Plants
1. The flower is the reproductive organ of higher plants.
2. The four main main parts of the flower are the sepals, petals, stamen, and pistil.
3. When conditions are right, the seed germinates, or starts to grow.

BUILDING VOCABULARY
Write the word from the list that best completes each sentence.

root hairs, fats, pollination, flower, glucose, vascular, phloem, stomates, photosynthesis, zygote

Green plants make their own food during a process called ___1___ . During this food-making process, carbon dioxide and water combine to form oxygen and a sugar called ___2___. Structures called ___3___ increase the surface area so that plants can take in enough water from the soil. After the water is absorbed, it is conducted by the ___4___ system from the roots to the stems and leaves. Carbon dioxide enters the leaves through structures called ___5___. Food, manufactured in the cells of the leaves of the green plant, is transported by a kind of tissue called ___6___. In addition to sugar, green plants make starch, proteins, and ___7___. The reproductive structure in higher plants is the ___8___. Pollen grains are transferred from the anther to the stigma during ___9___. The sperm and egg cells combine in the ovule during fertilization to form the ___10___.

SUMMARIZING
If the statement is true, write *true*. If the statement is false, change the *italicized* term to make the statement true.

1. Carbon dioxide and water combine to form glucose during *cellular respiration*.
2. *Herbaceous* stems are thick and hard.
3. Carbon dioxide enters the leaf through tiny openings called *stomates*.
4. The *spongy* layer of the leaf is located right below the upper epidermis.

CHAPTER REVIEW

5. Photosynthesis takes place in organelles called *mitochondria*.
6. Veins contain the plant's *vascular* system.
7. The *pistil* is the female reproductive structure of a plant.
8. Pollen grains are formed in the *style*.
9. A ripened ovary is called a *seed*.

INTERPRETING INFORMATION

A student set up the demonstration shown in Figure 7-17. Two days later, she found water droplets on the glass inside the beaker.

1. Where did the water droplets come from?
2. Name the structures through which water vapor escaped from the leaf.
3. In a repeat demonstration, the student coated the underside of the leaf with petroleum jelly. Did water droplets form? Why?

Figure 7-17

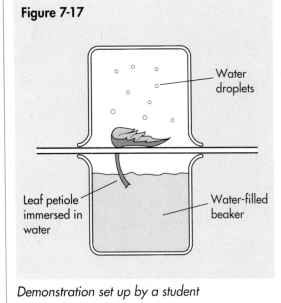

Water droplets

Leaf petiole immersed in water

Water-filled beaker

Demonstration set up by a student

THINK AND DISCUSS

Use the section number in parentheses to help you find each answer. Write your answers in complete sentences.

1. Name four parts of the leaf and explain how each part is an adaptation for photosynthesis. (7-1)
2. List four conditions that are necessary for photosynthesis to take place. (7-2)
3. Write summary equations for photosynthesis and cellular respiration. Compare the two processes. (7-3)
4. Cross-pollination results in greater variation than self-pollination. Why? (7-4)

GOING FURTHER

Do some research to learn how the Venus flytrap gets its food. Name some other plants with characteristics similar to those of the Venus flytrap.

COMPETENCY REVIEW

Questions 1 and 2 are based on the following experiment.

A student did an experiment to determine the effects of increasing amounts of light on the growth of bean seedlings. She used three groups of bean seedlings, each containing 20 plants. All seedlings were grown in the same kind of soil. She collected and recorded the data shown in Figure 7-18.

1. Based on the data, which one of the following conclusions can be drawn?
   a. As the amount of light increases, the growth rate of the plants decreases.

b. As the amount of light increases, the growth rate of the plants increases.
c. The amount of light has no significant effect on the plants' growth.
d. Only if the temperature were increased would the plants' growth rate increase.

2. Which one of the following conditions was not kept constant in this experiment?
  a. air temperature
  b. amount of water given
  c. amount of exposure to light
  d. type of soil

Questions 3, 4 and 5 are based on the following experiment.

Twelve germinated lima bean seeds were divided into four groups of three seeds each. One group was grown under red light, the second under green light, the third under blue light, and the fourth under white light. After three weeks, the height of each group of plants was measured to see which had grown most.

3. Which hypothesis would this experiment test?
  a. Different colors of light affect the growth rate of plants.
  b. Changes in temperature affect the rate at which lima bean seeds germinate.
  c. Yellow light slows the germination of lima bean seeds.
  d. Twelve is the best number of seeds for an experiment.

4. To improve this experiment you could
  a. grow all plants under white light.
  b. increase the number of lima bean plants in each of the four groups.
  c. add more water to all four groups.
  d. add another group of lima bean plants and grow them under yellow light.

5. Which tissue transports food from the leaves to other parts of the plant?
  a. phloem
  b. chloroplasts
  c. stomates
  d. xylem

Figure 7-18

Group	Temperature	Amt of water (mL) given daily	Amt of light (min./day)	Height of plants (cm) after 25 days
#1	30°C	10	20	19.2
#2	30°C	10	30	20.8
#3	30°C	10	40	21.7

CHAPTER 8

LIVING THINGS IN THEIR ENVIRONMENT

All living things depend on the environment in which they live for all of their basic needs. You, for example, depend on the plants and animals in your environment for the food you eat. You also depend on the environment for the air you breathe and for the materials from which your clothing is made. The wood, concrete, brick, or other materials that make up your home come from the environment as well.

Look at the owl and its environment pictured in Figure 8-1. Note the other organisms in the owl's environment. Which organisms would the owl depend on for food? Now look for the nonliving things in the owl's environment, such as sunlight and soil. In what ways does the owl depend on nonliving things?

Make a list of five organisms with which you are familiar. Think about the environment in which each organism lives. Describe how the survival of each organism depends on the living and nonliving things in its environment.

8-1 Ecology

■ *Objectives*

☐ *Describe the different levels of organization within an ecosystem.*

☐ *List the limiting factors that exist in an environment.*

☐ *Distinguish between a habitat and a niche.*

What makes up the environment of the frog in Figure 8-2? The frog lives in a pond. The pond contains living things,

Figure 8-1

Like all living things, the owl depends on its environment.

Figure 8-2

In what ways does a frog depend on its environment?

such as insects and plants, that the frog uses for food. The pond also contains non-living things, such as water and oxygen. The frog needs these materials to carry on its life processes.

Levels of Organization

The study of the interactions between organisms and their environment is called **ecology**. Ecologists group these interactions into several levels of organization. The first level of organization is the **population.** A population is a group of organisms of the same species that live in the same area. For example, all the squirrels living in a park make up a population of squirrels. All the trout living in a pond make up a population of trout.

All the populations living in the same area form a **community**, the next level of organization. Notice the variety of organisms in the field shown in Figure 8-3. All the populations in the field, such as grass, daisies, grasshoppers, robins, rabbits, owls, and mice, make up the field community.

Figure 8-3

What organisms live in a field community?

The living things in an environment are known as **biotic** (by-AT-ik) **factors**. However, an environment also contains nonliving things, or **abiotic** (AY-by-at-ik) **factors**. Abiotic factors include water, soil, minerals, sunlight, oxygen, and carbon dioxide gases.

The biotic and abiotic factors in an environment combine to form an **ecosystem.** The field ecosystem in Figure 8-3 includes both biotic and abiotic factors. You have already identified the biotic factors. What are the abiotic factors in this ecosystem?

Any of the abiotic or biotic factors in the ecosystem such as water, air, space, temperature, light, or food are called **limiting factors.** Limiting factors restrict the number of organisms that can live in an area. For example, soil contains only a limited amount of water and minerals. Therefore, only a certain number of plants can grow in an acre of soil. Thus, in a desert, where water is scarce, you will find plants scattered far apart. In a rain forest, where rainfall is heavy, trees grow close together.

The last level of organization of living things is the **biosphere** (BY-uh-sfiur). The biosphere includes parts of the earth where life exists. All of the ecosystems on Earth, including those in water, land, and air, make up the biosphere.

A C T I V I T Y

How Many Habitats Can You Identify around Your School?

Process Skills *observing, organizing information*

Materials paper, pencil

Procedure
1. Walk along the street or sidewalk surrounding your school. If there are no grounds or gardens around your school, visit a park.
2. Make a list of the habitats you can identify. Trees and bushes would represent a miniature forest. A lawn would represent a miniature field.
3. Describe the conditions in each habitat. For example, describe the temperature, amount of sunlight, amount of water, and so on.
4. Search for animals and plants in each habitat. List all the organisms you find in each habitat.

Conclusions
5. How is each animal or plant adapted for the habitat in which it lives?
6. Draw a habitat map that summarizes the information you have gathered. On your map, label each habitat you have identified.
7. Present your map to your class. Discuss with your teacher and classmates how the conditions in each habitat shown on the map differ.

Habitats and Niches

Different kinds of ecosystems exist throughout the biosphere. Each organism occupies a certain place in the ecosystem, called its **habitat.** For example, the habitat of a codfish is the part of the ocean where the fish swims, looks for food, and reproduces.

Many species may occupy a single habitat. Plants grow in the same soil where earthworms live. Deer, chipmunks, and rabbits may live in a forest along with foxes, wolves, and coyotes.

Although species share habitats, the needs and activities of each species within that habitat differ. The needs and activities of a species make up the **niche** of that species. The rabbits and groundhogs in Figure 8-4 live in the same field and thus have the same habitat. However, rabbits live above the ground, while groundhogs live underground. Rabbits and groundhogs eat different kinds of food and care for their young in different places. Thus, the rabbit and the groundhog each have their own niche within their habitat.

▬▬ Section 8-1 Review ▬▬

Write the definitions for the following terms in your own words.

1. **population**   2. **community**
3. **ecosystem**   4. **habitat**
5. **niche**

Answer these questions.

6. What is ecology?
7. Identify the levels of organization in the biosphere.
8. Distinguish between the biotic and abiotic factors in an ecosystem.
9. What would happen if two species had both the same habitat and niche?

Figure 8-4

Describe the differences in the niches of the rabbit and the groundhog.

8-2 Characteristics of the Ecosystem

■ *Objectives*
☐ *Illustrate how energy and matter flow through communities.*
☐ *Explain the role of the players in a food web, including producers and consumers.*
☐ *Describe the three cycles that occur in nature.*

An ecosystem needs a source of energy to keep it going. Without a source of energy, life on Earth could not exist. The sun is the primary source of energy for almost all ecosystems.

The Players

Energy enters the ecosystem when chlorophyll in the cells of algae and plants captures light energy from the sun. Through the process of photosynthesis, algae and plants use this energy to make food. Organisms that make their own food are **producers** in an ecosystem. Some of this food is used during cellular respiration. The rest is stored as sugar, starch, protein, and fat.

Animals are the consumers in an ecosystem. Consumers depend on plants or other animals for their food. Animals that feed directly on plants are called **primary consumers,** or **herbivores** (HUR-buh-vohurs). Cows and rabbits are primary consumers.

Animals that eat primary consumers are called **secondary consumers.** Secondary consumers include wolves, lions, and snakes. Some secondary consumers only eat meat. Meat-eating animals are called **carnivores** (KAR-nuh-vohurs). Other animals, including humans, eat both plants and animals. These animals function as both primary and secondary consumers and are known as **omnivores** (AHM-ni-vohurs).

Some secondary consumers are **predators,** animals that hunt and kill other animals for their food. The hawk in Figure 8-5 is a predator. It is about to capture a rabbit. The rabbit is an example of **prey,** animals that predators kill.

Some secondary consumers, called **scavengers**, do not kill other animals. They eat dead animals. You may have seen a vulture picking at a dead animal along the side of the road.

Figure 8-5

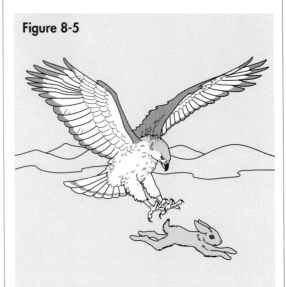

Which is the predator and which is the prey in this picture?

Scavengers are not the only living things that feed on dead organisms. Bacteria and fungi are **decomposers**, organisms that break down dead organisms and return nutrients to the soil. Plants absorb these nutrients and reuse them to make food.

Food Chains and Food Webs

The interaction among organisms as they obtain food is called a **food chain.** A food chain represents one path in which food travels in a community. By studying a food chain, you can see how food is transferred from one organism to another. The arrows in Figure 8-6 show the direction of the flow of food through a food chain. The chain begins with grass, a producer. What is the

Figure 8-6 A Typical Food Chain

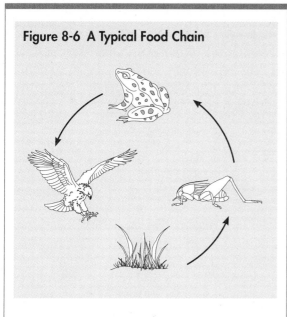

Figure 8-7

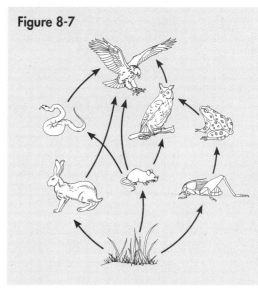

Which organisms are part of more than one food chain?

role of the other organisms in this food chain?

Most organisms eat more than one kind of food. Therefore, most organisms belong to more than one food chain. Different food chains combine and overlap, forming a **food web.** How many food chains can you find in the food web in Figure 8-7?

Energy Flow

Organisms need the chemical energy in food to carry out their life processes. As life processes are carried out, food energy is changed to heat energy. Heat energy leaves the organism and escapes into the environment. It is then no longer available for use by living things.

Organisms store food that is not used for life processes. Suppose a rabbit eats some grass. The energy stored in the grass is transferred to the rabbit. The rabbit uses some of this energy to carry on its life processes and stores the rest.

Ecologists use a model called an **energy pyramid** to show how energy moves through a food chain. Study the energy pyramid in Figure 8-8. Notice that the

Figure 8-8 An Energy Pyramid

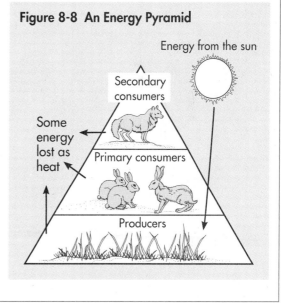

number of organisms decreases as you move up the food chain. Can you explain why this is so?

Matter Flow

Once energy is used, it cannot be used again. However, the matter that makes up the earth can be **recycled,** or used again and again. Matter that is recycled through the biosphere includes nitrogen, carbon, oxygen, and water.

Nitrogen Cycle Nitrogen is an element found in proteins and other compounds. In the nitrogen cycle, nitrogen compounds called **nitrates** are removed and then returned to the soil. Use Figure 8-9 to follow the steps of the nitrogen cycle. First, decomposing bacteria change proteins in dead organisms into ammonia. Then, **nitrifying bacteria** change ammonia into nitrates. In addition, **nitrogen-fixing bacteria,** which live in the roots of soybean and pea plants, change nitrogen in the atmosphere into nitrates. These nitrates are also released into the soil.

Plants absorb nitrates from soil and use the nitrates to make proteins. Animals eat plants and change plant proteins into animal proteins. When plants and animals die, the nitrogen cycle begins again.

Carbon Dioxide-Oxygen Cycle The cycling of carbon dioxide and oxygen through the biosphere is called the carbon dioxide-oxygen cycle. As Figure 8-10 shows, plants use carbon dioxide from the air to carry out photosynthesis. The process of photosynthesis releases oxygen into the air. Most organisms use this oxygen for cellular respiration. As a result of cellular respiration, carbon dioxide is returned to the air. Decaying organisms and burning fuel also release carbon dioxide into the air.

Water Cycle The cycling of water through the biosphere is called the water cycle. Use Figure 8-11 to trace the steps of the water cycle. The sun's energy causes water to **evaporate** into the air. Evaporation is the process by which water changes from a liquid to a gas, or vapor. Living things also

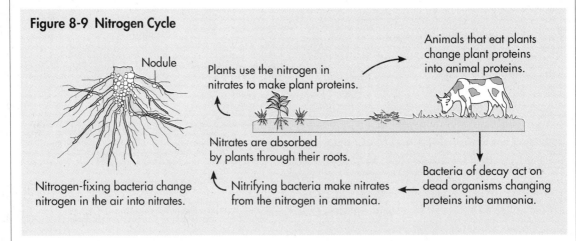

Figure 8-9 Nitrogen Cycle

Nodule

Plants use the nitrogen in nitrates to make plant proteins.

Animals that eat plants change plant proteins into animal proteins.

Nitrates are absorbed by plants through their roots.

Nitrogen-fixing bacteria change nitrogen in the air into nitrates.

Nitrifying bacteria make nitrates from the nitrogen in ammonia.

Bacteria of decay act on dead organisms changing proteins into ammonia.

Figure 8-10 Carbon Dioxide-Oxygen Cycle

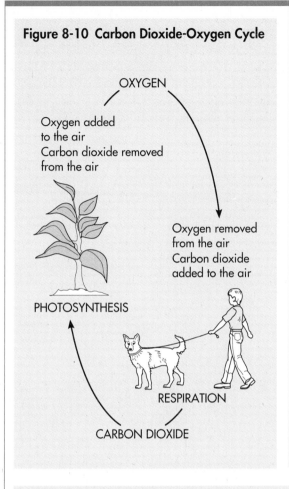

OXYGEN

Oxygen added to the air
Carbon dioxide removed from the air

Oxygen removed from the air
Carbon dioxide added to the air

PHOTOSYNTHESIS

RESPIRATION

CARBON DIOXIDE

return water vapor to the air. Plants release water as a waste product of both photosynthesis and cellular respiration. Animals also carry on cellular respiration, releasing water as a waste product into the air.

Eventually, water returns to the earth as **precipitation.** Precipitation includes rain, hail, sleet, and snow. Plants absorb this water from the soil. They use some of the water during photosynthesis. Some of the water in plants is passed on to animals when they eat the plants. Animals also drink water that has fallen to the earth. Through respiration and excretion, animals return water to the earth. The water cycle then begins again.

Symbiosis

Some organisms interact with each other in a special way called **symbiosis.** Symbiosis is a close, long-term relationship between two organisms. Three kinds of symbiosis have been identified.

Commensalism In one type of symbiosis, **commensalism** (kuh-MEN-suh-liz-um),

Figure 8-11 Water Cycle

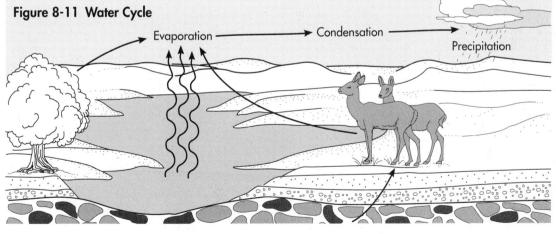

Evaporation → Condensation →

Precipitation

one organism benefits while the other is not affected. Figure 8-12 shows commensalism between a remora fish and a shark. The remora fish travels with the shark and feeds on scraps of the shark's food. The shark, however, is not affected by the remora.

The interaction between a barnacle and a whale is another example of commensalism. The barnacle cannot move. To get food, it attaches itself to the back of a whale. The whale carries the barnacle to sources of food. Like the shark, the whale is not affected by the relationship.

Mutualism   A relationship in which both organisms benefit is called **mutualism**. For example, the tick bird lives on the back of the rhinoceros. It feeds on ticks that live on the skin of the rhinoceros. The bird is well fed, and the rhinoceros is relieved of the ticks. Thus, both organisms benefit from the relationship.

Bees feed on nectar produced by flowers. As they gather nectar, the bees pollinate the flowers. The bees are fed, and the flowers reproduce. Why is this relationship another example of mutualism?

Parasitism   In **parasitism** (PAR-uh-suh-tiz-um), one organism benefits while the other is harmed. Look at the tapeworm in Figure 8-13. The tapeworm is a parasite that lives in the digestive system of another organism. The tapeworm attaches to the digestive

Figure 8-13

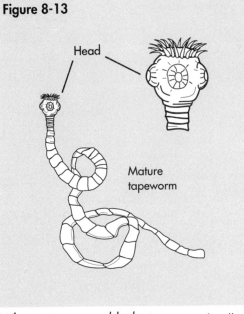

Head

Mature tapeworm

What structures enable the tapeworm to attach itself to its host?

Figure 8-12

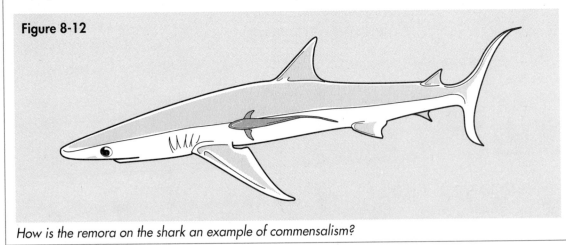

How is the remora on the shark an example of commensalism?

system and draws blood from it. The leech is another parasite that feeds upon the blood of other organisms.

▰▰▰ Section 8-2 Review ▰▰▰

Write the definitions for the following terms in your own words.

1. **primary consumer**
2. **secondary consumer**
3. **predator**
4. **scavenger**
5. **decomposer**

Answer these questions.

6. Explain why producers are considered to be the foundation for all communities.
7. Distinguish between herbivores, carnivores, and omnivores.
8. Describe the role of producers, consumers, and decomposers in a food web.
9. What is an energy pyramid?

8-3 Biomes

■ *Objective*
☐ *Describe the characteristics of the major terrestrial and aquatic biomes.*

If you traveled throughout the world, you would see many different **biomes** (BY-ohms). A biome is a large area of the earth that has a particular **climate.** Calculated over a long period of time, climate is the average yearly rainfall and temperature in an area. Climate determines the types of plant and animal life able to survive in a biome.

Terrestrial Biomes

Biomes on land are known as terrestrial biomes. Biologists have identified six major terrestrial biomes. Each one is characterized by the most plentiful species of plants and animals living there. Figure 8-14 on page 164 shows the distribution of the major terrestrial biomes. Refer to this figure as you read the description of each biome.

Tundra Find the biome in the far northern sections of the earth. This biome is a very cold and dry region called the **tundra.** Tundra winters are long, and the summers are short. Even in summer, the temperature rarely rises above 10° Celsius.

Ice and snow cover the ground for most of the year. In the summer, only the top part of the soil thaws. Because of the thin soil and dry conditions, only lichens, mosses, grasses, and low shrubs can grow in the tundra.

You may be surprised to learn that many animals live in the tundra. Ducks, geese, and other aquatic birds nest in the tundra during the summer. Most of these birds migrate south for the winter. Small mammals like lemmings, hares, and wolves live in the tundra, as well as larger animals like musk oxen and reindeer. Many of these animals feed on tundra plants.

Taiga The biome located just south of the tundra is the **taiga** (TY-guh). The winters here are long and cold, and the summers are short and warm. Enough rain falls in the taiga to support the growth of trees.

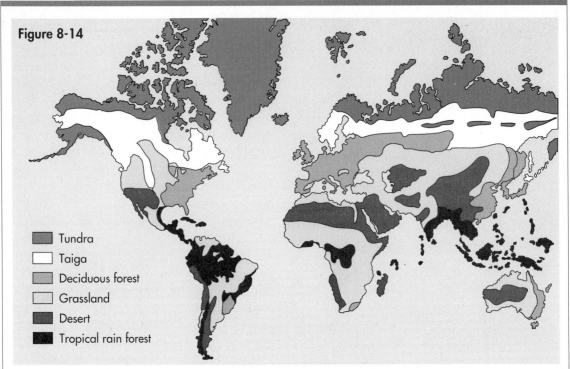

Figure 8-14

Tundra
Taiga
Deciduous forest
Grassland
Desert
Tropical rain forest

In which biome is the northeastern part of the United States located?

Forests in the taiga consist mainly of conifers, such as pines, spruces, and firs. These trees have cones and needle-shaped leaves with a waxy coating. The waxy coating prevents water loss, enabling the tree to store extra water. When the ground freezes, the tree uses the water it stored in the warmer months.

Animals that feed on plants of the taiga include moose, elk, and deer. These animals are the prey of bears and wolves. Hawks and owls feed on smaller mammals, such as mice.

Deciduous Forest South of the taiga is a biome called the **deciduous forest.** The deciduous forest includes most of the eastern United States. A moderate climate characterizes the deciduous forest. Winters are cold and summers are warm. Fall and spring temperatures are mild. Precipitation is plentiful throughout the year.

Many species of **deciduous trees,** such as hickory, beech, and maple, grow in this biome. Deciduous trees lose their leaves in the fall and grow new leaves in the spring. Figure 8-15 shows a deciduous tree and how it looks during the different seasons. What changes do you observe?

By shedding their leaves, deciduous trees prevent water loss during the winter. The soil freezes in the winter, and trees cannot absorb water. Since deciduous trees have no leaves in the winter, water does not evaporate from them.

Figure 8-15

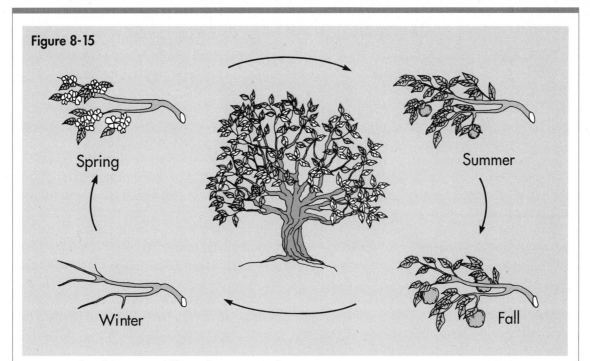

Spring

Summer

Winter

Fall

How is a deciduous tree different from a cone-bearing tree?

The moderate climate and abundant plant life of the deciduous forest support a large number of animals. Many birds nest in deciduous trees. Salamanders, snakes, squirrels, chipmunks, deer, wolves, skunks, and rabbits live on the forest floor.

Grassland The **grassland** biome includes much of the central United States. Grassland summers are hot and dry, and winters are cold and snowy. As you might guess, grasses are the dominant plant life in this biome. The rich grassland soil supports the growth of wheat, barley, and oats, as well as other grains that feed human populations. Grassland animals include prairie dogs, mice, and jackrabbits. Herds of grazing animals, such as bison and antelope, are also common.

Desert In the **desert** biome, rain seldom falls, and water is very scarce. Throughout the year, the temperature is hot during the day and cool at night. However, many species are adapted for survival in the desert. For example, cacti have spiny leaves that prevent water loss. Cacti also have thick stems in which water is stored.

Snakes, rabbits, lizards, and birds live in the desert. Large desert animals include fox, coyotes, and deer. Most desert animals hunt for food at night. Can you explain why?

Tropical Rain Forest You can find the **tropical rain forest** biome near the equator. Tropical rain forests are characterized by heavy rainfall and warm temperatures year-round. These conditions are ideal for plant growth. As a result, the tropical rain forest has the greatest number and variety of living things of any biome.

Trees grow very tall in the tropical rain forest. Their large, broad leaves form a dense canopy, or roof. The canopy shades the forest floor so completely that few plants grow there. Large numbers of vines grow around trees in the tropical rain forest.

Many kinds of amphibians, reptiles, birds, and mammals live in the canopy. Colorful parrots and macaws are abundant here. Tree frogs, snakes, monkeys, gibbons, and orangutans also dwell in the tropical rain forest. You can see the variety of tropical rain forest species in Figure 8-16.

Aquatic Biomes

Aquatic biomes are water biomes. Water biomes cover more than 75 percent of the Earth's surface. Lakes and rivers, which contain little salt, are **freshwater biomes.** The oceans, which contain saltwater, are **marine biomes.**

Marine Biomes Marine biomes include two areas, the intertidal zone and the ocean. Find these areas in Figure 8-17. The intertidal zone is under water during high tide and exposed to the air during low tide. Organisms that live in the intertidal zone are adapted for both water and land environments. Clams, mussels, oysters, and crabs live in the intertidal zone.

As you move farther away from land, the depth of the ocean increases. The greatest number of living things is found near the surface of the ocean. Light is plentiful here, and temperatures are the warmest. Algae and tiny plants and animals called **plankton** float near the ocean's surface. Many marine animals feed on plankton. Light can penetrate about 200 meters below the surface of the ocean. No plant life exists below this depth. Why?

Freshwater Biomes The two types of freshwater biomes are still-water and running water. Ponds and lakes are still-water biomes. Rivers and streams are running-water biomes.

Many kinds of organisms, such as fish and amphibians, live in ponds and lakes.

Figure 8-16 Typical Tropical Rain Forest

Figure 8-17

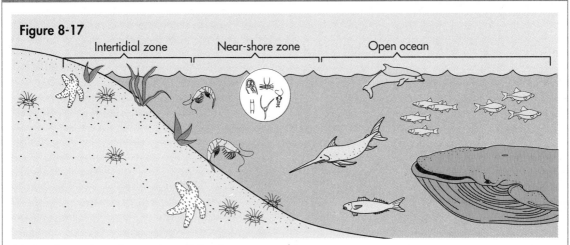

Intertidial zone   Near-shore zone   Open ocean

Notice the variety of organisms living in an ocean biome.

These animals feed on the abundant algae, water plants, and plankton. Eventually, erosion of their banks may cause ponds and lakes to fill in. The ponds and lakes may then become terrestrial biomes.

Streams and rivers have swift-flowing waters. Oxygen and minerals are more plentiful here than in still-water biomes. Many species of fish, such as trout, live in streams and rivers. Few plankton can withstand the swift-flowing water in streams and rivers. Therefore, freshwater animals feed on insects and insect larvae.

▬▬▬ Section 8-3 Review ▬▬▬

Write the definitions for the following terms in your own words.

1. **biome**
2. **climate**
3. **tundra**
4. **taiga**
5. **deciduous forest**

Answer these questions.

6. Compare the structure of plants in the deciduous forest, rain forest, and desert.
7. Why can the tropical rain forest support more life-forms than any other biome?
8. Imagine that you are a biologist. You notice that the aquatic plants and fish seem to be decreasing in numbers in a nearby lake. What could you do to increase the number of fish?

8-4 Biological Succession

■ *Objectives*
☐ *Explain the causes of biological succession.*
☐ *Distinguish between primary and secondary succession.*
☐ *Predict that succession will continue until the climax community is reached.*

Have you ever seen a garden or field that was left untended for a long period of time?

You probably would have seen weeds begin to grow, only to be replaced by taller weeds and shrubs. The types of animals living in the area would change as well. Change in a community like the one described here is called **biological succession.** During biological succession, a community changes through an orderly sequence of events over a period of time into a different community. Plant populations change first, followed by animal populations. Succession is a result of changes in the environment.

Primary Succession

Whenever areas without life begin to support life, **primary succession** occurs. For example, primary succession may begin on a bare rock. Figure 8-18 shows lichens growing on a bare rock. A lichen consists of an alga and a fungus living in a mutualistic relationship. The algae produces food used

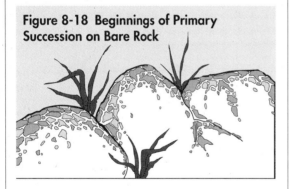

Figure 8-18 Beginnings of Primary Succession on Bare Rock

by both the algae and fungus. The fungus absorbs the water used by both organisms. Each organism helps the other to survive.

Lichens release chemicals that dissolve the surface of rock. The rock begins to crumble, forming the beginnings of soil. When lichens die and decay, nutrients are added to the soil. Seeds of small plants may land on this soil and germinate. In time, enough soil will be created for larger plants to grow.

As new species enter a community, they cause changes in the environment. These new conditions encourage the growth of other organisms. These changes in turn make the environment unsuitable for the current organisms. As a result, these organisms die out and are replaced by new organisms.

The final stage of succession is called a **climax community**. A climax community is characterized by organisms that are adapted for that environment and become permanently established there. The kinds of organisms that become permanently established depend on the climate and soil of that area. For example, oak-hickory and beech-maple forests are climax communities in the northeastern United States.

Secondary Succession

Recently, fires destroyed vast areas of Yellowstone National Park. Some biologists think that these fires are natural events that occur once every 200 to 300 years. They base their conclusions on long-term studies of forest succession that takes place after forest fires.

This type of succession is called **secondary succession.** Secondary succession occurs when natural events or human activities destroy or change an existing community. Secondary succession may occur when farmers cut down forests in order to grow crops. If farmers later abandon the fields, secondary succession will change the fields back to forests.

Observing

Figure 8-19 shows how succession can change a pond to a field. What changes take place in a pond over time?

1. What changes have taken place in the pond?
2. What kind of climax community has resulted from these changes?
3. What could have prevented succession from occurring in this pond?

Figure 8-19

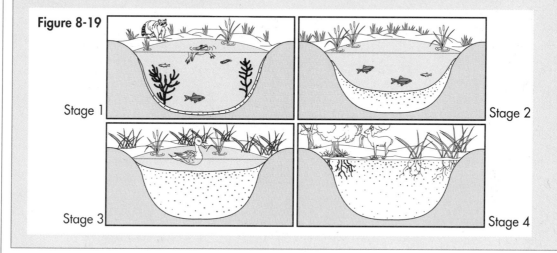

Stage 1
Stage 2
Stage 3
Stage 4

Section 8-4 Review

Write the definitions for the following terms in your own words.

1. **biological succession**
2. **primary succession**
3. **climax community**
4. **secondary succession**

Answer these questions.

5. What takes place during biological succession?

6. A rock slide brings many large boulders to the base of a mountain. Years later, the boulders are covered with lichens. Is this an example of primary or secondary succession? How do you know?
7. A farmer abandons a field. In time, grasses are replaced by weeds and then shrubs and trees. Is this an example of primary or secondary succession? How do you know?
8. What determines the type of climax community that will become established in an area?

SCIENCE, TECHNOLOGY, & SOCIETY

Solid Waste Management

Currently, Americans throw out about 160 million tons of garbage each year, or about 3.5 pounds per individual each day. In some parts of the United States, people are producing more garbage than there are places to dump it. The problem is especially severe in highly populated areas. Some people favor sending the garbage to less populated areas, where there is plenty of dump space. However, most people do not want other people's garbage dumped in their neighborhood.

Several steps can be taken to reduce the amount of space needed for garbage dumps. First, people must reduce the amount of garbage they produce. For instance, companies could reduce the amount of plastic, Styrofoam, and cardboard used in packaging. People can also reduce garbage by repairing big items, such as furniture, cars, and appliances, rather than buying new ones.

Another way to reduce garbage is to recycle it. Recycling changes trash items back to usable materials. For example, soda bottles and cans, newspapers, and cardboard boxes can be recycled. Metal, paper, and plastic wastes can be separated from other trash and sent to recycling centers. Recycling reduces the amount of trash deposited in dumps and helps pay for garbage pickup.

Most garbage is placed in large dump areas called landfills. Some landfill areas become building sites after they settle. Part of New York City, for example, is built on what formerly had been landfill space. However, landfills are temporary solutions to the garbage problem. To encourage recycling, planners are trying to limit the creation of new landfill space.

Follow-up Activity

Figure 8-20 shows how many years are left until landfill space in the United States is used up. In how many states will existing landfill sites be filled in less than five years? Go to the library and find out how long it will be before landfill sites are used up in your state.

Figure 8-20

U.S. MAINLAND

Years until landfill space gone	Number of states
Under 5	7
5 to 10	18
Over 10	23

CHAPTER REVIEW

Section 8-1 Ecology

1. Ecology is the study of the interaction of living things with one another and with their environment.
2. The populations of all organisms interacting in any given area form a community.

Section 8-2 Characteristics of the Ecosystem

1. Energy is supplied to an ecosystem by plants and other producers. Other organisms use the energy produced by plants.
2. Materials from dead and decaying plants and animals are recycled by decomposers.
3. Fungi and other decomposers cannot produce their own food and thus depend on dead and decaying animals and plants for their food.
4. Food chains and food webs represent pathways along which food flows.
5. The nitrogen cycle, carbon dioxide-oxygen cycle, and water cycle recycle matter through the biosphere.
6. The balance present in ecosystems is the result of complicated interactions among community members and between community members and the environment.

Section 8-3 Biomes

1. The six terrestrial biomes are tundra, taiga, deciduous forest, grassland, desert, and tropical rain forest.
2. The two aquatic biomes are freshwater and marine biomes.

Section 8-4 Biological Succession

1. Natural communities change through an orderly, predictable sequence of events. Over time, one community can be replaced by a quite different community. This series of changes is called biological succession.
2. The final community to be established in an area is known as the climax community.

BUILDING VOCABULARY

Write the term from the list that best matches each statement.

biosphere, mutualism, succession, deciduous forest, population, decomposers, abiotic factors, food web

1. a group of organisms of the same species living in the same area
2. all the nonliving things in the environment
3. all the interrelated food chains in a community
4. organisms that recycle material from dead organisms to the soil
5. close relationship in which both organisms benefit
6. areas of the earth that support life
7. biome characterized by trees that lose their leaves in winter
8. a process during which communities change in an orderly sequence of events

Explain the difference between the terms in each pair.

9. population, community
10. predator, scavenger

11. producer, consumer
12. mutualism, parasitism
13. primary succession, secondary succession
14. biotic factors, abiotic factors
15. tundra, taiga
16. habitat, niche
17. terrestrial biome, aquatic biome
18. primary consumer, secondary consumer

SUMMARIZING

Write the missing word for each sentence.

1. The study of living things and their environment is called ___.
2. Animals that are hunted and eaten by other animals are called___.
3. All the populations living in the same area form a(an) ___.
4. A (An)___ represents the path along which food travels in a community.
5. The flow of food energy through a food chain is represented by a(an) ___.
6. A barnacle attached to a whale shows a symbiotic relationship known as ___.
7. The biome in which rainfall and temperature are high all year is the ___.
8. A biome that is hot and dry year-round is the___.

INTERPRETING INFORMATION

Populations of deer live in an area located in Arizona known as the Kaibab Plateau. The deer are prey for wolves in this area. In the early 1900s, the U.S. government offered a cash reward for each wolf killed. By doing this, the government hoped to protect the deer from being hunted and killed by the wolves. The graph in Figure 8-21 shows the effects of the government's interference on the populations of deer and wolves on the Kaibab Plateau.

Figure 8-21

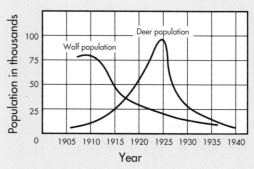

Changes in the wolf and deer populations in Kaibab Plateau

1. Describe the changes in the wolf and deer populations from 1905 to 1940.
2. What caused the population of wolves to decline?
3. What do you think would have happened to the populations of deer and wolves if the government had not interfered?

THINK AND DISCUSS

Use the section number in parentheses to help you find each answer. Write your answers in complete sentences.

1. List and describe the levels of organization in the biosphere. (8-1)
2. How are food chains, food webs, and energy pyramids related? (8-2)

3. Identify some of the limiting factors in the tundra, desert, and tropical rain forest. (8-3)
4. Give examples of the way biological succession encourages the growth of some organisms and discourages the growth of other organisms. (8-4)

GOING FURTHER

When logs burn, energy is released. Where does this energy come from? Use library books to research fossil fuels. Write a report in which you describe how each fossil fuel is formed. Trace the energy in fossil fuels back to the sun.

COMPETENCY REVIEW

Questions 1 and 2 are based on Figure 8-22.

1. Which statement is true concerning the use of large quantities of oil in the United States?
   a. The United States uses 26 percent of the world's oil.
   b. The United States releases 22 percent of the world's nitrogen oxides.
   c. The United States produces 26 percent of the world's carbon dioxide wastes.
   d. The United States produces less carbon dioxide waste from fossil fuel combustion than any other country.
2. What conclusions can be drawn from the data provided?
   a. The United States conserves fuel wisely.
   b. The United States should not be concerned with conserving oil, since there is plenty left in the Earth.

Figure 8-22 Facts about the U.S.

Percentage of world's population	5
Disposal of toxic waste	290 million tons
Percentage of world's oil used	26
Percentage of world's nitrogen oxides released	26
Percentage of world's carbon dioxide produced from burning of fossil fuels	22

   c. The United States releases 22 percent of the world's nitrogen oxides.
   d. The combustion of large amounts of fossil fuels by the United States is polluting the atmosphere.
3. An organism that uses other organisms for food is a (an)
   a. producer.   b. plant.
   c. algae.   d. consumer.
4. The primary source of energy for most ecosystems comes from (the)
   a. plants.   b. consumers.
   c. water.   d. sun.
5. The biome with the greatest variety of organisms is the
   a. desert.   b. tundra.
   c. tropical rain forest. d. deciduous forest.

CHAPTER 9

HOW PEOPLE AFFECT THE ENVIRONMENT

Perhaps you have heard about raging fires that have destroyed large sections of forest. When lightning causes a forest fire, the fire is a natural event. If that event occurs on a large scale, a disaster may result. Such a natural disaster took place in the summer of 1988 in Yellowstone National Park. See Figure 9-1. Lightning caused forest fires that destroyed entire ecosystems. As a result, many plant and animal species perished.

The fires at Yellowstone were a natural disaster. The fire disturbed the balance of nature in the park's ecosystem. Can you think of other natural disasters that could also destroy entire ecosystems?

Natural disasters are not the only events that may upset the balance of nature in an ecosystem. Human activities also may disturb ecosystems. Some human activities cause water and air pollution, which harm living things. The clearing of forests to make way for farmland has destroyed the habitats of many forms of wildlife. Human activities like these have negative effects on the ecosystem.

9-1 Upsetting the Balance

■ *Objectives*

☐ *Conclude that natural disasters such as flood, fire, earthquakes, and diseases can disturb the balance of nature.*

☐ *List and describe the effects of human activities on the balance of nature.*

A dramatic event such as the fire at Yellowstone calls attention to natural disasters. Headlines often report damage from natural disasters. Like forest fires, other natural

Figure 9-1

Forest fires upset the balance of nature.

disasters may destroy the habitats of living things. For example, the energy released by some earthquakes is great enough to disturb major landforms on the surface of the earth.

Severe storms may also damage the environment. Hurricanes and tornadoes are storms with strong winds. These natural events may knock down trees and cause floods.

Still another natural event that can disturb an ecosystem is disease. For example, a deadly disease recently wiped out an entire population of wolves. These wolves had preyed on deer populations in the same ecosystem. As the wolf population dropped, the deer experienced a population explosion. In fact, the deer population become so great that many deer, unable to find food, died.

Global Warming

Human activities also cause disturbances in the balance of the ecosystem. For example, many scientists believe that human activity is slowly increasing the temperature of the earth. The burning of fuel by power plants, factories, and automobiles has added a large amount of carbon dioxide to the atmosphere. Carbon dioxide acts like the panes of glass in a greenhouse. Study the model of a greenhouse in Figure 9-2. The panes of glass admit the sun's rays into the greenhouse but prevent heat from escaping. In a similar way, carbon dioxide prevents the escape of heat rays from the earth. The resulting increase in the temperature of the earth is known as **global warming**.

Many scientists think that global warming could change the climate of the earth.

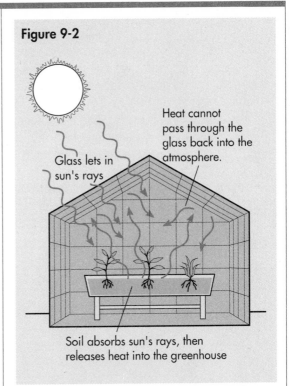

Figure 9-2

Glass lets in sun's rays

Heat cannot pass through the glass back into the atmosphere.

Soil absorbs sun's rays, then releases heat into the greenhouse

Compare the heating of a greenhouse to the process of global warming.

Areas near the equator may become too hot to support life. The climate of northern regions may become more like that of the tropics. The warm temperatures could melt polar ice caps, causing flooding in coastal cities.

Destruction of the Ozone Layer

Find an aerosol spray can and look at the label. Are the words "This product contains no chlorofluorocarbons" on the label? Chlorofluorocarbons, or CFCs, are gases that are used to force the contents from some cans of spray paint, deodorant, and hair spray. When you spray with one of these cans, CFCs escape into the atmosphere.

These CFCs may be destroying the **ozone layer**. Ozone is a gas that screens out harmful ultraviolet rays from the sun. Ultraviolet rays may cause cancer and other harmful effects. As Figure 9-3 shows, a layer of ozone lies above the earth's atmosphere. Reducing the ozone layer may put living things in greater danger from harmful ultraviolet rays. For this reason, some manufacturers no longer use CFCs in their spray cans.

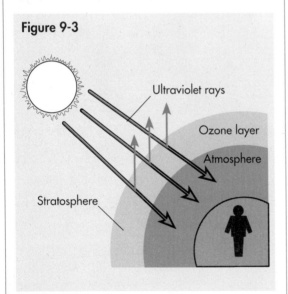

Figure 9-3

Ultraviolet rays

Ozone layer

Atmosphere

Stratosphere

How would the destruction of the ozone layer affect the amount of ultraviolet radiation reaching the earth?

Nuclear Waste Disposal

As you have seen, products that are intended to improve human life may also endanger the environment. Nuclear power is such a product. Nuclear power plants were built throughout the United States and Europe in order to provide cheap electricity. We now also know that nuclear power can also present safety risks. Radiation may leak from nuclear power plants into the atmosphere, causing mutations and cancer.

Improperly stored nuclear wastes may pollute water, soil, and living things. When one part of a food chain becomes polluted, other organisms in the food chain are poisoned as well. In addition, harmful mutations may be passed on to future generations.

Extinction

When an ecosystem is seriously damaged, species may become extinct. Destruction of forests and other ecosystems causes the extinction of about 100 plant and animal species every day. Most of these species live in the tropical rain forests of South America, Asia, and Africa. Tropical rain forests are home to more than 50 percent of the earth's species. People clear millions of acres of these forests each year to build homes, farms, and highways. As a result, animals like those shown in Figure 9-4 are dying out.

Overpopulation

Another example of imbalance in an ecosystem is **overpopulation.** Overpopulation exists when an ecosystem has more members of a species than it can support. Human overpopulation is a problem in many parts of the world. About 5 billion people inhabit the earth. As you can see from Figure 9-5, the human population is increasing at a very fast rate each year.

Ninety percent of this population growth is expected in countries that lack money or natural resources. These countries often

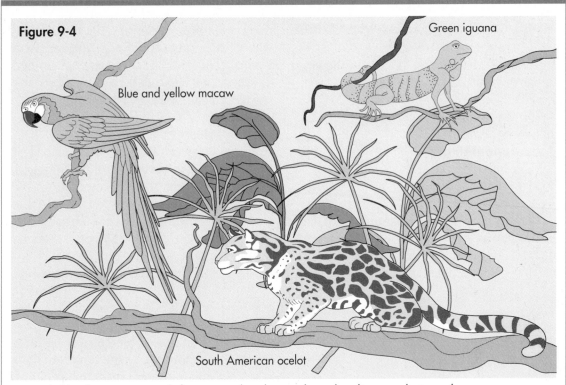

Figure 9-4

Blue and yellow macaw

Green iguana

South American ocelot

Animals like these may vanish forever as the places where they live are destroyed.

cannot feed and shelter all the people who live there. Starvation in northern Africa has already gained worldwide attention. In parts of India, people cannot buy enough food to survive.

As people try to meet the needs of a growing population, they may damage environments in other areas. People cut down forests to grow crops, but cutting down forests leads to soil erosion, floods, and loss of homes for wildlife. Pesticides that kill harmful insects may also kill helpful insects. Animals that feed on these insects become poisoned by pesticides. In addition, fields are overgrazed and overplowed from efforts to produce enough food for the growing human population.

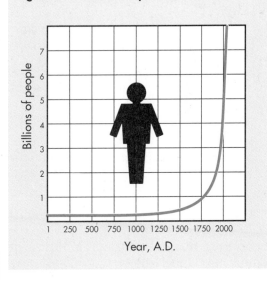

Figure 9-5 Human Population Growth

Billions of people

Year, A.D.

Write the definitions of the following terms in your own words.

1. **global warming**
2. **ozone layer**
3. **overpopulation**

Answer these questions.

4. Name three natural disasters that can destroy an ecosystem.
5. Explain the cause of global warming.
6. How can overpopulation lead to damage of environments?

9-2 Conserving Natural Resources

■ *Objectives*

☐ *Recognize that the earth's resources can be used up faster than they are recycled and therefore must be conserved.*

☐ *Identify soil, trees, water, forests, and wildlife as renewable resources and describe ways of conserving them.*

☐ *Conclude that recycling will increase the availability of renewable resources.*

☐ *Describe the effects of pollution on renewable resources.*

People use many materials from the earth to get food, build shelter, and meet other needs. These materials, including air, water, minerals, and fuels, are **natural resources.** The earth has a limited amount of natural resources. Some resources can be replaced; others cannot.

Kinds of Resources

Natural resources that can be replaced or recycled are called **renewable resources**. Water, soil, and forests are renewable resources. Water is recycled around the earth by means of evaporation and rainfall. Forests are replaced as seeds develop into new trees.

Materials that cannot be replaced or recycled are called **nonrenewable resources**. Minerals and energy resources such as coal, petroleum, and gas are examples of non-renewable resources. Non-renewable resources formed over millions of years. Millions more years are required to replace the nonrenewable resources that we use today.

Supplies of both renewable and nonrenewable resources are getting low. People can, however, avoid using up the supply of natural resources by practicing **conservation.** Conservation is the wise and careful use of natural resources.

Conserving Renewable Resources

Soil, water, air, forests, and wildlife are renewable resources. Renewal, however, requires time and effort. Often, renewable resources are used more quickly than they can be replaced. If this happens, the supply of resources may not be great enough to meet the needs of living things. The solution to this problem is to conserve renewable resources by using them wisely.

Soil Resources The survival of human beings depends on the availability of good soil. Soil contains the minerals that plants need to make food. Plants in turn are the source of food for all animals, including humans.

Soil is made of broken rock and substances formed from the decay of dead organisms and the wastes of living organisms. This decayed material contains nutrients and increases the soil's capacity to hold water. The process of building nutrient-rich soil is a slow one. Notice the different soil layers in Figure 9-6. In which layer do most plants grow?

Even the richest farm soil can be overused. Overuse results when too many crops are grown in soil and the soil loses nutrients. Farmers may return nutrients to the soil by adding natural fertilizers such as decaying leaves and manure.

Farmers may also restore nutrients to the soil by practicing crop rotation. Crop rotation is a system in which a different kind of crop is planted in a field every other year. For example, a farmer may plant corn one year and plant peas in the same field the following year. Different plants require different kinds and amounts of nutrients. Crop rotation conserves soil by making sure that the soil does not lose too much of one nutrient. In addition, the roots of pea plants contain bacteria that take nitrogen from the air and change it to a form that plants can use.

Sometimes rich topsoil is lost through **erosion**. Erosion occurs when wind blows topsoil or running water washes it away. The removal of forests increases soil erosion. Tree roots help hold the soil in place.

When tree roots are removed, erosion is more likely to occur. When the loss of topsoil is severe in an area, crops can no longer grow there.

Figure 9-6

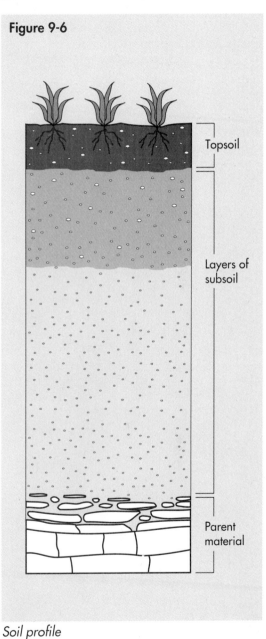

Soil profile

Several farming methods can help prevent soil erosion. Figure 9-7 shows three of these methods. They are contour plowing, strip cropping, and terracing. In each method, crops are planted so that water will not wash soil downhill. Planting crops that cover the ground and planting trees to protect fields from wind also help conserve soil.

Water Resources Most of our fresh water comes from reservoirs or from underground water. A reservoir is a lake in which fresh water is stored. Dams hold water in reservoirs and release it when it is needed. Supplies of underground water collect when rainwater seeps into the soil.

As the human population increases, the need for water steadily rises. The supply of water on the earth, however, remains the same. Water is neither gained nor lost. Rather, water is continuously being returned to the earth by the water cycle. If people use water faster than it is recycled, a shortage results.

Figure 9-7 Methods of Soil Conservation

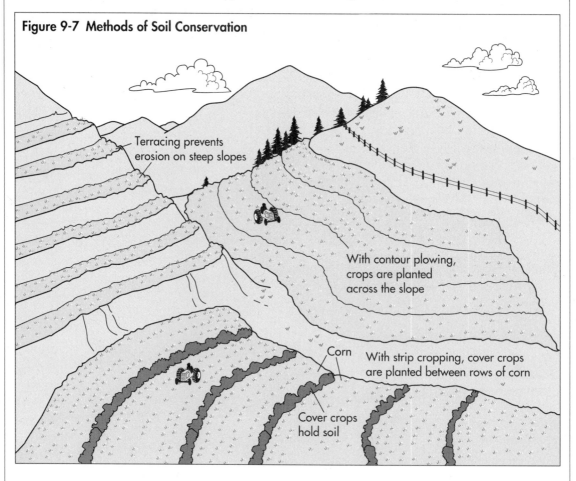

Terracing prevents erosion on steep slopes

With contour plowing, crops are planted across the slope

Corn

With strip cropping, cover crops are planted between rows of corn

Cover crops hold soil

Actually, less than half the water people use is returned to the environment in useable condition. Humans often add harmful materials, called **pollutants,** to the water supply. Figure 9-8 shows several examples of how pollutants get into water supplies. How many of these sources of pollution have you heard about?

One major source of water pollution is **sewage.** Sewage is the waste material that flows from toilets, drains, and sewers into rivers, lakes, or oceans. Sewage contains bacteria, some of which can cause disease. Water contaminated with sewage, therefore, is unfit to drink. In most populated areas, treatment plants remove harmful material from sewage before it is released into the water.

Nuclear power plants can also cause water pollution. They use cold water from rivers and streams to cool equipment. Heat released from the equipment raises the temperature of the water. The higher temperature causes increased growth of bacteria and algae. The large number of bacteria and algae use up oxygen supplies in the water. The reduced supply of oxygen causes many fish to die.

How can people conserve supplies of clean water? One way is by passing laws to protect water quality. Some laws prevent the dumping of pollutants into waterways. Other rules control the use of water during droughts. For example, during a drought, washing cars and watering lawns might be prohibited.

Figure 9-8 Sources of Water Pollution

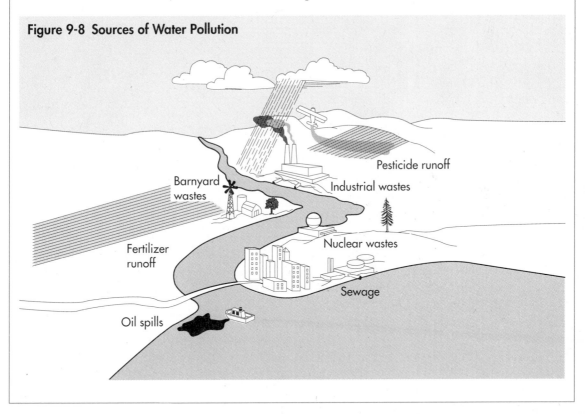

Pesticide runoff

Barnyard wastes

Industrial wastes

Fertilizer runoff

Nuclear wastes

Sewage

Oil spills

Estimating

How much water do you and your family use in one day? To help you find out, refer to Figure 9-9. Copy the table into your notebook. Estimate the number of times your family does each of these activities each day. Then fill in the last two columns of the figure.

Conclusions

1. How many gallons of water does your family use each day?
2. What steps can you and your family take to conserve water?
3. How many gallons a day could your family conserve if you followed those steps?

Figure 9-9 Water Use in the Home

Activity	Amount water used each time	Number of times	Total amount
Dishwashing	10 gallons		
Toilet	3 gallons		
Shower	25 gallons		
Bath	35 gallons		
Clothes washing	25 gallons		
Washing hands/face	0.25 gallons		

The process of **reforestation** also conserves water. Reforestation is the planting of seedlings to replace trees that have been cut down. The roots of trees hold soil in place, preventing erosion. As a result, rainwater can slowly seep into the ground and renew underground water supplies.

Air Resources The biggest threat to the air supply is pollution. When factories and motor vehicles burn fuels, they give off waste products that pollute the air. These pollutants include soot, dust, and gases such as sulfur dioxide, nitrogen oxide, carbon dioxide, and carbon monoxide.

Figure 9-10 shows the pollutants in auto exhaust. Carbon monoxide is poisonous to living things. Sulfur dioxide and nitrogen oxide may combine with rainwater to form acid rain. Acid rain has polluted the water in

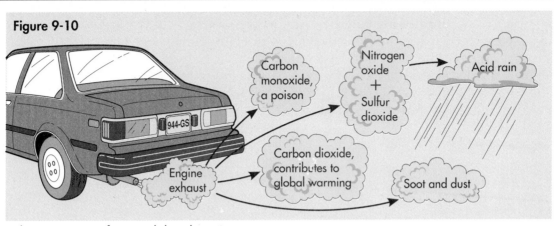

Figure 9-10

Carbon monoxide, a poison

Nitrogen oxide + Sulfur dioxide

Acid rain

Carbon dioxide, contributes to global warming

Soot and dust

Engine exhaust

What comes out of automobile exhaust?

some lakes and ponds, killing many species of fish. Other gas pollutants are now being studied as possible causes of lung cancer.

What can be done to protect the quality of the air? The government passes laws to monitor air-pollution levels. For example, new cars must have an air-pollution-control device. Factories must filter wastes before they escape through smokestacks. Many communities have passed laws against burning trash. The United States and other countries have banned the use of CFCs in spray cans.

Forest Resources People depend on forests for wood products and lumber. Forests provide beauty and places for camping and recreation. Forests also provide habitats, or places to live, for many kinds of wildlife.

Today many forests are in danger of being destroyed directly or indirectly by human activity. People often misuse and waste forests. Human carelessness has caused many forest fires. In addition, you have seen how the clearing of forests for farming leads to erosion and destruction of habitats.

What can be done to conserve forestland? Careful management of forests is important. Foresters like the person shown in Figure 9-11 might practice selective

Figure 9-11

Forestry workers examine and measure trees before they are cut. Why?

cutting, or the removal of mature trees to make room for younger trees. Removing weak and unhealthy branches, or even whole trees, also helps conserve forests.

As Figure 9-12 shows, individuals can also contribute to forest conservation.

Figure 9-12

What precautions should be taken when using a fire in a forest?

Conservation efforts can be as simple as carefully putting out all campfires that you start in the woods. Recycling paper and repairing wood furniture also helps conserve forest resources.

Wildlife Resources Look at the animals shown in Figure 9-13. Each of these animals is an endangered species. In other words, so few of these animals exist that they are in danger of becoming extinct. The survival of these animals depends on the ability of people to solve problems of the environment.

Why do people care about saving endangered species? Conserving wildlife is important in order to keep the balance in ecosystems. Each species is part of one or more food chains and food webs. If one species becomes extinct, other species may face food shortages or overpopulation.

A major cause of extinction is destruction of forests, swamps, and other natural habitats. Overhunting has also endangered many species. Wild turkeys are hunted for sport and for food. Rabbits, foxes, and

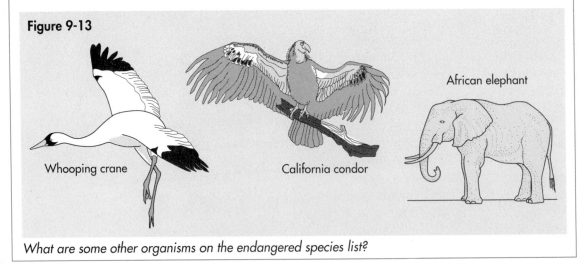

Figure 9-13

Whooping crane

California condor

African elephant

What are some other organisms on the endangered species list?

beavers are hunted for fur. Elephants are hunted for their ivory tusks. Plants are harvested for their fruit and flowers.

The United States has passed a number of laws to conserve wildlife. Hunting and fishing laws limit the amount of wildlife that can be taken, as well as the seasons in which they can be hunted. The Endangered Species Act outlaws the hunting of endangered species. The government has also set aside land called wildlife preserves, which protect the habitats of wildlife.

Other methods of wildlife conservation include raising and restocking of fish and game birds such as wild ducks. In addition, some endangered species, such as the panda, are being carefully bred in zoos. Scientists hope that such efforts will help endangered species reproduce and grow in numbers.

■■■ Section 9-2 Review ■■■

Write the definitions of the following terms in your own words.

1. **conservation**
2. **natural resource**
3. **erosion**
4. **pollutant**
5. **reforestation**

Answer these questions.

6. Explain how soil forms.
7. Describe the methods farmers use to conserve soil.
8. What is being done to help conserve fresh water and air?
9. Why are forests important?

10. What is being done to conserve forest and wildlife resources?

9-3 Conserving Nonrenewable Resources

■ *Objectives*

☐ *Categorize coal, oil, gas, and mineral resources as nonrenewable resources.*

☐ *State that recycling of minerals and development of new energy sources are needed.*

☐ *Conclude that all people have a responsibility to maintain the quality of the environment.*

Coal, oil, and minerals take millions of years to form. For this reason, they are considered nonrenewable resources. If people do not conserve nonrenewable resources, these resources will be used up in a very short time.

Minerals

A **mineral** is a natural, nonliving material that people take from the earth for various uses. Examples of minerals include iron ore and salt. The mineral calcite is used for building stone, in steel manufacturing, and in cement. Bauxite, a source of aluminum metal, is another kind of mineral. Metals such as gold and silver are also minerals.

To conserve the earth's supply of minerals, people must avoid using them wastefully. Careful mining is one step toward conservation. People can also conserve minerals by recycling. In recent years, many states have passed laws requiring that aluminum cans be recycled. Does your community have a recycling center like the one shown in Figure 9-14? Besides aluminium, products made of nickel, zinc, copper, and some other metals can be recycled also.

Figure 9-14

What happens to all of these aluminum cans?

Conservation of minerals can take place in several other ways. Substituting plentiful materials for scarce materials is one way. For example, some automobile parts are made of plastic instead of metal. Using more efficient mining and processing methods is another way of conserving minerals.

Fossil Fuels

Often people do not appreciate a resource until the supply of it runs out. In the 1970s the United States had a big oil shortage. The price of oil soared, and people had to wait in long lines at gas stations. People began to realize how much they depend on oil for heating homes, fueling cars, and producing electricity.

Oil, coal, and gas are **fossil fuels.** Fossil fuels formed from the remains of animals and plants that lived many millions of years ago. Oil and gas formed from billions of tiny sea animals and plants that died and were then buried under sediment on the ocean floor. Coal formed from the decayed remains of ancient ferns and trees that were buried under forest floors. Through the ages, heat and pressure changed the ancient plants and animals into fossil fuels.

Fossil fuels are nonrenewable energy resources. A barrel of oil, a tankful of gasoline, or a ton of coal once burned is gone forever. Conserving fossil fuels requires cooperation. For example, people can turn off lights and appliances that are not in use. In this way power plants that generate electricity burn less fossil fuel. People can also avoid unnecessary driving. What else can you do at home to conserve fossil fuels?

Another way to reduce our dependence on fossil fuels is to use other energy sources. In some areas, steam from underground sources, wind, and sunlight provide energy to heat homes and operate machinery.

The Future

As the human population continues to grow, people need to stay informed about ways to manage and conserve the earth's resources. Otherwise, resources such as water, air, and soil will become more polluted. The supply

Which Substances Can Be Naturally Recycled?

Process Skill observing

Materials filter paper, aluminum foil, plastic from a milk container, Styrofoam from a hot cup, orange peel, several leaves from trees, two flower pots, two sheets of plate glass, potting soil

Procedure

1. Fill two flower pots with potting soil.
2. Place small pieces of aluminum foil, styrofoam, and plastic on top of the soil in one flower pot. Cover the pot with a piece of plate glass.
3. Place small pieces of orange peel, filter paper, and some leaves on top of the soil in the second flower pot. Cover this pot with a sheet of plate glass.
4. After two weeks, observe the materials placed in each pot.

Conclusions

5. Which items showed evidence of decomposition? Which did not?
6. Why did only some of the items decompose?
7. How do items like plastic and Styrofoam, which do not decompose, affect the environment?
8. How can people prevent the buildup of large amounts of items that do not decompose?

---

of forest and wildlife resources will become more scarce. Energy and mineral supplies will shrink.

The first step people can take to conserve resources is to decide what is essential and nonessential in their lives. For example, people can save gasoline by walking, riding a bicycle, or using public transportation. People can save oil or gas by using less to heat their homes and wearing warmer clothing. People can also recycle wood, paper, metal, and glass products. Finally, people can urge government officials to seek long-term solutions to environmental problems. People can make sure industries obey laws designed to protect the environment.

Section 9-3 Review

Write the definitions for the following terms in your own words.

1. **mineral**
2. **fossil fuel**

Answer these questions.

3. How can people conserve mineral resources?
4. If fossil fuels form from decaying organisms, why are they considered nonrenewable resources?
5. How can people conserve fossil fuels?

SCIENCE, TECHNOLOGY, & SOCIETY

Land Use Management

Many states are taking steps to save their vacant land. Governments are trying to buy this land and use it for state forests and recreation sites. They wish to protect their vacant land from development by builders and industry.

As the human population grows and resources become scarce, people need new sources of minerals and fossil fuels. Some people want to mine lands that have been set aside for state forests, parks, and wildlife preserves.

Many ecologists, however, oppose the mining of these lands. They think that mining operations will change the character of these lands. The loss of habitats and extinction of wildlife species might result. These ecologists think that people need to conserve natural resources and, if necessary, learn to live with fewer comforts.

All citizens are affected by decisions about land-use management. These decisions may determine how you heat your home or whether you can enjoy parks or forest preserves. You can affect these decisions by conserving resources when possible and staying informed about land-use issues.

Follow-up Activity

Suppose you are a part of a planning committee that is meeting to discuss land use. The map in Figure 9-15 shows how land is used around your city. A group of people wants to buy the farmland across

the river and build houses on this land. Another group wants to begin mining operations in the forest preserve. Still another group wants to improve the sewage treatment plant. Each of these proposals will bring jobs and money to the city. How will each proposal affect the ecosystem? Write down what you would say at the meeting.

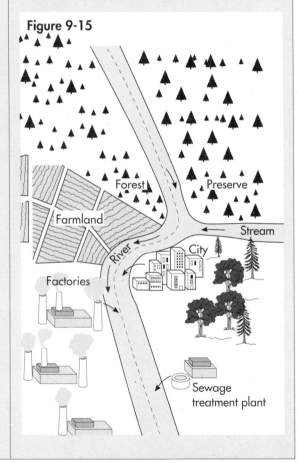

Figure 9-15

KEEPING TRACK

Section 9-1 Upsetting the Balance

1. Natural disasters such as earthquakes, storms, and disease may upset the balance of ecosystems.
2. Human activities can also upset the balance of ecosystems by causing global warming, destruction of the ozone layer, extinction of species, and overpopulation.

Section 9-2 Conserving Natural Resources

1. The supply of natural resources, including soil, water, air, forest and wildlife resources, fossil fuels, and minerals, is limited.
2. People can deplete the supply of renewable resources through overuse.
3. When a renewable resource such as water becomes polluted, it may not return to the environment in usable condition.
4. Conservation is the careful use of natural resources.

Section 9-3 Conserving Nonrenewable Resources

1. Minerals and fossil fuels are nonrenewable resources, which may eventually run out.
2. Minerals may be conserved by substituting more-plentiful materials, more-efficient production, and recycling.
3. Science and technology play major roles in conserving natural resources and finding other energy sources.

BUILDING VOCABULARY

Write the term from the list that best matches each statement.

nonrenewable, renewable, acid rain, erosion, carbon dioxide, conserve, ozone layer, resource, global warming, sewage

Some human activities may result in the loss of valuable natural ___1___. Forests, water, air, and soil are examples of ___2___ resources. Industrial pollution has caused the death of some fish in lakes affected by ___3___. Bacteria contained in ___4___ may contaminate the water supply. Cutting down forests may cause flooding and ___5___. Automobiles and factories discharge gases such as ___6___. This gas traps heat in the atmosphere, which may cause ___7___. CFCs used in spray cans have destroyed part of the ___8___. Some natural resources, called ___9___ resources, cannot be recycled. It is important to ___10___ these resources so that they do not disappear.

SUMMARIZING

If the statement is true, write *true*. If the statement is false, change the *italicized* term to make the statement true.

1. Forests and water are examples of *nonrenewable* resources.
2. When no living members of a species exist, that species is said to be *endangered*.
3. CFCs used in spray cans are slowly destroying the *ozone layer.*
4. A process in which seedlings are planted and left to grow into new trees is called *reforestation.*
5. Substances that harm the environment are known as *natural resources.*

CHAPTER REVIEW

INTERPRETING INFORMATION

Use Figure 9-16 to answer the following questions.

Figure 9-16

An average paper mill uses 180,000 tons of wood per year.

It uses enough energy to light Las Vegas for a week.

It gives off 31 billion liters of liquid waste.

It gives off an average of 62 grams of dioxin, a deadly poison.

1. Which natural resources does a paper mill use?
2. How much of these resources does it use a year?
3. How does a paper mill cause water pollution?

THINK AND DISCUSS

Use the section number in parentheses to help you find each answer. Write your answers in complete sentences.

1. How do natural disasters and human activities change ecosystems? (9-1)
2. Describe some negative effects of humans on the environment. (9-2)

3. What role do you think the government should play in protecting natural resources? (9-2)
4. Why are minerals and fossil fuels considered limited resources? (9-3)

GOING FURTHER

1. Plan a field trip to a sewage treatment plant. Learn what steps are involved in treating sewage.
2. Collect newspaper and magazine articles about the environmental problems and laws passed to protect the environment. Write a report about each problem and the solutions proposed.
3. Make a list of every piece of trash you throw away in one day. Divide your list into those items that can be recycled and those that cannot be recycled.
4. Research current state and federal laws designed to protect the environment. Write a report summarizing what is protected by each law. Suggest some new laws which you think the government should pass.

COMPETENCY REVIEW

1. Which of the following is not an effect of human population growth?
   a. overcrowding
   b. pollution
   c. shortage of food
   d. shortage of carbon dioxide

2. Which of the following is an example of a natural disaster?
   a. disappearance of the ozone layer
   b. water pollution
   c. global warming
   d. earthquake

3. Which one of the following is a nonrenewable resource?
   a. water   b. air
   c. mineral   d. tree

4. Endangered species
   a. are dangerous to humans.
   b. have become extinct.
   c. are nearing extinction.
   d. are becoming overpopulated.

5. Biologists are concerned about the clearing of tropical rain forest because
   a. wildlife habitats are being destroyed.
   b. erosion of soil and water will increase.
   c. less rain will fall.
   d. all of the above.

6. People are concerned about land use management because
   a. the human population is increasing.
   b. food is scarce.
   c. minerals are becoming scarce.
   d. all of the above.

Base your answers to questions 7 and 8 on Figure 9-17.

7. The figure suggests that the amount of carbon dioxide in the air
   a. is stable.
   b. is increasing.
   c. is decreasing.

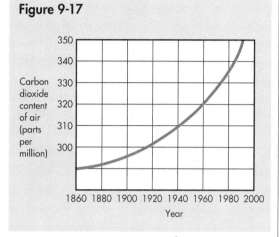

Figure 9-17

Carbon dioxide content of air (parts per million) / Year

d. will level off at the end of the century.

8. The greatest change in carbon dioxide concentration took place from
   a. 1860 to 1880.
   b. 1900 to 1920.
   c. 1940 to 1960.
   d. 1960 to 1980.

9. All of the following are responsible for causing global warming except the
   a. increase in air pollution by industry.
   b. efforts to reforest land.
   c. increase in air pollution by motor vehicles.
   d. burning of fossil fuels.

10. All of the following are methods of wildlife conservation except
   a. hunting and fishing laws.
   b. establishing wildlife preserves.
   c. breeding endangered species in zoos.
   d. introducing a foreign species into an ecosystem.

CHAPTER 10

STRUCTURE OF THE BODY

Have you ever watched construction workers building a skyscraper? Construction workers, like those shown in Figure 10-1, work in teams. Each team does a different kind of work. One team drives the trucks and works the bulldozers. Another team pours and levels the building's cement foundation. Each team of workers is specialized to do one job better than the others. Yet all of these teams work together as they build the skyscraper.

The cells of your body also work in teams. Cells, which are the smallest units of life, are like construction workers. Each cell has its own job. Yet each cell works with other cells like the teams on a construction crew. These "teams" of cells work together to perform the life processes that keep you alive. Like the boss of a construction crew, you are in charge of seeing that your body's team members do their jobs. Eating the right foods, getting the right amounts of exercise and rest, and developing good health habits are ways to help keep your body working properly.

10-1 Building the Parts of Your Body

■ *Objectives*

☐ *Describe the structure and function of major types of human cells.*

☐ *Identify the levels of organization that build the human body.*

Many different kinds of cells make up your body. Each kind of cell performs a specific job. The structure of each type of cell is

Figure 10-1

Teamwork helps build skyscrapers.

an adaptation for the specific job that it performs.

Human Cells

Look at the the nerve cell in Figure 10-2. Notice how long and thin it is. Like electric wires, nerve cells carry messages from one body part to another body part. Notice the flat, round shape of the skin cell. The structure of skin cells allows them to cover and protect your body. Muscle cells are long and flexible, like rubber bands. This structure enables muscles to stretch and contract.

Although the cells of the body have different structures and functions, they have several parts in common. Look again at the cells in Figure 10-2. Each cell contains a cell membrane, nucleus, and cytoplasm. Recall the job of each of these parts from Chapter 3. Other parts of the cell are too small to be seen with a compound microscope. Scientists use the electron microscope to observe the tiniest cell structures.

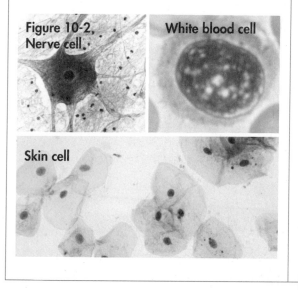

Figure 10-2. Nerve cell.

White blood cell

Skin cell

SKILL BUILDER

Observing

Scientists use microscopes to observe cells. They also take photographs of cells through a microscope.

1. Carefully study Figures 10-3 and 10-4, which show samples of the same kind of tissue. Figure 10-3 was taken through a compound microscope. Figure 10-4 was taken through an electron microscope.

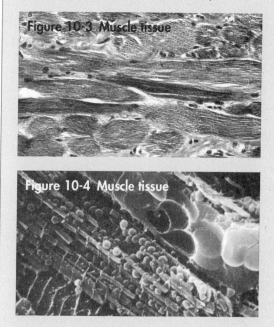

Figure 10-3 Muscle tissue

Figure 10-4 Muscle tissue

2. Compare the two photographs. What cell structures can you see in both photographs? Which photograph reveals the most detail?

3. Do some research to find out about the advantages and disadvantages of using electron microscopes.

Tissues

Cells of the same kind that do the same job make up **tissues.** For example, groups of skin cells form skin tissue. Groups of muscle cells form muscle tissue. Bone cells form bone tissue. The cells of each tissue work together to perform a specific function. For example, your skin cells work together to cover and protect the parts of your body. Figure 10-5 lists the five main groups of human body tissues.

Organs

If you were to list some body parts, you might include the heart, brain, stomach, and eyes. All of these parts are examples of **organs.** An organ is a group of tissues that work together to do a specific job.

Your leg is an organ. Look at the diagram of a leg in Figure 10-6. What tissues is it made of? Skin tissue covers and protects it. Bone tissue below the skin supports

Figure 10-6

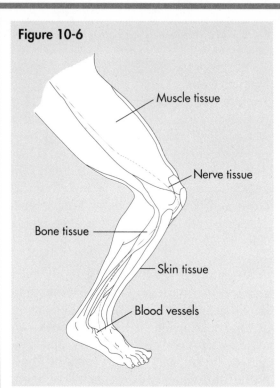

Why is the leg considered an organ?

Figure 10-5 Human Body Tissues

Tissue type	Description	Function
Muscle	Bundles of long, thin muscle cells that expand and contract	Move body parts
Nerve	Bundles of long, branching cells	Carry messages throughout body
Blood	Fluids in which red blood cells, white blood cells, and platelets flow	Carry food, oxygen, and wastes throughout body, fight disease, help clot blood
Skin	Broad, flat cells that form thin sheets	Cover body organs
Connective	Cells that form strong, stringy tissue	Hold parts of the body together

the leg and gives it shape. Muscle tissue moves the leg. Nerve tissue carries messages from the rest of the body and the environment to and from the leg. Look at the blue lines under the skin of your own leg. These lines are blood vessels. Blood vessels carry blood tissue throughout the leg and the rest of your body.

Organ Systems

Now you understand how teams of tissues work together to form the organs of your body. Organs also work together. Groups of organs form **organ systems.** An organ system is a group of organs that work together to carry on a certain life process.

The human digestive system is an organ system that includes the mouth, stomach, intestines, and other organs. The food that you eat passes through your digestive system. All of the organs of the digestive system work to turn the food into substances that can be used by your body. The human body is made up of several organ systems. Figure 10-7 lists some of these organ systems.

▬ Section 10-1 Review ▬

Write the definitions for the following terms in your own words.

1. **tissue**   2. **organ**
3. **organ system**

Answer these questions.

4. Give two examples of how the structure of a certain type of cell is well suited to its function.
5. What is the difference between a cell and a tissue?
6. Describe the functions of the five main groups of tissue in the human body.
7. What is the difference between an organ and an organ system?

Figure 10-7 Human Organ Systems

System	Organs	Function
Digestive	Mouth, esophagus, stomach, small intestine, liver, gall bladder, pancreas, large intestine, rectum	Breaks down food for use by cells
Circulatory	Heart, artery, vein, capillary	Transports materials to and from the body cells
Excretory	Kidney, ureter, bladder, urethra	Eliminates wastes produced by body cells
Nervous	Brain, spinal cord, nerves, sense organs	Transmits messages throughout the body

10-2 The Skeletal System

■ *Objectives*

☐ *Describe the structure and function of the skeletal system.*

☐ *Identify some minerals necessary for bone growth.*

You learned in Chapter 5 that all vertebrates, including humans, have an endoskeleton. An endoskeleton is a skeleton located inside the body. Together, the bones of your skeleton make up your **skeletal system.** The skeletal system is the framework that supports and protects your body. Without a skeleton, you could not walk or run. You could not even get out of bed in the morning.

In addition to providing support, your skeleton protects the organs in your body. Gently tap your head with your fist. Now tap your fist against the center of your chest. The hard bones you feel protect your brain, your heart, and your lungs.

Structure of the Skeleton

About 206 bones make up the human skeleton. How many of these bones can you see in Figure 10-8? Some bones, such as the bones in your fingers, are very tiny. Others, such as the bones in your arms or legs, are quite large. Some bones are long and thin. Others are broad and thick. Even though bones differ in shape and size, all bones are made up of bone tissue. All bones are strong and hard.

In addition, all bones are connected to other bones. At the ends of many bones is a soft material called **cartilage** (KART-ul-ij). Cartilage acts as a cushion where

bones come together. Cartilage is also present in body parts that do not have bones, such as the outer ear and the tip of the nose.

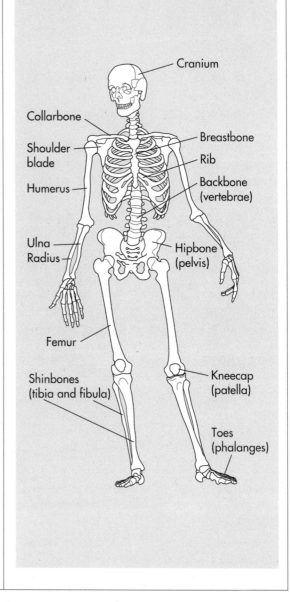

Figure 10-8 The Human Skeletal System

- Cranium
- Collarbone
- Shoulder blade
- Breastbone
- Rib
- Backbone (vertebrae)
- Humerus
- Ulna
- Radius
- Hipbone (pelvis)
- Femur
- Shinbones (tibia and fibula)
- Kneecap (patella)
- Toes (phalanges)

The Skull and the Spinal Column

Begin your study of the skeletal system by looking at the parts of the **skull.** The bones of the skull protect the brain from injury. Study the human skull in Figure 10-9. Notice how the bones in the skull are joined by toothed edges that fit closely together. The thick, hard bones form a solid covering around the brain.

Figure 10-9 also shows the **spine,** or backbone. Your spine runs up the middle of your back. Many small bones called **vertebrae** (VER-tuh-bray) make up your spine. These vertebrae fit together to form a strong yet flexible column. The column supports your body and also allows it to bend and move.

Look at the vertebrae that make up the spine. Each vertebra has a hole through its middle. All of these holes line up to form a long hollow tube. A thick rope of nerves called the spinal cord passes from the brain through the hollow center of the spine. The spine protects the spinal cord from injury. Between each vertebra, you can find disks of cartilage. These disks act as cushions or shock absorbers. They keep the vertebrae from rubbing against each other.

Find the **breastbone** in Figure 10-8. The breastbone runs up and down the top part of the chest. Seven pairs of curved bones called **ribs** are connected to the breastbone. The ribs curve all the way around to the spine. The next three pairs of ribs are not attached to the breastbone. Each of these ribs is attached to the rib just above it in the front and to the spine in the back. The bottom two pairs of ribs are attached to the spine only. Together, the 12 pairs of ribs form the **rib cage.** The rib cage surrounds and protects your heart and lungs.

Study the human skeleton in Figure 10-8. Find the shoulder blades, the collarbone, the hipbone, and the long bones in the arms and legs. What, do you think, is the function of each of these bones? What parts of the body do they support or protect?

Bone Formation

Sometime between the ages of 11 and 13, a person begins to grow rapidly. The skin,

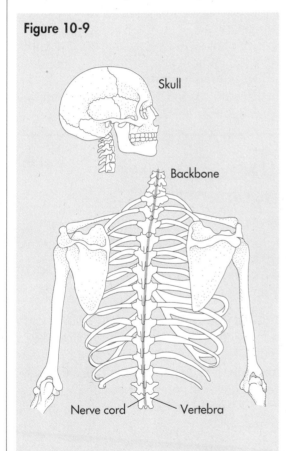

Figure 10-9

Skull

Backbone

Nerve cord — Vertebra

The cracks in the skull are actually places where bones in the skull fit together. Notice the vertebrae, which form the backbone.

muscles, arms, and legs all grow. The bones must grow too. To grow, bones need large amounts of two minerals, calcium and phosphorus. Calcium and phosphorus are carried to the bones by the bloodstream. They are stored by the bones and used in the hardening process of new bone cells.

Bone begins as cartilage and other soft tissue. As bone hardens, the calcium and phosphorus combine to form calcium phosphate, the substance that makes bone hard. Calcium phosphate also gives bone its strength and shape.

Look at the cross section of a bone in Figure 10-10. The center of the bone is filled with a soft, spongy tissue called **marrow.** Red blood cells are made in the marrow. You will learn more about red blood cells in Chapter 13.

Figure 10-10

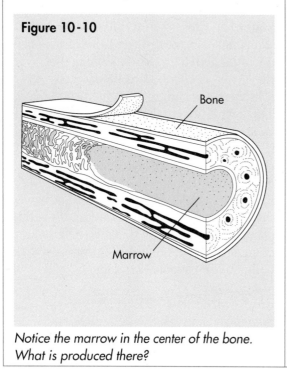

Bone

Marrow

Notice the marrow in the center of the bone. What is produced there?

Section 10-2 Review

Write the definitions for the following terms in your own words.

1. **cartilage**   2. **spine**
3. **vertebrae**   4. **rib cage**
5. **marrow**

Answer these questions.

6. What is the function of the skeletal system?
7. Distinguish between cartilage and bone.
8. What characteristics make your skull well suited to protect your brain?
9. How do the vertebrae work together to make your spine strong yet flexible?

10-3 Joints and Ligaments

■ *Objectives*
☐ *Relate the structure of the skeletal system to body movement.*
☐ *Name several kinds of joints.*

Extend your arm straight out. Move it up and down. Now pretend you are throwing a ball. Feel the circular movement in your shoulder as you go through these motions. Joints make movement possible.

Joints

Joints are places in the skeleton where bones are connected to each other. Joints are the movable parts of your skeleton. Elbows, shoulders, hips, and knees are all joints. Without joints, your body would be as rigid as a building. You could not do any of the activities you enjoy, such as playing baseball, writing, or walking.

Figure 10-11 shows the knee joint. The knee is an example of a **hinge joint.** A hinge joint works just like a door hinge. It allows a bone to bend back and forth. Notice, however, that hinge joints move bones back and forth only. For example, your knee joint bends your leg but does not let it twist or swing. Other hinge joints include your elbows and the knuckles in your fingers and toes.

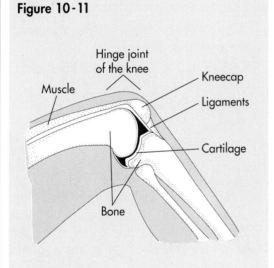

Figure 10-11

Unlike the knee joint, the shoulder joint allows your arm to move in many directions. A shoulder joint is a **ball-and-socket joint.** Ball-and-socket joints allow bones to move in a complete circle. Figure 10-12 shows a ball-and-socket joint. Notice how the ball-like end of the upper arm fits into the hollow socket of the shoulder bone.

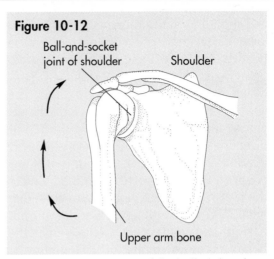

Figure 10-12

Notice how the structure of the ball-and-socket joint allows for circular motion.

Your hip also contains ball-and-socket joints. Your hip joint lets you move your leg in several different directions. Extend your leg out in front of you. Wave it around so that your foot draws circles in the air. You have just seen your hip joint in action.

Your body contains other kinds of joints as well. Figure 10-13 shows a pivot joint

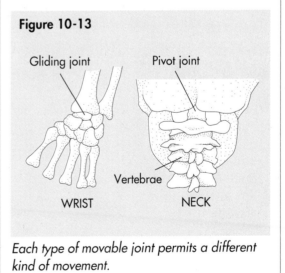

Figure 10-13

Each type of movable joint permits a different kind of movement.

and a gliding joint. Your neck has a pivot joint. The pivot joint lets you move your head up and down and from side to side. Your wrist has a special kind of joint called a gliding joint. Working together with a hinge joint, the gliding joint allows you to move your wrist in many different directions.

Some of the bones in your body are connected by **immovable joints.** Unlike the movable joints in your elbow, shoulder, neck, and wrist, immovable joints do not permit any movement. Recall that the bones in your skull are joined together by tightly-fitted toothed edges. These edges are examples of immovable joints.

Ligaments

Bones are held together by strong bands of connective tissue called **ligaments.** Ligaments are attached to the ends of each bone in a joint. When the joint moves, the ligaments stretch slightly but always stay tight enough to keep the bones from separating. Look again at the knee joint shown in Figure 10-11. Find the bands of ligaments that attach the bones to each other.

■ Section 10-3 Review ■

Write the definitions for the following terms in your own words.

1. **hinge joint**
2. **ball-and-socket joint**
3. **immovable joint**
4. **ligament**

Answer these questions.

5. What is the function of a joint?
6. Describe how a hinge joint and a ball-and-socket joint work. Name two examples of each of these joints in the human body.
7. Suppose your fingers had no hinge joints. Name three things you would not be able to do.
8. How do ligaments hold joints together?

10-4 The Muscular System

■ *Objectives*

☐ *Describe the structure and function of the muscular system.*

☐ *Explain how the skeletal and muscular systems work together.*

☐ *Recognize that muscles work in pairs.*

As you read this book, you are making all kinds of movements. Your eyes are blinking. Your head is moving back and forth. Your heart is beating, and your lungs are breathing in and out. After you finish reading, you may decide to take a walk. What makes each of these movements possible? Every movement that you make is controlled by muscles.

The human **muscular system** includes about 600 muscles. They differ in size, shape, and strength. Different kinds of muscles control different parts of your body. However, all muscles are alike in two important ways. All muscles are made up of muscle cells, and all muscles require large amounts of energy.

How Muscles and Bones Work Together

How do muscles make your body move? To find out, do this simple experiment. Let your arm hang down. Feel the muscle in the front part of your upper arm. Keep your hand on it as you slowly bend your elbow. Can you feel the muscle in your upper arm becoming thicker and shorter? Now lower your arm. Notice how the muscle becomes thinner and longer again.

Muscles move bones by becoming shorter or longer. Their shape and length change as the cells that make up the muscle become shorter and longer. As the muscles change shape, they pull on the bones to which the muscles are attached.

Figure 10-14A shows the muscles and bones of the arm. Strong cords of tissue attach the muscles to the bones. These cords are called **tendons**. To raise your arm, your bones, muscles, and tendons must interact in a precise way. First, the muscle in the front part of your upper arm grows shorter, or contracts. As this muscle

contracts, it pulls on the tendon. The tendon in turn pulls the bone in the forearm toward the upper arm. Your arm then rises.

How Muscles Work in Pairs

In order for your arm to move in either direction, your muscles must work in pairs. Look at Figure 10-14B. The muscle on the inside of the arm is the **biceps**, and the muscle on the outside is the **triceps**. To bend your arm, your biceps contracts, pulling the forearm toward the upper arm. At the same time, the triceps on the other side of the arm stretches. To extend your arm straight out, the biceps stretches, and the triceps contracts.

Muscles work in pairs in several other parts of your body. For example, your thigh muscles, the muscles in your upper leg, work in pairs. This pair of muscles is attached to bones in the lower leg. Your thigh muscles work together with the bones and tendons to bend or straighten your leg at the knee.

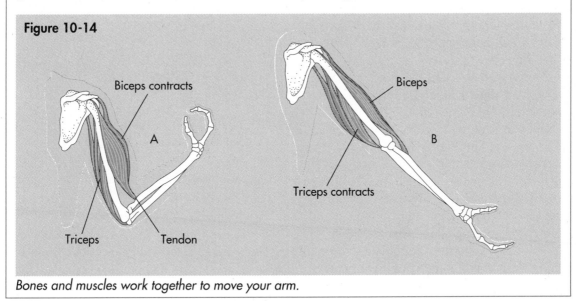

Figure 10-14

Biceps contracts

A

Triceps   Tendon

Biceps

B

Triceps contracts

Bones and muscles work together to move your arm.

Muscle Types

The muscles you have read about so far are **skeletal muscles.** Skeletal muscles are the muscles that move bones. Skeletal muscles are made of long, slender muscle cells. As Figure 10-15 shows, skeletal muscle cells have a striped appearance.

The skeletal muscles are **voluntary muscles.** That is, you control the movement of these muscles. Your brain must send messages telling them to contract and stretch.

Your body also contains **involuntary muscles.** You have no control over the movement of your involuntary muscles. These muscles do not move bones. They are found in the organs of your body, such as the stomach and small intestine.

The involuntary muscles in your organs are known as **smooth muscles.** Smooth muscles are made of short, slender muscle cells. Find the smooth muscle in Figure 10-15. Smooth muscles perform the squeezing action necessary to move food through the stomach and intestine. Because smooth muscles are involuntary, food automatically moves through the digestive system.

Your heart is a special kind of muscle called **cardiac muscle.** Find the cardiac muscle in Figure 10-15. Cardiac muscle is similar to skeletal muscle except that cardiac muscle fibers form a kind of net. This net of muscle contracts all at once when it is stimulated by nerve impulses. If you place your hand slightly to the left of the center of your chest, you will feel your heart muscle in action. Cardiac muscle is involuntary. It works automatically day and night to pump blood through your body.

Figure 10-15

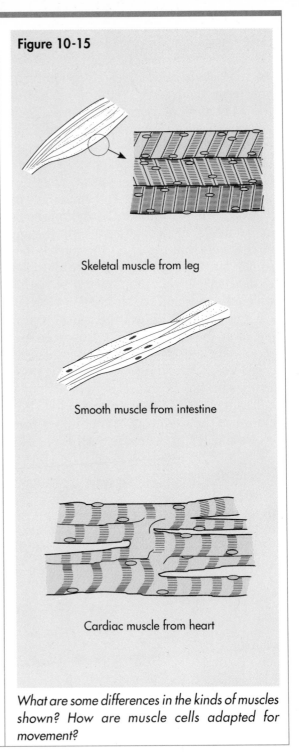

Skeletal muscle from leg

Smooth muscle from intestine

Cardiac muscle from heart

What are some differences in the kinds of muscles shown? How are muscle cells adapted for movement?

What Does Skeletal Muscle Tissue Look Like Under a Microscope?

Process Skill *using a microscope*

Materials piece of raw beef, pin, slide, cover slip, medicine dropper, water, iodine stain, microscope

The skeletal muscle tissue of a cow is very similar to human skeletal muscle tissue. In this activity, you will use a microscope to examine beef, which is a cow's skeletal muscle tissue.

Procedure

1. Use a pin to separate a thin piece of muscle tissue from a piece of raw beef.
2. Place the tissue in a drop of water on a clean slide. Stain it with a drop of diluted iodine.

Caution Do not touch your eyes or mouth with your fingers after handling chemicals. Wash hands afterwards.

3. Place a cover slip over the slide.
4. Examine your slide under the microscope. Describe each muscle cell. Can you make out any of its parts? Notice the shape of each muscle cell. Look for the bundles of muscle cells that make up muscle tissue.

Conclusion

5. Draw a diagram of the muscle tissue in your notebook. Show how the skeletal muscle cells are shaped and how they are bound together to form tissue. Compare your diagram to the skeletal muscle cells shown in Figure 10-15.

▬ Section 10-4 Review ▬

Write the definitions for the following terms in your own words.

1. **skeletal muscle**
2. **voluntary muscle**
3. **involuntary muscle**
4. **smooth muscle**
5. **cardiac muscle**

Answer these questions.

6. How do the muscles and bones in your arm work together to create movement?
7. Explain how your triceps and biceps work together to bend and extend your arm.
8. Name three muscle types and describe how they work.
9. Why is it important that smooth muscle and cardiac muscle work automatically?

SCIENCE, TECHNOLOGY, & SOCIETY

Using Transplants to Extend Human Lives

Imagine waiting for a phone call that could save your life. People waiting for an organ transplant have had to do this. They have waited days or weeks to hear whether the new heart, kidney, or liver their body needs could be found.

In an organ transplant, a surgeon transfers an organ from one person into another person's body. Healthy organs are obtained from those who have agreed to donate their organs in case of death. The organ is then given to someone whose organs are severely diseased or damaged.

In most cases, organ transplant surgery is complicated and risky. Some people do not survive the operation. Because the body recognizes the new organ as a foreign object, it often tries to reject the organ. Still, heart, kidney, and liver transplants have added months and even years to people's lives.

Follow-up Activity

Choose two of the four characters described here. In each character's voice, write a paragraph explaining your feelings and opinions about the operation.

Mary Jones, a 38-year-old mother of three, has had two serious heart attacks. Without a heart transplant, she will soon die.

Dr. Juan Alvarez, Mary's doctor, is an experienced heart surgeon. Two of his three heart transplant patients have died. The third patient is doing well. Dr. Alvarez thinks that Mary has a 70 percent chance of surviving a heart transplant. He thinks that a heart transplant would add at least two years to Mary's life.

Dr. John Cosby is another heart surgeon who was asked to give a second opinion about Mary's case. He does not think Mary will survive heart transplant surgery. He thinks that with medication, Mary can live for another year.

Bill Jones, Mary's husband, is urging Mary and Dr. Alvarez to agree to the operation. He feels that any means of extending his wife's life should be tried.

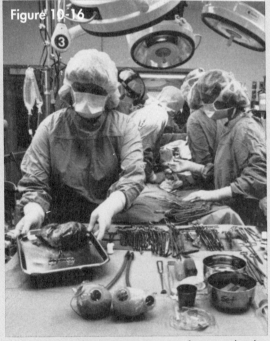

Figure 10-16

Organ transplant operations are long and risky.

KEEPING TRACK

Section 10-1 Building the Parts of Your Body

1. The human body is made of cells. Each kind of cell performs a specific job.
2. Cells that act together to do the same job form tissues.
3. Tissues that work together form organs.
4. Organs that act together are organized into systems.
5. The human body is made up of several organ systems, each of which performs a different job.

Section 10-2 The Skeletal System

1. The skeletal system, which includes the skull and spinal column, protects and supports the body. The skeletal system also contains some soft tissue called cartilage.
2. The spine is a strong, flexible column of bones that supports the body and allows it to bend and move.
3. Bones need calcium and phosphorus to grow.

Section 10-3 Joints and Ligaments

1. Joints are movable parts of the skeleton where bones connect to each other.
2. Types of joints include hinge, ball-and-socket, pivot, and gliding joints.

Section 10-4 The Muscular System

1. The skeletal and muscular systems work together to move the human body.
2. Muscles work in pairs to move bones.
3. The muscular system consists of voluntary and involuntary muscles. Skeletal muscle is voluntary. Smooth muscle and cardiac muscle are involuntary.

BUILDING VOCABULARY

Write the term from the list that best completes each sentence.

skull, smooth, tissues, ribs, cardiac, voluntary, organs, tendons

Groups of cells that work together to do the same job are called ___1___. The heart, brain, and stomach are all ___2___. The bones that protect the heart and lungs are the 12 pairs of ___3___. The bones that protect the brain make up the ___4___. Bones are attached to muscles by ___5___. Two kinds of muscles are ___6___ muscles and involuntary muscles. Involuntary muscle in organs is called ___7___ muscle. The heart is made of ___8___ muscle.

Explain the difference between the terms in each pair.

9. skeletal system, muscular system
10. tendons, ligaments
11. biceps, triceps

SUMMARIZING

If the statement is true, write *true*. If the statement is false, change the *italicized* term to make the statement true.

1. The smallest unit of organization of the human body is the *nucleus*.
2. An organ is made up of different kinds of *tissues*.

3. The *lung* is an organ that pumps blood through the body.
4. A group of organs that carry on a life process is called a *tissue*.
5. The *muscular* system supports the body.
6. The *skull* protects the brain from injury.
7. The vertebrae fit together to form the *rib cage*.
8. Bones are connected at the *joints*.
9. The shoulder joint is a *hinge* joint.
10. Red blood cells are made in the *bone marrow*.

INTERPRETING INFORMATION

Use Figure 10-17 to answer the following questions.

1. What is the recommended dietary allowance for calcium for a 12-year-old girl?
2. Your teacher would like to know how much calcium he or she needs each day. What would you need to know before you could provide an answer? Why would you need this information?
3. Construct a graph of the information in Figure 10-17. On the horizontal axis, label the age in years. On the vertical axis, label the amount of calcium in milligrams.

THINK AND DISCUSS

Use the section number in parentheses to help you find each answer. Write your answers in complete sentences.

1. Give two examples of how the structure of a cell is related to its function. (10-1)

Figure 10-17 Recommended Dietary Allowances for Calcium and Phosphorus

Age (years)	Calcium (mg)	Phosphorus (mg)
Infants 0.0-0.5	360	240
Infants 0.5-1.0	540	360
Children 1-10	800	800
Males 11-18	1200	1200
Males 19+	800	800
Females 11-18	1200	1200
Females 19+	800	800
Pregnant Females	+400	+400

2. Why is the human leg considered to be an organ? (10-1)
3. What are two important functions of the human skeletal system? (10-2)
4. Explain how tendons, ligaments, muscles, and bones help you lift an object. (10-3)
5. How does cardiac muscle tissue help your heart perform its job? (10-4)

1. Ask your teacher to show you a model of the human body. Find and name some of the organs and organ systems. Describe how each organ system works with the others to keep the body alive.
2. Use a first aid book to find examples of sports injuries. List the symptoms of each and the first aid treatment. Identify each as a skeletal or muscular injury.

COMPETENCY REVIEW

1. Each part of the human body, including the heart, kidney, and stomach, is known as a(an)
   a. organ.   b. tissue.
   c. cell.   d. system.
2. Which tissue covers and protects body parts?
   a. nerve   b. skin
   c. muscle   d. blood
3. Which tissue carries messages from organ to organ?
   a. nerve   b. skin
   c. muscle   d. blood
4. Which tissue carries oxygen and helps fight disease?
   a. nerve   b. skin
   c. muscle   d. blood
5. Which organ is made of cardiac muscle tissue?
   a. liver   b. heart
   c. brain   d. skull
6. Which of the following terms includes all the others?
   a. cell   b. organ
   c. tissue   d. organ system

7. Human muscles and bones work together to
   a. carry messages from organ to organ.
   b. pump blood throughout the body.
   c. move the parts of the body.
   d. cover and protect the parts of the body.

Use Figure 10-18 to answer Questions 8-10.

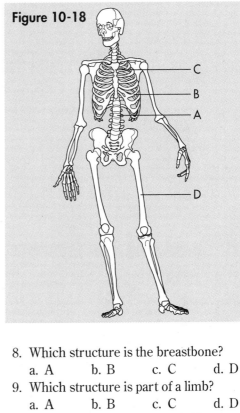

Figure 10-18

8. Which structure is the breastbone?
   a. A   b. B   c. C   d. D
9. Which structure is part of a limb?
   a. A   b. B   c. C   d. D
10. If you were running, you would use voluntary muscles attached to which structure?
    a. A   b. B   c. C   d. D

CHAPTER 11

NUTRIENTS IN FOODS

Have you ever watched a machine at work? The machine shown in Figure 11-1 is used by farmers to harvest crops. Its gasoline engine supplies the machine with the energy it needs to do the work of cutting grain. Like a machine, your body does work, too. You work when using your muscles to walk. You work when you carry an object from place to place. Your heart works to pump blood to all parts of your body. Even breathing is work for your body. For your body to carry on these and other life processes, it needs energy. What fuel provides you with the energy you need? That fuel is the food you eat.

If you have a balanced diet, your food supply comes from both plant and animal products. Plants such as wheat are the producers in a food chain. During photosynthesis, the wheat changes the sun's energy into chemical energy. This energy is stored in the grains. When you eat a slice of bread made from this wheat, you become a consumer in the food chain.

Other animals eat plants, too. In turn, many humans eat animals. When you eat meat that comes from an animal, you become a consumer in another food chain.

11-1 Nutrients for Energy and Growth

■ *Objectives*

☐ *Compare the energy values of different foods.*

☐ *List and describe the functions of the major nutrients required by the human body.*

You have probably heard the expression, "You are what you eat." The food you eat and how your body uses that food are

Figure 11-1

A machine is used to harvest crops.

what **nutrition** is all about. Nutrition is the study of food and how the foods you eat make you healthy. Food provides the energy you need for life processes, including growth and repair of body tissues.

Eating the proper amounts of nutritious foods is especially important for teenagers. In your teenage years, you experience rapid growth. Your body's need for energy is great. Only proper amounts of the right kinds of foods will supply you with the materials needed for growth and provide the energy needs of your body.

What Is Food?

In your own words, write a definition of food. Compare your definition to those given in dictionaries and other reference books. Scientists define food as any material taken into your body that is used by your body cells for growth and repair. It also provides the energy you use in work and play.

Nutrients and Their Uses

No doubt you have watched a house being built. Can you list some of the materials that are used to build it? Your list may include bricks, cement blocks, pipes, and wood.

Just as a house cannot be built without special materials, your body cannot grow without **nutrients**. Nutrients are the substances in foods that your body needs to survive. Your body changes the nutrients in foods to simpler materials that your cells can use. Some of these materials are used in the growth and repair of cells. Other nutrients provide the energy you need to study, work, and play. Your body produces energy by combining food with oxygen in the process of cell respiration.

Measuring the Energy in Foods

Each activity you do requires energy. Your every movement, from the beating of your heart to even the blinking of your eyelids, uses energy. This energy comes from the food you eat. However, different types of food provide different amounts of energy. Scientists measure the energy in food by measuring the amount of heat given off when that food is burned.

The unit of measurement for the amount of heat given off when a food is burned is a **calorie**. A calorie is the amount of heat needed to raise the temperature of one gram of water one degree Celsius. One kilogram-calorie, or **Calorie,** is equal to 1,000 calories. The energy values for foods are expressed in Calories. For example, one egg has about 75 Calories.

The Energy Nutrients

Foods provide energy to your body so you can carry out activities. Some foods provide more energy than others. Nutritionists call these foods the high-energy foods. These high-energy foods include carbohydrates, fats and oils.

Carbohydrates Often before a basketball game or track meet, an athlete will eat an orange or other fruit. Do you know why? Oranges are rich in glucose, a simple sugar. Glucose provides quick energy. A basketball player who has just eaten an orange may perform better with an increased energy supply.

How Can You Measure the Energy Value in Food?

Process Skills performing measurements

Materials 250 mL beaker, thermometer, long needle, cork, shelled walnut, Bunsen burner, water, ring stand with ring

When the temperature of one gram of water goes up by one degree Celsius, one calorie of heat has been added to the water sample. If the temperature of one kilogram of water (1000 mL) goes up by one degree, then one Calorie (1000) calories has been added. In this activity, you will burn a walnut and calculate how much heat is given off by measuring how much the temperature of the water above it rises.

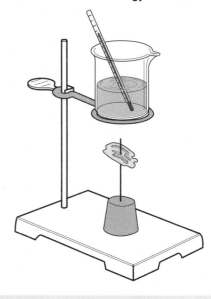

Figure 11-2 Laboratory setup to determine the amount of energy in a food

Procedure

1. Add 100 mL of water to a 250 mL beaker. Take the temperature of the water and record.
2. Push a long needle all the way through a cork. Place a shelled walnut on the tip of the needle. Place the cork under the beaker as shown in Figure 11-2.
3. Light the Bunsen burner. Use the burner to start the walnut burning. As soon as the nut starts to burn by itself, remove the Bunsen burner.
4. After the walnut has burned completely, take the temperature of the water again.

Conclusions

5. How many degrees was the temperature of the water raised?
6. If one calorie will raise the temperature of one gram of water one degree Celsius, how many calories were released when the walnut burned? (Hint: You used 100 grams of water. So the number of calories = the change in temperature × 100).
7. To find how may Calories were released, divide your answer to number 6 by 1000.
8. Do you think that the water received every calorie of heat from the burning walnut? Why or why not?

Glucose is part of a group of nutrients known as carbohydrates. Carbohydrates are divided into two groups. **Simple carbohydrates** are foods that contain sugar. **Complex carbohydrates** contain starches such as those found in bread, rice, and pasta. Figure 11-3 shows several foods that are rich in carbohydrates.

Figure 11-3 Simple Carbohydrates

Do you include these high-energy foods in your daily diet?

How does your body use carbohydrates? After you eat complex carbohydrates, your digestive system breaks them down into glucose. Glucose is absorbed quickly into the bloodstream, where it is transported to the cells of your body.

When glucose molecules reach the mitochondria in your cells, they are used in cellular respiration. In cellular respiration, glucose undergoes **oxidation.** During oxidation, glucose combines with oxygen, releasing energy for life processes.

Fats and Oils Sugars and starches are not the only high-energy foods your body needs. **Fats** are nutrients that provide energy too. Figure 11-4 shows several foods that are high in fat.

Figure 11-4 Fats and Oils

Can you name other foods that are rich in fat and oil?

Why are fats and oils valuable nutrients? Like carbohydrates, fats and oils are good sources of energy. As a matter of fact, fats and oils provide even more energy, gram for gram, than carbohydrates

How Can You Test for Carbohydrates?

Process Skills *making observations, using a control*

Materials three test tubes, test tube rack, Benedict's solution, glucose, apple slices, hot water bath, shallow dish, cornstarch, water, iodine, wax pencil, test tube holder

Procedure

Testing for Sugar

1. Label three test tubes 1, 2, and 3. Place the test tubes in a rack. Add 15 to 20 drops of blue Benedict's solution to each tube.
2. To test tube 2 add a small amount of glucose and stir.
3. To test tube 3 add several small slices of apple.
4. Place all three test tubes in a hot water bath as shown in Figure 11-5.

A color change from blue to brick red indicates the presence of simple sugar.

Testing for Starch

5. Place a small amount of cornstarch in a shallow dish. Add enough water to make a paste.
6. Add two drops of iodine. A blue-black color indicates the presence of starch.

Conclusions

7. Which test tubes showed a color change?
8. What nutrient is found in apple?
9. What was the control in this activity?
10. What nutrient is found in cornstarch?
11. What other foods would show a positive test for starch? Try this test on these foods to see if you are correct.

Figure 11-5 Testing for Sugar with Benedict's Solution

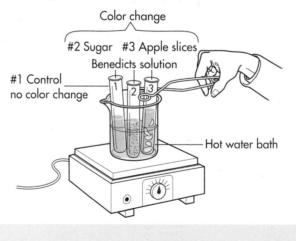

provide. Oils and fats are also used to build cell membranes.

Your daily diet should include some oils and fats. Figure 11-6 lists some foods that are rich in oils and fats. Study the list carefully. Does your daily diet include moderate amounts of some of these foods?

Your body digests fats into simpler substances called **fatty acids** and **glycerol** (GLIS-uh-rawl). The bloodstream carries fatty acids and glycerol to your cells. There, some of the fatty acids and glycerol are used to build the cell membranes. Your cells can also change some of these fatty acids and glycerol molecules into sugar. These sugars can then provide energy.

You can easily test foods for the presence of oil or fat. Rub a piece of the food on a brown paper bag. If it contains oil or fat, the food will leave a shiny spot on the paper. Try this test with different foods, including meats and nuts. Do they contain oils or fats?

Proteins

Have you eaten any eggs, fish, cheese, or meat today? If so, then you have eaten foods rich in the nutrient protein. Figure 11-7 shows several foods that contain protein. Why are proteins useful to you?

Look in the mirror. Study your hair, your nails, and your skin. Now flex your muscles. All of these body parts are made

Figure 11-7

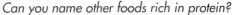

Can you name other foods rich in protein?

of protein. Other organs of your body, including your heart, lungs, and kidneys, contain large amounts of protein. In fact, next to water, protein is the most plentiful substance in your body.

In order for you to grow, your cells must grow and increase in number. Damaged cells must be repaired or replaced. Since many parts of cells are made of protein, your cells cannot grow unless you eat foods that contain protein.

What would happen if you did not eat enough protein? Scientists have performed many experiments to test the importance of protein to the diet. In one experiment, mice were given corn as their only protein food. Corn contains some kinds of protein but lacks many other proteins. After several weeks, the mice became ill and died. Other mice were given a diet containing a

Figure 11-6 Foods Rich in Fats and Oils			
Butter	Margarine	Peanut butter	Sesame oil
Bacon	Mayonnaise	Peanut oil	Soybean oil
Corn oil	Olive oil	Safflower oil	Sunflower seeds

variety of protein foods. They remained healthy. Humans need a variety of protein foods too.

Figure 11-8 lists a variety of foods rich in protein. Notice that most of the foods in this list come from animals. However, many protein-rich foods come from plants, including peanuts, peas, beans, and grains.

Your body must change animal and plant proteins into a form that can be used by your cells. Follow the steps of this process in Figure 11-9. First, your digestive system changes proteins into simpler substances called amino acids. These amino acids then enter the bloodstream, where they are carried to all of your cells.

In the cells, these amino acids are recombined to form human proteins. Your cells use these proteins for growth and repair.

Minerals and Vitamins

Food provides the energy your body needs. However, your body needs food for more than just energy. Foods contain minerals and other substances that are used in the growth and repair of cells.

Minerals   You probably know that milk is important for developing strong bones and teeth. Milk is a rich source of calcium and phosphorus. Calcium and phosphorus are minerals that make your bones and teeth

Figure 11-8 Foods Rich in Protein

Beef	Eggs	Milk	Shrimp
Bologna	Fish	Peanut butter	Tuna
Cheese	Frankfurter	Pork	Turkey
Chicken	Ham	Scallops	Yogurt

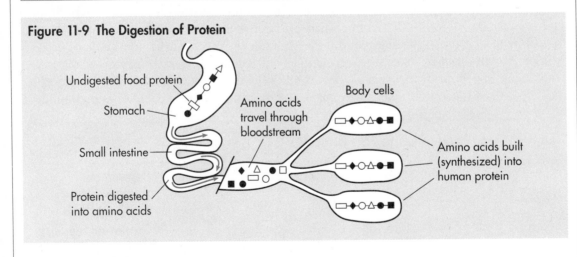

Figure 11-9 The Digestion of Protein

strong and healthy. If your diet lacks these minerals, your bones and teeth will become brittle and weak.

Your body also needs the mineral iron. Red blood cells need iron in order to carry oxygen to all your cells. The cells of people whose blood contains low levels of iron do not receive enough oxygen. As a result, not enough energy will be released from glucose. People who do not have enough iron in their diet often feel tired.

Sometimes, a shortage of a certain mineral can cause disease. For example, a shortage of iodine in the diet causes the thyroid gland to work overtime. The thyroid is located in the neck. When a thyroid is overworked, it becomes very swollen. This swollen gland is called a goiter. Adding iodine to the diet can cure a goiter or prevent one from forming. Salt manufacturers now add iodine to table salt. Seafoods are also an important source of iodine. Figure 11-10 shows foods rich in minerals.

Vitamins Even if you eat enough carbohydrates, fats, proteins, and minerals, you might not have a balanced diet. You also need a variety of **vitamins.** Vitamins are chemicals found in small quantities in certain foods. Many experiments have proven the importance of vitamins in the diet. In one experiment, a scientist gave rats a diet consisting only of carbohydrates, fats, proteins, and minerals. No vitamins were included in this diet. The rats became ill and died. Rats that received a diet that included vitamins stayed healthy and lived longer.

Humans may also become ill if their diet lacks certain vitamins. For example, a lack of vitamin C causes a disease called

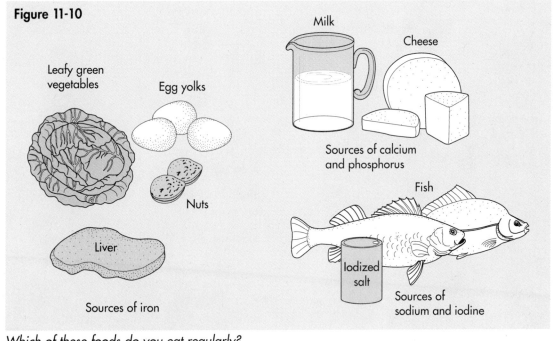

Figure 11-10

Leafy green vegetables

Egg yolks

Nuts

Liver

Sources of iron

Milk

Cheese

Sources of calcium and phosphorus

Fish

Iodized salt

Sources of sodium and iodine

Which of these foods do you eat regularly?

scurvy. About 200 years ago, scurvy was a very common disease. Then people discovered that eating limes and other citrus fruits prevented scurvy. Citrus fruits are rich in vitamin C. Today, scurvy is rare in the United States.

People who do not eat enough of the proper foods may not get enough of certain vitamins. These people suffer from **vitamin deficiency** (di-FISH-un-see). Figure 11-11 lists several vitamins that are important to your health. It also identifies

Figure 11-11 Vitamins Important to Your Health

Vitamin	Foods	Use by body	Deficiency disease
A	Liver, eggs, yellow vegetables and fruits	Healthy skin, eyes, bones, teeth	Night blindness, skin disorders
B_1 (thiamine)	Whole grains, liver, most vegetables	Normal working of heart, energy release from foods	Beriberi, cardio-vascular disorders
B_2 (riboflavin)	Poultry, eggs, cheese, whole grains, green vegetables	Healthy skin, energy release from proteins and fats	Poor vision, early aging, sore mouth and tongue
B_6 (niacin)	Whole grains, leafy vegetables, yeast	Growth, healthy digestive and nervous systems	Pellagra, skin disorders
B_{12}	Liver, cheese, milk, meat	Red blood cells	Anemia
C (ascorbic acid)	Citrus fruits, tomatoes	Healthy bones and teeth, resistance to infection, healthy blood vessels	Scurvy, bleeding gums, sores in mouth
D	Milk, eggs, fish oils, sunlight	Healthy bones and teeth	Rickets, poor teeth
E	Leafy vegetables, whole grains, vegetable oils	Healthy cells	Torn red blood cells, muscular dystrophy
K	Leafy vegetables	Normal blood clotting	Bleeding (hemorrhaging)

foods that contain these vitamins and the symptoms of various vitamin deficiencies. Study this table and compare it with the foods you eat. Decide whether or not you need to add different foods to your diet.

Water

Of all the substances your body needs, water is the most important. As you learned in Chapter 2, life processes cannot take place without water.

Water makes up about two thirds of your body weight. Some of your cells are as much as 90 percent water. Water makes up about 92 percent of the liquid part of your blood. The wastes from your kidneys and sweat glands are mostly water as well.

To stay healthy, you should have at least six to eight glasses of water a day. You do not have to depend entirely upon liquids for your water supply. Much of the food you eat contains water too.

■■■ Section 11-1 Review ■■■

Write the definitions for the following terms in your own words.

1. **nutrition**   2. **oxidation**
3. **nutrient**   4. **vitamin**
5. **Calorie**

Answer these questions.

6. Distinguish between a Calorie and a calorie.
7. What does the digestive system do with the nutrients in your food?
8. What happens during oxidation?

9. Sometimes, people who wish to lose weight eliminate all fats and oils from their diet. Is this a good idea? Why or why not?
10. What is a vitamin deficiency disease? Name three diseases caused by a vitamin deficiency and state the cause of each disease.

11-2 Food Additives

■ *Objectives*

□ *List and describe the functions of food additives.*

□ *Evaluate the advantages and disadvantages of using food additives.*

Have you ever read the fine print of a food label? Read the salad dressing label shown in Figure 11-12. Which ingredients are familiar foods?

Figure 11-12

Ranch-Style
SALAD DRESSING

INGREDIENTS: Water, Soybean oil, Vinegar, High fructose corn syrup, Salt, Garlic, Dried onion, Sugar, Dried red bell peppers, Xanthan gum for consistency, Spice, Lemon juice, Annatto and caramel for color, Calcium disodium EDTA to preserve freshness

Uses of Food Additives

Do you add salt, sugar, pepper, or vinegar to any of the foods you eat? If you do, then you are using a **food additive**. A food additive is a chemical that is added to food to improve it in some way.

The chemicals used as food additives may come from natural or artificial sources. Natural food additives come from plants and animals. For example, sugar comes from sugarcane and corn syrup comes from the corn plant. Carrageenan, an additive that thickens food, comes from seaweed. Gelatin, another food thickener, comes from the bones of animals. Monosodium glutamate, or MSG, is a plant product that makes food taste more flavorful.

Artificial additives are produced in laboratories. Saccharin, for example is an artificial sweetener. EDTA is an artificial **preservative** that prevents foods from losing their natural color and from spoiling.

Types of Food Additives

Food additives are classified into five major groups. Each group has a different purpose. Notice in Figure 11-13 which foods contain which types of additives.

Flavoring Agents Flavoring agents are additives that improve the flavor of foods. Natural flavoring agents include cinnamon, clove, vanillin, and garlic. Artificial flavoring agents are chemicals that resemble the flavorings found naturally in foods.

Coloring Agents Coloring agents include natural and artificial additives. Food manufacturers use them to make foods look good to eat. For example, a green coloring agent is added to mint ice cream to give

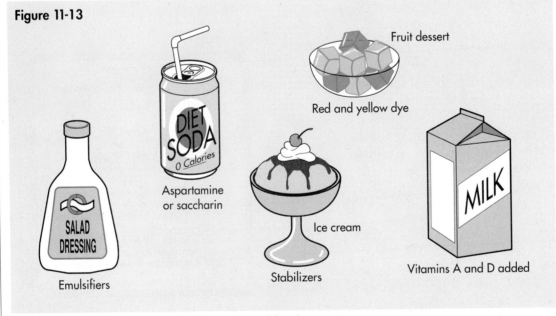

Figure 11-13

Fruit dessert

Red and yellow dye

DIET SODA 0 Calories
Aspartamine or saccharin

SALAD DRESSING
Emulsifiers

Ice cream
Stabilizers

MILK
Vitamins A and D added

Food additives can be found in many packaged foods.

it an attractive look. Other foods to which coloring agents are added include hot dogs, oranges, and margarine.

Preservatives   As stated before, preservatives are food additives that keep foods from spoiling. Some preservatives, such as BHT and BHA, keep fats and oils from turning rancid. Others stop the growth of mold, bacteria, and yeast. Sodium propionate slows the growth of mold in breads. Nitrates prevent bacteria from growing on cured meats and smoked fish.

Texture Agents   Texture agents include emulsifiers, stabilizers, and thickeners. Emulsifiers hold together substances that would ordinarily separate, such as oil and water. Salad dressings usually contain emulsifiers. Stabilizers and thickeners give foods a uniform texture. For example, stabilizers keep bits of chocolate from separating in chocolate milk. They also prevent ice crystals from forming in ice cream. Thickeners make foods look and taste thicker and richer than they really are. Gelatin and carrageenan are food thickeners.

Nutritional Supplements   Some food additives improve the nutritional value of foods or replace nutrients that were lost in food processing. Vitamins and minerals are the most often used nutritional supplements. For example, vitamins A and D are added to milk. Iodine is added to salt. Cereals are enriched with iron and other minerals.

Safety of Food Additives

Are food additives safe? Many are, but some are not. Figure 11-14 lists several food additives. Note which additives should be avoided, which should be used with caution, and which are considered safe.

Figure 11-14 Frequently Used Food Additives

Avoid these	Use these with caution	These are considered safe
Artificial colorings:	Artificial coloring Yellow No. 6	Alginate
Blue Nos. 1 and 2	BHA	Ascorbic acid
Citrus Red No. 2	BHT	Beta carotene
Green No. 3	Caffeine (for adults)	EDTA
Red Nos. 3 and 4	Carrageenan	Gelatin
Yellow No. 5	MSG (for adults)	Gums: arabic, guar,
Caffeine (for children)		locust bean, etc.
MSG (for children)		Lecithin
Saccharin		Mannitol

For example, scientists have found that MSG is harmful to many people. Feeding MSG to infant mice destroyed nerve cells in parts of their brains. Because of these findings, MSG is no longer added to baby foods. Although some adults have an uncomfortable reaction to MSG, scientists are uncertain of the effects of MSG on the health of adults.

Some artificial food dyes have been linked to cancer in laboratory animals. As a result, the Food and Drug Administration has banned these coloring agents from use in foods. These food dyes include red dye numbers 2 and 4, carbon black, and yellow dye numbers 1, 2, 3, and 4.

Many scientists are concerned about the use of many of the additives used in foods. They question the safety of using nitrates and nitrites as preservatives in cured meats and smoked fish. Scientists are also researching the effects of artificial sweeteners like saccharin and aspartamine on human health.

To reduce your intake of unsafe additives, you can follow these guidelines. Eat "real" rather than imitation foods. Fresh fruits, vegetables, and juices do not contain additives. Canned and frozen products do contain additives. Reduce your use of salt and sugar, the two leading additives. In large amounts, salt and sugar are dangerous to your health. Reading food labels carefully will help you reduce the amount of food additives in your diet.

▰▰▰ Section 11-2 Review ▰▰▰

Write the definitions for the following terms in your own words.

1. **food additive**
2. **preservative**

Answer these questions.

3. Why are flavoring agents and coloring agents added to foods?
4. What are preservatives?
5. Name three additives that are known to be dangerous to human health. Why are they dangerous?
6. Why are nutritional supplements added to foods?
7. For lunch, a student ate a hot dog and a diet soft drink. Explain why this lunch is not healthy.

11-3 A Balanced Diet

■ *Objectives*

☐ *Prepare a menu for a daily well-balanced diet.*

☐ *List ways to reduce fat and salt content in your diet.*

You have learned about nutrients and why they are important for good health. Now, take a look at your own eating habits. Are you getting the right amounts of each nutrient from the foods you eat? How can you find out?

Comparing Menus

To help you think about these questions, study Figure 11-15. It shows two different lunch menus. Which lunch would provide more of the nutrients needed for cell growth and repair and energy?

Look at lunch 1. The foods in this lunch contain too many carbohydrates and not enough protein, vitamins, and minerals. On the other hand, lunch 2 is well balanced. It includes all the major nutrients, including carbohydrates, fats, proteins, vitamins, and minerals. Eating well-balanced meals satisfies the needs of your growing body.

Now examine your daily diet. List every food that you ate yesterday. Include breakfast, lunch, dinner, and snacks. After you have made your list, look at the food chart in Figure 11-16. This chart shows the four basic food groups. These food groups are milk, meat, fruits and vegetables, and breads and cereals. The chart also lists some examples of foods from each group. You should eat foods from each group for a well-balanced diet.

Each food group includes foods rich in one or more nutrients. For example, all the foods in the meat group are rich in protein. The foods in the milk group are rich in calcium. Knowing the nutrients in these groups is the first step in selecting a well-balanced diet.

Figure 11-15 Comparing Two Lunches

Lunch 1	Lunch 2
Ham sandwich	Turkey sandwich
Apple pie	Green salad
Ice cream	Apple
Bottle of soda	Glass of skim milk
Candy bar	Raisins and nuts

Figure 11-16 The Four Food Groups

Food group	Food	Nutrient
Milk group	Milk, hard cheese, ice cream, yogurt, cottage cheese	Fat, protein, carbohydrates, minerals
Meat group	Beef, veal, pork, lamb, fish, poultry, eggs, beans, peas, nuts, seeds, peanut butter	Protein, fat
Vegetable-fruit group	Potatoes, oranges, grapefruit, dark green or yellow vegetables, fruits such as apples, pears, peaches	Carbohydrates, some vitamins and minerals
Cereal group	Bread, cereal, cornmeal, grits, macaroni, spaghetti, noodles, rice	Carbohydrates

Interpreting Data from a Graph

Figure 11-17 compares the human diet during the early 1900s with the diet of today. Study the figure, then answer the following questions.

1. Which nutrient provided the greatest source of calories in each time period?

2. Compare the intake of fat in the early 1900s to the intake of fat today.

3. More people die of heart attacks today than ever before. Suggest a reason for this change. Base your answer on what you have learned about nutrition and on the information in Figure 11-17.

Figure 11-17

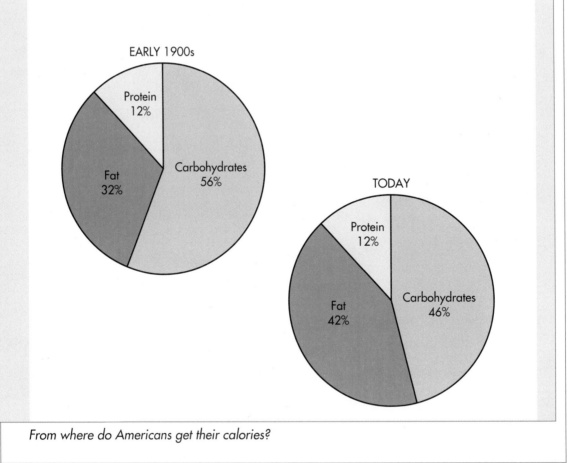

EARLY 1900s

Protein
12%

Fat
32%

Carbohydrates
56%

TODAY

Protein
12%

Fat
42%

Carbohydrates
46%

From where do Americans get their calories?

Now look again at the list of foods that you ate yesterday. Did you eat several servings of foods from each group? If the answer is yes, you are probably eating a well-balanced diet.

Eating to Stay Well

Do illnesses like heart disease, high blood pressure, cancer, and diabetes run in your family? Experiments have shown that people whose diet is high in fat, sugar, salt, and food additives are more likely to get these diseases. On the other hand, you can reduce the risk of getting these diseases by cutting down on these substances.

The menu in Figure 11-18 shows that good-tasting foods can also be nutritious. The menu is very low in fat and low in calories. It is also low in salt. Eating meals such as these can help keep you healthy. The following list also contains a number of suggestions for healthy eating. You may wish to share these suggestions with your family.

1. Flavor your foods with herbs and spices instead of salt.
2. Use jam instead of butter and mustard instead of mayonnaise. Use low-fat yogurt instead of cream and low-fat cottage cheese instead of cream cheese.
3. Trim fat from meat before cooking it. Eat chicken without the skin. Eat more fish.
4. Have fruit and fruit ices for dessert. Limit your intake of rich cakes and ice cream, which are high in fat.
5. Read food labels carefully. Do not buy foods that are high in salt and food additives. Avoid foods with coconut and palm oil, lard, or butter.
6. Avoid foods that are high in sugar.
7. Eat foods with adequate starch and fiber.

▬ Section 11-3 Review ▬

Answer these questions.

1. What is meant by a balanced diet?
2. Make a list of what you ate for dinner last night. Was your meal well balanced? Why or why not?
3. What advice on diet would you give to a friend whose relatives suffer from heart disease? Write a breakfast, lunch, and dinner plan for this friend.

Figure 11-18 A Healthy Menu of Tasty, Low-fat Meals

Breakfast	Lunch	Dinner

Orange juice
Whole-wheat toast
  with butter and jelly
Low-fat milk
	Turkey sandwich on whole-wheat bread
	  with lettuce, tomato, and mustard
	Pea soup
	Fruit
		Chili with corn tortillas
		Cucumber and
		  pepper salad
		Fruit ice

Total calories for the day approx. 1800 Fat content approx. 20%

SCIENCE, TECHNOLOGY, & SOCIETY

From Where Will Food of the Future Come?

Throughout the world, people depend on plants for food energy. However, space for growing crops is limited, especially as world population increases rapidly. In some countries, the population has grown faster than the food supply, resulting in hunger and starvation.

How can technology help feed a hungry world? One way is by developing the best possible seeds. These seeds may grow in many climates and produce more nutritious crops.

Another type of technology, called genetic engineering, is also changing the foods we eat. In genetic engineering, the chromosomes of plants are changed to give the plant desirable characteristics. For example, a genetically engineered "super-tomato" might be large, tasty, and hardy. However, genetic engineering may also introduce harmful characteristics into plants. It may also force out plants that originally grew in an environment.

Another way to grow more food is through hydroponics. Hydroponics involves growing plants indoors in containers of water rather than in a field of soil. You have learned that plants need sun, soil, water, carbon dioxide, and space to grow. How, then, can plants live indoors?

A hydroponic plant such as the one in Figure 11-19 gets its minerals from the water that constantly bathes its roots. Artificial lights take the place of the sun.

Because plants are exposed to light for long periods of time, they are harvested quickly. Lettuce can be ready to eat in less than a month. However, the lights also use a great deal of electricity. They make hydroponics an expensive farming practice.

Follow-up Activity

Imagine you are called in to help two different countries solve the problem of growing more food. One country has plenty of land and the people are farmers. The other country has many crowded cities. Which new ways of growing plants would you recommend to each country? Why?

Figure 11-19 Hydroponic gardening

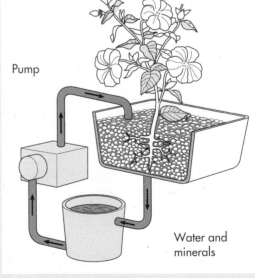

Pump

Water and minerals

CHAPTER REVIEW

KEEPING TRACK

Section 11-1 Nutrients For Energy and Growth

1. The human body needs food for energy and for growth and repair of tissues.
2. Nutrition is the study of food and of eating for good health.
3. The amount of stored energy in foods is measured in Calories.
4. Important nutrients in the human diet include carbohydrates, fats, proteins, minerals, vitamins, and water.

Section 11-2 Food Additives

1. Food additives are chemicals that improve the taste, texture, appearance, or nutrient value of foods, or keep foods from spoiling.
2. Some food additives are dangerous to human health and should be avoided.

Section 11-3 A Balanced Diet

1. The human diet should include foods from each of the four basic food groups. These groups include milk, meat, fruits and vegetables, and breads and cereals.
2. Eating the right amounts and kinds of foods is important for good health.

BUILDING VOCABULARY

Write the word from the list that best completes each sentence.

fats, nutrients, glycerol, minerals, simple, salt, food groups, complex, fatty acids, vitamin deficiency

The ___1___ in foods provide energy and are used for cell growth and repair. The digestive system breaks down ___2___ carbohydrates into ___3___ carbohydrates such as glucose. ___4___ are the nutrients that provide the greatest amount of energy. These nutrients are broken down into two substances, ___5___ and ___6___. Calcium and iron are examples of nutrients called ___7___. Diseases such as scurvy result from a ___8___. If some members of a family have high blood pressure, the family members should limit their intake of ___9___. When planning their diet, people should eat foods from the four ___10___.

SUMMARIZING

If the statement is true, write *true*. If the statement is false, change the *italicized* term to make the statement true.

1. Your body requires *energy* to carry on its life processes.
2. The study of food and how it makes you healthy is called *botany*.
3. The unit of measure of the amount of heat given off when a food is burned is a *calorie*.
4. Carbohydrates include sugars and *proteins*.
5. An essential nutrient for repair in the body is *starch*.
6. Scurvy is a disease caused by a *vitamin deficiency*.
7. Food additives called *nutritional supplements* make foods stay fresh longer.
8. The mineral *iron* is now added to table salt.

INTERPRETING INFORMATION

Use Figure 11-20 to answer the following questions.

1. Which activities require the fewest calories?
2. If you weighed 100 pounds, how many Calories would you burn off in two hours of studying?
3. How do the number of calories used in one hour of bicycling compare to the number of calories used for walking?

THINK AND DISCUSS

Use the section number in parentheses to help you find each answer. Write your answers in complete sentences.

1. Name five important nutrients. Explain why each one is important. (11-1)

2. Milk contains proteins, fat, carbohydrates, and minerals. Why might nutritionists refer to milk as a "perfect" food? (11-1)
3. Why would a doctor put a patient on a high-protein diet after the patient has undergone surgery? (11-2)
4. List five types of food additives. Explain the use of each type of additive. (11-2)
5. It has been said that good nutrition is a balancing act. Make a list of the groups of foods that a person should eat each day for a well-balanced diet. (11-3)

GOING FURTHER

1. Scientists think that too much saturated fat and cholesterol in the diet is dangerous to human health. Use library books to learn about these substances and their negative effects. Make a list of foods that are rich in these substances.

Figure 11-20 Amount of Calories Needed for Some Activities

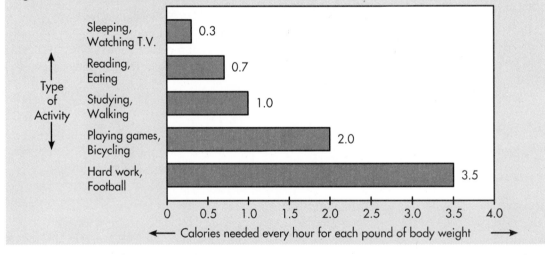

2. Some pesticides used on fruits and vegetables may endanger human health. Use the library to research the pesticides alar and captan. How dangerous are they? Should children be allowed to eat fruits and vegetables sprayed with these pesticides?

3. During photosynthesis, plants use carbon dioxide and release oxygen. Therefore, in an undisturbed environment, a balance between oxygen and carbon dioxide exists.
   a. Suppose that, as a result of an oil spill, many ocean plants are destroyed. What effect will this oil spill have on the balance of carbon dioxide and oxygen in the environment? Explain your answer.
   b. With expansion of cities comes a loss of valuable farmland. What effect will this have on the amount of oxygen released into the atmosphere by plants? Explain your answer.

COMPETENCY REVIEW

1. Which of the following is not a nutrient?
   a. sugar
   b. water
   c. iron
   d. energy

2. The nutrients that provide most of our energy needs are
   a. carbohydrates and fats.
   b. fats and proteins.
   c. proteins and minerals.
   d. minerals and carbohydrates.

3. When you drink a glass of milk, you are part of which food chain?
   a. grass → human → cow
   b. grass → cow → human
   c. human → cow → grass
   d. cow → grass → human

4. A person's energy needs are generally greatest between the ages of
   a. 1 and 5.
   b. 6 and 11.
   c. 12 and 17.
   d. 18 and 23.

5. What are the main nutrients in a turkey sandwich on whole grain bread?
   a. glucose and calcium
   b. fat and minerals
   c. protein and carbohydrates
   d. vitamin C and iron

6. A balanced diet is best represented by which of the following groups?
   a. cake, hot dog, french fries, orange drink
   b. candy, potato chips, hamburger, coffee
   c. cereal, tuna fish, carrots, milk
   d. soda, pretzels, fried chicken, cookies

7. Which is an important mineral found in milk?
   a. iron
   b. salt
   c. iodine
   d. calcium

8. It is recommended that fresh fruits and vegetables be washed thoroughly before they are eaten so as to remove
   a. salts.
   b. MSG.
   c. pesticides.
   d. artificial colors.

9. One reason for the shortage of nutritious food throughout the world is
   a. overpopulation.
   b. additives.
   c. oxidation.
   d. all of these.

10. Why are preservatives used in foods?
    a. to increase the number of Calories
    b. to improve the taste
    c. to make the food stay fresh longer
    d. to keep ingredients from separating

CHAPTER 12

YOUR DIGESTIVE SYSTEM

Have you tried any new foods lately? At an international food fair, you can sample delicious foods from all over the world. You can enjoy the aroma of fried rice from China and filled tacos from Mexico. You might taste African dishes of meat and peanuts in spicy sauce. Your hands could get sticky from a Greek dessert rich with nuts and honey. Of course, you could try a slice of pizza, a favorite of many Americans.

Eating your way through a street fair can be a treat. The variety of foods to choose from may seem endless. Yet, no matter how different the foods look and taste, they still break down into nutrients. To stay healthy, all people need nutrients such as those shown in Figure 12-1.

How do these nutrients enter the cells of your body? After you chew a bite of pizza, can the cells of your cheek and tongue absorb the food? No, your body must first process the food you chew. The molecules that make up pizza dough, cheese, and tomato sauce are too large for your cells to use. Your body must break down these large molecules into smaller and smaller ones. The small molecules can travel through your bloodstream and nourish your cells.

12-1 The Role of the Digestive System

■ *Objectives*
☐ *Explain the function of the digestive system.*
☐ *Label a diagram of the digestive system.*

The process of digestion consists of two parts. The first part is called **physical digestion**. During physical digestion, food is broken into smaller pieces. Your teeth physically digest food when you chew.

Figure 12-1

Scientists can analyze the nutrients found in pizza such as carbohydrates, proteins, and fats.

What Foods Are Soluble in Water?

Process Skills observing

Materials four 150-milliliter beakers, water, starch, dextrose, two test tubes, iodine, Benedict's solution, hot water bath, two funnels, filter paper

Are carbohydrates soluble in water? In this activity, you will test the solubility of two carbohydrates, starch and a simple sugar called dextrose.

Procedure

1. Mix five grams of starch in a beaker containing 100 milliliters of water. Mix five grams of dextrose in another 100 milliliters of water. Stir both mixtures well.
2. Pour a small amount of the starch mixture into a test tube. Test for the presence of starch by adding two drops of iodine. If starch is present, the iodine will turn blue-black.
3. Pour a small amount of the sugar mixture into another test tube. Test for the presence of sugar by adding ten drops of Benedict's solution. Place in a hot water bath. If sugar is present, the solution will turn brick red.
4. Set up two funnels and filter some of each mixture into beakers A and B. Follow the procedure shown in Figure 12-2. The liquid that passes through the funnel into the beaker is called the filtrate.
5. Test filtrate A for the presence of starch. Test filtrate B for the presence of sugar.

Conclusions

6. Which is soluble in water, starch or dextrose? How do you know?

Figure 12-2

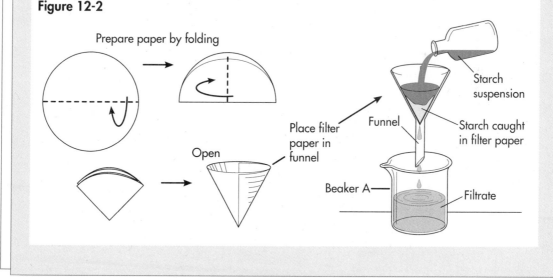

Prepare paper by folding

Open

Place filter paper in funnel

Funnel

Starch suspension

Starch caught in filter paper

Beaker A

Filtrate

The small pieces of chewed-up food have more surface areas on which digestive juices can work.

During **chemical digestion**, the nutrients in foods are changed into smaller molecules that can dissolve in water. Molecules that can dissolve in water are **soluble** molecules. Only soluble molecules can pass through cell membranes and be absorbed into your bloodstream.

Most food molecules, however, are not soluble. These **insoluble** molecules do not dissolve in water and cannot pass through cell membranes. During digestion insoluble molecules are broken down into soluble molecules so that they can enter cells.

The organs of your **digestive system** break food down into nutrients your cells can use. Food passes through several organs as it is digested. Other organs, called **accessory organs,** do not directly digest food. They produce chemicals that are used in digestion. Refer to Figure 12-3 as you read about the organs of the digestive system in the sections that follow.

Section 12-1 Review

Write the definitions for the following terms in your own words.

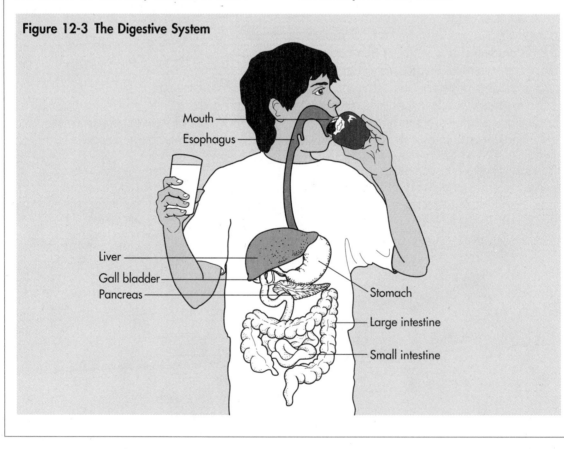

Figure 12-3 The Digestive System

Mouth

Esophagus

Liver

Gall bladder

Pancreas

Stomach

Large intestine

Small intestine

1. **physical digestion**
2. **chemical digestion**
3. **digestive system**
4. **accessory organ**

Answer these questions.

5. What is the role of the digestive system?
6. Why is physical digestion considered to be a preparation for chemical digestion?
7. Distinguish between soluble and insoluble molecules.

12-2 Digestion in the Mouth

■ *Objective*
☐ *Describe the role of the mouth in digesting food.*

The food you eat enters your body through your **mouth**. Digestion begins in the mouth when you chew food. Your teeth physically digest food by breaking it into small pieces.

While you chew, **saliva** mixes with your food. Saliva is a mixture of juices produced by the **salivary glands**. Find the salivary glands in Fig 12-4. Small tubes carry saliva

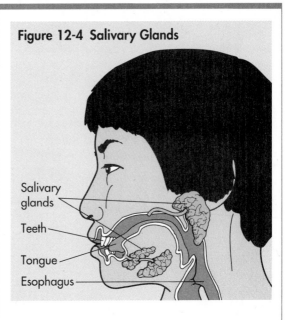

Figure 12-4 Salivary Glands

Salivary glands
Teeth
Tongue
Esophagus

from the salivary glands to your mouth. When your mouth waters, your salivary glands are at work. Saliva moistens food and makes it easier to swallow.

In addition, an enzyme in saliva begins to break down insoluble starch molecules into soluble sugar molecules. Recall that an enzyme causes or speeds up chemical reactions. Enzymes control many of the chemical reactions that take place during digestion. Figure 12-5 shows the function of saliva in digesting a slice of bread.

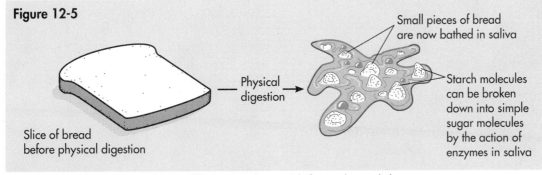

Figure 12-5

Small pieces of bread are now bathed in saliva

Physical digestion

Starch molecules can be broken down into simple sugar molecules by the action of enzymes in saliva

Slice of bread before physical digestion

Notice how saliva acts on the smaller pieces that result from physical digestion.

Predicting

A student sprinkles a few grains of starch into a drop of water on a microscope slide. She then adds two drops of iodine solution. The starch grains turn a blue-black color.

Then the student adds a bit of saliva to the mixture of starch, water, and iodine on the microscope slide. Within half an hour, the grains of starch lose their black color and disappear.

1. Explain why the color change takes place.
2. Why do the starch grains disappear?
3. Predict what would happen if the student heated and tested the mixture with Benedict's solution. Explain your prediction.

Section 12-2 Review

Write the definitions for the following terms in your own words.

1. **mouth**
2. **saliva**
3. **salivary gland**

Answer these questions.

4. Name the structures in the mouth that are involved in digestion.
5. What role do enzymes play in digestion?

6. Does saliva function in physical digestion, chemical digestion, or both? Explain your answer.

12-3 Digestion in the Stomach

■ *Objective*

☐ *Describe the role of the stomach in digesting food.*

After the food is chewed and moistened in your mouth, it passes down a tube at the back of your throat. This tube is called the **esophagus**. To feel the movement of the muscles in your esophagus, swallow two or three times. This muscle movement is called **peristalsis** (per-uh-STAHL-sus). As Figure 12-6 shows, peristalsis is a series of rhythmic, wavelike actions that move food along the esophagus.

Food moves down the esophagus to a pouchlike organ called the **stomach.** In your stomach, peristalsis continues to break down food physically and soften it. Peristalsis also mixes food with secretions called **gastric juice**.

Gastric juice is produced in small gastric glands located in the stomach wall. Find the gastric glands in Figure 12-7. Gastric juice is a mixture of several chemicals that help digest different foods. One of these chemicals, hydrochloric acid, must be present for other chemicals to do their job.

Gastric juice also contains an enzyme called **pepsin.** As the stomach gives off hydrochloric acid, pepsin breaks down proteins in the foods you have eaten. Even

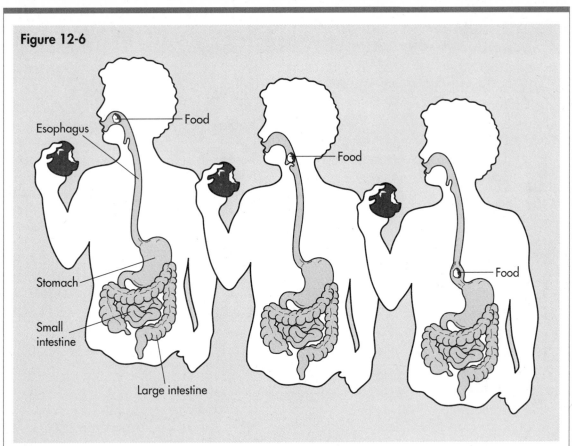

Figure 12-6

Esophagus

Food

Food

Food

Stomach

Small
intestine

Large intestine

Peristalsis moves food along the esophagus into the stomach.

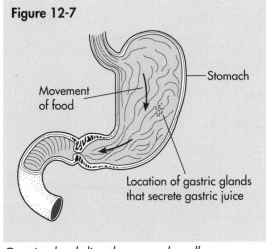

Figure 12-7

Movement
of food

Stomach

Location of gastric glands
that secrete gastric juice

Gastric glands line the stomach wall.

after passing through the stomach, however, food is not yet ready to enter your cells. Food must still be broken down to even simpler forms.

The process of digestion described is how the digestive system typically works. However, there are some conditions that can slow down or disrupt the digestive process. One common digestive problem is an upset known as **indigestion.** Indigestion happens when spoiled food irritates the lining of the stomach or small intestine. Eating too much food at one time can also produce indigestion.

What Kind of Digestion Takes Place in the Stomach?

Process Skills *interpreting observations, using a control*

Materials hard-cooked egg white, four test tubes, wax pencil, water, test tube rack, pepsin, 0.5 percent hydrochloric acid solution, incubator

The white of an egg contains a protein called albumen. In this activity, you will find out what substances must react with protein for digestion to occur.

Procedure

1. Place two pea-sized pieces of hard-cooked egg white into each of four test tubes.
2. Use a wax pencil to number the test tubes one, two, three, and four. Add two centimeters of water to each test tube. Place test tube one in a test tube rack.
3. To test tube two add a pinch of pepsin. Place the test tube in the test tube rack.
4. To test tube three add a small amount of 0.5 percent hydrochloric acid solution. **Caution** Use acid according to teacher's directions.
5. To test tube four add both a pinch of pepsin and a small amount of 0.5 percent hydrochloric acid solution. Place both test tubes in the test tube rack.
6. Place the test tube rack in a warm spot, preferably in an incubator. Examine the test tubes after 24 hours. Examine the test tubes again several days later.
7. Construct a data table in which you record the changes you observe in each test tube.

Conclusions

8. In which test tube was the egg white broken down, or digested, most completely? Explain your results.
9. What was the control in this experiment.
10. The contents of which test tube would most closely match the contents of your stomach? Why?

■■■ Section 12-3 Review ■■■

Write the definitions for the following terms in your own words.

1. **esophagus**   2. **peristalsis**
3. **stomach**   4. **indigestion**

Answer these questions.

5. How does food move from your mouth to your stomach?
6. Compare physical and chemical digestion in the stomach.
7. How are gastric juices and saliva similar?

12-4 Digestion in the Small Intestine

■ *Objectives*

☐ *Describe the role of the small intestine in digesting food.*

☐ *Explain the role of the accessory organs in digestion.*

As food continues its path through the digestive system, it moves from the stomach to the **small intestine.** Partly digested food enters the small intestine through a valve at the lower end of the stomach. The small intestine is a coiled tube about seven meters long, located below your stomach. Look back at Figure 12-3, which shows the digestive system, to find the small intestine.

Completion of Digestion

Remember that enzymes in your mouth change some starches to sugar. Recall, too, that proteins are partially digested in the stomach. Digestion is completed in your small intestine.

Muscles in the walls of the small intestine squeeze and push food along. Tiny glands in the wall of your small intestine produce intestinal juices. As these juices mix with the food, they help complete the digestion of sugars, fats, and proteins.

The accessory organs produce substances that aid in digestion. Find the **pancreas** in Figure 12-8. This organ produces a liquid called pancreatic juice. Pancreatic juice flows from the pancreas to the small intestine. Pancreatic juice completes the digestion of sugars and starches. It also digests proteins and fats.

Find the **liver** and **gall bladder** in Figure 12-8. The liver produces a chemical called **bile**. The gall bladder stores bile until it is needed. The bile then flows through a duct into the small intestine. Bile helps **emulsify** (ee-MUHL-si-fy), or break apart, large pieces of fat into tiny particles. The small pieces of fat are then digested chemically in the small intestine by pancreatic juices.

Figure 12-8

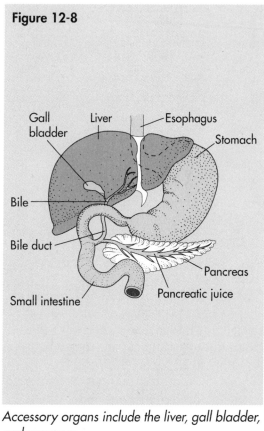

Accessory organs include the liver, gall bladder, and pancreas.

By the time food passes through the small intestine, digestion is nearly complete. Starches, sugars, proteins, and fats have been broken down into molecules that are soluble in water. Figure 12-9 summarizes the processes that take place during chemical digestion.

Figure 12-9 Some Examples of Chemical Digestion

Nutrient	Digestive juice	Where digestion occurs	End product
Starch	Saliva Pancreatic and intestinal juices	Mouth Small intestine	Simple sugars
Protein	Gastric, pancreatic, and intestinal juices	Stomach and small intestine	Amino acids
Fat	Pancreatic and intestinal juices	Small intestine	Fatty acids, glycerol

Absorption of Digested Food

The soluble end products of digestion are able to enter your bloodstream. This process is known as **absorption**. Water in your blood dissolves and carries these digested nutrients to all parts of your body. Even as you read, your bloodstream is carrying nutrients throughout your body.

How are digested foods in the small intestine absorbed by your blood? The walls inside your small intestine are lined with many microscopic, fingerlike bumps called **villi** [VIL-eye]. The singular term is *villus*. Villi are adapted to absorb food into the bloodstream.

Look at the villi in Figure 12-10. Each villus is covered by a thin, moist layer of cells. Within each villus are many tiny blood vessels. Digested food passes through the villus wall into these blood vessels. As the digested food passes through, it is absorbed and dissolved into the blood.

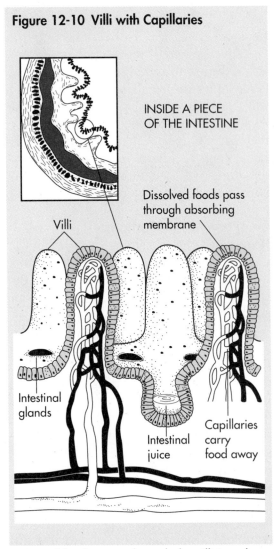

Figure 12-10 Villi with Capillaries

INSIDE A PIECE OF THE INTESTINE

Villi

Dissolved foods pass through absorbing membrane

Intestinal glands

Intestinal juice

Capillaries carry food away

Digested food passes through the villi into the capillaries.

Write the definitions for the following terms in your own words.

1. **pancreas**
2. **liver**
3. **gall bladder**
4. **bile**
5. **absorption**

Answer these questions.

6. Describe digestion in the small intestine.
7. List the end products of digestion.
8. What is the role of the villi in digestion?

12-5 The Large Intestine

■ *Objectives*
☐ *Describe the role of the large intestine in digesting food.*
☐ *Distinguish between indigestible and undigested foods.*

Some of the foods that enter the small intestine cannot be digested and absorbed into the bloodstream. These foods are called **indigestible** foods, or **roughage**. Examples of indigestible foods include the tough fibers of vegetables and tiny bits of cartilage from meat. In addition, some digestible foods may not be completely digested in the small intestine. These foods are called **undigested** foods.

Undigested and indigestible foods make up your body's solid wastes. These materials pass from the small intestine into the large intestine. The large intestine is only about 1.5 meters long, but it is much larger in diameter than the small intestine. Trace the path of the large intestine in Fig. 12-3. Notice that it goes up one side toward the stomach, across the body, and down the other side.

The walls of the large intestine absorb water from the solid wastes. The water passes into the bloodstream. The waste materials that remain in the large intestine form **fecal material**. The opening at the end of the large intestine is called the anus. Fecal material passes out of the body through the anus.

Several species of bacteria live in the large intestine. These bacteria live off your body's undigested matter. The bacteria make vitamins such as B$_{12}$ and K. These vitamins are necessary for your good health.

■■ **Section 12-5 Review** ■■

Write the definitions for the following terms in your own words.

1. **indigestible**
2. **roughage**
3. **fecal material**

Answer these questions.

4. Distinguish between undigested and indigestible foods.
5. What happens in the large intestine?
6. How do humans and the bacteria that live in their large intestines benefit each other?

SCIENCE, TECHNOLOGY, & SOCIETY

Environmental Hazards and Human Health

Many harmful substances find their way from the environment into the human digestive system. One group of harmful substances are chemicals called insecticides. Farmers use insecticides to destroy insects that damage food crops.

If not properly washed, raw fruits and vegetables may remain covered with insecticides. If a person eats this food, the insecticide will pass through the digestive system and eventually be absorbed into the bloodstream. The bloodstream will carry the insecticide to the cells of the body. Some insecticides may change these normal cells into cancer cells.

Lead was once used in many house paints. Many children, however, developed lead poisoning by eating chips of paint containing lead. Lead poisoning can cause blood disorders, severe intestinal pains, nerve damage, and even death. Today it is illegal to use lead in paints.

Even drinking water may contain poisonous chemicals from industrial waste dumps. Drinking this contaminated water may result in cancer, birth defects, and other disorders. Governments have passed laws against dumping harmful chemicals into public water supplies. They have also banned the use of dangerous insecticides and house paint containing lead. Other harmful substances in the environment may not yet be identified, however. Scientists continue to do research to test the safety of our food and water supplies.

Follow-up Activity

Suppose you are a farmer whose crops are threatened by insect damage. You depend on the money you earn from selling your crops. You are also concerned, however, about keeping the environment safe. In a class discussion, talk about possible solutions to this problem. Which solution is best for your farm and for the environment?

Figure 12-11 The Health Effects of Some Pesticides

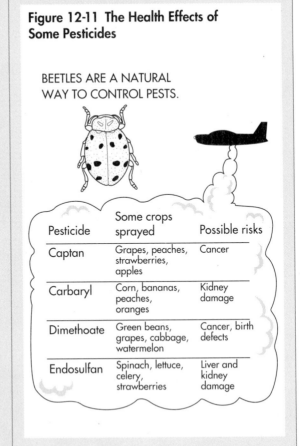

BEETLES ARE A NATURAL WAY TO CONTROL PESTS.

Pesticide	Some crops sprayed	Possible risks
Captan	Grapes, peaches, strawberries, apples	Cancer
Carbaryl	Corn, bananas, peaches, oranges	Kidney damage
Dimethoate	Green beans, grapes, cabbage, watermelon	Cancer, birth defects
Endosulfan	Spinach, lettuce, celery, strawberries	Liver and kidney damage

CHAPTER REVIEW

Section 12-1 The Role of the Digestive System

1. Some nutrients are made of very large molecules that must be changed to smaller molecules that can be used by cells.
2. The digestive system breaks down food physically and chemically. Digested food is absorbed into the bloodstream.

Section 12-2 Digestion in the Mouth

1. Digestion begins in the mouth. The teeth physically digest food. This action provides a greater surface area on which digestive juices can act.
2. Saliva changes starch molecules into soluble sugar molecules.

Section 12-3 Digestion in the Stomach

1. As a result of peristalsis, food moves along the esophagus into the stomach.
2. Gastric glands in the wall of the stomach secrete gastric juice, which chemically digests protein.

Section 12-4 Digestion in the Small Intestine

1. Juices produced in the small intestine help complete the digestion of sugars, fats, and proteins.
2. Chemicals from the liver and pancreas assist in chemical digestion in the small intestine.
3. The end products of digestion are absorbed into tiny blood vessels located in the villi, which line the small intestine.

Section 12-5 The Large Intestine

1. Indigestible and undigested materials make up fecal material, which moves through the large intestine and is eliminated by the body.
2. Water is absorbed from the fecal material. Fecal material passes out of the body through the anus.

BUILDING VOCABULARY

Write the term from the list that best matches each description.

small intestine, large intestine, peristalsis, villi, mouth, emulsify

1. organ where digestion begins
2. process that moves food along in the esophagus
3. what bile does to large pieces of fat
4. organ in which most digestion occurs
5. structures in the small intestine where digested food is absorbed into the bloodstream
6. organ in which solid wastes form

Explain the difference between the terms in each pair.

7. soluble molecule, insoluble molecule
8. physical digestion, chemical digestion
9. small intestine, large intestine
10. hydrochloric acid, pepsin
11. saliva, gastric juice
12. undigested material, indigestible material

CHAPTER REVIEW

SUMMARIZING

Write the missing term for each sentence.

1. The ___ is a digestive organ that measures about seven meters in length.
2. Chemical digestion of protein begins in the ___.
3. A substance called ___, produced by the liver, helps to physically digest large chunks of fat.
4. The end products of digestion can be absorbed into the bloodstream because they are ___ in water.
5. Food that the body cannot digest is known as indigestible material, or ___.
6. A chemical used to test for the presence of sugar in food is called ___.
7. ___ digestion takes place when you chew food.
8. Iodine is used to test for the presence of ___.
9. Most digestion takes place in the ___.
10. Food moves through the digestive system by the process of ___.

INTERPRETING INFORMATION

A science teacher wanted to demonstrate the digestion of various foods. She placed three different foods into three test tubes, as shown in Figure 12-12. Then she added either bile, gastric juice, or saliva to each test tube. Study the results of her experiment and then answer the following questions.

1. To which test tube was bile added?
2. To which test tube was saliva added?

3. To which tube was gastric juice added?
4. Explain your answers to questions 1–3.

Figure 12-12

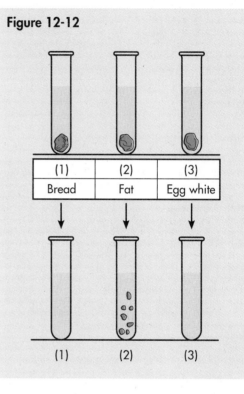

THINK AND DISCUSS

Use the section number in parentheses to help you find each answer. Write your answers in complete sentences.

1. Why must insoluble nutrients be digested into soluble ones? (12-1)
2. Why is it an advantage to chew your food before swallowing it? (12-2)
3. Compare the process of digestion in the mouth and stomach. What is similar about

digestion in these two organs? What is different? (12-3)

4. What is similar about the salivary glands, gastric glands, and intestinal glands? (12-4)

5. The large intestine is much shorter than the small intestine, but is named the large intestine. Why? (12-5)

GOING FURTHER

How do patients who have had their gall bladder removed have to change their diet? Use library books to find the answer.

COMPETENCY REVIEW

Base your answers to questions 1 and 2 on Figure 12-13.

Figure 12-13

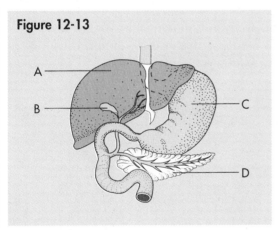

1. Pancreatic juice is produced in this organ.
   a. A   b. B
   c. C   d. D

2. Bile is stored in this organ.
   a. A   b. B
   c. C   d. D

3. An organ in which chemical digestion does not take place is the
   a. mouth.
   b. stomach.
   c. small intestine.
   d. large intestine.

4. Which organ produces hydrochloric acid?
   a. mouth   b. esophagus
   c. stomach   d. large intestine

5. The end products of digestion enter blood vessels in the
   a. pancreas.   b. mouth.
   c. villi.   d. esophagus.

6. Salivary glands, gastric glands, and intestinal glands all produce chemicals called
   a. hormones.   b. sugars.
   c. starches.   d. enzymes.

7. Identify the path food follows through your body.
   a. stomach, esophagus, small intestine, large intestine
   b. mouth, esophagus, stomach, small intestine
   c. small intestine, esophagus, large intestine, stomach
   d. mouth, esophagus, large intestine, small intestine

8. A person who had most of his stomach surgically removed would later have difficulty digesting
   a. sugar.   b. starch.
   c. fats.   d. proteins.

9. Gastric juice is to protein as saliva is to
   a. fat.   b. oil.
   c. starch.   d. enzymes.

CHAPTER 13

YOUR CIRCULATORY SYSTEM

A siren wails during the middle of the night. An ambulance stops at the entrance of a hospital emergency room. A rescue team brings in an accident victim on a stretcher. He has several injuries and has lost a large amount of blood. Doctors and nurses check his heartbeat, as shown in Figure 13-1, and hook him up to equipment that will give him the blood he needs to stay alive.

What is this life-saving liquid called blood? People have long known that blood is necessary for life. The presence of a heartbeat is the first sign that someone is alive. For many years, however, people did not really know what blood was and how it kept people alive. They believed that blood had special powers. Good health was associated with "good blood" and sickness with "bad blood."

Today, the heart and blood are much less mysterious subjects. We know how the heart works and what blood is made of. In this chapter you will learn about how these organs and tissues keep you alive.

13-1 Absorption and Transport

■ *Objectives*

☐ *Explain how soluble molecules are absorbed into the bloodstream.*

☐ *Describe the process of diffusion.*

☐ *Explain the role of the circulatory system.*

You have learned that your bloodstream carries oxygen and nutrients to all the cells of your body. How do important materials such as the end products of digestion

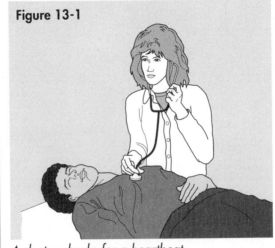

Figure 13-1

A doctor checks for a heartbeat.

pass into your bloodstream? How are they carried to all the cells of your body? The organs that work to transport these materials throughout your body make up the **circulatory system** (SUR-kyuh-luh-tohr-ee).

Your circulatory system carries out two important activities. One activity is absorption. Recall from Chapter 12 that during absorption, the end products of digestion pass from the small intestine through cell membranes into the bloodstream. Absorption also occurs as oxygen passes from the lungs through cell membranes into the bloodstream.

The other activity of the circulatory system is transport. **Transport** is the process by which nutrients and oxygen are carried to every cell in your body. In addition, wastes such as salts and carbon dioxide are transported out of your cells. Figure 13-2 shows how nutrients, gases, and wastes move in and out of cells.

Diffusion

In order for materials to be absorbed and circulated in your body, they must move. Molecules move by a type of energy called **kinetic energy** (kuh-NET-ik). Kinetic

energy keeps molecules moving constantly. The more kinetic energy molecules have, the faster they move.

You can observe the kinetic energy of molecules in action. Simply add a few drops of food coloring to a glass of water. The food coloring will spread evenly throughout the water in the glass, as shown in Figure 13-3. The molecules of

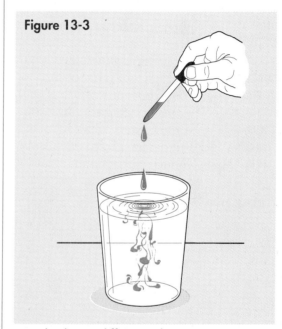

Figure 13-3

Food coloring diffuses in the water.

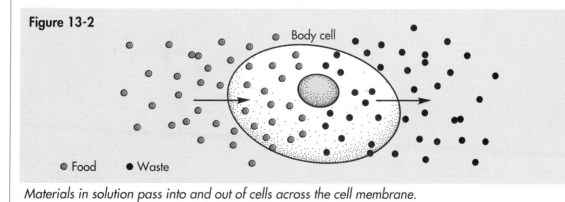

Figure 13-2

Body cell

● Food ● Waste

Materials in solution pass into and out of cells across the cell membrane.

food coloring move from the area containing many molecules to an area containing few molecules. This movement is called **diffusion** (dif-YOO-zhun).

Figure 13-4 demonstrates how diffusion works. In the first picture, a sugar cube has been dropped into water. The cube contains many sugar molecules. The water contains none. The sugar molecules leave the sugar cube, dissolve in the water, and then diffuse into the spaces between the water molecules.

Diffusion enables the molecules your body needs to reach all your cells. For instance, glucose is one of the end products of digestion. Several hours after you eat a large meal, your small intestine contains large numbers of glucose molecules. Your bloodstream contains fewer

glucose molecules. The glucose molecules therefore diffuse from the small intestine into the bloodstream.

To do so, however, glucose molecules must first move through the cell membranes. They begin by crossing the cell membranes of the cells that make up the wall of your small intestine. Then they diffuse across the wall of the blood vessels and into your bloodstream. How do glucose and other molecules pass through cell membranes? To understand how this movement takes place, you need to learn about some of the properties of the cell membrane.

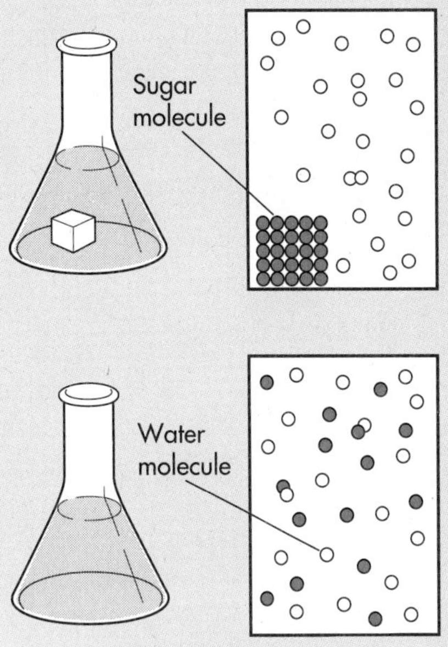

The Cell Membrane

A cell membrane surrounds each of your cells. As shown in Figure 13-5, the cell membrane is made of fat and protein molecules. The combination of fat and protein gives the cell membrane special characteristics. The molecules work together to

Figure 13-4

Figure 13-5

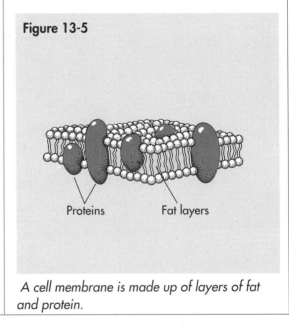

A cell membrane is made up of layers of fat and protein.

How Can You Observe Diffusion through a Membrane?

Process Skills *making a model, drawing a hypothesis*

Materials bottle of perfume, test tube, rubber band, nonwaterproof cellophane membrane, beaker, starch suspension, iodine solution

Open a bottle of perfume. Stand close to it. Soon you will detect the smell of perfume in the air. How soon after you opened the bottle did you smell the perfume in the air? How far from the bottle did you stand?

Diffusion takes place through the air. You know that diffusion also takes place in living cells. Small molecules can diffuse through a living cell membrane but large molecules cannot. You can observe diffusion in action by using a piece of nonwaterproof cellophane as a model of a cell membrane.

Procedure

1. Fill a test tube with a starch suspension. Use a rubber band to fasten a nonwaterproof cellophane membrane over the open end of the test tube, as shown in Figure 13-6.
2. Turn the test tube over and place it into a beaker containing an iodine solution. Observe what happens to the starch suspension.

Conclusions

3. Why did the starch suspension turn blue-black?

4. What process caused this color change?
5. Did starch molecules move from the test tube through the cellophane or did iodine move into the test tube? Explain your answer.

Figure 13-6

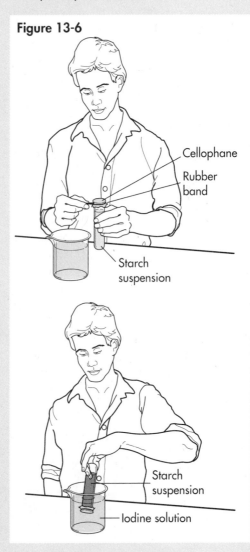

Cellophane

Rubber band

Starch suspension

Starch suspension

Iodine solution

form a barrier between the inside and outside of the cell. Substances cross the cell membrane by moving through spaces between the fat and protein molecules.

As you learned in Chapter 3, a cell membrane is a semipermeable membrane. Some materials can permeate, or pass through, a semipermeable membrane, and others cannot. Only water-soluble molecules can pass through a cell membrane. Water-soluble molecules include oxygen, carbon dioxide, and the end products of digestion. Larger insoluble molecules such as proteins and starch cannot pass through the cell membrane. These insoluble molecules must first be chemically digested.

The process by which water diffuses across the cell membrane is called **osmosis** (ahs-MOH-sus). Osmosis is one of the most important processes that take place in living things. Cells consist mostly of water. The materials needed for life processes constantly move through this water and across cell membranes.

Look at the arrows in Figure 13-7. They show that simple sugar molecules move

Figure 13-7

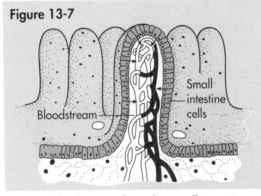

Bloodstream

Small intestine cells

Digested food moves from the small intestine into the bloodstream.

from the small intestine through semipermeable cell membranes into the bloodstream. Based on what you know about diffusion, can you explain why the sugar molecules travel in that direction?

Section 13-1 Review

Write the definitions for the following terms in your own words.

1. **circulatory system**
2. **kinetic energy**
3. **diffusion**
4. **osmosis**

Answer these questions.

5. By what process do molecules pass through a semipermeable cell membrane?
6. What kind of molecules can pass through the cell membrane? What kind of molecules cannot pass through the cell membrane?
7. Distinguish between diffusion and osmosis.
8. Explain how a molecule of digested food enters the bloodstream.

13-2 The Heart and Circulation

■ *Objectives*

☐ *List the parts of the circulatory system.*

☐ *Trace the flow of blood through the body.*

☐ *Explain the role of valves in preventing the backward flow of blood.*

Digested material from the small intestine enters your bloodstream. The bloodstream transports digested materials to all the cells of your body. The bloodstream also transports oxygen from your lungs to all your cells. Finally, waste products formed in your cells enter the bloodstream. The bloodstream transports wastes to organs like your kidneys and your lungs. Your kidneys and lungs eliminate these waste products from your body. In this section, you will learn how the circulatory system transports materials throughout your body.

Your Heart at Work

The **heart** is a pump made of a kind of muscle called cardiac muscle. The heart sends blood through your blood vessels to all your cells. Did you ever feel your heart pound after you climbed a flight of stairs? Later, as you rested, your heartbeat returned to normal.

Most of the time, you are not aware of your heartbeat. You only notice it when your heart beats quickly. Your heart beats constantly, however, day and night.

Look at the heart in Figure 13-8. The heart is slightly larger than a fist and weighs about 300 grams. The heart is located in the center of your chest cavity, just under your breastbone. Its thick, strong muscles pump blood to every part of your body. Your heart pumps about 70 times a minute, over 100,000 times a day. How many times does it pump in a month, in a year?

During a medical checkup, your doctor listens to your heart with an instrument called a stethoscope. Gently place the fingers of your right hand on the inside of

Figure 13-8

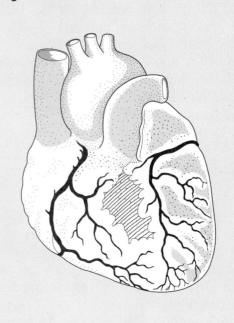

Your heart is about the size of your fist.

your left wrist. What do you feel? You are actually feeling a surge of blood called the **pulse** as your heart pumps blood through the vessels in your wrist. You can feel the pulse in your wrist because the blood vessels there are very close to the surface of the skin. You can also find your pulse at the side of your neck and in your temples.

Every time your heart beats, you can feel a pulse beat. Thus you can use your pulse to determine how fast your heart is beating. Simply measure the number of times your pulse beats per minute.

Structure of the Heart

The human heart is similar to that of most mammals. Your teacher may have a sheep or beef heart that you can study. These hearts are very much like the human heart. Compare the animal heart with the human heart shown in Figure 13-8. What similarities do you see?

Study the outside of the heart and note its shape. Find the small blood vessels on the surface. These vessels carry food and oxygen to the cells of the heart. They also remove waste products. Find the larger blood vessels at the top of the heart. Some of these vessels take blood away from the heart. Other vessels bring blood back to the heart.

With your teacher's supervision, use a knife to carefully cut the animal heart in half. Look at the thick wall of muscle that divides the right and left sides of the heart. Also find this thick wall of muscle in Figure 13-9.

The heart is divided into four chambers. Find the chambers of the human heart in Figure 13-9. Both the right and left sides

of the heart have upper and lower chambers. Each upper chamber is called an **atrium** (AY-tree-um). The plural of *atrium* is *atria*. The lower chambers are **ventricles** (VEN-trih-kul). Blood constantly moves through the chambers of your heart. The arrows in Figure 13-9 show the direction in which the blood enters, fills, and then leaves the heart.

After the blood circulates through the body, it returns to the right side of the heart. As it moves through the body, the blood releases oxygen to all the body cells.

At the same time, blood picks up carbon dioxide and other wastes from the body cells. This blood returns to the heart through the right atrium. The blood flows from the right atrium to the right ventricle. From there it is pumped to the lungs. Blood enters the lungs through a vessel called the **pulmonary artery**, which comes out of the right ventricle. The pulmonary artery branches into two vessels to carry blood to the right and left lungs.

In the lungs the blood gives up carbon dioxide and takes up oxygen by diffusion. The oxygen-rich blood leaves the lungs through a vessel called the **pulmonary vein** and returns to the left atrium. The circulation of blood from the heart to the lungs and back to the heart is known as **pulmonary circulation**.

Then, the blood moves from the left atrium to the left ventricle. From the left ventricle, oxygen-rich blood is pumped through the **aorta** (ay-ORT-uh) and continues to circulate through your body. The aorta is the largest artery in your body. It is large and strong enough to withstand the pressure of the blood as it leaves the

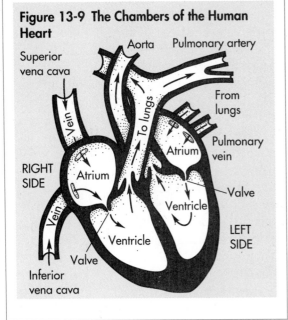

Figure 13-9 The Chambers of the Human Heart

Superior vena cava
Aorta
Pulmonary artery
From lungs
Vein
To lungs
Pulmonary vein
Atrium
RIGHT SIDE
Atrium
Valve
Vein
Ventricle
Ventricle
LEFT SIDE
Valve
Inferior vena cava

heart. The heart pumps three to four liters of blood into the aorta each minute.

Circulation of the blood from the heart to the body systems and back to the heart is known as **systemic circulation**. Find two large veins in Figure 13-10 called the **superior vena cava** and the **inferior vena cava**. Through these two large veins, blood returns from the body to the right atrium.

As you can see, the heart is a double pump. The right atrium receives blood that has circulated through your body. The right ventricle pumps oxygen-poor blood to the lungs. The left atrium receives oxygen-rich blood from the lungs. The left ventricle pumps oxygen rich blood to the body. Both of these pumps work at the same time. The muscular walls of the heart keep the oxygen-poor blood and the oxygen-rich blood from mixing.

Your left ventricle is about three times as muscular as the right ventricle. Do you know why? The right ventricle pumps blood only a short distance to your lungs. However, the left ventricle must pump blood over a much longer distance to all the parts of your body.

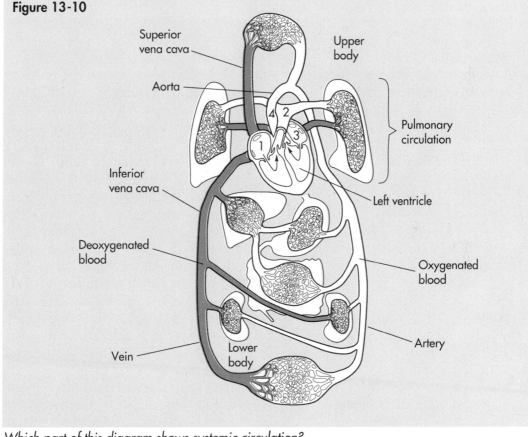

Figure 13-10

Which part of this diagram shows systemic circulation?

What keeps blood from flowing in the wrong direction? The upper and lower chambers of the heart are separated by **valves.** Valves are flaps of tissue that open and close to keep the blood flowing in one direction. Find the valves in Figure 13-9. The valves open to allow the blood to flow from the atria to the ventricles. As the ventricles pump blood out of the heart, these valves shut to prevent the blood from flowing backward into the atria. When doctors listen to your heart through a stethoscope, they can hear the valves snap shut.

The following steps summarize the path of blood through the body Each step corresponds to the numbers in Figure 13-10. Use this figure to trace the path of blood.

Step 1.   Blood enters the right side of the heart from the body.

Step 2.   Blood is pumped into the lungs by the pulmonary artery.

Step 3.   Blood returns from the lungs to the left side of the heart.

Step 4.   Blood is pumped into the aorta and travels to the rest of the body.

■■■ Section 13-2 Review ■■■

Write the definitions for the following terms in your own words.

1. **heart**   2. **atrium**
3. **ventricle**   4. **aorta**
5. **valve**

Answer these questions.

6. Give an example of something that causes the pulse rate to change.

7. Explain how oxygen-rich blood gets from your heart to other parts of your body.
8. Distinguish between the systemic circulation and the pulmonary circulation.
9. Describe characteristics of the heart that adapt it for pumping blood through the body.

13-3 Your Blood Vessels

■ *Objective*

☐ *Identify the structure and function of an artery, vein, and capillary*

You know that blood is carried in blood vessels. The circulatory system includes three types of blood vessels. Blood vessels that carry blood away from the heart are called **arteries.** Blood vessels that carry blood to the heart are called **veins.**

In Figure 13-10 you noticed the large artery called the aorta leading away from the heart. Notice that the aorta branches into smaller arteries. The branches lead to your arms and legs, as well as your kidneys, intestine, brain, and other organs. The branches carry blood containing food and oxygen to all your cells. Valves called semilunar valves are found at the base of each of these branching arteries. The semilunar valves prevent backflow of blood to the heart.

Most of your arteries transport oxygen-rich blood. Oxygen-rich blood is called **oxygenated** (AHK-sih-juh-nayt-ed) blood.

One artery, the pulmonary artery, carries oxygen-poor blood, or **deoxygenated** blood, away from your heart to your lungs. This blood becomes oxygenated in the lungs.

The walls of your arteries are thick and tough, but they are also flexible. Arteries expand as they receive spurts of blood pumped under pressure from the heart. Most arteries lie deep below the skin. However, arteries in your wrist, neck, and temples lie close to the surface. In these places you may easily feel your pulse.

Look at the system of veins and arteries in Figure 13-11. Trace an artery from the heart to an arm. Notice that, as the artery divides and divides again, it gets smaller and smaller. The smallest arteries are called **arterioles** (are-TEER-ee-ohls). The arterioles branch into clusters of tiny microscopic blood vessels called **capillaries** (KAP-uh-ler-ee).

Capillaries are the most abundant blood vessels in the body. They pass through all of the tissues and organs of your body. Capillaries are found close to every cell in

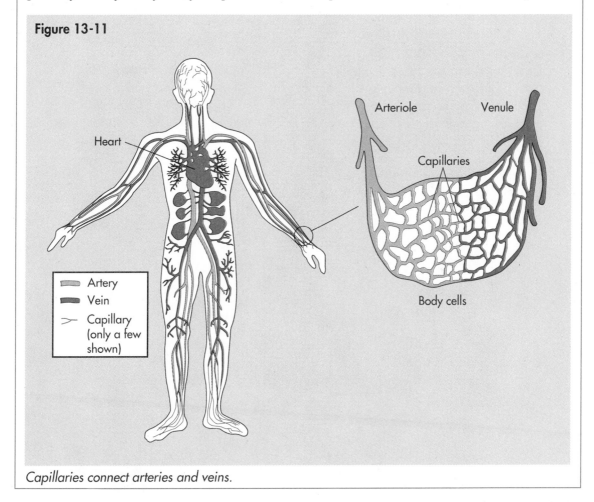

Figure 13-11

Heart

Arteriole   Venule

Capillaries

Body cells

Artery

Vein

Capillary (only a few shown)

Capillaries connect arteries and veins.

How Can You Observe Circulation in a Goldfish's Tail?

Process Skills *observing, using laboratory equipment*

Materials fish net, goldfish bowl, goldfish, cotton, petri dish, microscope, microscope slide

In this activity, you will observe the flow of blood through capillaries.

Procedure

1. Dip a small fish net into a fish tank. Catch a goldfish and remove it from the tank. Wrap its head and gills in a piece of wet cotton. Make sure the goldfish stays moist.
2. Place the fish in a petri dish with its tail near the center of the dish as shown in Figure 13-12. Cover the fish's tail with a microscope slide.
3. Place the petri dish on the microscope stage. Examine the blood circulating through the fish's tail, using low power. Observe the blood spurting through the narrow capillaries.
4. Switch from low to high power. Draw the cells flowing inside the capillaries.
5. When you are finished, carefully place the fish back in the water. Do not keep the fish out of the tank for more than 10 or 15 minutes.

Conclusions

6. What kind of cells did you see?
7. How many blood cells can pass through the capillaries at a time?
8. If possible, compare your observations with the capillaries in other animals such as in the tails of tadpoles or the webbing between a frog's toes.

Figure 13-12

your body. Capillary walls are usually just one cell layer thick. Thin capillary walls allow food and oxygen to diffuse through them to the cells.

In your cells, food and oxygen combine to release energy. Water and carbon dioxide are waste products of this reaction. These cellular wastes diffuse from your cells into your capillaries. Then your blood carries these wastes back into tiny veins called **venules** (VEEN-yels). Venules combine into larger and larger veins that finally reach the heart.

Look at the blue lines under the skin on the back of your hand. These blue lines are actually your veins. The blood in your hand has traveled a long distance from your heart. First your heart pumped it to your arteries in rapid spurts. Your arteries carried the blood to your hand. Then the blood flowed into clusters of tiny capillaries. The blood then entered the veins, which carried the blood back to your heart.

How does your blood move from your hands and feet back toward your heart? What stops your blood from moving away from your heart between beats? Valves in your veins keep blood moving in the right direction. These valves prevent your blood from flowing backward, away from your heart. Valves are like tiny doors. When they are open, blood flows toward your heart. When they are closed, valves prevent blood from flowing away from your heart. Figure 13-13 shows how the valves in your veins keep blood from flowing away from your heart.

Your blood spurts rapidly through your arteries. Blood flows more slowly in your veins because the blood in your veins is

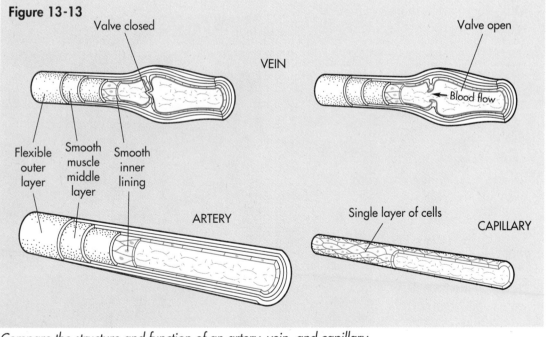

Figure 13-13

Valve closed

VEIN

Valve open

Blood flow

Flexible outer layer

Smooth muscle middle layer

Smooth inner lining

ARTERY

Single layer of cells

CAPILLARY

Compare the structure and function of an artery, vein, and capillary.

farther from the force exerted by the heart. Your artery walls are thick and elastic. They are suited for fast blood flow. The walls of your veins are thinner and less elastic. They are suited for slow blood flow.

▬▬ Section 13-3 Review ▬▬

Write the definitions for the following terms in your own words.

1. **artery**   2. **vein**
3. **arteriole**   4. **capillary**
5. **venules**

Answer these questions.

6. How are arteries adapted for receiving blood from the heart?
7. Why must capillaries come in contact with every cell in the human body?
8. What role do valves play in the transport of blood?

13-4 Your Blood

■ *Objectives*
☐ *List the parts of the blood.*
☐ *Describe the functions of each of the parts of the blood.*

If you are ill or injured, your doctor will probably obtain a sample of your blood. By examining blood under a microscope, doctors can identify signs of many diseases or other problems. Your blood contains cells and fluids that carry food, oxygen, and wastes through your body. Blood also contains cells that fight disease and heal wounds.

Your Red Blood Cells at Work

Red blood cells are one part of blood that doctors may observe. Red blood cells are also called **erythrocytes** (ih-RITH-ruh-syt). Look at the human red blood cells in Figure 13-14. Notice their disklike shape.

Erythrocytes pick up oxygen from your lungs and carry it to all of the cells of your body. Oxygen is carried in a protein called **hemoglobin.** Each red blood cell in your body contains hemoglobin. When you breathe, oxygen molecules attach themselves to hemoglobin molecules in your lungs. The oxygenated hemoglobin gives blood its bright red color. The hemoglobin molecules carry oxygen from your lungs, through your blood, to the other parts of

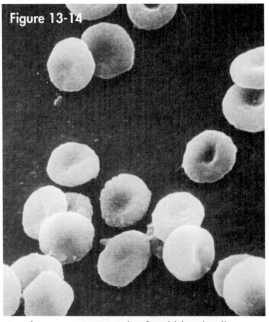

Figure 13-14

An electron micrograph of red blood cells

your body. As your red blood cells deliver oxygen to your body cells, your blood loses its bright red color.

Mature human red blood cells have no nucleus. For this reason, red blood cells cannot reproduce. They live only for a short time. Each red blood cell remains active for about 120 days. Your body must continue to replace its red blood cells. As you may recall from Chapter 10, new red blood cells are made in the bone marrow, the soft red center of your bones.

Your cells need oxygen to release energy from food. If your body cells do not get enough oxygen, you will feel tired. After examining a person's blood, a doctor may find that the red blood cells are in short supply. In this case, the body cells will not get enough oxygen to meet their needs. Then the body's energy supply drops.

A lack of iron in the diet may cause the shortage of red blood cells. Hemoglobin is rich in iron. If the body has too little iron, it cannot make hemoglobin. To increase the number of red blood cells, a doctor may prescribe a diet rich in iron. Iron-rich foods include liver, green vegetables, and grains.

With the added iron, the body can make more hemoglobin. As the supply of hemoglobin increases, the body can make more red blood cells. The body will once again have sufficient amounts of red blood cells to supply its cells with oxygen.

Your White Blood Cells at Work

Your blood also contains many types of white blood cells. White blood cells are also called **leucocytes** (LOO-kuh-syts). White blood cells are also made in your bone marrow. Figure 13-15 shows what white blood cells look like under the high power of a microscope. Notice the large nucleus in the center of the leucocytes. Because leucocytes have no hemoglobin, they are colorless.

White blood cells are larger than red blood cells. There are also fewer white blood cells than red blood cells. In fact, your blood usually contains only one white blood cell for about every 600 red blood cells.

White blood cells are the disease fighters of your body. They can seek out foreign materials such as disease-causing bacteria. White blood cells surround and take in bacteria, thus protecting the body from disease.

Normally, each drop of human blood contains 5000 to 9000 white blood cells. When bacteria invade your body, white blood cells multiply rapidly. For example, if

Figure 13-15 White Blood Cells

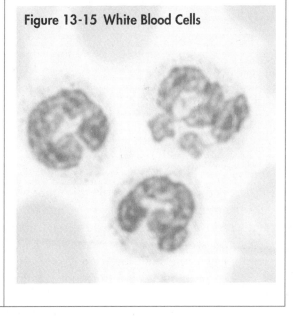

you cut yourself, bacteria may enter your skin. The number of white blood cells in your blood will then increase rapidly. The bloodstream carries these large numbers of white blood cells to the cut. There, the white blood cells surround and destroy the bacteria.

Have you ever had a cut or scrape that became infected? The yellow fluid that formed around the wound was **pus**. Pus is made of living and dead bacteria, white blood cells, and blood **plasma**. Plasma is the liquid part of blood. A wound that contains pus is called an **infection**. To prevent an infection from developing, always wash a wound with soap and water.

In most cases your body wins the battle against harmful bacteria. White blood cells fight the bacteria, and an infection soon goes away. Sometimes, though, bacteria grow and reproduce so quickly that your white blood cells cannot destroy all of them. Such cases require a doctor's care. The doctor will clean the wound and prescribe medicine to help your body destroy harmful bacteria.

If you do cut yourself, your blood can stop a wound from bleeding by forming a blood clot. Special parts of the blood called **platelets** play an important role in forming a blood clot. Figure 13-16 shows platelets being formed.

Your Blood Plasma

Plasma is the liquid part of blood. About 90 percent of plasma is water. The rest contains dissolved nutrients, wastes, minerals, gases and special proteins. Some of these proteins help the body fight disease. Other special proteins, called hormones, help

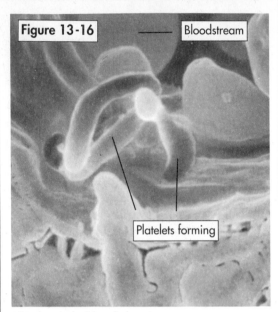

Figure 13-16 — Bloodstream — Platelets forming

Platelets help blood clot.

control the activities of your body and make them work together.

Plasma delivers the dissolved materials to cells of your body. Your blood plasma also carries dissolved waste produced by your cells to your kidneys, skin, and lungs. These three organs work to eliminate wastes.

Plasma changes constantly as it flows through your circulatory system. For example, plasma picks up digested food from the villi of the small intestine. The plasma gives up this digested food to feed the cells of your body. Plasma gives up carbon dioxide wastes as it flows into the capillaries in the lungs.

Blood plasma carries food to all your body cells and carries wastes away from your body cells. Your red blood cells carry oxygen to all parts of your body while the white blood cells help you fight harmful bacteria.

Inferring

Studying a sample of blood begins with placing blood in a test tube and then spinning it at high speed. The spinning separates blood into its different parts. The test tubes in Figure 13-17 contain two blood samples.

1. What percentage of the blood samples is a liquid without cells?
2. In each sample, which blood cells are the more numerous?
3. In each sample, what percentage of the blood contains white blood cells and platelets?
4. One of these blood samples is normal. The other is from someone with an infection. Can you identify which is which? Explain your answer.

Figure 13-17

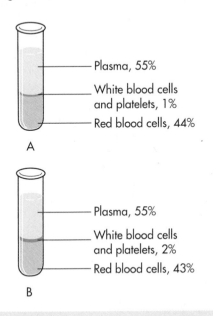

Plasma, 55%

White blood cells and platelets, 1%

Red blood cells, 44%

A

Plasma, 55%

White blood cells and platelets, 2%

Red blood cells, 43%

B

■ Section 13-4 Review ■

Write the definitions for the following terms in your own words.

1. **blood**
2. **erythrocyte**
3. **leucocyte**
4. **plasma**
5. **platelet**

Answer these questions.

6. Why are erythrocytes unable to reproduce?
7. What materials are carried in blood plasma?
8. Why are leucocytes called the disease fighters of the body?
9. What is pus made of? When does pus form?

Using Tropical Oils

You have probably heard about cholesterol. It is a fatty substance found in the blood and all body cells. Although your body needs some cholesterol, too much can cause heart disease.

Scientists believe that as people age, the linings of their arteries become coated with cholesterol. These cholesterol deposits cause the openings of the arteries to become narrower and narrower. If an artery near the heart becomes completely blocked, blood cannot pass through. A heart attack could result.

Some people have an inherited tendency to produce too much cholesterol. Others eat too many cholesterol-rich foods. These foods include red meat, eggs, whole milk, and certain oils. Palm oil and coconut oil, known as tropical oils, are especially high in cholesterol.

Tropical oils are often used to add flavor to baked goods. Scientists, though, have proven that tropical oils raise cholesterol levels. Now many food companies have stopped using tropical oils in their products. Packages like the one shown in Figure 13-18 have become a common sight on grocery store shelves.

Some producers of tropical oils claim they have evidence that palm oil actually lowers cholesterol levels. American scientists, however, claim that the evidence is misleading. The scientists say that palm oil does indeed raise cholesterol.

Figure 13-18

Many foods are now made without tropical oils.

Follow-up Activity

Look at the foods you have at home. Study the packages and the food labels. How many of these foods contain tropical oils? How many packages include a statement like "This product contains no tropical oils"? Share your findings with your classmates.

13-1 Absorption and Transport

1. Soluble molecules are absorbed into the bloodstream by diffusion.
2. Osmosis is the process of the diffusion of water.
3. The cell membrane is semipermeable, which means it lets only selected molecules diffuse through.

13-2 Human Circulation

1. The circulatory system carries digested food, water, and oxygen to cells. It transports carbon dioxide and other wastes away from the cells.
2. The circulatory system consists of the heart, blood, arteries, veins, and capillaries.
3. The heart is a muscular pump made of four chambers, including the right and left atria and the right and left ventricles.
4. Systemic circulation is the circulation of blood from the heart to the body and back to the heart.
5. Pulmonary circulation is the circulation of blood from the heart to the lungs and back.

13-3 Your Blood Vessels

1. Arteries carry blood away from the heart to all the body cells.
2. Veins carry blood from the body cells back to the heart.
3. Capillaries are tiny blood vessels in which food, oxygen, and wastes are exchanged between blood and the cells.

13-4 Your Blood

1. Red blood cells, or erythrocytes, flow in the plasma. Erythrocytes contain hemoglobin molecules, which carry oxygen through the bloodstream.
2. White blood cells, or leucocytes, help fight disease by surrounding bacteria.
3. Platelets contain chemicals that help the blood clot.

Write the term from the list that best matches each statement.

infection, pulse, superior vena cava, inferior vena cava, hemoglobin, pus, pulmonary artery, pulmonary vein, oxygenated, deoxygenated, systemic, pulmonary

The surge of blood you feel if you place your fingers on your wrist is your ___1___. ___2___ circulation is the circulation of blood from the heart to the lungs and back. ___3___ circulation is the circulation of blood from the heart to the body and back. Blood enters the lungs through the ___4___. It leaves the lungs through the ___5___. Blood returns to the right atrium through two veins, the ___6___ and ___7___. Blood that returns to the heart from these two veins is ___8___. Blood that leaves the lungs and enters the heart is ___9___. The oxygen-carrying protein in red blood cells is called ___10___. Sometimes a yellowish liquid called ___11___ forms around a wound. The presence of this liquid means that a(n) ___12___ has developed.

SUMMARIZING

If the sentence is true, write *true*. If the statement is false, change the *italicized* term to make the statement true.

1. Molecules that can pass through the cell membrane are *insoluble*.
2. The diffusion of water is called *osmosis*.
3. In your heart, *valves* prevent blood from flowing backward.
4. Pulmonary blood vessels connect the heart to the *liver*.
5. The blood vessels that carry blood away from the heart are the *veins*.

INTERPRETING INFORMATION

Use Figure 13-19 to answer the following questions.

1. Which artery shows a buildup of cholesterol on its walls?
2. What threat to health does this buildup represent?
3. What foods most likely caused this buildup?

Figure 13-19

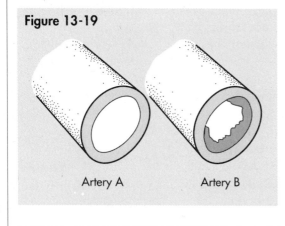

Artery A   Artery B

THINK AND DISCUSS

1. Name two life processes that depend on diffusion. (13-1)
2. Trace the path of blood through the heart. Name the parts of the heart through which the blood flows. (13-2)
3. Why are valves necessary for normal blood flow? (13-3)
4. What might a white blood cell count of 12,000 mean? (13-4)

GOING FURTHER

1. How do cigarette smoking, cholesterol, diet, and the excessive use of salt or caffeine affect the circulatory system? Write a report about the effects of one of these subjects. Refer to your local library, the American Cancer Society, or the American Heart Association for information.
2. Find out the causes of the condition called hypertension. Why is hypertension called a "silent killer"? How is this condition treated?
3. Dangerous chemicals (poisonous substances) from the environment sometimes find their way into the cells of the human body. What are some sources of these dangerous chemicals? How do these chemicals get to human cells? Make a list of some of these dangerous chemicals and the effects they may have on cells. Do some library research to find this information.

COMPETENCY REVIEW

1. Salts and simple sugar molecules do not have to be digested because they are
   a. water soluble.

b. able to diffuse.

c. small.

d. all of the above.

2. The two halves of the U-shaped tube shown in Figure 13-20 are separated by a nonwaterproof membrane. What would you expect to happen?

a. Only starch molecules will diffuse from side A to side B.

b. Only simple sugar molecules will diffuse from side A to side B.

c. Both starch and simple sugar molecules will diffuse from side A to side B.

d. No molecules will diffuse from side A to side B.

Figure 13-20

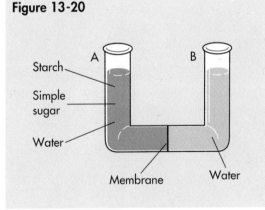

3. The function of the heart is to

a. digest food.

b. filter wastes from the blood.

c. manufacture red blood cells.

d. pump blood.

4. Which part of the blood transports digested nutrients?

a. red blood cells   b. plasma

c. white blood cells   d. platelets

5. Blood flows in which direction?

a. arteries to capillaries to veins and back to the heart

b. veins to capillaries to arteries and back to the heart

c. capillaries to arteries to veins and back to the heart

d. capillaries to veins to arteries and back to the heart

6. Blood pressure is a measure of how hard the blood is being pushed through

a. veins.   b. capillaries.

c. arteries.   d. valves.

7. The function of blood is to

a. digest food.

b. manufacture proteins.

c. build cells.

d. carry materials through the body.

8. Which is true of red blood cells?

a. They are larger than white blood cells.

b. They transport oxygen.

c. They destroy bacteria.

d. They repair wounds.

9. A patient with too few platelets in the blood would have difficulty with

a. blood clotting.

b. getting enough oxygen.

c. getting enough nutrients.

d. removing cellular wastes.

10. Doctors in the 1700s could not study capillaries because capillaries are

a. colorless.   b. weak.

c. microscopic.   d. rare.

CHAPTER 14

YOUR RESPIRATORY SYSTEM

Each day you breathe thousands of times, yet probably think very little about the fact that you are breathing. Breathing is a basic human function. Though you might live without food and water for several days, you can live only for a few minutes without oxygen.

People usually do not think about breathing unless they are having trouble doing so. Imagine, for example, your are beginning to climb to the top of a high mountain. Getting to the top will not be easy. Mountain climbers often become tired, dizzy, and short of breath.

What causes such problems? Tiredness, dizziness, and breathlessness are all signs of lack of oxygen. High in the mountains there is less oxygen in the air. Therefore, your body must work overtime to get enough oxygen. You must take several breaths to get the same amount of oxygen you would get in one breath down below.

Take a deep breath and slowly let it out. As you breathe in, you can feel your **lungs** fill with air. The lungs, shown in Figure 14-1, are organs of the body that help you breathe.

14-1 Parts of Your Respiratory System

■ *Objectives*

☐ *Describe the structure and function of the parts of the respiratory system.*

☐ *Explain what causes breathing rates to change.*

The lungs and other parts of the body that take in oxygen make up your **respiratory system**. These organs are shown in Figure 14-2. Use this figure to trace the path of air as it moves through your body.

Figure 14-1

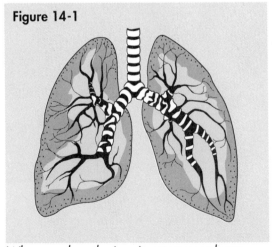

When you breathe in, air enters your lungs.

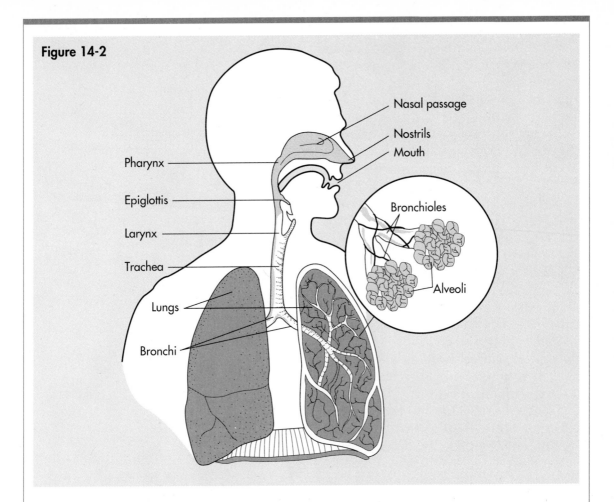

Figure 14-2

Nasal passage

Nostrils

Mouth

Pharynx

Epiglottis

Larynx

Trachea

Lungs

Bronchi

Bronchioles

Alveoli

Most of the air you breathe enters through your nose. The two openings in your nose where air enters are called **nostrils**. From the nostrils, air moves into your **nasal passages**, two tunnels that lead to the throat.

The nasal passages are lined with membranes that are coated with a moist, sticky substance called **mucus**. Mucus traps dust and bacteria in the air. Some of the cells that line the nasal passages have tiny hairlike cilia. The cilia move back and forth. This action pushes the mucus containing dust and bacteria back toward the nostrils. You may force out this mucus when you sneeze or blow your nose. The nasal passages also contain many tiny capillaries. The capillaries warm the air as it moves through the nasal passages.

The warmed and cleaned air moves from the nasal passages to the pharynx (FAR-ings), the area at the back of your throat. From the pharynx, air moves into the **trachea** (TRAY-kee-uh), or windpipe. The trachea is also lined with mucus, which traps still more dust in the air.

If you move your fingers gently up and down your neck, you can feel your trachea. The trachea is a tube made of rings of soft cartilage. These rings keep the tube open so that air can pass through it.

The upper part of the trachea is called the **larynx.** The larynx contains the vocal cords. Vocal cords are the structures that enable you to speak. They are made of flexible bands of tissue that stretch across the larynx. When you speak, air moves up from the lungs, causing the vocal cords to vibrate. These vibrations produce your voice.

The larynx contains the **glottis,** a slit-like entrance to the trachea. Located above the glottis is a small flap of tissue called the **epiglottis.** Find the glottis and epiglottis in Figure 14-3. The epiglottis opens when you speak or breathe. It closes when you eat, thereby preventing swallowed food from entering the trachea.

The trachea divides into two bronchial tubes, or **bronchi** (BRAHN-ky); the singular form is *bronchus*. The bronchi are the tubes that carry air to the lungs. A double membrane called the **pleura** covers and protects the lungs.

Inside each lung the bronchus branches into even smaller tubes called **bronchioles.** Each bronchiole ends in a cluster of microscopic air sacs called **alveoli** (al-VEE-uh-ly); the singular form is *alveolus*. The millions of alveoli give the lungs their spongy appearance.

Notice in Figure 14-4 that a network of capillaries surrounds each alveolus. Oxygen diffuses from each alveolus into the blood inside of the network of capillaries. Carbon dioxide diffuses from the blood into each alveolus. The carbon dioxide

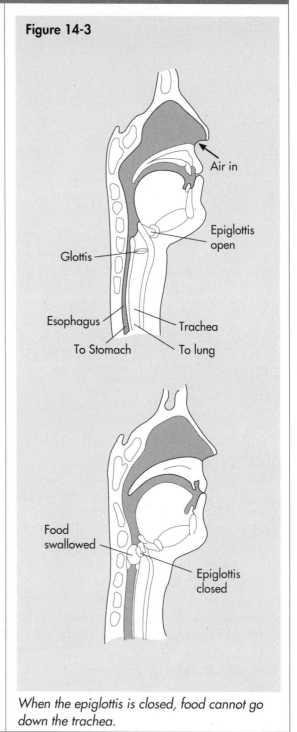

Figure 14-3

When the epiglottis is closed, food cannot go down the trachea.

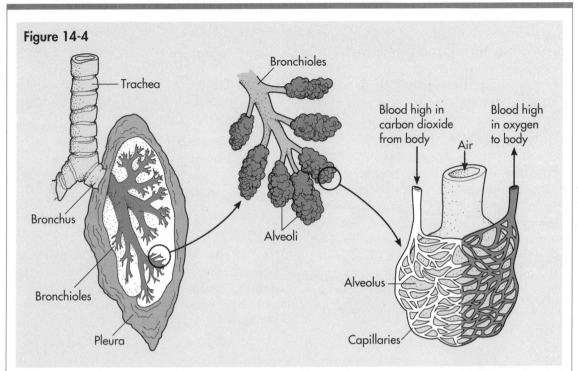

Figure 14-4

Trachea

Bronchioles

Bronchus

Bronchioles

Alveoli

Pleura

Blood high in carbon dioxide from body

Air

Blood high in oxygen to body

Alveolus

Capillaries

Alveoli are very small, but they have an important job. Your lungs contain up to 700 million alveoli.

What Gas Do You Breathe Out?

Process Skill forming and testing a hypothesis

Materials graduated cylinder, limewater, two 100 milliliter beakers, glass marker, drinking straw

Procedure
1. Limewater is a solution that turns milky white in the presence of carbon dioxide. Use a graduated cylinder to measure 50 milliliters of limewater.
2. Label two 100 milliliter beakers A and B. Pour 25 milliliters of limewater into each beaker.
3. Use a drinking straw to blow air bubbles into beaker A. Repeat several times.
   Caution Only breathe out into the limewater.
4. Compare the appearance of the limewater in both beakers.

Conclusions
5. What differences did you observe in the two beakers?
6. Explain this difference.

passes from the lungs up through the trachea. It is then breathed out through the nose and mouth.

The amount of carbon dioxide in your blood determines how often you need to breathe. The more carbon dioxide your blood contains, the more often you breathe. When you exercise, the amount of carbon dioxide in your blood increases. How would exercise affect your breathing rate?

In addition to carbon dioxide, you also breathe out water vapor. Thus, the breathing process helps control the amount of water in your body. Have you noticed how a windowpane or mirror fogs up when you breathe on it? The water vapor that leaves your lungs forms visible water droplets when it reaches the glass.

▬▬ Section 14-1 Review ▬▬

Write the definitions of the following terms in your own words.

1. **respiratory system**   2. **trachea**
3. **larynx**   4. **lung**

Answer these questions.

5. Name the parts of the respiratory system that air passes through when you breathe.
6. What is the function of the epiglottis?
7. Why are the alveoli surrounded by a network of capillaries?
8. What determines how often you breathe?
9. When you breathe out on a cold day, a mist forms. Explain why.

14-2 The Stages of Respiration

■ *Objectives*
☐ *Identify the three stages of human respiration.*
☐ *Describe what occurs during external, internal, and cellular respiration.*

The process of respiration occurs in three stages. During the first stage, you breathe, and oxygen is exchanged for carbon dioxide in your lungs. This first stage is called external respiration. During the second stage, the bloodstream transports oxygen to your body cells. The second stage is called internal respiration. During the third stage, oxygen combines chemically with food to release the energy needed for life processes. As you learned in Chapter 2, this process is called cellular respiration.

External Respiration

You know the path air takes to reach the alveoli. What, though, actually draws air into your lungs? To find out, look at Figure 14-5. Find the **diaphragm** (DY-uh-fram), a thick sheet of muscle under the lungs. Above the diaphragm find the ribs, or bones, that surround and protect the lungs.

Place your hands over your ribs and take a deep breath. You can feel your ribs pushing upward and outward. When you draw air into your lungs, you **inhale**. Now release the air through your nose and mouth. Do you feel your ribs move inward? When you release your breath, you **exhale**. The muscles of your diaphragm and your ribs help you inhale and exhale.

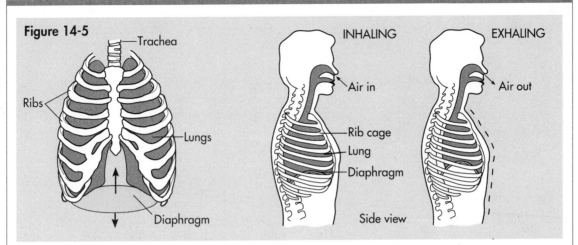

Figure 14-5

Trachea

Ribs

Lungs

Diaphragm

INHALING

Air in

Rib cage

Lung

Diaphragm

Side view

EXHALING

Air out

Where is your diaphragm when you inhale? Where is it when you exhale?

Figure 14-6 shows a model of your breathing system. Pulling the rubber sheet down creates more space in the bell jar for air. The air pressure inside the bell jar becomes lower than the air pressure in the surrounding air. As a result, outside air rushes through the opening in the tube and into the balloons to fill the space. The balloons become larger as they fill with air.

Pushing the rubber sheet up leaves less space in the bell jar. The air pressure inside the bell jar becomes greater than the air pressure outside. The balloons are squeezed. Air is forced out of the balloons through the opening in the tube. The balloons collapse.

The action of the bell jar model is similar to what happens when you breathe. Think of the bell jar as your chest cavity, the balloons as your lungs, and the rubber sheet as your diaphragm. The balloons fill with air when you pull down the rubber sheet.

Likewise, as your diaphragm moves down, your lungs fill with air and your ribs push outward. The volume of your chest

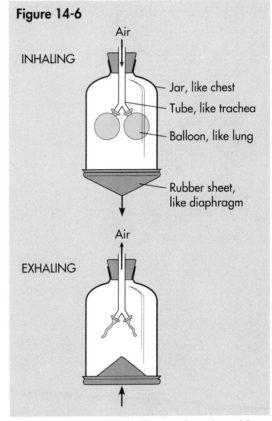

Figure 14-6

INHALING

Air

Jar, like chest

Tube, like trachea

Balloon, like lung

Rubber sheet, like diaphragm

EXHALING

Air

What happens to the balloons when the rubber sheet is forced upward?

What Is the Volume of Your Lungs?

Process Skills *measuring, using experimental data*

Materials two balloons, tape measure, partner

Procedure

1. Copy the table in Figure 14-7 into your notebook.
2. Exhale as you normally do into a balloon. Quickly pinch the balloon so that no air escapes.

Figure 14-7 Measuring Lung Volume

Student	Circumference Normal Breath	Circumference Deep Breath
Yourself		
Partner		

3. Have your partner use a tape measure to determine the circumference of the balloon at its widest point. Record the circumference in the table.
4. Take as deep a breath as you can. Hold it and then exhale as much air as possible into the balloon. Have your partner measure and record the circumference of the balloon. Record the circumference in the table.
5. Switch places with your partner. Repeat steps 2, 3, and 4, using another balloon.

Conclusions

6. Compare the measurements you obtained after breathing normally and after taking a deep breath. Explain the difference.
7. Compare your partner's numbers with your own. What might cause lung volume to differ from one individual to another?

cavity increases. The air pressure inside the chest cavity is lower than the air pressure outside your body. Air enters your lungs to even out the air pressure.

Air is forced out of the balloons when you push the rubber sheet up. Similarly, your ribs push inward and the space in your chest cavity decreases when your diaphragm moves up. The air pressure inside your chest cavity is now greater than the air pressure outside. The difference in air pressure forces air out of your lungs.

Internal Respiration

Air enters your lungs when you inhale. This air is rich in oxygen. How does oxygen move from your lungs to other parts of your body?

Recall from Chapter 13 that the right side of your heart pumps oxygen-poor blood through the pulmonary arteries to your lungs. The pulmonary arteries that bring the blood from the heart branch into clusters of capillaries as they enter the lungs. These tiny clusters of capillaries surround the air sacs, as shown in Figure 14-8. After you inhale, the air sacs contain a great deal of oxygen. Blood in the capillaries around the air sacs has very little oxygen. The oxygen passes from the air sacs into the blood by diffusion.

The hemoglobin molecules in your red blood cells attach to the oxygen molecules. These hemoglobin molecules carry oxygen from your lungs back through pulmonary veins to your heart. Then the heart pumps this oxygen-rich blood through the aorta to all other parts of your body.

Cellular Respiration

All the cells of your body need energy. In this way, your body is like a car engine. A car engine runs on the energy produced by burning fuel. The cells of your body also get their energy from burning fuel. The fuel is digested food. It "burns" when it reacts with oxygen inside each of the body cells.

The Nature of Burning   As you learned in Chapter 11, the process during which digested food reacts with oxygen is called oxidation. Both types of fuel, gasoline and digested food, are made of carbon and hydrogen compounds. When these fuels burn, they break up into individual atoms of carbon and hydrogen. The carbon atoms

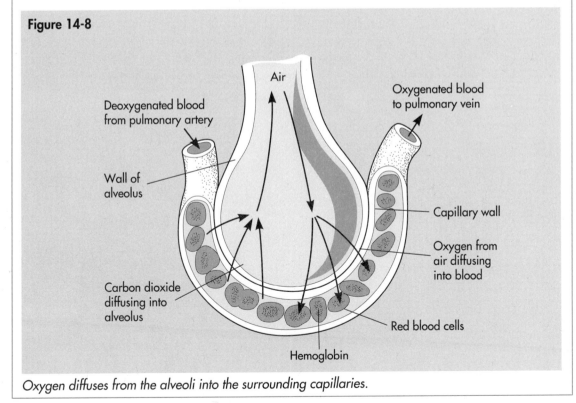

Figure 14-8

Air

Deoxygenated blood from pulmonary artery

Oxygenated blood to pulmonary vein

Wall of alveolus

Capillary wall

Oxygen from air diffusing into blood

Carbon dioxide diffusing into alveolus

Red blood cells

Hemoglobin

Oxygen diffuses from the alveoli into the surrounding capillaries.

combine with oxygen, forming carbon dioxide. The hydrogen atoms combine with oxygen, forming water. This process releases a great deal of energy. You can observe this energy in the form of light and heat from a fire. When the fuel is used up, burning stops.

Oxidation occurs quickly in a car engine. Oxidation can also occur slowly, however. In fact, it may happen so slowly that you do not even notice it. For example, the rusting of iron is a slow form of oxidation. Iron combines with oxygen in the air. The rust you see is a compound called iron oxide. As rust forms, heat is released very slowly. Look at Figure 14-9. Which picture shows a slower form of oxidation?

Oxidation in your body cells also takes place slowly. Digested food combines slowly with oxygen, and energy is released. Cup your hands and breathe into them. Notice that the air you exhale is warm. The oxidation that takes place in your cells produces your body heat.

The Cell's Energy Cycle The energy produced by your cells is released very slowly. Your body can use this energy only after a great deal of it has collected, however. How are large amounts of this energy collected and stored?

Figure 14-10 illustrates the energy cycle of cells. Your cells store energy in large molecules called **ATP** molecules. When ATP molecules are broken down, they form smaller molecules called **ADP**. This process releases the energy that your body uses to breathe, move, or think.

When you need energy, your body breaks down more ATP molecules. As a result, the number of ATP molecules decreases and the number of ADP molecules increases. How does your body rebuild its supply of ATP? Building up the ATP supply requires the energy from the oxidation of more food. The cycle of building and breaking down ATP occurs over and over again in all your cells.

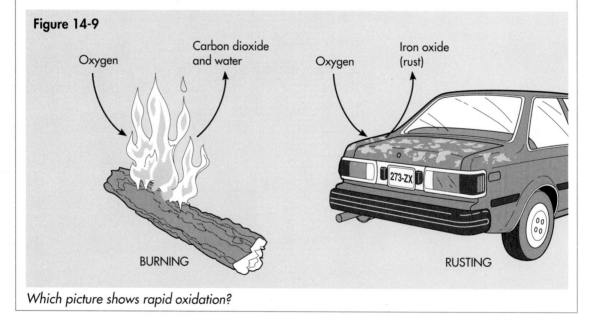

Figure 14-9

Oxygen

Carbon dioxide and water

BURNING

Oxygen

Iron oxide (rust)

273-ZX

RUSTING

Which picture shows rapid oxidation?

Figure 14-10

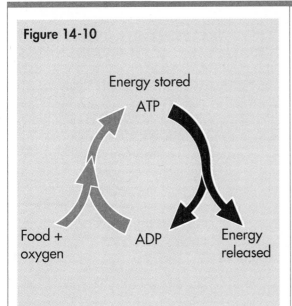

Energy stored

ATP

Food + oxygen

ADP

Energy released

During cellular respiration, food and oxygen combine to produce energy. That energy is stored in the ATP molecule. When ATP breaks down into ADP, energy is released.

■■■ Section 14-2 Review ■■■

Write the definitions of the following terms in your own words

1. **inhale**
2. **exhale**
3. **diaphragm**
4. **ATP**
5. **ADP**

Answer these questions.

6. List and describe the three stages of respiration.
7. How do the rib cage and the muscle in the diaphragm assist in the breathing process?

8. How would exercise affect the rate of cellular respiration in your body? How could you test your hypothesis?
9. Briefly compare ATP and ADP.

14-3 Health Hazards and Your Respiratory System

■ *Objectives*

☐ *Cite evidence that a relationship exists between air pollution and respiratory diseases.*

☐ *List several examples of occupational health hazards.*

☐ *State the negative effects of smoking tobacco on the respiratory system.*

You do not have to look very far to find some form of air pollution. Soot and smoke pour out of the smokestacks and chimneys of factories and homes. Filthy exhaust shoots out from the tailpipes of trucks, buses, and cars. Each of these sources dumps pollutants into the air. Air pollution tends to be especially serious in cities and industrial areas. Wherever air is polluted, pollutants threaten human health in a number of ways.

The Effects of Air Pollutants

Many air pollutants contain chemicals that may harm your respiratory system. For example, some air pollutants make breathing more difficult. Others help cause diseases of the respiratory system. Scientists have found that people who live or work in highly polluted areas are more likely to get respiratory diseases. Figure 14-11 summarizes harmful effects of air pollutants.

Some places present greater health risks than others. For example, people who live near coal-burning power plants often suffer the effects of pollution. Burning coal produces sulfur compounds that pass into the air. When sulfur compounds are inhaled, they may damage the respiratory system.

Sulfur compounds in combination with soot and smoke particles may cause **bronchitis.** Bronchitis is an inflammation of the bronchial tubes. The lining of the bronchi becomes very thick and produces too much mucus. People with bronchitis cough a great deal to expel this mucus from their lungs.

Air pollutants also increase the risk of **emphysema.** Emphysema is a disease that causes the breakdown of the alveoli walls. Alveoli become very enlarged and lose their ability to expand and contract. As a result, holes form in the lungs. The destruction of alveoli leaves fewer places for oxygen to enter the bloodstream. A person with emphysema also has difficulty exhaling because these holes trap air. Figure 14-12 shows the lung tissue of an emphysema patient.

Polluted cities are not the only places where people are exposed to air pollutants. In some factories and mines, workers may be exposed to harmful chemicals. Such chemicals are known as occupational pollutants. Some occupational pollutants are **carcinogens** (kar-SIN-uh-juns), or substances that cause **cancer.** Cancer is a disease having characteristics of uncontrollable growth and spread of abnormal cells. These abnormal and rapidly growing cells form a mass of tissue called a tumor.

Figure 14-12

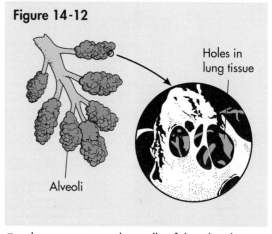

Emphysema causes the walls of the alveoli to break down, forming holes in the lung tissue.

Figure 14-11 AIR POLLUTANTS MAY

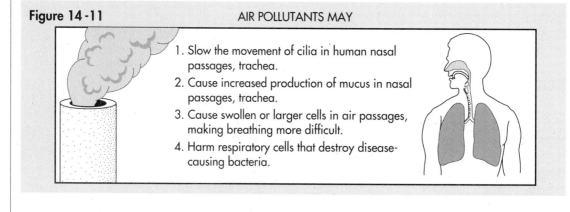

1. Slow the movement of cilia in human nasal passages, trachea.
2. Cause increased production of mucus in nasal passages, trachea.
3. Cause swollen or larger cells in air passages, making breathing more difficult.
4. Harm respiratory cells that destroy disease-causing bacteria.

Identifying a Variable

Read the paragraphs below. Then answer the questions.

Occupational pollutants include arsenic, lead, potash, cadmium, and coal tar. Exposure to any of these substances may cause lung disease. Sometimes scientists suspect a link between certain pollutants and lung disease, but it is hard to establish a clear relationship. For example, a workplace may contain many occupational pollutants. In this case, scientists may have difficulty isolating the pollutant that causes disease.

Finding links between pollutants and disease is becoming more difficult because some lung diseases may not appear until years after the person has left the workplace. Besides, many people will not take part in medical studies that try to show connections between pollutants and disease.

1. To find out the causes of lung disease, scientists must test one variable at a time. What variable would be involved in such a test?
2. Name two reasons why scientists have difficulty showing a connection between certain pollutants and lung disease.

Cigarette Smoking and Health

Look at the warning label on the cigarette package shown in Figure 14-13. What effects does smoking tobacco have on the human respiratory system? Have you considered taking up smoking? What you read may convince you not to smoke.

Cigarette smoke is produced by the burning of tobacco. Cigarette smoke contains dozens of different chemical compounds. Some of these compounds have been found to be hazardous to your health.

Nicotine The most dangerous substance in cigarette smoke is **nicotine.** In large amounts, nicotine can kill a person almost instantly. A cigarette contains only a small amount of nicotine. Even in small amounts,

however, nicotine affects the body. It speeds up the heartbeat. It narrows the blood vessels, which raises blood pressure. Nicotine also affects the nervous system.

Figure 14-13

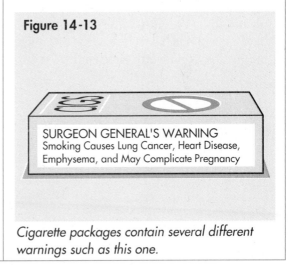

SURGEON GENERAL'S WARNING
Smoking Causes Lung Cancer, Heart Disease, Emphysema, and May Complicate Pregnancy

Cigarette packages contain several different warnings such as this one.

Carbon Monoxide Cigarette smoke also contains a gas called carbon monoxide. When a person inhales cigarette smoke, carbon monoxide enters the lungs. This carbon monoxide prevents oxygen from reaching the cells of your body.

Recall that oxygen is carried from the lungs to all of your cells by red blood cells. Hemoglobin in the red blood cells attaches to oxygen, carries it through the body, and releases it where it is needed. However, carbon monoxide can attach to hemoglobin even more easily than oxygen can. As Figure 14-14 shows, carbon monoxide then reaches the cells instead of oxygen. Cells cannot use carbon monoxide and, without oxygen, cells cannot survive.

Tar The filter of an unsmoked cigarette is white. After only a few puffs of the cigarette, though, the filter turns dark brown. The substance that causes this color change is **tar.** Tar is a yellowish, sticky substance made of many different chemicals. The cigarette filter absorbs some tar but not all of it. The tar that is not absorbed by the filter enters the lungs.

Many studies have shown that chemicals in tar from cigarette smoke cause lung cancer. In one study, mice were placed in a smoking machine that kept the air filled with tobacco smoke. After several months many of the mice died from lung cancer. Mice from the same family that were not placed in a smoking machine did not develop lung cancer. Many other experiments using other kinds of animals have shown similar results.

Experiments have also proven that tar causes cells in the lining of the bronchial tubes and air sacs to grow rapidly and form tumors. These tumors may develop into cancer. Tumors may block the bronchial tubes, which causes difficulty in obtaining air. Some of the cells in these tumors may even enter the bloodstream, where they are carried to other organs. Once inside the other organs, cancer cells grow rapidly and form more tumors. Cancer can spread throughout the body in this way. From these experiments, scientists have concluded that heavy smokers have a greater chance of developing lung cancer than do nonsmokers. To see how smoking damages the lungs, compare the healthy and cancerous lungs in Figure 14-15.

Smoking and Disease Scientists have also identified a link between smoking and

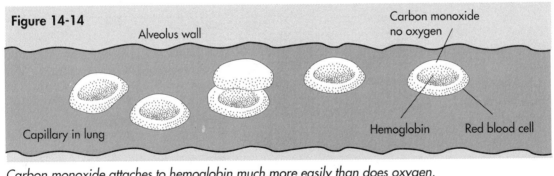

Figure 14-14

Carbon monoxide
no oxygen

Alveolus wall

Capillary in lung

Hemoglobin   Red blood cell

Carbon monoxide attaches to hemoglobin much more easily than does oxygen.

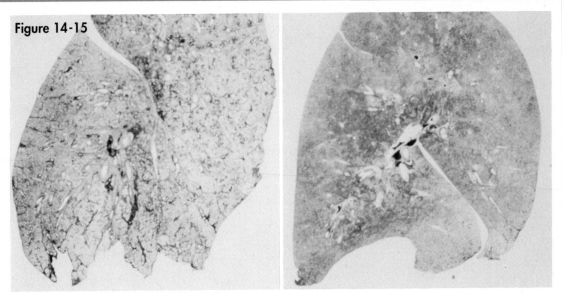

Figure 14-15

The smoker's lung on the left contains deposits not found in a healthy lung.

other respiratory diseases. These diseases include emphysema, bronchitis, and influenza. Each of these diseases affects the breathing tubes and lungs. These diseases are more common in smokers than in nonsmokers. These diseases also become worse as a person continues to smoke.

Many forms of heart disease are also connected with tobacco smoking. Studies show that the death rate from heart disease is much higher in people who smoke than in people who do not smoke. In addition, more smokers experience hardening of the arteries than do nonsmokers.

At some point in your life, you will have to decide whether or not to smoke. You will want to keep in mind the link between smoking and disease. Not smoking will greatly reduce your chances of getting heart or lung disease.

Section 14-3 Review

Write the definitions of the following terms in your own words.

1. **bronchitis**   2. **emphysema**
3. **carcinogen**   4. **nicotine**
5. **tar**

Answer these questions.

6. How do air pollutants affect the human respiratory system?
7. Why are respiratory diseases more common in urban areas than in rural areas?
8. Describe three substances in cigarette smoke that are hazardous to human health.
9. How does carbon monoxide interfere with breathing?
10. What is a tumor?

Science, Technology, & Society

Occupational Health Hazards

When you breathe, you expect to inhale clean, fresh air. Some people breathe and work in unhealthful environments, however. What makes the environments unhealthful are job-related pollutants in the air.

One job-related pollutant is asbestos. People exposed to asbestos have a greater chance of developing lung cancer than people not exposed to asbestos. Asbestos is a lightweight material commonly found in nature. Asbestos is also fireproof. For this reason, it was used for many years in shingles and other building materials, as Figure 14-16 shows.

In the 1970s, scientists discovered that lung cancer occurred more frequently among people who worked near asbestos.

These people breathed in asbestos fibers that had flaked off from pipes or walls. Scientists also discovered that most of the asbestos workers who got lung cancer were smokers.

In one study, nonsmoking asbestos workers got lung cancer at a normal rate. Coworkers of the same age who were smokers, however, developed lung cancer eight times more often. From these results, scientists concluded that asbestos increases the risk of lung cancer when it is combined with cigarette smoke.

Federal laws now forbid the use of asbestos in building materials. Millions of dollars have been spent to remove asbestos from existing buildings. By the time the danger of asbestos was known, however, many people had been exposed to asbestos, even in their own homes. Some of these people are now suffering from lung cancer and other respiratory diseases.

Follow-up Activity

Write a paragraph from the point of view of one of the people described below.

Ernest is a retired 72-year-old who is very ill with emphysema. He is suing his old employer, the Hasper Asbestos Company, for $1 million in damages.

Fred is a 45-year-old executive at Hasper. He does not think that the company owes damages to an employee who left the company more than ten years ago.

Figure 14-16 Uses of Asbestos

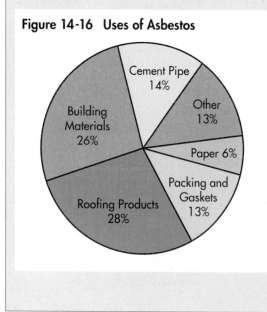

Cement Pipe 14%
Other 13%
Building Materials 26%
Paper 6%
Packing and Gaskets 13%
Roofing Products 28%

Section 14-1 Parts of Your Respiratory System

1. The respiratory system consists of the nose, trachea, bronchi, and lungs.
2. The breathing rate is determined by the amount of carbon dioxide in the blood.

Section 14-2 The Stages of Respiration

1. In the respiratory system, oxygen and carbon dioxide are exchanged between the external environment and the cells of the body.
2. The exchange of gases takes place first between the lungs and the blood and then between the blood and the body cells.
3. Cellular respiration releases energy from digested food by combining food with oxygen.

Section 14-3 Health Hazards and Your Respiratory System

1. Diseases such as bronchitis, lung cancer, and emphysema have been linked to air pollution.
2. Substances in tobacco smoke, including carbon monoxide, nicotine, and tar, have been linked to respiratory diseases such as lung cancer and emphysema.

Write the term from the list below that best matches each description.

alveoli, mucus, pleura, ATP, emphysema, cancer

1. This membrane covers and protects the lungs.
2. The cell's energy is stored in these large molecules.
3. This disease is characterized by the uncontrolled growth of cells.
4. This lung disease results in the breakdown of the walls of the alveoli.
5. These tiny air sacs make up the lungs.
6. A moist, sticky substance that traps dust and bacteria from the air.

Explain the difference between the terms in each pair.

7. nostrils, nasal passage
8. bronchus, bronchiole
9. glottis, epiglottis
10. inhale, exhale
11. pharynx, larynx
12. ADP, ATP

Write the term that best completes each statement.

1. The nasal passages are lined with a moist sticky substance called _____.
2. The trachea is a tube made of rings of soft _____.
3. Located above the glottis is a small flap called the _____.
4. The trachea divides into two _____.
5. Each alveolus is surrounded by a network of _____.
6. The breathing rate is determined by the amount of _____ gas in the blood.

7. _____ from cigarette smoke prevents oxygen from attaching to hemoglobin.
8. The process whereby glucose combines chemically with oxygen in human cells is called _____ _____.
9. The diaphragm moves down and the rib cage expands when you _____.
10. Chemicals known to cause cancer are called _____.

INTERPRETING INFORMATION

A scientist conducted an experiment to see how the amounts of certain gases in the air affect breathing rate. The experiment took place in a room where the contents of air could be changed. Subjects were asked to breathe normally. Figure 14-17 shows the results of the experiment. Use the figure to answer the questions.

1. What happened to the breathing rate when the amount of oxygen in the air was changed?

2. What happened to the breathing rate when the amount of carbon dioxide was changed?
3. Which gas controls breathing rate? How do you know?

THINK AND DISCUSS

Use the section number in parentheses to help you find each answer. Write your answer in complete sentences.

1. What do you think happens when you "swallow the wrong way"? (14-1)
2. How are the lungs adapted for the exchange of gases? (14-1)
3. What happens to the rib muscles and diaphragm when you exhale? (14-2)
4. How are oxygen and carbon dioxide gases exchanged during breathing? (14-2)
5. What are some effects of air pollutants on the structure and function of the respiratory system? (14-3)
6. Name some things you can do to protect the health of your respiratory system. (14-3)

Figure 14-17   Contents of Air Inhaled

Content of Air Inhaled	Number of Breaths per Minute
Normal Carbon dioxide/Increased oxygen	25
Normal Carbon dioxide/Decreased oxygen	25
Normal oxygen/Increased Carbon dioxide	28
Normal oxygen/Decreased Carbon dioxide	22

What changes have occurred in the smoking habits of Americans since a connection was found between cigarette smoking and cancer? Have young adults changed their views about smoking? Do some research to find out.

COMPETENCY REVIEW

1. What process takes place in organ 3, shown in Figure 14-18?
    a. heating of the air
    b. filtering of dust particles
    c. exchange of oxygen and carbon dioxide
    d. blocking of food from the trachea

Figure 14-18

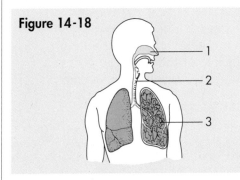

2. Particles of cigarette smoke in the lungs may most directly affect
    a. the digestion of food.
    b. the absorption of oxygen.
    c. the production of red blood cells.
    d. the flow of saliva.
3. Which of the following is not an air pollutant?
    a. asbestos   b. carbon monoxide
    c. sulfur dioxide   d. oxygen
4. Energy is released from digested food
    a. when oxygen is inhaled into the lungs.
    b. when carbon dioxide passes from the blood into the lungs.
    c. after oxygen is absorbed into the cells.
    d. as oxygen travels through the blood.
5. The digestive system is related to the stomach as the respiratory system is related to the
    a. heart.   b. lung.
    c. artery.   d. capillary.
6. To study the effect of exercise on the breathing rate, the breathing rate should be measured
    a. before exercise but not after.
    b. before, during, and after exercise.
    c. only before exercise.
    d. only after exercise.
7. Oxygen is absorbed into the capillaries after it reaches the
    a. muscles.   b. alveoli.
    c. stomach.   d. small intestine.
8. In order for oxygen to enter the lungs,
    a. the chest cavity must become larger.
    b. the chest cavity must become smaller.
    c. the diaphragm must lift up.
    d. the diaphragm must not move.
9. The process by which digested food combines with oxygen is known as
    a. circulation.
    b. chemical digestion.
    c. cellular respiration.
    d. nutrition.
10. A substance in the environment that causes cancer is a(an)
    a. carcinogen.   b. hormone.
    c. enzyme.   d. nutrient.

CHAPTER 15

YOUR EXCRETORY SYSTEM

Have you ever seen a 26-mile running marathon? Runners need a great deal of energy to run such a long distance. During the race, the runners lose a great deal of fluid. If you look along the sidelines, you may see trainers and assistants giving drinks to passing runners. The runners need to drink fluids during the race to replace the fluids lost by sweating and breathing out.

You have learned that energy comes from food that combines with oxygen during cellular respiration. Cellular respiration must take place rapidly in runners to provide the energy that moves the muscles. At the same time, the waste products, such as water and heat, are released at a fast rate. Some of these waste products are released as sweat, and some are released in air exhaled from the lungs. Breathing onto a mirror, as shown in Figure 15-1, gives evidence of the heat and water released in breath. The organs that remove these wastes make up your **excretory** (EK-skruh-tohr-ee) **system**.

15-1 The Role of Your Excretory System

■ *Objectives*

☐ *State two functions of the excretory system.*

☐ *Describe the structure and function of the skin as an excretory organ.*

☐ *Explain how perspiration forms.*

As long as you live, your cells produce wastes. The wastes produced by such activities as respiration are called metabolic,

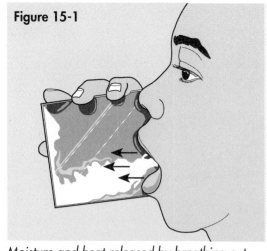

Figure 15-1

Moisture and heat released by breathing out

or **excretory wastes**. For example, carbon dioxide and water are produced as your cells oxidize food.

Your cells produce other excretory wastes. Your blood carries amino acid molecules to your cells. When amino acid molecules are oxidized, a waste product called **urea** forms. Because urea contains the element nitrogen, it is referred to as a **nitrogenous** (ny-TRAJ-uh-nus) **waste**.

Urea is an excretory waste. If urea is not removed from your body, it will collect in your cells. In large amounts, urea is poisonous and causes cell damage.

Excretory wastes such as water, carbon dioxide, nitrogenous wastes, and salts leave your cells and enter your blood. The removal of wastes from your cells, blood, and eventually your body is the process of excretion. During excretion, excretory wastes are removed from your body.

Recall that excretion is not elimination. Excretion only refers to removal of wastes from the cells. You learned in Chapter 12 that undigested and indigestible wastes leave the digestive system as solid wastes.

Because these materials never enter body cells, however, they are not excretory wastes.

The process of excretion does more than rid your body of harmful substances. It also maintains the proper water balance in your body. Water balance refers to the concentration of water and salts in body fluids. Your body contains a great deal of water and salts. In order for you to stay healthy, the concentration of water and salts must stay within a certain range.

Removing Wastes through Your Lungs

In Chapter 14 you read about the role of your lungs in respiration. The exchange of carbon dioxide and oxygen takes place in the lungs. Excretion also takes place through the lungs. When you exhale, wastes such as carbon dioxide and water leave your body. Air sacs provide a large surface area through which these wastes diffuse from the capillaries to the lungs. Figure 15-2 shows how excretory wastes are formed as a result of life processes.

Figure 15-2

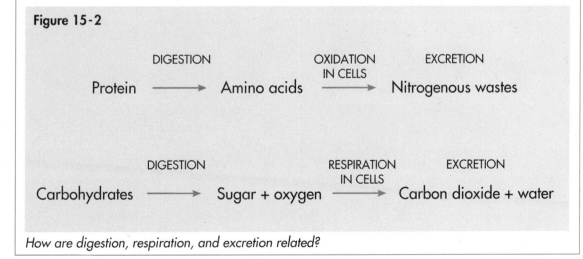

How are digestion, respiration, and excretion related?

Removing Wastes through Your Skin

Excretory wastes also leave the body through the skin. The skin is the largest organ of your body. Figure 15-3 shows the many types of tissue that make up the skin. These tissues include thousands of **sweat glands.** Sweat glands excrete wastes including salts, urea, and water from the blood.

The blood that reaches your skin cells has a high concentration of these wastes. Sweat glands have a low concentration of wastes. Many capillaries surround the sweat glands. Excretory wastes diffuse from the capillaries to the sweat glands.

Wastes then pass from the sweat glands to the skin and leave the body through tiny openings called **pores**. The mixture of wastes and water that leaves through these pores is called sweat, or **perspiration**.

You have probably noticed that you perspire more and breathe faster when you exercise. Your cells must oxidize large amounts of glucose to produce the energy needed for exercise. The increased rate of oxidation produces large amounts of carbon dioxide and water. Your body gets rid of these waste products. It removes water through heavy perspiration. It removes carbon dioxide through exhaling.

Perspiration also helps cool your body. During exercise, your body produces more heat. Your body must have a way of cooling itself, or you will overheat. When you perspire, sweat evaporates from the surface of your skin and cools your body.

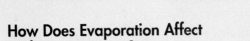

A C T I V I T Y

How Does Evaporation Affect Body Temperature?

Process Skills describing observations, explaining a relationship

Materials rubbing alcohol, two cotton balls, timer, water

In this activity, you will feel the effects of evaporation by dabbing some rubbing alcohol on your skin.

Procedure
1. Pour a small amount of rubbing alcohol onto a cotton ball.
2. Dab the cotton ball onto your wrist.
3. Start the timer immediately after you dab the cotton on your wrist. Stop the timer as soon as the liquid evaporates. Record the amount of time that elapses.
4. Observe how your skin feels as evaporation occurs.
5. Wet a second cotton ball with water. Repeat steps 2, 3, and 4.

Conclusions
6. Which liquid evaporated faster? Which made you feel cooler?
7. What is the relationship between evaporation rate and the ability to cool?
8. What effect does the evaporation of sweat from your skin have on your body temperature?
9. Why do you sweat more on a hot day than on a cool day?

Figure 15-3

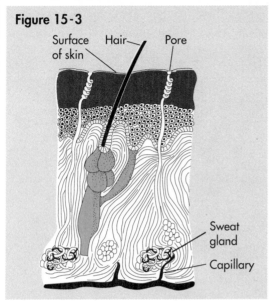

Surface of skin — Hair — Pore

Sweat gland

Capillary

Where does sweat leave the body?

▬▬ Section 15-1 Review ▬▬

Write the definitions for the following terms in your own words.

1. **excretory system**
2. **nitrogenous waste**
3. **sweat gland**
4. **perspiration**

Answer these questions.

5. How are wastes excreted through the lungs?
6. What is meant by water balance?
7. How do excretory wastes pass from the blood into the sweat glands?
8. Why do you feel hotter on a humid day than a dry day if the temperature is the same?

15-2 Removing Wastes Using Your Kidneys and Liver

■ *Objectives*

☐ *Describe the structure and function of the kidney.*

☐ *Explain how urine forms.*

☐ *Describe the role of the liver in excretion.*

You have learned how your lungs and skin help rid your body of excretory wastes. Other excretory organs also help rid your body of wastes. They help maintain the correct water balance in your body as well.

The Kidneys

The **kidneys** are bean-shaped organs about ten centimeters long, located below the middle of the back. As Figure 15-4 shows, one kidney is a little lower than the other. The kidneys filter wastes from the blood

Figure 15-4

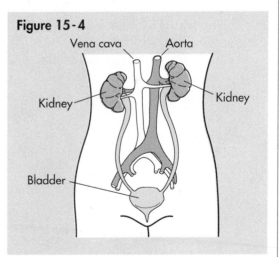

Vena cava — Aorta

Kidney — Kidney

Bladder

The kidneys are fist-sized organs located on the right and left side of the spine.

and recycle water and other usable materials. Each minute about one liter of blood passes through the kidneys.

Figure 15-5 shows a close-up view of the kidney. Find the large artery that enters each kidney. This large artery eventually

Figure 15-5

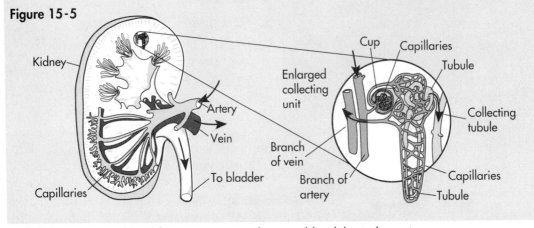

Each kidney receives blood from an artery and returns blood through a vein.

Evaluating a Hypothesis

A student complains of pain in the lower back. The school nurse notices that the student's ankles look swollen and that her eyes look puffy. The nurse immediately suspects a kidney disease. The nurse pulls out the chart shown in Figure 15-6. Suppose you are the school nurse.

1. Why should you hypothesize that this student has a kidney disease?
2. What other questions would you ask this student to support your hypothesis? Use the information in the chart to help you.
3. What test could be performed to help identify that the student has a kidney disease?

Figure 15-6 Signs of Kidney Disease

1. Puffiness around the eyes, especially in children

2. Gradual swelling of parts of the body, such as ankles

3. Lower back pain just below the rib cage

4. Increase in the number of times urination occurs

5. Pain during urination, or change in urine color

6. High blood pressure, which can be tested with a blood pressure cuff

branches into groups of capillaries. A cup-shaped structure surrounds each group. Each kidney contains about one million of these structures.

Water, sugar, minerals, and wastes from the blood pass from the capillaries into the cups. These materials pass from the cups to long, narrow tubules. There, the sugar, minerals, and most of the water return to the blood. This filtered blood enters the veins and returns to the heart.

Meanwhile, the wastes and excess water collect in the tubules, forming **urine.** Urine consists mainly of water, salts, and urea. The many tubules merge into one large tube that leaves each kidney. These tubes carry the urine to a sac called the **urinary bladder**. When the bladder becomes full, the urine passes to a tube that leads out of the body.

The Liver

You know that urine contains urea. Urea comes from the breakdown of amino acids by the liver. Look at the liver shown in Figure 15-7. The liver is a large, heavy organ that may weigh up to 1500 grams.

Recall from Chapter 12 that your liver produces bile which helps digest fats. In addition to this important role in digestion, the liver also plays an important role in excretion.

Your liver removes worn-out red blood cells from your bloodstream and destroys them. After the red blood cells are destroyed, iron remains in the liver. This iron is returned to the bloodstream, where it is carried to the bone marrow. In the bone marrow, iron is reused to make new red blood cells.

Figure 15-7

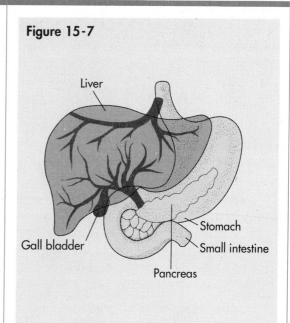

The liver is the heaviest organ in the body.

▬ Section 15-2 Review ▬

Write the definitions for the following terms in your own words.

1. **kidney** 2. **urine**
3. **urinary bladder**

Answer these questions.

4. What is the role of the kidney?
5. What happens to excretory wastes that the kidneys filter from the blood?
6. Why does your body not lose all the water and nutrients that filter out of the blood and into the kidneys?
7. How does the liver recycle iron in your body? What do you think would happen to your body if it did not recycle iron?

SCIENCE, TECHNOLOGY, & SOCIETY

Artificial Kidneys

What happens when a person's kidneys stop working? Poisonous excretory wastes collect in the blood. If the wastes are not removed, the person will die.

Kidney disease was once a leading cause of death. Scientists, however, have developed ways to remove wastes from the blood of a person with diseased kidneys. One such development is the artificial kidney. The artificial kidney cleans the blood by removing wastes.

Figure 15-8 shows a patient hooked up to an artificial kidney machine. The tubes placed in an artery and vein in the arm connect the patient to the machine. The machine cleans blood from the artery with a washing solution. Then the cleaned blood returns through the vein to the patient's body. Patients use the artificial kidney two or three times a week.

The first artificial kidneys were too large to move around. Many patients today, however, use portable artificial kidneys that can be carried from place to place. These patients can do most everyday activities without following a special schedule.

Like all technologies, artificial kidney machines come with costs and burdens. They are very expensive. For this reason, only a limited number of machines have been made, although there are many individuals who need them. Therefore, patients often must wait for a machine to become available.

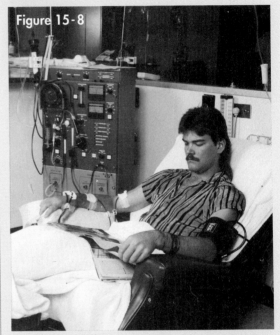

Figure 15-8

This person is being treated with an artificial kidney machine.

Follow-up Activities
1. The artificial kidney machine works on a principle called dialysis. What is dialysis? Do library research to find out.
2. Some patients have another choice besides the artificial kidney machine. This choice is called CAPD, for continuous ambulatory peritoneal dialysis. Just what is CAPD? Why is it more convenient to use than an artificial kidney machine? Do library research to find out.

Section 15-1 The Role of Your Excretory System

1. The excretory system removes wastes from the blood and eventually from the body.
2. Excretory wastes include water, carbon dioxide, salts, and nitrogenous wastes.
3. The excretory system consists of the lungs, skin, kidneys, and liver.
4. The skin removes excretory wastes from the blood as perspiration, or sweat.
5. When sweat evaporates from the surface of the skin, the body temperature decreases.

Section 15-2 Removing Wastes Using Your Kidneys and Liver

1. The kidneys eliminate excretory wastes from the blood as urine.
2. Excretory wastes that pass from the blood into the kidney tubes collect in the urinary bladder.
3. The liver breaks down excess amino acids into urea.
4. The liver destroys worn-out red blood cells.

Write the term from the list that best matches each statement.

bladder, kidneys, pores, urea, red blood, perspiration, excretory, urine

The wastes of your cells are called metabolic or ___1___ wastes. These wastes are filtered from the blood in your lungs, skin, and ___2___. Your skin contains thousands of openings called ___3___. Through these openings ___4___, a mixture of excretory wastes and water, leaves your body. Excretory wastes filtered from the blood are carried by tubes from the kidneys to the urinary ___5___.

These wastes leave the bladder in the form of ___6___. The liver breaks down excess amino acids into a nitrogenous waste called ___7___. The liver also destroys worn out ___8___ cells.

If the sentence is true, write *true*. If the sentence is false, change the *italicized* term to make the statement true.

1. The wastes of your cells are called *solid* wastes.
2. Urea is an example of a *nitrogenous* waste.
3. The *oil* glands excrete wastes including salts, nitrogenous wastes, and water from the blood.
4. As you perspire, sweat evaporates from the surface of your skin, helping to *warm* your body.
5. The kidneys are *bean-shaped* organs.
6. Wastes filtered from the blood by your kidneys make up *sweat*.
7. Excretory wastes are stored in the *gall* bladder.
8. Worn-out red blood cells are destroyed in the *liver.*
9. The liver is part of both the *skeletal* and excretory systems.
10. The *kidneys* help maintain the correct water balance in your body.

CHAPTER REVIEW

INTERPRETING INFORMATION

The following statements describe the structures with key letters shown in Figure 15-9. Match each statement to the letter of the structure it describes.

Figure 15-9

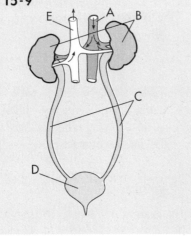

1. Urine collects here before it passes out of the body.
2. Blood is filtered as it passes through millions of tubes in these structures.
3. Blood enters the kidneys through this blood vessel.
4. Newly cleaned blood enters this blood vessel.
5. Urine leaves the kidneys through these structures and is carried to the bladder.

THINK AND DISCUSS

Use the section number in parentheses to help you find each answer. Write your answers in complete sentences.

1. Discuss the role of the skin in removing wastes. (15-1)
2. Sometimes runners take salt tablets after they run a race. Why might they do this? (15-1)
3. How is urine similar to perspiration? Compare the processes by which urine and perspiration are formed. (15-1, 15-2)
4. If not for your kidneys, you would have to drink great amounts of water each day to meet your body's water needs. How do your kidneys recycle water? (15-2)
5. The liver breaks down amino acids into urea and helps in the digestion of fats. How does the liver affect blood? (15-2)

GOING FURTHER

1. Ask your teacher to show you models of the skin and the kidney. Find the blood capillaries in each model. Then write a short description of the role of the blood capillaries in each organ.
2. A federal law requires that city sewage be treated before being dumped into waterways. Visit a library to learn how human wastes are treated today. Make a list of the main points.

COMPETENCY REVIEW

1. Which statement is true of the excretory system?
   a. It consists of the stomach, small intestine, and large intestine.
   b. It consists of bones and cartilage.
   c. It removes cellular wastes from the blood and from the body.

d. It eliminates solid wastes from the large intestine.

2. Which organ is not part of the excretory system?
   a. liver
   b. lung
   c. kidney
   d. stomach

3. Which statement about the kidney is true?
   a. It helps control the water and mineral balance in the body.
   b. It produces red blood cells.
   c. It destroys red blood cells.
   d. It produces bile.

4. Which organ removes cellular wastes from the blood?
   a. testis
   b. esophagus
   c. gall bladder
   d. kidney

5. If a person's skin is covered with paint, which process will be affected?
   a. removal of carbon dioxide
   b. absorption of oxygen
   c. removal of perspiration
   d. production of bile

6. Which of the following is not an excretory waste?
   a. feces   b. water
   c. urea   d. salt

7. The digestive system is related to the small intestine as the excretory system is related to the
   a. kidneys.   b. heart.
   c. gall bladder. d. pancreas.

8. Water, salt, and urea are removed from the blood by the
   a. liver and lungs.
   b. sweat glands.
   c. pancreas and gall bladder.
   d. kidneys and liver.

Use Figure 15-10 to answer questions 9 and 10.

Figure 15-10

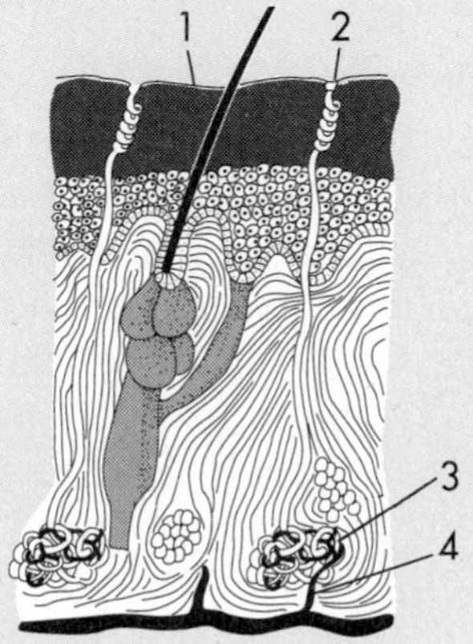

9. In which structure is perspiration produced?
   a. 1
   b. 2
   c. 3
   d. 4

10. Which structure excretes perspiration from the skin?
    a. 1
    b. 2
    c. 3
    d. 4

CHAPTER 16

YOUR NERVOUS SYSTEM

Imagine returning home from school to find the aroma of your favorite food filling the air. Before you even enter the kitchen, you may know what is being served for dinner. How do you react to this aroma? You probably begin to feel hungry. Perhaps your mouth begins to water. Recall from Chapter 2 that such reactions are called responses.

When you smell your favorite food, you are reacting to a change in your environment. Some responses are simple, such as blinking when dust gets in your eye or pulling your fingers away from a hot object. Other responses are more complex. Solving a mathematics problem and playing a musical instrument involve complex responses.

You respond with the help of your **nervous system**, shown in Figure 16-1. The nervous system includes all the organs that help you respond to changes in your environment. In this chapter you will learn about the organs that make up the nervous system. You will also learn how the nervous system helps control your life processes.

16-1 The Sense Organs

■ *Objectives*

☐ *State the role of the nervous system.*

☐ *List the five sense organs.*

☐ *Explain the role of the sense organs in changing stimuli into impulses.*

Stop reading this book for a moment. Close your eyes. Listen to the sounds around you. You might hear a door closing, a person talking, or music playing. You might even hear traffic or birds outside.

Figure 16-1 The Nervous System

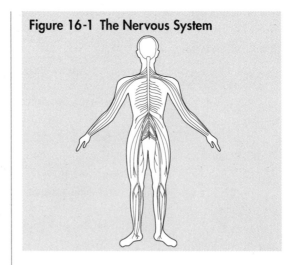

Each of these sounds is an example of a stimulus. As you learned in Chapter 2, a stimulus is any change or disturbance in the environment. Sights and smells are other examples of stimuli. As a living thing, you are constantly receiving and responding to stimuli.

What makes you aware of stimuli? How do you learn about your environment? Your eyes, ears, mouth, nose, and skin help keep you in touch with your environment. These structures are all parts of the nervous system, and they are called **sense organs**.

Sense organs contain special nerve cells called **receptors**. Each type of receptor senses a certain kind of stimulus. For example, the receptors in your eyes sense only light, and the receptors in your ears sense only sound. When a receptor receives a stimulus, it sends a message to the brain. The brain interprets the message so that the body can carry out an appropriate response.

The Eye

Your eyes are paired sense organs that receive light. They enable you to see things in the world around you. The eyeball is one of the best-protected organs in the body. The hard bones of the skull surround it almost entirely. Only the front part of the eye is not protected by the skull. The eyelid is a movable cover that protects the front of the eye.

Figure 16-2 shows the structure of the eye. Find the opening in the front of the eye; this is called the **pupil**. Look at your own pupil in a mirror. Notice how dark the pupil is. Surrounding the pupil is a circle of colored muscle called the **iris**. What color are your irises? The muscles of the iris control the amount of light that enters the eye. In bright light, the iris widens and the pupil narrows so that less light enters the eye. In darkness, the iris narrows and the pupil widens, allowing more light to enter the eye.

Follow the diagram that traces the path of light through the eye in Figure 16-2. Light first passes through the **cornea**. The cornea is a transparent layer that covers the pupil and iris. The cornea prevents dust and other objects from entering the eye. From the cornea, light passes through the pupil and then through a part of the eye called the **lens**. The lens bends the light rays that come into the eye. It aims light toward the **retina** (RET-nuh),

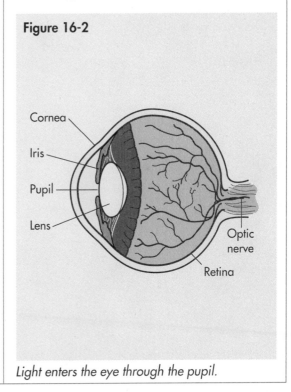

Figure 16-2

Cornea

Iris

Pupil

Lens

Optic nerve

Retina

Light enters the eye through the pupil.

the inner lining of the eye. The retina is like a screen where the pictures of light are projected. A tiny upside down image forms on the retina. Find the image in Figure 16-3. Eye muscles control the shape of the lens. This control enables you to see objects that are very near as well as those that are far away.

The back of the retina contains two kinds of light-receiving cells called cones and rods. The cones let you see colors in bright light. The rods let you see black and white and objects in dim light.

Rods and cones are connected to nerves in the retina. These nerves merge together to form the **optic nerve**. The upside-down image formed on the retina passes along the optic nerve to the brain in the form of electrical messages. The brain interprets these electrical messages and you see the object right side up.

Figure 16-3

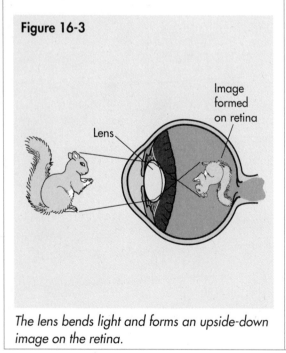

Lens

Image formed on retina

The lens bends light and forms an upside-down image on the retina.

The Ear

The sense organs that process sounds are the ears. To understand how you hear, you need to know how sound is produced and how it travels. Sounds are produced when objects vibrate. Gently place your thumb under your larynx and say hello. As you speak, you will feel a vibration. Vibrations occur as the larynx gently and rapidly pushes and pulls the air. This action rapidly squeezes air particles back and forth, producing air-pressure waves. These waves travel through the air to the ear. What happens to these air-pressure waves when they reach the ear?

The waves first reach the outer ear, which directs sounds through a short tube to the **eardrum**. The eardrum is a thin sheet of tissue that stretches across the inside of the outer ear. Find the eardrum in Figure 16-4. When sounds enter the ear, they strike the eardrum, causing it to vibrate back and forth.

Notice that the eardrum is attached to the middle ear. The middle ear consists of three tiny bones: the hammer, anvil, and stirrup. The hammer is attached to the eardrum. As the eardrum vibrates, the hammer also begins to vibrate. The hammer passes the vibration on to the anvil and then to the stirrup. Finally, the vibrations reach the inner ear.

The inner ear contains a coiled, snail-shaped structure called the **cochlea** (KOH-klee-uh). The inside of the cochlea is lined with small hairs. These hairs stimulate the ends of nerves that are connected to the brain.

When the vibrations begun in the eardrum reach the inner ear, liquid in the cochlea vibrates. The hairs that line the cochlea pick up these vibrations. The vibrations are changed to messages that are carried by nerves to the brain. The brain then translates these messages into the sounds you hear.

Hearing is not the only function of your ears. Look again at Figure 16-4. Find the **semicircular canals** in the inner ear. These loop-shaped tubes help you keep your balance. Like the cochlea, the semicircular canals are filled with liquid and lined with many tiny hairs. When your head changes position, the liquid in the semicircular canals moves. The tiny hairs sense where the liquid is. The hairs then stimulate nerves that send messages to the brain. The brain interprets these messages so that you know the position of your head and the rest of your body. You use this information to make the movements necessary to maintain your balance.

The Nose

At the beginning of this chapter, you were asked to imagine the odor of your favorite food. What are odors? What enables you to smell them?

Odors come from molecules that escape from substances such as steaming hot foods. As these molecules float through the air, they may drift by your nose. These molecules enter your nose when you breathe.

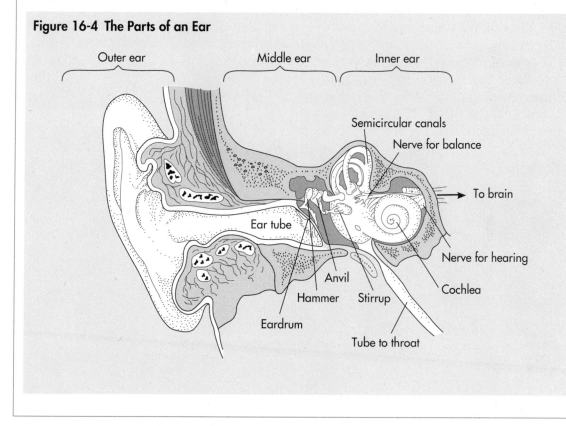

Figure 16-4 The Parts of an Ear

Outer ear   Middle ear   Inner ear

Semicircular canals
Nerve for balance
To brain
Ear tube
Nerve for hearing
Anvil
Cochlea
Hammer   Stirrup
Eardrum
Tube to throat

The lining of the nose is covered with tiny nerve endings, as shown in Figure 16-5. These nerve endings are sensitive to different types of molecules. The molecules you breathe in stimulate different nerve endings. These stimulated nerve endings, in turn, send messages through nerves to the brain. The brain interprets these nerve messages as odors. Your brain can detect up to 10,000 different kinds of odors.

The Tongue

If you were asked to describe the taste of sugar, you would probably say that it is sweet. What exactly is taste? Taste is the sense you use to detect molecules in the foods you eat. When you chew food, molecules of the food dissolve in saliva. Your taste buds sense these dissolved molecules.

Your tongue is covered with about 9000 **taste buds**. Taste buds are made of groups of nerve endings that sense the different flavors in foods. Taste buds respond to bitter, sour, salty, and sweet tastes. Study Figure 16-6 to see what parts of the tongue sense each kind of taste. Taste buds at the back of the tongue detect bitter tastes. Taste buds along the side of the tongue detect sour tastes. Taste buds located at the tip of the tongue detect salty and sweet tastes.

Your taste buds connect with nerves in the tongue. These nerves in turn connect to the brain. Tastes received by your taste buds are sent as messages through the nerves to the brain. The brain translates these messages, enabling you to decide what you are tasting.

Have you ever wondered why foods seem to have little flavor when you have a cold? The reason is that the senses of smell and taste are very closely related. If you have a stuffy nose and cannot smell your food, your ability to taste will be lessened too.

Figure 16-5

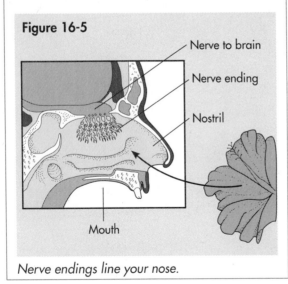

Nerve to brain

Nerve ending

Nostril

Mouth

Nerve endings line your nose.

Figure 16-6

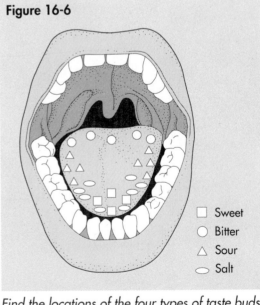

☐ Sweet
○ Bitter
△ Sour
⬭ Salt

Find the locations of the four types of taste buds on the tongue.

What Senses Do You Use to Taste Food?

Process Skills *observing*

Materials paper towels; small pieces of apple, potato, carrot, and onion

Procedures
Note: Work in pairs for this activity.
1. Fold a paper towel into a blindfold. Cover your partner's eyes with the blindfold. Have your partner tightly hold his or her nose closed.
2. Give your partner a taste of each of the foods, one at a time.
3. Ask your partner to chew each food and then tell you what it is. Make sure your partner's nose is closed while all four foods are tasted.
4. Repeat steps 1-3, but without holding the nose. This time, give the foods to your partner in a different order.

Conclusions
5. Did your partner correctly identify more foods with the nose closed or open?
6. Explain the difference in the results.

The Skin

"Don't touch the stove. It's hot!" "This shower is ice cold!" "This scraped knee really hurts!" Heat, cold, and pain are all familiar sensations. You feel these and many other sensations with your skin. Your skin can recognize five different types of stimuli. These stimuli are heat, cold, pressure, pain, and touch.

Each type of stimulus is recognized by a different kind of receptor in the skin. Figure 16-7 shows the location of some of these receptors. Some areas of the skin have more of one kind of nerve ending than other areas do. For example, the tips of your fingers and your forehead are more sensitive to touch than are other parts of the skin. When nerve endings in your skin are stimulated, a message is sent to your brain. Your brain interprets the message as one of the five sensations.

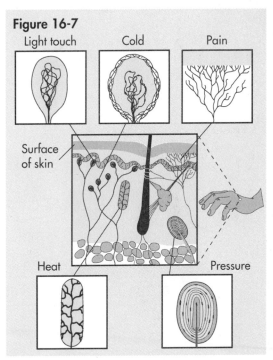

Figure 16-7

Light touch Cold Pain

Surface of skin

Heat Pressure

Several kinds of touch receptors are found at different depths below your skin.

Write the definitions for the following terms in your own words.

1. **nervous system**
2. **receptor**
3. **retina**
4. **eardrum**
5. **taste bud**

Answer these questions.

6. What is the function of a sense organ? Name the five sense organs.
7. Explain how each structure of the eye helps you see.
8. Identify the three main parts of the ear. Describe the role of each part in hearing.
9. Why do your fingertips and forehead contain more nerve endings than other parts of your skin?

16-2 Structure and Function of the Nervous System

■ Objectives

☐ *Describe the structure and function of a neuron.*

☐ *Describe the functions of three kinds of neurons.*

You know that nerves carry messages from your sense organs to your brain. In this section, you will learn how the structure of the nervous system is adapted for carrying messages throughout the body. You will also learn about the make-up of these messages, or **impulses**.

Neurons and Impulses

Messages are carried to your brain by nerve cells, or **neurons.** As you can see in Figure 16-8, neurons have many structures found in other cells of your body.

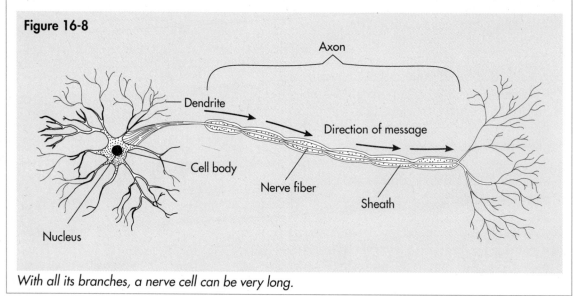

Figure 16-8

Axon

Dendrite

Direction of message

Cell body

Nerve fiber

Sheath

Nucleus

With all its branches, a nerve cell can be very long.

Each neuron has a nucleus that floats in cytoplasm. A cell membrane surrounds the cytoplasm. The nucleus, cytoplasm, and cell membrane make up the part of the cell known as the cell body.

Neurons also have structures that other cells do not have. Neurons have long, threadlike nerve fibers that extend from the cell body. Each neuron has two types of nerve fibers. The long fiber that extends from the cell body is the **axon.** The axon carries impulses away from the cell body. Each axon is surrounded by a protective coating called a sheath.

The neuron also has many shorter fibers called **dendrites.** Dendrites pick up impulses from the other parts of the body. For example, they might pick up messages from your eyes, skin, or taste buds. Dendrites also pick up messages from other neurons.

Impulses move along a neuron in one direction. Follow this movement in Figure 16-9. Impulses begin in the dendrite, pass into the cell body and from there travel through the axon. The axon then carries the message to the dendrites in the next neuron.

Look at the two neighboring neurons in Figure 16-9. Notice that they do not touch each other. The space between them is called a **synapse** (SIN-aps). To pass from one neuron to the next, an impulse must cross this synapse.

An impulse is actually a weak electrical current. It begins in a dendrite, moves into the cell body, and then travels through the axon to the end of the neuron. How does the electrical impulse travel across the synapse?

When the electrical impulse reaches the end of the axon, it causes the ends of the axon to produce a chemical. This chemical travels across the synapse to the dendrites of the neighboring neuron. The chemical then starts new electrical impulses in the dendrites of the neighboring neuron.

Types of Neurons

The nervous system includes three types of neurons. Each type of neuron has a different job to perform. Each carries messages to and from different parts of the body.

Neurons that carry messages from receptors in the sense organs to the spinal

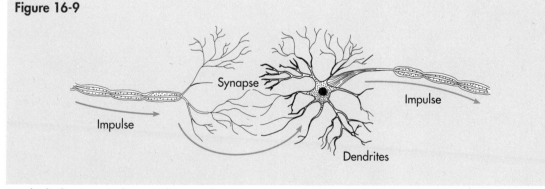

Figure 16-9

In which direction is the impulse traveling?

cord and brain are **sensory neurons**. The spinal cord and the brain contain **associative neurons** that take in all the information collected by your sensory neurons. Associative neurons interpret this information and send an impulse to a **motor neuron**. Motor neurons carry messages to your muscles, causing your muscles to move.

Figure 16-10 shows how all these neurons work together. If a doctor taps your knee, sensory neurons in your skin detect this tap. An impulse travels through your sensory neurons to the associative neurons in your spinal cord. Immediately, another impulse is sent back through a motor neuron to the muscle in your leg. This impulse causes your leg muscles to contract, and you kick your leg.

This kick, called a knee jerk, is an example of a **simple reflex**. A simple reflex is a reaction that you do not have to learn to do. Such reactions occur in a split second. Your **brain**, the organ that is the control center of your body, is not always involved in simple-reflex actions. Can you think of some other simple-reflex actions?

Neurons form a complex system in which organs of the body are connected to other organs. Each neuron in your body contains nerve fibers. As Figure 16-11 shows, these neurons are bound together like the wires in a telephone cable. These bundles of neurons form nerves. Your nerves branch out through your body, sending impulses from one part to another. Parts of your body then react to these impulses.

Figure 16-10 The Knee-Jerk Reflex

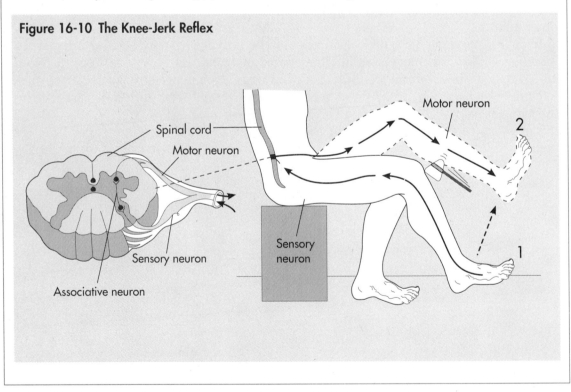

Figure 16-11

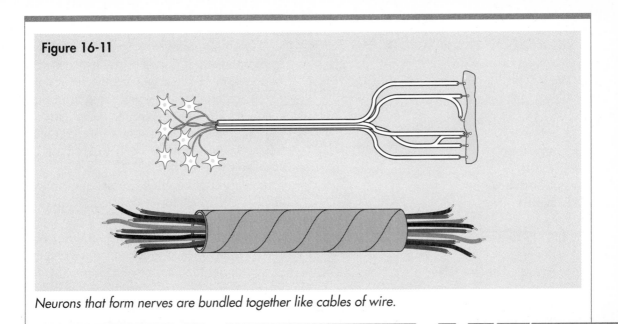

Neurons that form nerves are bundled together like cables of wire.

A C T I V I T Y

What Is a Simple Reflex?

Process Skills *observing; determining a relationship*

Materials clear plastic wrap, paper, thread

In this activity you will work with a partner to demonstrate some simple reflexes. As you do each activity, identify the stimulus and the response. Construct a data table in which you describe the stimulus and response.

Procedure

1. Ask your partner to hold a piece of clear plastic in front of his or her face. Throw a loosely wadded ball of paper, aiming at your partner's eyes. Watch your partner's eyes to see the response. Describe the response in your table.

2. Obtain a piece of sewing thread from your teacher. After your teacher has demonstrated this procedure, have your partner gently tickle the inside of his or her nostril. Describe your partner's response.

3. Ask your partner to sit with crossed legs so that one leg swings freely. Taking care not to hurt your partner, firmly strike just below his or her knee cap with the edge of your hand. Before doing this, ask your teacher to demonstrate. If you apply the stimulus at the proper place, the leg will swing outward. Describe your partner's response.

Conclusions

4. What is similar about each response?
5. Which of these activities demonstrates a simple reflex? How do you know?

Section 16-2 Review

Write the definitions for the following terms in your own words.

1. **neuron**
2. **synapse**
3. **axon**
4. **dendrite**
5. **brain**

Answer these questions.

6. What is an impulse? How does an impulse travel across a synapse?
7. Describe the three types of neurons.
8. What is a simple reflex?
9. Without looking, a girl chases a baseball into the street. She suddenly sees a car moving toward her. Trace the path that nerve impulses take for her to avoid being hit by the car.

16-3 Complex Reflexes and Voluntary Actions

■ *Objectives*

□ *Trace the path of an impulse from a sensory neuron to a motor neuron.*

□ *Distinguish between a simple reflex and a complex reflex.*

□ *Distinguish between a voluntary and an involuntary action.*

Blinking your eyes when something comes close is a simple reflex. You were born with the ability to show this reflex. Your brain does not need to process any information in a simple reflex. Other reflexes, called **complex reflexes,** are more involved. They occur almost as quickly as a simple reflex. The actions in a complex reflex, however, must be triggered by an impulse from the brain.

Imagine touching a hot object, as shown in Figure 16-12. How would you respond? You would quickly move your hand away to avoid burning your fingers. What signals the muscles in your arm to perform the movements that pull your fingers away?

First, your skin feels the hot object. The message "hot" is carried by sensory neurons to associative neurons in your spinal cord. Immediately, another impulse is sent from the spinal cord through motor neurons to the muscles in your arm. This part of your reaction is a simple reflex. At this point, however, the associative neuron carries another impulse from the spinal cord to the brain. The brain gets the message, "hot."

The brain then sends out impulses through associative neurons. These impulses reach motor neurons in the head, eyes, vocal cords, and other parts of the body. The muscles that receive these impulses respond in various ways. These muscles turn your head and eyes toward your hand and cause you to scream, "ouch." The entire process takes place in an instant. This complex reflex, however, takes just a little longer than the simple reflex that caused your hand to pull back from the hot object.

The knowledge that you burned yourself arrives after the simple-reflex action

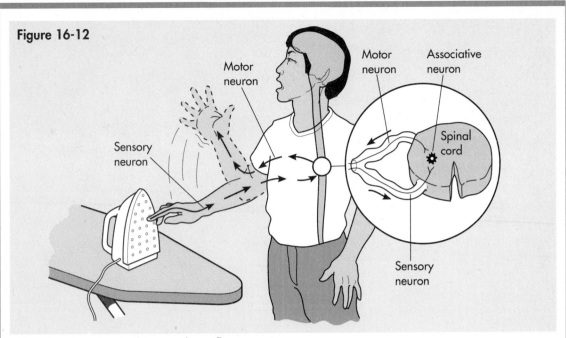

Figure 16-12

Motor neuron

Sensory neuron

Motor neuron

Associative neuron

Spinal cord

Sensory neuron

What is happening in this complex reflex?

took place. In this way, your nervous system protects you from further harm.

Actions that you think about before doing are called **voluntary actions**. Voluntary actions are controlled entirely by the brain. For example, you hear your teacher ask a question. Sensory neurons from your ear carry this message in the form of impulses to your brain. The brain quickly interprets the message, understands the question, and forms the answer.

In a flash, impulses are sent from the brain through other associative neurons and motor neurons to many parts of your body. These impulses trigger several actions. You raise your hand. Your head and eyes move toward the teacher. Perhaps you smile. All of this happens in just a fraction of a second, yet you still control these actions.

Section 16-3 Review

Write the definition for the following term in your own words.

1. **complex reflex**

Answer these questions.

2. What is the difference between a complex reflex and a simple reflex?
3. Describe how the complex reflex of pulling a hand away from a hot object takes place.
4. What is a voluntary action?
5. Suppose you cross your left knee over your right knee and begin kicking your left foot out. Is this a voluntary action? Why?

16-4 Parts of the Nervous System

■ *Objectives*
☐ *Describe the functions of the central nervous system.*
☐ *Label a diagram of the brain.*

Your nervous system is divided into two main parts. One part includes the brain and the spinal cord. The other part includes the nerves that connect the brain and spinal cord with the rest of the body.

Central Nervous System

The brain and the spinal cord make up the **central nervous system**. Find the brain and spinal cord in Figure 16-13. Impulses are interpreted in the central nervous system and are then directed through nerves to other parts of the body for an appropriate response.

Spinal Cord   The spinal cord carries messages between the brain and other body structures. The spinal cord also serves as a center for many reflex actions. Look back at the reflex action shown in Figure 16-12. What role does the spinal cord play in allowing this reflex action to take place? How does the brain become informed of what is happening?

The Brain   Humans have the most highly developed brain of all animals. The highly developed brain gives humans an increased ability to think, reason, and create. The brain is divided into three parts. Find these parts in Figure 16-14.

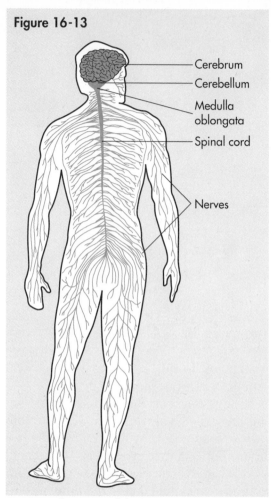

Figure 16-13

Cerebrum
Cerebellum
Medulla oblongata
Spinal cord

Nerves

How are the parts of the nervous system connected?

The largest part of the brain is the **cerebrum** (suh-REE-brum). The cerebrum is about the size of a softball. Its surface is folded and wrinkled. The cerebrum controls most voluntary actions. It controls the muscles you use to walk, hit a baseball, or comb your hair. The cerebrum enables you to think, learn, reason, and remember. Finally, the cerebrum

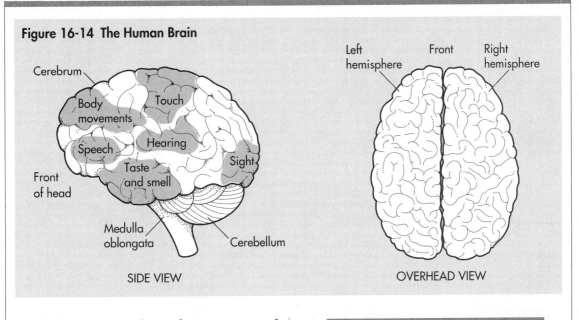

Figure 16-14 The Human Brain

Cerebrum

Body movements

Touch

Speech

Hearing

Taste and smell

Sight

Front of head

Medulla oblongata

Cerebellum

SIDE VIEW

Left hemisphere

Front

Right hemisphere

OVERHEAD VIEW

receives messages from the receptors of your sense organs.

The cerebrum is divided into the left hemisphere and the right hemisphere. The left hemisphere, or half, controls the movement of the right side of the body. The right hemisphere controls the movement of the left side of the body. Each hemisphere is further divided into sections called lobes. Each lobe controls different activities of the body, such as seeing, speaking, and moving.

The **cerebellum** (ser-uh-BEL-um) is located in the back of the brain and underneath the cerebrum. The cerebellum works with the cerebrum to **coordinate,** or organize, the movements of the skeletal muscles. Suppose that you decide to throw a ball. Nerves carry the message of your decision from your cerebrum to the cerebellum. The cerebellum, through a series of impulses, coordinates the muscles you use to throw the ball.

SKILL BUILDER

Determining Relationships

Have you ever seen a gymnast doing a headstand?

1. Describe the actions required of the gymnast to do a headstand. Write a short paragraph explaining how the parts of the body work together to do the headstand.
2. Think of other activities such as walking, writing, or catching a baseball. List the body parts involved in doing these activities. Explain how each of these activities involves the coordinated efforts of body parts.
3. Research the role of the cerebellum in organizing your voluntary muscles so that you can perform all the activities listed above.

The cerebellum also works with the semicircular canals to maintain balance. The semicircular canals send impulses to the cerebellum. The cerebellum then coordinates your muscles so that you can walk or stand straight without losing your balance. What parts of the brain is the athlete in Figure 16-15 using?

The third part of your brain is the **medulla oblongata** (muh-DUL-uh ab-lawn-GAT-uh). The medulla oblongata lies just below the cerebellum at the base of the brain. It connects the brain to the spinal cord. The medulla oblongata controls the movements of the involuntary muscles, which are the muscles that you do not control. For example, the medulla oblongata controls the cardiac muscles that pump your blood. It also controls the smooth muscles that line your digestive system and the muscles in your rib cage and diaphragm that enable you to breathe.

Peripheral Nervous System

The **peripheral nervous system** includes all the nerves, or neurons, that are not part of the central nervous system. All the body's sensory and motor neurons are part of the peripheral nervous system. The peripheral nervous system carries all the messages between the central nervous system and the rest of the body.

Look again at Figure 16-13. Notice that the nerves extend from the spinal cord to all the other parts of the body. These nerves make up the peripheral nervous system.

The peripheral nervous system is made up, in part, of the **voluntary nervous system.** The voluntary nervous system

Figure 16-15

This athlete has extraordinary coordination.

includes all the sensory neurons in the sense organs. It also includes the motor neurons that go from the brain and spinal cord to the voluntary muscles.

The peripheral nervous system is also made up of the involuntary or **autonomic nervous system**. The autonomic nervous system includes all the neurons that lead to and from the internal organs, such as the lungs, stomach, and heart. All these neurons are connected to the medulla oblongata. The autonomic nervous

What Controls Your Breathing Rate?

Process Skills measuring; inferring

Materials timer

Your breathing rate is controlled by the amount of carbon dioxide in your blood. If you hold your breath, the amount of carbon dioxide in your blood increases. Even though you stop exhaling, your cells continue to oxidize glucose and add more carbon dioxide to your blood.

As the carbon dioxide-rich blood flows to your brain, the medulla oblongata sends impulses to involuntary muscles in your diaphragm and rib cage making them contract. You resume breathing to eliminate carbon dioxide wastes.

Procedure

1. While sitting still, count the number of times you breathe per minute. Record your breathing rate.
2. Now hold your breathe as long as comfortably possible. Exhale and immediately count the number of breaths taken during the next minute. Record your results.

Conclusion

3. Explain why the number of breaths per minute was greater the second time you counted them.

system regulates involuntary actions. Involuntary actions happen automatically and are not under your control. They include processes such as respiration, digestion, and circulation.

▬ Section 16-4 Review ▬

Write the definitions for the following terms in your own words.

1. **central nervous system**
2. **peripheral nervous system**
3. **coordinate**
4. **voluntary nervous system**
5. **autonomic nervous system**

Answer these questions.

6. What is the function of the central nervous system?
7. Describe the functions of the three parts of the brain.
8. Explain how the cerebellum and the cerebrum coordinate the movements of your muscles when you throw a ball.
9. Suppose you entered a room where the air contained high levels of carbon dioxide. What part of your brain would respond to these conditions? What would it do?

SCIENCE, TECHNOLOGY, & SOCIETY

Laser Surgery to Save Sight

In most kinds of surgery, surgeons use such tools as knives and clamps. Now, however, physicians can perform some types of surgery without using a knife. Instead they use a laser, a concentrated beam of light that can be aimed with great accuracy. Figure 16-16 illustrates this new technology being used in eye surgery.

The advantage of laser surgery is that the laser cuts more cleanly than a knife.

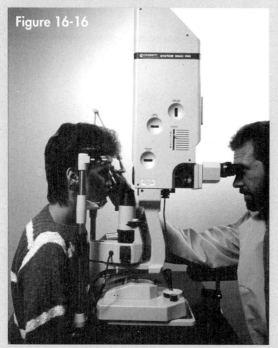
Figure 16-16

Lasers have been especially successful in eye surgery.

Little bleeding occurs because the laser seals the blood vessels. A laser can destroy a tumor in the eye without hurting healthy tissue. It can also restore a detached retina to its proper place.

Laser surgery can correct many types of eye problems. For example, a condition called a cataract causes cloudy vision in many older people. Cataracts can now be removed with a ten-minute laser treatment. In other people, the retina contains too many blood vessels. This condition may cause blindness. A laser can be used to make a tiny burn that dries up the extra blood vessels. This simple procedure can save a person's eyesight.

Laser surgery has been used mainly to treat disorders that lead to blindness. Laser surgery can also correct less serious vision problems, however. For instance, nearsighted people cannot see faraway objects. Eyeglasses or contact lenses can correct this problem. But hundreds of nearsighted people have had laser surgery to correct their problem. Some of them may never have to wear glasses again.

Follow-up Activity
1. Do you think having laser surgery to correct a slight vision problem is worth the risk and expense?
2. Would you feel the same if surgery could save your eyesight? Discuss.

■■■■■■■■ KEEPING TRACK ■■■■■■■■

KEEPING TRACK

Section 16-1 The Sense Organs

1. The nervous system regulates and controls all body activities.
2. Sense organs, including the eyes, ears, mouth, nose, and skin, receive stimuli from the environment.
3. Sense organs change stimuli into electrical impulses that are carried through nerves to the spinal cord and brain. The brain interprets stimuli and directs the proper response.

Section 16-2 Structure and Function of the Nervous System

1. Nerves are made up of neurons, which are adapted for carrying impulses from one part of the body to another.
2. Impulses are weak electrical currents that travel along a nerve in one direction only.
3. Simple reflexes are inborn reactions that do not have to be learned.

Section 16-3 Complex Reflexes and Voluntary Actions

1. Complex reflexes involve the brain, spinal cord, and several other organs.
2. Voluntary actions are actions that you think about before you do them.

Section 16-4 Parts of the Nervous System

1. The central nervous system consists of the brain and spinal cord.
2. The peripheral nervous system consists of all the sensory and motor neurons that are not part of the central nervous system.

BUILDING VOCABULARY

Write the term from the list that best matches each description.

medulla, sense organ, cochlea, associative neuron, lens, semicircular canal, muscle, simple reflex, cerebrum, impulse, optic nerve, cornea

1. structure that bends light rays to form an image in the eye
2. structure that receives stimuli from the environment
3. message carried by nerve cells
4. transmits messages from sensory neurons to motor neurons
5. transmits messages from the eye to the brain
6. snail-shaped structure in the ear
7. response that does not involve the brain
8. tissue that receives messages from motor neurons
9. part of the brain that receives information from sense organs
10. part of the brain that controls heartbeat
11. transparent covering over the eye
12. structure that helps maintain balance

Explain the difference between the terms in each pair.

13. stimulus, response
14. motor neuron, sensory neuron
15. cerebrum, cerebellum
16. synapse, impulse

SUMMARIZING

Write the missing term for each statement.

1. The eyes, ears, and nose are called ___ organs.
2. The space between two neurons is the ___.
3. A change in the environment that brings about a response is called a ___.
4. Blinking when dust gets in your eye is an example of a ___.
5. The two main parts of the nervous system are the central nervous system and the ___ nervous system.
6. The part of the brain that controls balance is the ___
7. The part of the brain that enables you to answer this question is the ___.
8. The part of the brain that controls breathing and heartbeat is the ___.
9. Nerve cells in the spinal cord are called ___ neurons.
10. Each nerve cell has one long fiber called a(an) ___.

INTERPRETING INFORMATION

Study Figure 16-17. Identify the part or parts of the brain associated with the following activities.

1. You see your friend in the lunchroom.
2. You think about the solution to a math problem.
3. Peristalsis moves your food along your digestive system.
4. You throw a ball in gym class.

Figure 16-17

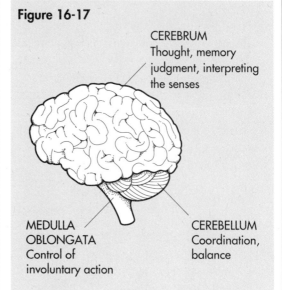

CEREBRUM
Thought, memory judgment, interpreting the senses

MEDULLA OBLONGATA
Control of involuntary action

CEREBELLUM
Coordination, balance

THINK AND DISCUSS

Use the section number in parentheses to help you find each answer. Write your answers in complete sentences.

1. Besides adding pleasure to our lives, why are taste and smell important senses? (16-1)
2. How is the structure of a neuron suited to its activity? (16-2)
3. You are sleeping soundly when your alarm clock goes off. Describe the simple and complex reflexes involved in jerking awake and turning off the alarm. (16-3)
4. A person under the influence of alcohol may stagger when walking, show poor judgment, and have slurred speech. Name the parts of the brain that alcohol affects and the ways it affects them. (16-4)

1. Describe an experience you have had in which you used your reflexes to avoid a serious injury.
2. Drugs such as marijuana, crack cocaine, and heroin affect the nervous system. Use reference books to learn about studies that show the effects of these drugs on the nervous system.

COMPETENCY REVIEW

1. A speck of dust enters your eye and your eye fills with tears. Which organ system caused this response?
   a. digestive   b. nervous
   c. circulatory   d. excretory
2. Which part of the brain enables you to think?
   a. cerebrum
   b. cerebellum
   c. medulla
   d. skull
3. Which statement is true of the retina?
   a. It allows light into the eye.
   b. It can only detect colors.
   c. An upside-down image forms on it.
   d. It bends light to form an image.
4. Which is not a sense organ?
   a. eye   b. ear
   c. nose   d. throat
5. You shudder when your warm shower turns icy. This response is called a
   a. simple reflex.
   b. voluntary action.
   c. learned behavior.
   d. reasoning behavior.

6. The brain and spinal cord make up the
   a. voluntary nervous system.
   b. central nervous system.
   c. peripheral nervous system.
   d. autonomic nervous system.
7. The part of the brain that regulates muscle coordination is the
   a. medulla oblongata.
   b. cerebrum.
   c. cerebellum.
   d. skull.
8. Which type of neuron connects the spinal cord with muscle cells?
   a. associative neuron
   b. sensory neuron
   c. motor neuron
   d. simple neuron
9. Which letter in Figure 16-18 represents the neuron that carries this impulse from the sense organ to the spinal cord?
   a. A   b. B
   c. C   d. D
10. The kind of behavior shown in Figure 16-18 is a (an)
    a. voluntary act.   b. simple reflex.
    c. habit.   d. abnormal act.

Figure 16-18

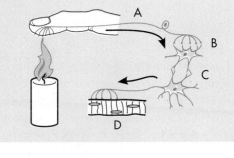

CHAPTER 17

YOUR ENDOCRINE GLANDS

Imagine that you are running a very close second in a bicycle race, such as the one shown in Figure 17-1. You are about to reach the finish line. Suddenly you have a burst of energy. You charge past your opponent and win the race. You wonder how you get that sudden burst of energy.

Far away in another location, an earthquake has just shaken a town. People are running away from collapsed buildings. A mother knows her son is trapped under a collapsed wall. Quickly, the mother lifts a huge piece of the wall to free her son. Where did she get such strength?

Both situations show how the human body can perform when a person is excited or frightened. The substance that causes these increases in energy is called a **hormone**. Hormones are chemical messengers that regulate many body processes. The hormone in the examples above is called **adrenaline** (uh-DREN-el-un). It speeds the heartbeat and breathing rate, bringing more oxygen to muscle cells. The increase in oxygen gives muscles more energy for running or lifting.

17-1 Endocrine Glands and Hormones

■ *Objectives*

☐ *Distinguish between duct glands and ductless glands.*

☐ *State the function of the endocrine system.*

☐ *Compare the function of the nervous system and the endocrine system.*

Organs that produce hormones make up your **endocrine system** (EN-duh-krun).

Figure 17-1

Adrenaline may help a cyclist win the race.

These organs include several **endocrine glands**. An endocrine gland releases, or **secretes**, hormones into the bloodstream.

Not all of your glands are endocrine glands. Look closely at the sweat gland in Figure 17-2. In Chapter 15 you learned how sweat glands in your skin secrete perspiration. Notice that a tube, or duct, leads from the base of the sweat gland to the surface of the skin.

Unlike sweat glands, endocrine glands do not have ducts. For this reason, endocrine glands are called ductless glands. The hormones produced by endocrine glands pass directly into the bloodstream. The bloodstream can therefore absorb hormones quickly and carry them throughout the body.

The endocrine glands perform a variety of functions. They work with the nervous system to coordinate and control body functions. You learned that the nervous system helps control body activities by keeping you in touch with changes in the environment. The nervous system also helps keep the conditions inside your body constant. Your body depends on the actions of hormones, however, to respond to the messages of the nervous system.

Figure 17-3 summarizes the functions of the nervous and endocrine systems, which work together to control body functions. For example, hormones produced by

Figure 17-2

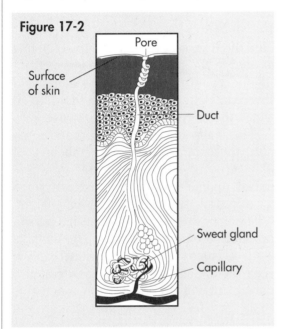

Notice the duct that carries perspiration to the surface of the skin.

Figure 17-3 Control and Regulation

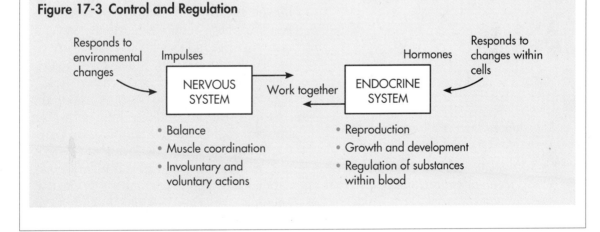

endocrine glands help control processes such as reproduction, growth, and development. Hormones also control the level of nutrients and minerals in your body, such as sugar and calcium. In fact, hormones control and regulate almost every activity that takes place in your body usually without you being aware of them.

Section 17-1 Review

Write the definitions for the following terms in your own words.

1. **hormone**
2. **endocrine system**
3. **endocrine gland**
4. **secrete**

Answer these questions.

5. How do duct glands and ductless glands differ from each other?
6. What is the function of the endocrine system?
7. Describe the role of the nervous system and the endocrine system.

17-2 The Work of the Endocrine Glands

■ *Objectives*
☐ *Label the endocrine glands on a diagram of the human body.*
☐ *Explain the function of the thyroid, parathyroid, adrenal glands, pancreas, and sex glands.*

Scientists have learned about the function of the endocrine glands by performing experiments. Figure 17-4 shows the names and locations of glands that make up the endocrine system. Refer to this figure as you read about the functions of each gland.

Thyroid Gland

Find the **thyroid gland** in Figure 17-4. It is located in the neck below the larynx. The thyroid gland produces a hormone called **thyroxin**. Thyroxin controls the rate at which the body breaks down glucose.

What happens if a person produces too little thyroxin? Very slow metabolism of glucose occurs, so very little energy is produced. An individual with too little thyroxin feels tired and sluggish and may gain weight.

The opposite reaction occurs if a person produces too much thyroxin. The metabolism of glucose in this individual occurs very rapidly and too much energy is produced. An individual with too much thyroxin may feel nervous, lose weight, and experience a rapid heartbeat.

Normal levels of thyroxin are important for normal growth and development. In one experiment, scientists surgically removed the thyroid gland from a tadpole. As you know, tadpoles normally develop into frogs. Tadpoles whose thyroids are removed, however, grow into larger tadpoles. They never develop frog characteristics.

Scientists have also learned about the thyroid gland by studying humans whose thyroid glands do not function properly. Children who have low levels of thyroxin may experience physical and mental retardation. In other people, the thyroid may become enlarged. This enlargement,

Figure 17-4

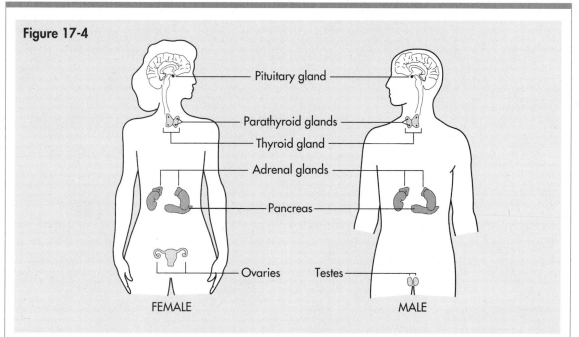

Pituitary gland

Parathyroid glands

Thyroid gland

Adrenal glands

Pancreas

Ovaries

Testes

FEMALE

MALE

The endocrine glands of a human female and male.

shown in Figure 17-5, is called a **goiter**. People who have goiters often feel sluggish and gain weight. This evidence further proves the importance of the thyroid gland in normal metabolism.

Goiters result from a lack of iodine in the diet. Iodine is one of the elements used to produce thyroxin. If the thyroid receives too little iodine, it cannot produce enough thyroxin. The thyroid swells because it is working overtime trying to produce enough thyroxin. Goiters were once a common disorder. Now, however, salt manufacturers add iodine to table salt, so most people get enough iodine in their diet, and goiters are rare problems.

Parathyroid Glands

Behind the thyroid gland are four tiny glands called the **parathyroid glands**.

Figure 17-5

What is this enlargement in the neck called? What gland has caused the enlargement?

These glands make parathyroid hormone, which controls the levels of calcium and phosphorus in the blood. Proper amounts of calcium and phosphorus are required for healthy growth of bones and teeth and of muscles and nerves. The proper amount of calcium is also needed for blood to clot.

Parathyroid hormone works by releasing calcium from bone tissue into the blood. As a result, the calcium level in the blood rises. Suppose that the parathyroid glands become too active. Then the amount of parathyroid hormone in the blood becomes abnormally high. As a result, too much calcium is removed from the bones, causing the bones to become soft.

If the parathyroid glands work too slowly, the amount of parathyroid hormone in the blood becomes too low. As a result, not enough calcium is removed from the bones, creating a shortage of calcium in the blood. This condition may cause uncontrollable muscle contractions or even convulsions.

Adrenal Glands

At the beginning of this chapter, you read about adrenaline, a hormone that increases the heartbeat and breathing rate. Adrenaline and other hormones are produced by the **adrenal glands**. As Figure 17-4 shows, you have two adrenal glands, one on top of each kidney.

Adrenaline provides extra energy during times of stress. When you are frightened, angry, or excited, the adrenal glands secrete adrenaline into the bloodstream. When adrenaline reaches the heart, it causes the heart to beat faster. Adrenaline also travels to your respiratory system, where it increases the breathing rate.

Adrenaline increases the amount of sugar, as well as oxygen, in the blood. The increased amounts of oxygen and sugar give you more energy. The energy burst that results from a surge in adrenaline has enabled some people to perform superhuman tasks. For example, one man lifted an overturned car off of the body of a friend.

Pancreas

In Chapter 12 you learned that the pancreas has an important role in digestion. The pancreas also functions as an endocrine gland. It produces two hormones, **insulin** and **glucagon**. Both of these hormones control the sugar level in your blood.

Insulin causes glucose to leave the blood and enter the cells of the liver. As a result, the blood glucose level drops. Once inside the liver, glucose is changed into starch. Glucagon has the opposite effect of insulin. Glucagon causes starch in your liver cells to break down into glucose. Then glucose leaves the liver to enter the blood. As a result, the blood glucose level rises.

You may know someone who has the disease **diabetes**. A diabetic person does not produce enough insulin. As a result, glucose cannot be removed from the blood. The kidneys remove some of the excess glucose from the blood, and it is excreted from the body in urine.

Because glucose is unable to reach the body cells, diabetics often lose weight. As the body attempts to excrete the glucose from the blood, it produces greater amounts of urine. As a result, diabetics urinate frequently and lose too much water.

Diabetes can prove fatal if it is not treated. Diabetics can control the disease by taking insulin, either by pills or injections. Diabetics must also limit the amount of sugars and starches in their diets.

What happens if glucagon levels are abnormally low? Recall that glucagon causes starch in your liver cells to be converted to glucose. The glucose is then returned to the blood, where it is distributed to the cells. Individuals with lower than normal levels of glucagon have low glucose levels in their cells. This low-level glucagon condition is called **hypoglycemia**. People with hypoglycemia often lack energy and feel tired much of the time.

Sex Glands

The endocrine system also plays an important role in human reproduction. You learned about the sex glands, the testes and ovaries, in Chapter 4. These glands are called **gonads**. Find the testes and ovaries in Figure 17-4. These glands produce the reproductive cells, or gametes. They also produce hormones that regulate sexual development. Some of these hormones are listed in Figure 17-6.

Testes   The testes are the male sex glands. They are located in a pouch outside the body wall. The testes produce a hormone called **testosterone** (teh-STAS-tuh-rohn). Under the influence of testosterone, the testes produce male reproductive cells called sperm cells. Testosterone also influences the development of male secondary sex characteristics. Secondary sex characteristics are those that do not relate directly to the reproductive organs. In males, these characteristics include the development of facial and body hair, the deepening of the voice, and broadening of the shoulders and chest.

Ovaries   The ovaries are the female sex glands. Ovaries are located in the abdominal cavity. They produce the sex hormones **estrogen** and **progesterone**. Under the influence of these hormones, the ovaries

Figure 17-6   Hormones Produced in Sex Glands

Glands	Hormone	Function
Male testes	Testosterone	Helps produce sperm Helps develop secondary sex characteristics
Female ovaries	Estrogen	Helps develop secondary sex characteristics
	Progesterone	Helps develop egg cells
		Prepares body for reproduction

Analyzing

Use the information in Figure 17-7 to answer the following questions.
1. Name two hormones produced by the pancreas.

2. What role do these two hormones play in regulating blood glucose levels?
3. Suppose you eat a meal high in sugar. How will this high sugar intake affect the endocrine system?

Figure 17-7

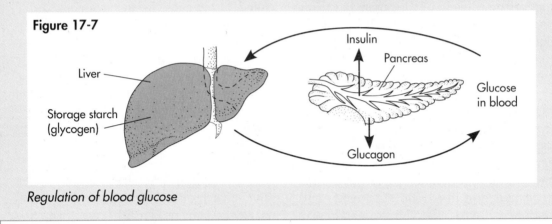

Regulation of blood glucose

produce female reproductive cells called egg cells. Estrogen and progesterone also influence the development of female secondary sex characteristics. In females, secondary sex characteristics include the growth of breasts and the widening of the hips. In addition, estrogen and progesterone play a role in regulating the menstrual cycle, which will be discussed in Chapter 20.

▬▬ Section 17-2 Review ▬▬

Write the definitions for the following terms in your own words.

1. **thyroid gland**
2. **adrenal gland**
3. **parathyroid gland**
4. **insulin**
5. **gonad**

Answer these questions.

6. Describe ways in which scientists have learned about the endocrine glands.
7. Explain how the thyroid gland controls the cell's metabolism.
8. How does the pancreas regulate the amount of sugar in the blood?
9. Suppose a person is being chased by a dog. How would the adrenal glands respond? What might the effects be?
10. What is the role of the sex glands?

17-3 Regulation and Control

■ *Objectives*

☐ *Explain how your endocrine system uses negative feedback.*

☐ *Explain how the pituitary gland regulates the other endocrine glands.*

☐ *Explain how the hypothalamus works with the endocrine system to regulate life processes.*

You may know that a device called a thermostat regulates the temperature inside your home. When you set the thermostat at a desired temperature, the thermostat helps keep this temperature. If the temperature drops, the thermostat turns the heating system on. After the temperature rises, the thermostat turns the heating system off.

The thermostat works by a **negative feedback system**. In a negative feedback system, a change in one part of the system shuts off another part of the system. Thus, an increase in room temperature signals the thermostat to turn off heat. See how negative feedback works in Figure 17-8.

Like the thermostat, the endocrine system is controlled through negative feedback. An endocrine gland called the **pituitary** (puh-TOO-uh-ter-ee) **gland** acts as the thermostat, or regulator, of your endocrine system. This gland regulates the activities of the other endocrine glands.

Pituitary Gland

Find the pituitary gland in Figure 17-9. The pituitary gland is a pea-shaped gland

Figure 17-9

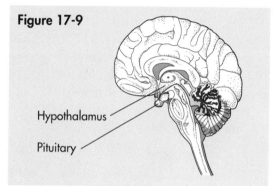

Hypothalamus

Pituitary

The pituitary gland hangs from a small part of the brain called the hypothalamus.

Figure 17-8

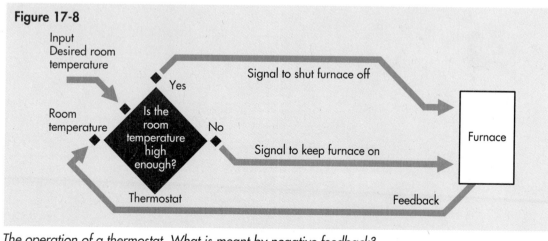

The operation of a thermostat. What is meant by negative feedback?

located at the base of the brain. Hormones produced by the pituitary gland control the activities of the other endocrine glands.

Thyroid-stimulating Hormone One hormone produced by the pituitary gland is TSH. TSH stands for thyroid-stimulating hormone. TSH enters the bloodstream, where it is carried to the thyroid gland. Here TSH stimulates the thyroid to produce thyroxin. Thyroxin then travels to the body cells, where it increases metabolism. The increased metabolism causes a rise in body temperature.

Under the influence of TSH, the level of thyroxin in the blood rises. The increased thyroxin level signals the pituitary to stop producing TSH. This action in turn causes the thyroid gland to stop producing thyroxin. As a result, the level of thyroxin in the blood falls. When the thyroxin level falls below a certain level, the pituitary gland produces more TSH, starting the process once more. Figure 17-10 shows how this negative feedback system regulates cell metabolism.

Follicle-stimulating Hormone In females, the pituitary gland produces follicle-stimulating hormone, or FSH. The bloodstream carries FSH from the pituitary to the ovaries. FSH causes the ovaries to produce estrogen. Under the influence of FSH, the level of estrogen in the blood rises.

The increased amount of estrogen in the blood signals the pituitary to stop producing FSH. The level of FSH decreases, causing the ovary to stop producing estrogen.

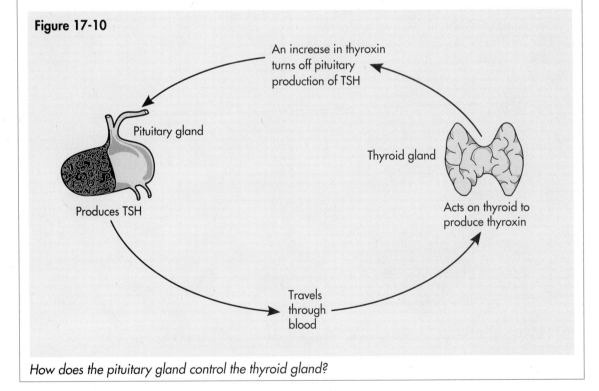

Figure 17-10

An increase in thyroxin turns off pituitary production of TSH

Pituitary gland

Thyroid gland

Produces TSH

Acts on thyroid to produce thyroxin

Travels through blood

How does the pituitary gland control the thyroid gland?

When the estrogen level drops too low, the pituitary gland starts producing FSH, starting the process over again. Figure 17-11 shows the negative feedback system that regulates amounts of FSH and estrogen.

Growth Hormone Not all pituitary hormones act on other glands. For example, the pituitary gland produces a hormone called GH, or growth hormone. GH stimulates bone and muscle growth. The action of GH determines how tall you will grow. If the pituitary gland produces too little GH during childhood, bones and muscles grow very slowly. A condition known as pituitary **dwarfism** may result. As Figure 17-12 shows, pituitary dwarfs have a short body but their body parts are in proper proportion to one another. Mental and sexual development are also normal.

In other instances, the pituitary gland produces too much GH during childhood. This results in excessive growth, a

Figure 17-12

A pituitary dwarf produces too little growth hormone during childhood.

Figure 17-11

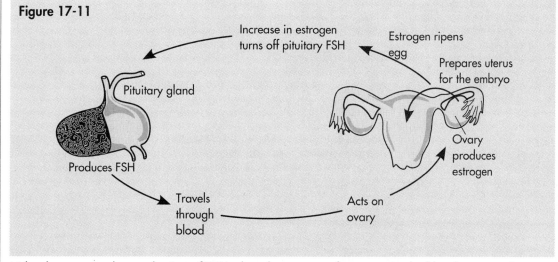

Increase in estrogen turns off pituitary FSH

Estrogen ripens egg

Prepares uterus for the embryo

Pituitary gland

Produces FSH

Travels through blood

Acts on ovary

Ovary produces estrogen

What happens to the production of FSH when the amount of estrogen in the blood increases?

condition called **giantism**. Figure 17-14 shows an example of a person whose pituitary gland has produced too much growth hormone.

The Hypothalamus
You learned earlier that the endocrine system and the nervous system work together to control life processes. The organ that

What Can You Infer about the Activities of the Endocrine Glands?

Process Skills inferring, showing a relationship

Procedure
1. Read the description of each of the five cases listed in Figure 17-13.
2. On a separate piece of paper, write the letters A through E. Beside each letter, write the name of the gland involved in each case.
3. Using Figure 17-4 as a guide, draw an outline of a human body next to your answers. Then draw in the endocrine gland from your list of answers. Label the glands with the correct name and the letters from each case.

Conclusions
4. Which gland produces a hormone that responds to stress?
5. Which gland produces the hormone most related to growth?

Figure 17-13

Case	Description
A	A boy is abnormally tall even though other family members are of average height.
B	A girl is eating normally, but she has still gained a lot of weight. She feels tired and sluggish.
C	A surge of energy enables a swimmer to overcome her opponent and win the race.
D	A man's blood sugar level continues to rise. He is always thirsty and hungry.
E	A boy is trapped under an overturned car. A friend lifts the car off the boy.

Figure 17-14

A giant produces too much growth hormone.

links these two systems is the **hypothalamus.** As you can see in Figure 17-9, the hypothalamus is the small region of the brain just below the cerebrum. The hypothalamus is considered part of both the nervous system and the endocrine system.

As an organ of the nervous system, the cells of the hypothalamus produce chemicals which regulate body temperature and the amount of water in the body. The hypothalamus also controls your appetite and sleep. When you feel hungry, thirsty, or tired, your hypothalamus is telling you that your body needs food, water, or sleep.

As an endocrine organ, the hypothalamus produces some hormones that regulate the production of hormones by other endocrine glands. For example, the hypothalamus produces a hormone that helps regulate body temperature.

Body temperature is regulated by the hypothalamus in the following way. The hypothalamus secretes pituitary-stimulating hormone, or PSH, which stimulates the pituitary to produce TSH. As you know, TSH stimulates the thyroid gland to produce thyroxin. An increase in thyroxin stimulates cell metabolism and, as a result, increases the body temperature.

When the level of thyroxin in the blood rises to normal, the hypothalamus stops secreting PSH. As a result, the pituitary stops producing TSH, and the thyroid reduces its secretion of thyroxin. The hypothalamus, by acting as controller of body temperature, thus serves as a link between the nervous and endocrine systems.

Section 17-3 Review

Write the definitions for the following terms in your own words.

1. **negative feedback system**
2. **pituitary gland**
3. **hypothalamus**
4. **dwarfism**
5. **giantism**

Answer these questions.

6. How does the pituitary gland control the activities of the other glands?
7. What role does the pituitary gland play in controlling metabolism?
8. Why, do you think, is the pituitary gland sometimes called the master gland?

SCIENCE, TECHNOLOGY, & SOCIETY

Programming Bacteria to Produce Hormones

Most of the insulin used to treat diabetics is obtained from cows and sheep. Now, however, scientists can obtain human insulin, as shown in Figure 17-15, from bacteria. Scientists can obtain other human hormones from bacteria as well. They program the genes of certain bacteria so that the bacteria produce human hormones.

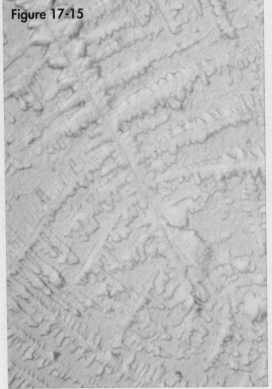

Figure 17-15

Human insulin can be produced by specially-programmed bacteria.

Scientists begin to program bacteria by first obtaining the human genes that contain instructions for producing the desired hormone. Sometimes they get these genes from the chromosomes of human cells. They may also build the necessary genes in the laboratory.

Suppose scientists want to program bacteria to produce insulin. First they obtain the human insulin gene. Then they inject this gene into the bacteria. The insulin gene becomes part of the genetic material of the bacteria. Now the bacteria contain the instructions necessary to make human insulin.

As the bacteria reproduce, so does the human gene for insulin production. Because bacteria reproduce quickly, a large amount of insulin can be produced in a short period of time. This process is much quicker and cheaper than using cows and sheep as sources of insulin.

Scientists have used a similar technique to program bacteria to produce human growth hormone (GH). In recent years, growth hormone from bacteria has been given to children who do not manufacture enough GH of their own. As a result, children who would otherwise be pituitary dwarfs may grow to a normal height.

Follow-up Activity
Many people in the United States, including children, have diabetes. Find out how diabetes is detected.

KEEPING TRACK

Section 17-1 Endocrine Glands and Hormones
1. The endocrine system consists of glands that secrete hormones directly into the bloodstream.
2. Hormones help control body functions.

Section 17-2 The Work of the Endocrine Glands
1. The thyroid and adrenal glands produce hormones that regulate cell metabolism.
2. The pancreas produces hormones called insulin and glucagon which control the amount of glucose in the blood.
3. The parathyroid gland produces parathyroid hormone, which controls the amount of calcium and phosphorous in the bloodstream.
4. The testes and ovaries produce sex hormones, which control the production of sex cells and influence secondary sex characteristics.

Section 17-3 Regulation and Control
1. The pituitary gland controls the activities of the other endocrine glands through negative feedback.
2. The hypothalamus works with the pituitary gland to regulate the endocrine system.
3. The endocrine system and the nervous system work together to coordinate and control body activities.

BUILDING VOCABULARY

Write the words from the list that complete the sentences.

diabetes, thyroxin, goiter, hypoglycemia, estrogen, glucagon, progesterone, pituitary, testosterone, adrenaline

The ___1___ gland controls the activities of other endocrine glands. The adrenal gland secretes a hormone called ___2___. The pancreas secretes a hormone called ___3___, which causes starch in the liver to break down into glucose. A shortage of this hormone causes a disease called ___4___. A person who does not produce enough insulin may develop a disease called ___5___.

The thyroid gland produces ___6___, which controls the rate at which cells metabolize glucose. A lack of this hormone may lead to an enlargement of the thyroid, called a ___7___. The ovaries produce eggs under the influence of two hormones, ___8___ and ___9___. The testes produce the hormone ___10___ which develops secondary sex characteristics.

SUMMARIZING

If the sentence is true, write *true*. If the sentence is false, change the *italicized* term to make the statement true.

1. Endocrine glands are often called *duct* glands.
2. Endocrine glands secrete chemicals called *perspiration*.
3. A person with diabetes does not produce enough *adrenaline*.
4. Normal levels of *thyroxin* are important for normal metabolism, growth, and repair.
5. The *pancreas* releases calcium from bone tissue into the blood.

6. The ovary secretes a hormone called *estrogen*.
7. The *pituitary* gland is located on top of the kidney.
8. The *pituitary* gland produces TSH and FSH.

INTERPRETING INFORMATION

Use Figure 17-16 to answer the following questions.

1. Compare the amounts of glucose in the blood of a normal person and a diabetic immediately after eating.
2. At what time was the glucose level highest in both people?
3. Why did the glucose levels for both people drop after reaching their peak?
4. Use the information in this line graph to create two bar graphs.

Figure 17-16

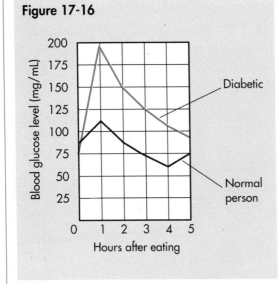

THINK AND DISCUSS

Use the section number in parentheses to help you find each answer. Write your answers in complete sentences.

1. How do endocrine glands communicate with each other and with the other organs of the body? (17-1)
2. Explain why the adrenal glands are sometimes called the "glands of combat" because of the effects of hormones. (17-2)
3. What would happen if the parathyroid glands failed to function? (17-2)
4. How does regulation of your body temperature act as a negative feedback system? (17-3)

GOING FURTHER

Some diabetics can take insulin in tablet form. Others must inject the insulin directly into their bloodstream. Do some research to find out why.

COMPETENCY REVIEW

1. Which statement about the endocrine glands is correct?
   a. They secrete hormones.
   b. They are duct glands.
   c. They are made of neurons.
   d. They secrete perspiration.
2. Which gland helps control the glucose level in the blood?
   a. ovary   b. parathyroid
   c. pancreas   d. testes

Use Figure 17-17 to answer questions 3 and 4.

Figure 17-17

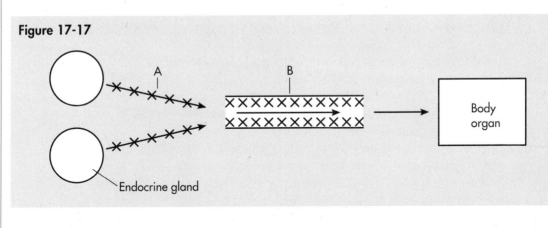

Endocrine gland

Body organ

3. What activity is taking place at letter A?
   a. Electrical messages travel through nerves.
   b. Hormones enter the bloodstream.
   c. Digestive juices enter the bloodstream.
   d. An endocrine gland secretes sugar.
4. Letter B represents a
   a. nerve.   b. duct.
   c. blood vessel.   d. cell.
5. The glands above the kidneys secrete
   a. insulin.   b. glucagon.
   c. estrogen.   d. adrenaline.

Use Figure 17-18 to answer questions 6 and 7.

6. The diagram illustrates that endocrine glands
   a. digest food.
   b. transport nutrients.
   c. coordinate and control body activities.
   d. eliminate body wastes.
7. After gland B produces hormone 2,
   a. gland A produces hormone 1.
   b. gland B produces hormone 1.

   c. hormone 1 turns on gland B.
   d. gland A stops producing hormone 1.
8. Which statement describes the function of an endocrine gland?
   a. The thyroid gland regulates metabolism.
   b. Sweat glands produce perspiration.
   c. Salivary glands secrete saliva.
   d. Gastric glands produce enzymes.

Figure 17-18

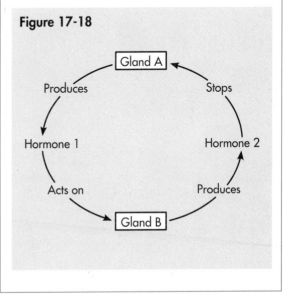

Gland A

Produces   Stops

Hormone 1   Hormone 2

Acts on   Produces

Gland B

CHAPTER 18

YOUR BEHAVIOR

To a scientist, **behavior** is any response of an organism to a stimulus from the environment. For example, a boy lifts a hot frying pan and drops it. A baby cries until it is fed. A gymnast rides a unicycle. A student solves a math problem. In each case, the person is reacting to a stimulus from the environment.

In order to carry out these and other forms of behavior, you must obtain information from your surroundings. Senses, such as sight or hearing, give you this information by receiving stimuli. Then parts of your nervous system work together so that you can behave or respond in the right way. An example of such a stimulus is shown in Figure 18-1. When your eyes see the red traffic light, your brain tells you not to cross the street. You react by waiting for the light to change to green.

Your behavior includes everything you do. Eating, breathing, blinking, talking, walking, and thinking, are all examples of behaviors you do each day. There are, of course, different kinds of behavior. You are born with the ability to carry out some forms of behavior. Other forms are learned as you live in the world.

18-1 Inborn Behavior

■ *Objectives*
☐ *Define behavior.*
☐ *Distinguish between a reflex and an instinct.*

The kind of behavior that you were born with the ability to do is called **inborn behavior**. You have been performing inborn behavior since you were born. You cried when you were uncomfortable. You swallowed when food was put into your mouth.

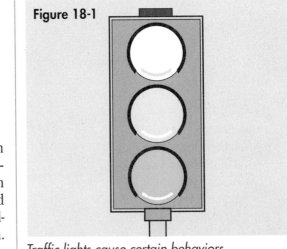

Figure 18-1

Traffic lights cause certain behaviors.

You did not have to learn these behaviors. You did them automatically.

In Chapter 16, you studied one kind of inborn behavior, reflexes. In a reflex, a certain stimulus always causes the same response. For example, the stimulus of touching a hot object with your hand causes you to quickly respond by moving your hand away. You did not learn how to move your hand when it touched the hot object, but did it automatically.

There are many other inborn reflexes that are parts of you. Can you name some? Perhaps you named blinking. When you have dust in your eye, your body reacts automatically to that stimulus by blinking. Even if you try not to blink, you probably will. Blinking is one example of a reflex. It is, therefore, an inborn behavior. For the most part, you cannot control your reflexes. They happen automatically to protect you. Can you explain how blinking protects you?

Instincts

An **instinct** is a complex pattern of inborn behavior. The major difference between a reflex and an instinct is that a reflex is simple and an instinct is not. In Figure 18-2, the bird is performing an example of instinctive behavior. Building a nest is a complicated task. The bird must find the proper tree, find the proper materials, and then put them all together in the correct order.

Figure 18-2 also shows a spider spinning a web and a butterfly flying away from its cocoon. These also are examples of inborn behavior. The bird, the spider, and the butterfly were not taught to

Figure 18-2

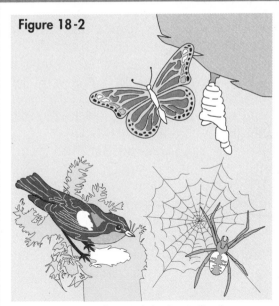

The bird, the spider, and the butterfly show instinctive behavior.

SKILL BUILDER

Stating a Hypothesis

A scientist wanted to demonstrate that a female rat caring for her young is an example of an instinct. The scientist took a litter of white rats away from its mother as soon as the rats were born. The mother had no chance to care for her young. Each of the rats grew up alone. When they were old enough, the females were mated and later gave birth.

1. Do you think that these new mothers cared for their young even though they were not cared for themselves? Explain your answer.
2. Now state your answer in the form of a hypothesis.

perform the tasks shown. Instead, they were born with these abilities.

Do you have a cat, a dog, a rabbit, or other pet? Has your pet ever given birth? If she did, you probably saw an example of caring for the young, which is another example of instinctive behavior. Animals are not taught to care for their young. The behavior, therefore, is inborn.

If you think about it, you can probably make a long list of instincts that are inborn in many animals. You have already read about a few, such as nest building, web spinning, and caring for young. There are many others, such as a dog wagging its tail, a chicken sitting on its eggs, and a fish knowing how to swim. Inborn behaviors, both reflexes and instincts, play important roles in the survival of animals.

Instincts are not as common in people, except when they are very young. A mother places a bottle in a newborn baby's mouth, and the baby begins to suck. Sucking is a form of inborn behavior. It is an instinct. Grasping is another example of instinctive behavior. If you hold your finger against the palm of a baby's hand, the baby will grasp it tightly. As humans grow and learn, they seem to depend less on instinctive behavior.

■■■ Section 18-1 Review ■■■

Write the definitions of the following terms in your own words.

1. **behavior**
2. **instinct**

Answer these questions.

3. What is meant by inborn behavior?
4. How can reflexes protect you?
5. What is the difference between an instinct and a reflex?
6. Imagine that you are reading in a quiet room. The wind blows a door shut behind you. The noise makes you jump. Have you acted on instinct or reflex? How do you know?

18-2 Learned Behavior

■ *Objectives*

☐ *Distinguish between inborn behavior and learned behavior.*

☐ *Compare conditioning to habit formation.*

☐ *Explain why conditioning and habit formation are examples of learned behavior.*

As humans mature, they seem to depend less on inborn behavior and more on **learned behavior**. Learned behavior is behavior that you were not born with, but which you had to acquire. Spelling is an example of learned behavior. Think of a word that you can spell. You could not have spelled it when you were two or three days old because you were not born with the ability to spell. You had to acquire, or learn, this ability.

Other examples of learned behavior include a dog learning to do a trick and a child learning how to ride a bicycle. Figure 18-3 shows some of these examples of learned behavior. Can you think of more?

One possible result of learned behavior is your ability to do something that you

There are many examples of learned behavior.

could not do before learning the behavior. Another result could be a change in the way you usually do something. Everything that you learn comes from one of the different kinds of learning.

Conditioning

One kind of learning is **conditioning**. Conditioning happens when an organism responds to a replacement stimulus the way it responded to an original stimulus. To help you understand conditioning, recall eating your favorite food, whatever that may be. When the food was in your mouth, your mouth probably watered. This was a response to a stimulus, food.

Suppose your favorite food was not actually present, but you thought about it. Would your mouth still water? If your mouth watered at the thought of the food, you had a conditioned reflex. The second stimulus, the thought of your favorite food, had replaced the original stimulus, the food itself.

Many years ago a scientist named Ivan Pavlov did some behavior experiments using a dog. Pavlov began by giving the dog food. The taste of the food acted as a stimulus. When given the food, the dog's mouth began to water. Every time Pavlov gave the dog the original stimulus of food, the dog had the same response.

In the next part of the experiment, shown in Figure 18-4, each time Pavlov gave the dog food, he also rang a bell. Now the dog received two stimuli, the food and the bell, at the same time. Each time the dog's response was the same. Finally, Pavlov rang the bell without giving the dog any food, as shown in Figure 18-5. Pavlov had replaced the original stimulus with a new one, ringing the bell. How do you think the dog responded?

The dog's mouth watered as if it were going to be fed. In the dog's brain the two stimuli, food and the ring of the bell, had come to mean the same thing. As a result, either stimulus produced the same response. The dog had been conditioned so that its mouth watered in response to either the original stimulus, the food, or the substituted stimulus, the sound. The dog had learned something new through conditioning.

Can you think of other examples of conditioned reflexes that can develop in a pet? Here is a hint. Think about training a dog to do a new trick. What kinds of rewards would you offer? Why is training an animal an example of conditioned behavior?

Habits

A **habit** is a chain of learned responses that becomes automatic as a result of repetition. The way you tie your shoelaces is an example of a habit. Other habits are shown in Figure 18-6.

Habits are rarely forgotten. Riding a bicycle is a good example. Have you ever heard the saying, "Once you learn to ride a bike, you never forget how"? People who learn to ride a bicycle when they are young still remember how years later. This is true even for those who have not ridden a bicycle for many years.

Habits, like reflexes, are automatic acts. You don't have to think about doing them. Instead, you do them automatically. Unlike reflexes, habits are learned.

At first, a habit has to be learned step by step. For example, to learn to tie your shoelaces, first you had to watch someone else do it, as is shown in Figure 18-7. Perhaps the process was explained to

Figure 18-4

What stimulus causes the dog to respond like this?

Figure 18-5

What stimulus is the dog responding to now?

Figure 18-6

The way you do things at an early age may become a lifelong habit.

Figure 18-7

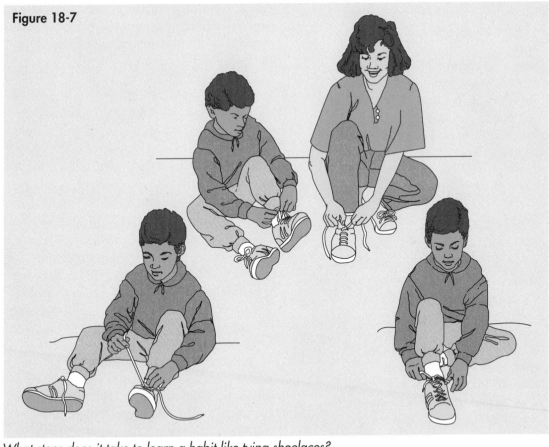

What steps does it take to learn a habit like tying shoelaces?

How Can You Condition Your Classmates?

Process Skill *designing an experiment, concluding*

Materials partner, pencil, and timer

Besides animals, people sometimes can be conditioned, too. Here is a little conditioning experiment you can try on your class and your friends.

Procedure

1. Tell your partner to tap the pencil on the desk every time you say the word *tap*.
2. Say the word *tap*. Your partner should respond by tapping. Repeat the word *tap* two more times with five seconds in between.
3. The next time, clap your hands as you say the word *tap*. Keep doing this for about one minute.
4. Now, without losing the five second rhythm, clap your hands but don't say the word *tap*.

Conclusions

5. What did your partner do when you clapped your hands without speaking? Explain why.
6. If you have a pet such as a hamster, you can condition it. You could start by noticing how your hamster responds every time you feed it. The hamster might run for the dish when you present food. Explain how you would condition the hamster to react to a second stimulus.

you. Then you tried to tie your own shoelaces. You may not have gotten it quite right the first time, the second time, or even the third. In fact, you may have tried tying your shoelaces many times before you could do it without really thinking about what you were doing. When you reached the point where you tied your shoelaces automatically, tying your shoelaces had become a habit.

Why are habits important? Habits can make difficult tasks easier. If you have a baby brother or sister, you may know how hard it is to learn to walk. A baby tries to walk over and over again. The baby usually falls down many times. It may take weeks or even months to learn the habit of walking. Once a child learns this habit, however, walking is easy.

Imagine what walking would be like if it were not a habit. Each time you wanted to go somewhere you would have to start by learning to walk again. It would take a long time to get anywhere. Think of some other habits that have helped make your life easier.

Learning a Habit As with all learning, there are certain steps you must follow to learn a habit. The first step is wanting to learn. You must have a reason for learning the habit. A baby like the one shown in Figure 18-8 may learn to walk because walking is an easier way to get from place to place than crawling is.

A baby may also learn to walk because walking pleases the baby's parents. You learn to spell difficult words for many reasons. It may make you feel good knowing you can spell a word such as *behavior*.

Figure 18-8

Describe the steps it takes to learn how to walk.

What Are the Characteristics of a Habit?

Process Skills *designing an experiment, stating conclusions*

Materials partner, paper, and pencil

Procedure

1. Ask your partner to write down what you say on a piece of paper. Tell your partner not to dot any *i* or to cross any *t* in the words they write.
2. Now rapidly read the three sentences in Figure 18-9 to your partner.
3. Was your partner successful in accomplishing this task? If not, why not?
4. Ask your partner to write his or her name with the hand he or she does not usually write with. Have your partner repeat writing with a different hand several times a day for a week.
5. Why is it hard to write with a different hand on the first try? How long does it take to get better at it?

Conclusions

6. How long does it take to form habits?
7. Why is repetition important in forming a habit?

Figure 18-9

Tibby is a little kitten. Tibby climbed up the big tree on the thirteenth day of April. It took some time for the little kitten to climb back down the tree.

Maybe it pleases your teacher or it helps you to pass a spelling test.

Sometimes you are not aware of the reasons for learning a behavior. Do you have a habit of biting your fingernails? Why do you think you have this habit? Did you say to yourself, "I think I want to learn how to bite my nails"? You may have a nervous habit like biting your nails, cracking your knuckles, or tapping your pencil. Even though you don't know why you do it, you have formed a habit.

The second step in learning is practice. In order to learn to do something, you have to do it over and over until you do it right. A baby trying to walk may keep falling down. But with much practice, the baby learns to take one step and then two, until the baby can walk across the room. In the same way, you learn to spell words by practicing them. You read them over and over. You write them 10, 20, or even 30 times. Finally, you can spell the words without having to think about them. It has become automatic. Spelling them is a habit.

The third step in learning is the enjoyment of learning what you practiced. Have you ever seen the pleasure on a baby's face when she walked across the room for the first time? Do you remember how happy you felt when you spelled a difficult word correctly? These feelings make you feel better about the habit. They make you practice it even more. They make the habit permanent.

There are many kinds of behavior that you can learn. Perhaps you might want to learn how to roller skate or ice skate. You may want to learn how to shoot baskets, ride a unicycle, or knit a scarf. Go and learn something new. Keep records of your time as you continue to practice. Remember, the more you practice a new behavior, the easier it will become, until it finally becomes a habit. Then you will do it automatically.

Learning a habit is quite simple. There are three steps that must be followed. First, you must want to learn the habit. Second, you must practice doing it. Finally, you have to feel good about learning that habit.

Breaking a Habit Sometimes, people learn bad habits as well as good habits. Smoking is an example of a bad habit. Bad habits are harmful to the person who has learned them. A person with a bad habit may try to break, or unlearn, the habit.

Many people smoke cigarettes. They probably started smoking because it made them feel good, or important, or just part of the gang. They had a reason to smoke. They did it often. They enjoyed it. Smoking became a habit.

Many smokers eventually realize that smoking is bad for their health. Smoking can cause many serious diseases, including cancer and heart attacks. For this and many other reasons, smokers may try to break the habit of smoking. What can be done to help people who have learned bad habits?

Although a bad habit cannot be forgotten, it can be replaced. Figure 18-10 suggests some habits that can replace smoking. The steps for replacing a habit are the same as for learning a new habit. You must want to learn, you must practice the new habit, and you must feel good about it.

The problem is that breaking a habit is usually very difficult. A person must want

Figure 18-10

12 THINGS TO DO INSTEAD OF SMOKING CIGARETTES.

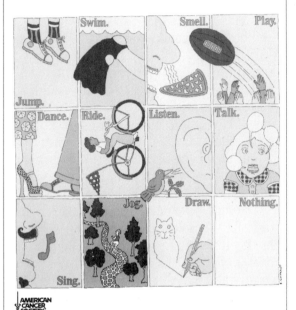

to change. He or she must practice the new habit while trying not to practice the bad habit any longer.

Nevertheless, breaking a bad habit can be done. Many people, for instance, have stopped smoking. They wanted to change because they realized how dangerous smoking is. They practiced their new habit, perhaps chewing sugarless gum instead of smoking. Finally, they felt a lot better about their health. Once people start to feel the benefits of breaking bad habits, it becomes much easier to avoid practicing them.

Write the definitions of the following terms in your own words.

1. **conditioning**   2. **habit**

Answer these questions.

3. What is meant by learned behavior?
4. How does inborn behavior differ from learned behavior?
5. One of your friends has a pet fish. Each time your friend feeds the fish, it swims to the surface. Your friend begins shining a light on the fish each time it is fed. In this way, the fish learns to swim to the surface when it sees the light. The fish does this even when no food is offered. What kind of learning has taken place? How do you know?
6. List examples of some habits. How are habits formed?

18-3 Ways We Learn

■ *Objectives*

☐ *Identify three methods through which human learning takes place.*

☐ *Relate reasoning to problem solving.*

So far, you have studied various kinds of inborn and learned behavior. These include instincts, reflexes, and habits. All these kinds of behavior become automatic. You have seen examples of these kinds of behaviors in people as well as in animals.

Automatic behavior is not the only kind of behavior, however. You have the ability to learn other forms of behavior. This ability to learn is called **intelligence**. Intelligence is partly an ability to solve problems you've never experienced before. As a human, your brain is highly developed. As a result, you have the ability to reason, to use tools, to speak, to memorize, and to understand the environment around you. You are able to use your intelligence to learn new things.

Learning by Trial and Error

One method of learning is by **trial and error**. Trial and error is trying possible solutions until the correct one is found.

Suppose you have a set of 15 or 20 keys, but only one of them will unlock the treasure chest shown in Figure 18-11. How can you find out which is the correct key? You try the first one. If it opens the lock, you have been successful. If the lock does not

Figure 18-11

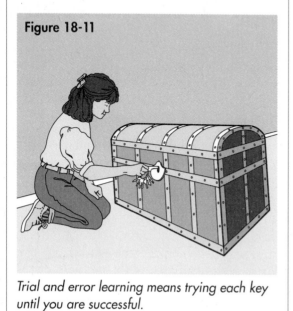

Trial and error learning means trying each key until you are successful.

open, you try the next key. You keep on trying keys until you are successful. This is an example of using trial and error to solve problems.

Thomas Edison used the same trial-and-error method to solve the problem of what material to use in his light bulb. Edison tried one material after another. Finally, he found the one that glowed the brightest and did not burn out quickly.

Learning by Past Experience

In a few years you will be old enough to drive a car. Learning to drive a car is not easy. There are many things you must remember to do at the same time. You might, however, find it easy to drive, even the first time you sit behind the steering wheel. Why?

You may have past experiences in **memory** that help you learn to drive. Memory is the knowledge you have gained from past experiences. As a child, you may have watched your parents drive the car. Perhaps you learned to ride a bicycle or rode in a go-cart. If so, you have learned certain skills and stored them in your memory. These skills are some of the same skills you need to drive a car. You can use the knowledge you have gained and stored from other experiences to help you learn a new skill.

Learning from Others

Humans have the ability to learn from one another. That is why you can learn from those who have already learned many of the things you are trying to learn. People can teach you what they already know. This can make your learning easier. You

What Is the Nature of Trial and Error Learning?

Process Skills forming generalizations, stating conclusions

Materials picture of a maze, pointer, timer

Procedure
1. Ask your teacher to provide you with a copy of the maze in Figure 18-12.
2. Set the timer.
3. Using a pointer, try to find a path through the maze. Don't be surprised if you have to backtrack several times before you succeed.
4. After solving the maze, go through it again.
5. Compare the time it took you to successfully solve the maze each time.

Conclusions
6. Did you take longer to solve the maze the first time or the second? Why?
7. Why is learning the path through a maze an example of trial and error learning?

Figure 18-12

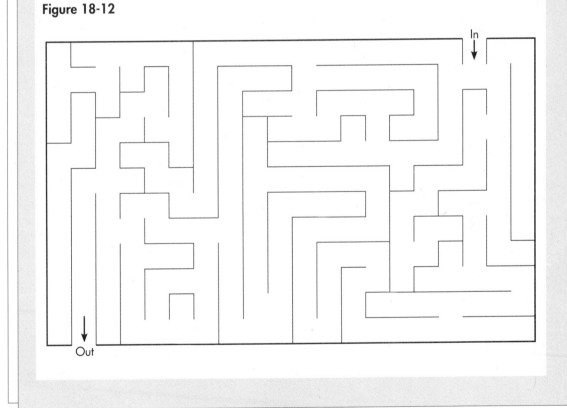

In

Out

How Do You Learn from Past Experiences?

Process Skills *stating conclusions*

Materials paper and pencil

Each individual is different from every other individual because each has a different combination of past experiences. This may cause people to have different reactions to the same situation. In this activity, you will be able to observe some of these differences.

Procedure

1. Read the list of words in Figure 18-13 to your partner.
2. As you say each word, ask your partner to write the first word that comes to mind.

Conclusion

3. Do you think that two or more classmates will come up with the same list of response words? Why or why not?

Figure 18-13

Chair	City
House	Money
Gold	Alcohol
Teacher	Apple
Cat	Barn
Family	Car
Drug	Food
School	Candy

learn in this way when a teacher shows you how to hold a pencil, write in script, or use a computer. Figure 18-14 shows some other examples of people learning from each other. When you use an encyclopedia or dictionary, you are learning from others too.

Learning by Reasoning

Most of your learning is done by **reasoning**. Reasoning is the power to think in an orderly and sensible way. For example, look back to the set of keys and the treasure chest in Figure 18-11. Instead of using a trial and error method, try just one key. If it does not fit the lock, you can reason that other similar keys will not fit either. You can then eliminate those similar keys. Now you have a much smaller number of keys to try. You can continue this process of eliminating unusable keys until you find the key that opens the lock.

Reasoning is one of the most important skills people possess. Reasoning helps solve

Figure 18-14

You can learn many things from others.

many problems. Think about some personal problems that you have faced and how you found solutions. Did you use reasoning? Success in learning depends greatly on your ability to think and reason clearly and to solve your problems.

Using Reasoning to Solve a Problem

A family is faced with the following decision. The company that employs the mother is relocating to another city. The mother was offered a job with the company in its new location. Should she and the other members of her family move to the new city?

1. Pretend that this family comes to you to help them make their decision. Make a list of the information you think you should gather before discussing possible decisions with them. Why would you ask for each of these bits of information?
2. Explain how you use reasoning to help this family solve this problem.

Section 18-3 Review

Write the definitions for the following terms in your own words.

1. **intelligence**   2. **trial and error**

Answer these questions.

3. What is reasoning?
4. List four ways in which you learn.
5. What is the advantage of reasoning over trial and error learning?
6. Why is the ability to learn helpful for human survival?

SCIENCE, TECHNOLOGY, & SOCIETY

Scanning the Brain

Medical science has long searched for a way to view the brain without causing any harm. The result is new technologies that provide images of the brain.

In 1979, Godfrey Hounsfield, an English electronics engineer, built the first CAT scanner. CAT stands for computerized axial tomography. The CAT scanner, shown in Figure 18-15, uses X rays to form images of parts of the brain. With it, a doctor can see abnormalities in brain tissue, such as those caused by tumors.

In the mid-1980s, a technique called magnetic resonance imaging, or MRI, was invented to scan the brain without using X rays. In MRI, a powerful magnetic field is produced by a large magnet strong enough to stop watches and cause bunches of keys to fly through the air. The magnet causes the hydrogen atoms in normal brain tissue to line up in a certain way. If brain tissue is abnormal, however, the hydrogen atoms line up in a slightly different way, and the abnormal tissue is revealed.

Both scanners have drawbacks, however. For one thing, doctors do not yet know the long-term and perhaps damaging effects of large dosages of X rays or magnetic fields on normal brain tissue. Both scanners are expensive to build and, because of their size, must be housed in a large, separate area. The total cost is often millions of dollars.

Follow-up Activity

Do some research to find out if scanners are used in hospitals in your area. Does the improved diagnosis the scanners provide outweigh their cost and possible risks?

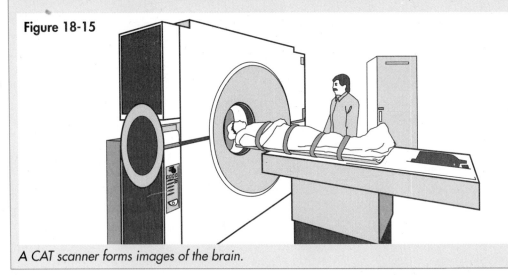

Figure 18-15

A CAT scanner forms images of the brain.

KEEPING TRACK

Section 18-1 Inborn Behavior

1. Behavior is any response of an organism to a stimulus from the environment.
2. Inborn behavior is behavior that you were born with the ability to do.
3. Instincts are complicated patterns of inborn behavior.

Section 18-2 Learned Behavior

1. Learned behavior is behavior that you were not born with but had to learn how to do.
2. Conditioning is a kind of learning in which an organism responds in the same way when a new stimulus is substituted for the original stimulus.
3. Habits are responses to stimuli that become automatic as a result of constant repetition.

Section 18-3 Ways We Learn

1. Humans possess intelligence or the ability to learn.
2. Humans learn by trial and error, past experiences, and reasoning.
3. Memory is the knowledge you have gained from past experiences.
4. Reasoning is the power to think in an orderly and sensible way.

BUILDING VOCABULARY

Write the term from the list that best matches each description.

trial and error, instinct, memory, conditioning, reasoning, habit

1. the ability to roller skate
2. the ability to sing the words to your favorite song
3. finding your way through a maze
4. finding a solution to a problem
5. the ability of a baby to suck
6. teaching your dog a new trick

Explain the difference between the terms in each pair.

7. stimulus, response
8. instinct, reflex
9. inborn behavior, learned behavior
10. conditioned response, habit
11. trial and error, reasoning

SUMMARIZING

Write the missing term for each sentence.

1. A reaction of an organism to a stimulus is called a ___.
2. The ability of a bird to build a nest is a kind of inborn behavior called an ___.
3. Conditioning is one example of a type of behavior called ___ behavior.
4. A ___ is a kind of response that becomes automatic as a result of constant repetition.
5. Intelligence is defined as the ability to ___.
6. You solve most problems through ___.
7. Thomas Edison used the ___ method to find the best material to use in his light bulb.
8. Behaviors can usually be classified as either inborn behavior or ___ behavior.
9. The ability to move your fingers away from a hot object is an example of a kind of behavior called a ___.

INTERPRETING INFORMATION

A scientist experimented by asking 20 students to read a copy of the word lists in Figure 18-16 three times. Then she asked the students to turn the lists over and rewrite each list in the correct order. The number of students who did so is shown below each list.

Figure 18-16

List A	List B	List C
Sep	Grass	Scientists
May	House	Do
Res	Teacher	Experiments
Nix	Meat	To
Mes	Table	Answer
Tus	Afternoon	Their
Auf	Bell	Questions

Students writing list correctly.		
1	3	18

1. Which list was correctly rewritten by the greatest number of students?
2. How can you explain the results?
3. Which helped students the most, thinking, reasoning, or memory?

THINK AND DISCUSS

Use the section number in parentheses to help you find the answer. Write your answer in complete sentences.

1. Why are reflexes and instincts considered to be forms of inborn behavior? (18-1)
2. What kind of behavior is shown by birds that fly south? (18-2)
3. Explain how a habit is formed.
4. Explain why teaching a dog a new trick is conditioning. (18-2)
5. How does your ability to reason help you learn? (18-3)

GOING FURTHER

1. Imagine that a close relative tells you that he wishes to stop smoking. Outline a plan of action he could take to break his bad habit.
2. Scientists believe that information is stored in your memory in the form of chemicals. Do some library research to investigate the chemical nature of your memory. Summarize your findings and present them to the class.

COMPETENCY REVIEW

1. All of the following are examples of inborn behavior except
   a. pulling your fingers away from a hot stove.
   b. salivating when you taste food.
   c. blinking when dust enters your eyes.
   d. learning how to ride a bicycle.
2. Which one of the following is an example of a human instinct?

a. A baby grasps an object.

b. A child learns to speak.

c. An adult gets to work on time.

d. A teacher asks questions in class.

3. People sometimes salivate when they smell food. This reaction is an example of a
   a. conditioned response.
   b. stimulus.
   c. habit.
   d. memory.

4. Which of the following is an example of a habit?
   a. solving a math problem
   b. riding a bicycle
   c. answering a question in class
   d. finding your way through a maze

5. The ability to learn is called
   a. memory.   b. reasoning.
   c. intelligence.   d. instinct.

6. Which statement about a habit is true?

a. It is a form of inborn behavior.

b. It must be learned.

c. A bad habit can never be broken.

d. A habit must be thought about before it is done.

7. The ability to use what you have learned in the past to solve a new problem is known as
   a. conditioning.   b. repetition.
   c. transporting.   d. reasoning.

8. A type of behavior that becomes automatic as a result of constant repetition is known as a
   a. stimulus.   b. fact.
   c. habit.   d. thought.

9. The person in Figure 18-17 is training the dog by using
   a. conditioning.
   b. trial and error learning.
   c. reasoning.
   d. ability to memorize.

Figure 18-17 Training

CHAPTER 19

HEALTH AND DRUGS

Since ancient times, people have taken medicines to relieve pain or help cure illnesses. Several thousand years ago in Egypt, for example, a common remedy for intestinal pain was to drink castor oil. Native North Americans traditionally have used many herbs for the relief of pain caused by disease.

Today, people in the United States spend billions of dollars a year on pain relievers and cold remedies. Drugstore shelves, like the ones shown in Figure 19-1, are lined with easily available medicines. Some drugs, however, must be taken only under a doctor's care. That is because drugs, when taken incorrectly, can harm the body or mind.

Still other drugs are illegal, or against the law. They are illegal because these drugs may have extremely harmful effects. People who use illegal drugs often start doing so because they are not aware of how drugs affect the body.

Are you the kind of person who says no to drugs? Knowing the facts about drugs is the first step toward making wise decisions about them. This chapter will give you some important information about drugs and how they can affect you.

19-1 A Healthy Balance

■ *Objectives*

☐ *Explain what is meant by good health.*

☐ *List the benefits of being fit.*

☐ *Explain what is meant by a positive self-image.*

As you grow older, you will make decisions that will affect your health. Health is more than just not being sick. Good health is a state of complete physical, mental, and social well-being. A healthy

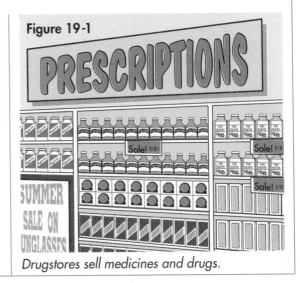
Figure 19-1

Drugstores sell medicines and drugs.

person usually eats well-balanced meals and gets enough rest and exercise. A healthy person is both energetic and physically fit.

What is meant by **physical fitness**? Physical fitness is the ability to do all normal daily activities, with energy left over to handle emergencies. When you are fit, all the body systems that you have learned about in previous chapters work better than if you were not fit. Physical fitness improves the body's ability to fight off disease. A physically fit person is also more likely to stay alert. If you are alert, you can identify possible dangers and protect your own safety. Figure 19-2 lists examples of the ways that keeping fit helps you stay healthy.

Keeping fit usually requires exercising regularly. Exercise does more than keep your body healthy. It can also help reduce stress or feelings of sadness or anger. All people feel unhappy sometimes, and these feelings are perfectly normal. Healthy, well-balanced people do not let emotions gain control of their lives, however. They find ways to solve problems before they become too hard to deal with.

When people are fit, they are likely to have a good **self-image**. Self-image is the idea you have of yourself. When you have a positive self-image, you feel good about yourself. You focus on your strengths rather than your weaknesses.

Like many other people, you may wish to improve your self-image. You may want

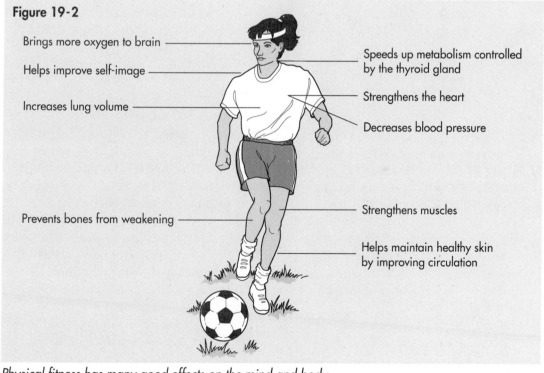

Figure 19-2

Brings more oxygen to brain

Helps improve self-image

Increases lung volume

Prevents bones from weakening

Speeds up metabolism controlled by the thyroid gland

Strengthens the heart

Decreases blood pressure

Strengthens muscles

Helps maintain healthy skin by improving circulation

Physical fitness has many good effects on the mind and body.

to get better at something. The way to improve your self-image is to set a goal to improve in a specific area. Start by setting small goals. Accomplishing these goals may give you the confidence to set higher ones. If you do not make progress at first, you might seek help from an adult you respect.

Adolescence is the time when many people form a self-image and learn decision-making skills. You begin to make choices about how you will live as an adult. These choices may involve avoiding behaviors that will harm your health. Some of these behaviors will be discussed in the next sections.

■■■ Section 19-1 Review ■■■

Write the definitions for the following terms in your own words.

1. **physical fitness**   2. **self-image**

Answer these questions.

3. What does it mean to be healthy?
4. What are some mental and physical benefits of being fit?
5. Joe is well liked, good in sports, and gets good grades in every subject except history. Yet he often feels that he is not worthwhile, especially when he gets a poor grade in history. What term describes Joe's feelings about himself? How can he improve them?
6. Make a list of decisions you will have to make in the future.

19-2 Some Important Choices

■ *Objectives*
☐ *Define drug abuse.*
☐ *List some of the reasons why teens use drugs.*
☐ *Distinguish between over-the-counter and controlled drugs.*
☐ *Describe the effects of five types of controlled drugs on the human body.*

Think about some of the decisions you will have to make in the next several years. For example, you will decide what courses to take in high school. You will decide whether to go to college and what kind of job you eventually will get.

One very important decision you will make is whether or not to use drugs. To make an informed decision about drugs, it is important to know the facts about them. Many communities have started campaigns warning teens about the harmful effects of drugs on the body. Storekeepers in these communities may display signs like the one shown in Figure 19-3.

A **drug** is a chemical taken into the body that affects the body in some way. For example, aspirin is a drug that reduces pain and fever. Antibiotics are drugs that fight infections caused by bacteria. Tranquilizers are drugs that calm people down or help them sleep. Modern medicine depends on drugs to prevent, treat, or cure many illnesses.

Other drugs have no medical benefit and are not safe to use. Even helpful drugs can be dangerous if they are not used

Figure 19-3

SAY NOPE TO DOPE.

PUS OP

Sto 9a

Are there signs like this in your neighborhood?

properly, however. The improper use of drugs is called **drug abuse**.

Drug Use and Abuse

Teenagers may use drugs for a variety of reasons. Many teens use drugs because they want to be part of a crowd. They think they will be accepted by others if they do what their friends are doing. Some young people copy the drug habit of their parents. Studies show that young people whose parents use drugs are more likely to become drug users than people whose parents do not use drugs. Still others use drugs to escape from the problems and conflicts of their difficult lives. Often these teens have a poor self-image and few friends. They may feel unloved and alone.

Some young people use drugs simply because they are curious. They may hear that drugs will make them feel good, and they want to experience these effects. The effects, however, do not last long. Many times the drug user will have to use the drug again and again to get the same feeling. Meanwhile the drug can seriously endanger the user's health.

Drugs belong to one of two groups. One group is **over-the-counter drugs**, or OTC drugs. They can be bought in a drug store or supermarket without a doctor's prescription. Aspirin, cold tablets, and many kinds of cough syrups are over-the-counter drugs. Some of these are shown in Figure 19-4.

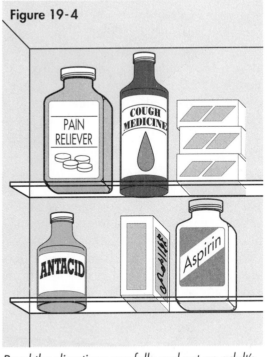

Figure 19-4

PAIN RELIEVER

COUGH MEDICINE

ANTACID

Aspirin

Read the directions carefully and get an adult's permission before taking any over-the-counter drugs.

The other group of drugs includes **controlled substances**, or controlled drugs. Controlled substances include prescription drugs and illegal drugs. A prescription is a set of instructions from a doctor that enables a patient to buy a certain drug. Prescription drugs are used to treat a variety of illnesses or injuries. People may abuse prescription drugs, however, by not using them according to the doctor's instructions.

Illegal drugs cannot be obtained with a prescription. They are considered to have no medical use or other benefits. It is a crime to use or sell these drugs.

Any drug can be dangerous if it is abused. Abusing some drugs may cause an **addiction** to the drug. An addiction is a state in which a person can no longer function normally without a particular drug. Addiction results from a **physical dependency** on a drug. Physical dependency means that the abuser's body develops a tolerance for the drug. When this happens, the drug abuser finds that more and more of the drug is needed to get the same feeling.

As a person takes more and more of a drug, more and more damage is done. Unless the drug abuser can break the drug habit or stop using the drug, the abuse might lead to death. Can an addicted person stop abusing drugs? Yes. However, curing drug abuse is very difficult, long, and painful. When a person becomes physically dependent on a drug, the body cannot work properly without the drug. Stopping drug use can cause **withdrawal**, a set of symptoms that includes pain, fever, nausea, and diarrhea.

People who cannot stop using drugs on their own may enter a hospital or other treatment center. There, doctors and counselors, like the one shown in Figure 19-5, help the drug abuser recover from the addiction. This may involve helping people to overcome a **psychological dependency** on the drug. Psychological dependency occurs when a person has a strong craving, or emotional need, for a drug. Overcoming psychological dependency can take months or even years. People who do not conquer their psychological dependence often return to drug abuse.

Kinds of Controlled Drugs

Controlled drugs can be divided into five groups. They are grouped according to what they are made of and how they affect the human body. Each group contains drugs that are often abused.

Narcotics Heroin, opium, morphine, and codeine are examples of **narcotics**. They dull the nervous system and cause drowsiness. Narcotics also slow down the respiratory system. They may also give the user a sense of well-being called a high. Some narcotics have medical uses as pain killers. Codeine is used in many cough syrups. All narcotics can cause physical dependence, however, and must be taken under a doctor's care.

Heroin is an illegal drug and is considered the most dangerous of narcotics. It is most often seen as a white or brownish powder. Beginners are likely to sniff the powder. Others might dissolve it in water and inject it just beneath the skin.

Injecting the drug this way is called skin popping. Long-term abusers inject heroin into a vein using a needle. This kind of injection is called mainlining, and it exposes the user to a variety of infections. Sharing needles causes the spread of diseases like AIDS. Mainlining can result in collapsed veins and other dangerous conditions. No matter how heroin is taken, however, repeated use leads to addiction.

When injected into veins, heroin reaches the brain very rapidly and almost immediately produces a powerful effect. The early effects of heroin may include nausea and vomiting. Afterward, the user feels relaxed and enters a dreamlike state. Feelings of peace, warmth, and well-being are

Figure 19-5

A person addicted to drugs may seek help from a counselor.

common. In this condition, which may last several hours, sensitivity to pain is reduced. Breathing becomes shallow and less frequent. The pupils of the eye decrease in size.

With repeated use of heroin, the body begins to adjust to its effects. Users require increasingly larger amounts of the drug to achieve the same results. They develop physical and psychological dependence. The body responds not only to the presence of the drug but to its absence. The dependence becomes so great that severe withdrawal symptoms result when heroin use stops.

Addiction is not the only risk that heroin users face. A sufficiently large amount of the drug can cause an **overdose**. Overdose victims may lose consciousness or go into a coma. Breathing rate, blood pressure, and body temperature all drop, and victims may stop breathing and die.

Hallucinogens   Some drugs, such as LSD and PCP, are **hallucinogens** (huh-LOOS-un-uh-juns). Hallucinogens are illegal drugs. They affect the brain and nervous system but not other parts of the body. Thus they do not cause physical dependence. A person under the influence of hallucinogens is said to be on a trip. LSD and PCP cause people to have illusions, nightmares, and hallucinations in which they see or hear things that are not there. An overdose of hallucinogens can result in frightening or dangerous hallucinations. One person on LSD, convinced she could fly, stepped from an upper-story window to her death.

PCP comes in tablets or capsules in a variety of shapes and sizes. The powdered form is also called angel dust. PCP can be smoked, snorted, swallowed, or injected. Most users smoke a marijuana cigarette sprinkled with PCP powder. The effects of the drug depend on how much is taken, how it is taken, and who takes it. PCP often disturbs memory, judgment, and concentration, which can in turn produce strange behavior. More PCP users die from accidents caused by the strange behavior than from the actual chemical effect of the drug. Many PCP users continue to experience the effects of PCP long after they have stopped taking it.

Stimulants Drugs that speed up the heartbeat, raise blood pressure, prevent sleep, and reduce appetite are called **stimulants**. Some stimulants have medical uses and are prescribed by doctors. All stimulants can produce physical dependence. An overdose of stimulants can cause hallucinations and possibly death.

Caffeine is a mild stimulant found in coffee, tea, chocolate, and some over-the-counter drugs. Amphetamines are strong stimulants, also known as speed or uppers. Many amphetamines are prescription drugs, but they are extremely dangerous and addictive if abused.

You have probably heard a great deal about the stimulant **cocaine**. Cocaine is a white powder that comes from the leaves of the coca plant, shown in Figure 19-6. It is also known as coke and snow. Most cocaine users snort, or inhale, the powder through the nose. Once inhaled, cocaine is absorbed quickly by the bloodstream.

Figure 19-6

Cocaine is made from the leaves of the coca plant, which grows in the mountains of South America.

A solid, highly concentrated form of cocaine is called **crack**. Most often crack is placed in the top of a glass pipe to which a flame is applied. The flame heats and vaporizes the crack, and the smoke is inhaled through the pipe stem. The drug is named for the cracking sound the heated mixture makes.

The immediate effects of cocaine or crack include enlarging of the pupils and a narrowing of the blood vessels. In addition, blood pressure, heart rate, breathing rate, and body temperature increase. At first the user may feel pleasant, energetic, and confident. Other users feel tense and edgy. As these effects wear off, however, the user feels depressed or let down.

Crack produces the most dramatic effects. It reaches the brain almost immediately. A rapid high is followed by a strong low. Crack leaves the user craving more. As a result, crack is very addictive. Dependency on cocaine and crack is so strong that these drugs dominate all aspects of an addict's life. This addiction could last a lifetime.

Figure 19-7 shows how severely cocaine and crack affect the body. Heart attacks and respiratory failure may occur. Cocaine and crack may cause brain seizures and strokes. Users who share needles to inject cocaine may infect themselves with hepatitis or AIDS. Cocaine and crack may interfere with normal behavior by damaging the brain.

Depressants Drugs that slow down the body's systems are **depressants**. They have the opposite effect of stimulants. They slow the heart rate and breathing rate and lower body temperature. Depressants include barbiturates and tranquilizers, which are prescribed to help a person

sleep or reduce anxious feelings or tension. Depressants are also known as downers. Most depressants are taken as pills, like those shown in Figure 19-8. Like stimulants, however, most depressants cause physical dependence that can lead to addiction or illness. An overdose of depressants can cause death. Depressants should not be taken except under a doctor's care.

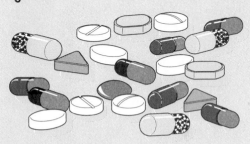

Stimulants and depressants often come in tablet or capsule form.

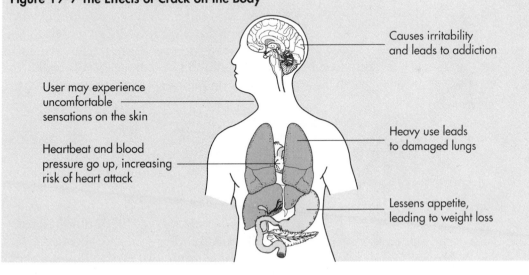

Figure 19-7 The Effects of Crack on the Body

Causes irritability and leads to addiction

User may experience uncomfortable sensations on the skin

Heartbeat and blood pressure go up, increasing risk of heart attack

Heavy use leads to damaged lungs

Lessens appetite, leading to weight loss

Marijuana One of the most common illegal drugs is **marijuana**, also called grass, pot, and weed. Marijuana comes from the hemp plant, *Cannabis sativa,* shown in Figure 19-9. A marijuana cigarette, or joint, is made from the dried leaves, stems, and buds of the plant.

Although marijuana does not cause physical dependence, psychological dependence on the drug is common. Marijuana affects different people in different ways, but it usually gives the user a high, increases the appetite, and acts as a mild depressant. Other immediate effects include an increase in heartbeat and pulse rate, bloodshot eyes, and a dry mouth and throat. The use of marijuana may decrease short-term memory. It may also alter the sense of time. Users often have difficulty concentrating, slower reactions, and loss of coordination. These effects reduce the person's ability to do such things as drive a car or operate machinery. An overdose of marijuana is not fatal, but it can lead to serious mental distress.

Some studies suggest that marijuana has no long-term effects. Other studies, though, show that heavy marijuana use does damage the body. Psychological dependence on marijuana may lead to problems with school, work, or personal relationships. The drug can become the most important part of a person's life.

Young people who start using marijuana regularly often lose interest in their schoolwork. The effects of marijuana can interfere with learning by damaging thinking, reading, comprehension, and mathematical skills. Research shows that students do not remember what they have learned when they are high.

The use of marijuana, crack, and other drugs by teenagers has increased in recent years. Many researchers believe that a lack of knowledge about drugs leads to increased drug use. The information in this chapter should help you make an informed decision about drugs.

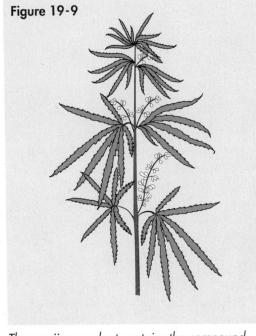

Figure 19-9

The marijuana plant contains the compound THC, which produces marijuana's effect on the body.

▬ Section 19-2 Review ▬

Write the definitions for the following terms in your own words.

1. **narcotic**
2. **hallucinogen**
3. **stimulant**
4. **depressant**
5. **marijuana**

Answer these questions.

6. What is meant by drug abuse?
7. What are some reasons why individuals abuse drugs? Suggest some alternatives to drug use.
8. Distinguish between stimulants and depressants.
9. What is crack? Why is it so dangerous?
10. If marijuana does not cause physical dependence, why is it considered dangerous?

19-3 Alcohol Abuse

■ *Objectives*
☐ *Describe the effects of alcohol on the brain and other organs.*

☐ *List the reasons why people drink alcohol.*
☐ *State some ways that alcoholics and their families can get help.*

In recent years, the number of adolescents who use alcohol has increased dramatically. By some estimates, millions of teenagers now have a drinking problem. How did their problems arise? What are the facts about alcohol?

The Effects of Alcohol

Figure 19-10 shows some effects of alcohol on the body. Alcohol is a chemical made of carbon, hydrogen, and oxygen. Like carbohydrates, which also contain these elements, alcohol can provide energy to your cells. Alcohol, however, is

Figure 19-10

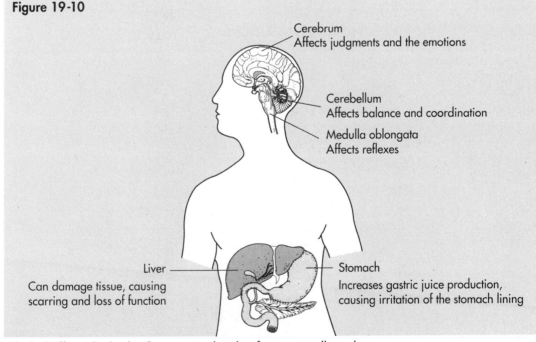

Cerebrum
Affects judgments and the emotions

Cerebellum
Affects balance and coordination

Medulla oblongata
Affects reflexes

Liver
Can damage tissue, causing scarring and loss of function

Stomach
Increases gastric juice production, causing irritation of the stomach lining

Alcohol affects the body almost immediately after it is swallowed.

not considered a good food source. It may damage the brain, heart, liver, and other organs. For these reasons, alcohol is considered a dangerous drug.

The digestive system cannot break down alcohol. After alcohol is swallowed it passes quickly through the digestive system into the bloodstream. The alcohol is then carried to all the organs. The brain absorbs more alcohol more quickly than any other organ. Alcohol affects the brain less than one minute after it is swallowed.

Recall from Chapter 16 that the human brain has three main parts. The cerebrum is the part of the brain that controls thinking, memory, and judgment. It also controls many voluntary movements of the body. The cerebellum controls balance and coordination. The medulla oblongata controls involuntary acts like breathing.

When someone drinks, alcohol affects the cerebrum first. As a result, a person's reaction time increases. Alcohol also affects the ability to judge distances. For this reason, driving a car after drinking is very dangerous. Most states have strict laws against drinking and driving.

Alcohol may also affect the part of the cerebrum that controls emotions. A person under the the influence of alcohol may feel extremely happy or sad, calm or nervous. Because everyone is different, alcohol affects people differently. Figure 19-11 summarizes some of the effects of alcohol on the body. In many states, a car driver with 0.10 percent of alcohol in the blood is subject to arrest.

Alcohol may also affect the cerebellum and the medulla oblongata. When alcohol reaches the cerebellum, a person

Figure 19-11 Effects of Blood Levels of Alcohol

Drinks per hr	Percent of alcohol in the blood	Effects
1	0.02-0.03	Feeling of relaxation
2	0.05-0.06	Slight loss of coordination
3	0.08-0.09	Loss of coordination; trouble talking and thinking
4	0.11-0.12	Slowed reaction time; lack of judgment
7	0.20	Difficulty thinking; loss of motor abilities
14	0.40	Unconsciousness; vomiting may occur
17	0.50	Deep coma; if breathing ceases, death

What Is the Relationship between Age and Motor Vehicle Accidents?

Process Skill *making a graph*

Materials graph paper, pencil

Motor vehicle accidents are a leading cause of teenage deaths in the United States. Many of these accidents involve teenagers who were driving while drunk.

Procedure
1. Study the data in Figure 19-12.
2. On a separate sheet of paper, place these data in a bar graph. Plot age along the horizontal axis and number of deaths along the vertical axis.

Conclusions
3. In 1988, which age group experienced the greatest number of deaths in motor vehicle accidents?
4. In most states young people can get a driver's license at 16 years of age. What can you infer from your graph using this information?

Figure 19-12 Teenage Deaths Resulting from Motor Vehicle Accidents in 1988

Age	Number of deaths
13	226
14	369
15	533
16	1094
17	1456
18	1827
19	1739

5. Total up the number of teenage deaths resulting from motor vehicle accidents in 1988. Do some research to find out what is being done by student and parent organizations to reduce this statistic.

experiences loss of coordination and balance. Activities like threading a needle, hitting a baseball, and driving a car then become difficult. A person who drinks too much even has trouble standing straight or walking in a straight line. If a person drinks a great deal of alcohol, the medulla oblongata may be affected. If this happens, the person's life is in danger. If reflexes such as breathing or swallowing stop or even slow down, death may result.

Alcohol affects the stomach and liver as well as the brain. In the stomach, alcohol can cause the gastric glands to produce too much gastric juice. This juice is a strong acid. As more and more acid enters the stomach, the stomach lining becomes irritated.

The liver removes alcohol from the bloodstream. The liver breaks alcohol down into water and carbon dioxide. Too much alcohol, however, can damage the liver, and a disease called **cirrhosis** (suh-ROH-sus) may develop. Too much alcohol destroys healthy liver cells, and the dead cells are replaced by scar tissue. The scar tissue cannot remove alcohol from the blood or carry on the regular

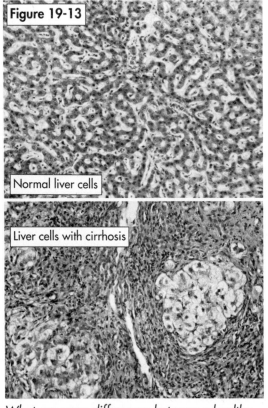

Figure 19-13

Normal liver cells

Liver cells with cirrhosis

What are some differences between a healthy liver and one damaged by cirrhosis?

liver function of breaking down fats. Figure 19-13 compares healthy liver cells with those damaged by cirrhosis.

Causes of Drinking Problems

One or two drinks may make a person feel stronger, funnier, or smarter. People may think they are more alert or in better control of themselves. For this reason, many people think alcohol is a stimulant. In fact, alcohol is a depressant. It slows down thinking, reasoning, heartbeat, and blood pressure.

The depressive effects of alcohol are made clear by one tragic statistic. In the United States thousands of people every year die in automobile accidents in which the driver had been drinking alcohol. You have probably heard the saying "Drinking and driving don't mix." Alcohol is too strong a depressant to be used when a person has to do anything that requires alertness.

Some people think that they will not get drunk if they drink beer or wine. This idea is incorrect. Figure 19-14 shows that the glass of beer, the glass of wine, and the glass of hard liquor contain the same amount of alcohol.

For most people, a drink now and then has few harmful effects. Many people, however, drink alcohol more than just once in a while. Some people cannot control the amount they drink. Others drink to escape problems, to calm their nerves, or to gain confidence. For these people, alcohol becomes a crutch that keeps them from solving their problems. In such cases, people are abusing, not using, alcohol.

Figure 19-14

Beer

Wine

Liquor

Each of these drinks contains about 15 milliliters of pure alcohol.

For people who abuse alcohol, drinking can become a daily habit. They become psychologically dependent on alcohol. They may even drink just to get through the day.

If alcohol abuse continues, the body becomes tolerant of alcohol. Little by little, a person needs more alcohol each day in order to feel as "good" as the day before. As a result, the person drinks more and more alcohol, and more and more damage is done to the body. In time, a physical dependency on alcohol develops, and not drinking can actually make the abuser feel ill.

Someone who has a drinking problem is an **alcoholic**. An alcoholic cannot control his or her drinking. Some alcoholics do not stop drinking until they are drunk or until they pass out. Even people who have only one or two drinks a day are potential alcoholics, however, if they have to drink. They are not drinking simply to enjoy a drink. They are drinking because they *must* drink.

Helping the Alcoholic

Doctors and scientists now recognize alcoholism as a disease. Although thousands of alcoholics do recover, they seldom do so by themselves. Unlike a cold or a fever, alcoholism does not go away in a few days. In order to recover from this illness, the alcoholic must first realize that illness exists. Most important, the alcoholic must want to be helped.

Fortunately, alcoholics can seek help from a number of places. The best known organization is Alcoholics Anonymous, often called AA. Alcoholics Anonymous members are alcoholics who have given up drinking. The group gives advice and help to anyone who wants to give up drinking. Because the people giving the help once had the same problem, they understand what the alcoholic is going through. Their understanding makes it easier for the alcoholic to accept help and treatment.

Alcoholism hurts other people besides the alcoholic. The other people may be the parents, children, relatives, or friends of the alcoholic. These people also might need help because they cannot cope with the person who drinks. They might not know how to help the alcoholic friend or relative.

Alateen is an organization that helps teenagers whose parents are alcoholics. Al-Anon is an organization that helps adults whose husbands, wives, or friends are alcoholics. In both groups, members discuss

Interpreting Information

Study the data presented in Figure 19-15. Then answer the questions that follow.

1. What percentage of the youth and young adults polled tried marijuana in 1985?
2. Which of the drugs listed was used most often by youth and young adults in 1974 and in 1985?
3. Which drugs were used more frequently in 1985 than in 1974? Answer this question for youth and young adults.
4. Which drugs were used less frequently in 1985 than in 1974? Answer this question for youth and young adults.

Figure 19-15 Drug Use Among Youth and Young Adults in 1974 and 1985

	Percentage of users			
	Youth (12-17 years)		Young adults (18-25 years)	
Substance	1974	1985	1974	1985
Alcohol	54.0	55.9	81.6	92.8
Cigarettes	52.0	45.3	68.8	76.0
Marijuana	23.0	23.7	52.7	60.5
Cocaine	3.6	5.2	12.7	25.2
Heroin	1.0	less than 1	4.5	1.2

Source: U.S. National Institute on Drug Abuse, National Household Survey on Drug Abuse ways to help alcoholics in their life. Posters like the one shown in Figure 19-16 tell young people where to get help.

Figure 19-16

Alateen posters leave space for local phone numbers and addresses where young people may find help.

They also discuss ways to help themselves cope with the problems of living with an alcoholic in the family.

Drinking and Teenagers

Studies show that a high percentage of teenagers in the United States have tried alcohol. The same studies show that many of the teenagers who drink have a serious problem. They cannot control their drinking. In other words, they are well on their way to becoming alcoholics.

Young people drink for many reasons. Many young people learn to drink from their parents or other adults. "If they drink, so can I," say many teenagers.

Other teenagers drink because they want to be a part of the crowd. They want to be accepted by others. Some teenagers think that drinking will make them attractive. They see ads in newspapers and magazines that make drinking look glamorous. Still other teenagers drink because they are unhappy. They feel alone or unloved and want to forget their problems.

Should you drink alcohol? You know some of the facts about alcohol and alcoholism. You must decide based on what you know and the advice of adults around you. When you are old enough to drink legally, you can make the choice that is right for you.

▰ Section 19-3 Review ▰

Write the definitions for the following terms in your own words.

1. **cirrhosis**   2. **alcoholic**

Answer these questions.

3. Describe some of the harmful effects of alcohol on the human body.
4. What are some organizations that help alcoholics and their loved ones? How do these organizations help?
5. Think of a saying or slogan that would help discourage teenagers from drinking.

SCIENCE, TECHNOLOGY, & SOCIETY

Testing for Alcohol Abuse

Driving while under the influence of alcohol can be deadly, as well as illegal. In many places, a 0.1 percent concentration of alcohol in the blood is the legal limit. Law enforcement officers now use technology to prevent accidents by catching people who go over the limit.

A police officer may stop a driver who appears to be under the influence of alcohol. The driver may be weaving in and out of traffic or driving too fast or too slowly. If the officer has a reason to stop the driver, a breath test may be given on the spot.

During a breath test, the person breathes into the small chamber of a breath tester, such as the one shown in Figure 19-17. Attached to the chamber is a tiny silicon chip. This chip can measure small electrical charges in the air. Alcohol in a person's breath changes the amount of electrical charge that the chip measures. The chip automatically calculates the content of alcohol in a person's blood from the amount of alcohol in the breath. The breath tester gives the officer a readout of the amount of alcohol in the individual's blood.

If the test shows a blood alcohol concentration over the legal limit, the officer might bring the person to the police station where another test is given. In this breath test, a person blows into a different kind of chamber. A beam of infrared light is passed through the chamber. If there is alcohol on

Figure 19-17

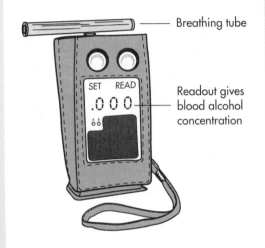

A person breathes into the tube of this portable breath tester.

the breath, it will absorb the infrared light in a certain way. The testing device then calculates the amount of alcohol in the blood from the amount in the breath.

Follow-up Activity
In some places where drunk driving is common, roadblocks are put up to stop people in their cars. Then random tests can be made to see whether people have been drinking. Some people think that random tests are an invasion of privacy and should not be allowed. Others think random tests are a good idea. What do you think? Have a class discussion.

■■■■■■ KEEPING TRACK ■■■■■■

Section 19-1 A Healthy Balance

1. Good health is a condition in which you have complete physical, mental, and social well-being.
2. Fitness improves the function of many body systems, guards against disease, increases alertness, and helps provide a good self-image.
3. During adolescence, teenagers form a self-image and make choices that will affect their future.

Section 19-2 Some Important Choices

1. A drug is a chemical that, when taken into the body, affects the body.
2. Some drugs help cure disease or have other benefits if they are used properly. Other drugs are dangerous and can damage the human body.
3. Over-the-counter drugs can be purchased without a doctor's prescription, whereas controlled drugs require a prescription.
4. Drug abuse is the improper use of drugs and may often lead to dependency on the drug or addiction to it.
5. Five types of controlled drugs are narcotics, hallucinogens, stimulants, depressants, and marijuana.

Section 19-3 Alcohol Abuse

1. Alcohol is a depressant that decreases the activity of the nervous system, slows the heartbeat and blood pressure, and has damaging effects on the stomach and liver.
2. An alcoholic is a person who has developed a physical and psychological dependency on alcohol.
3. Agencies that help alcoholics and their families include Alcoholics Anonymous, Al-Anon, and Alateen.

■■■■■■ BUILDING VOCABULARY ■■■■■■

Write the term from the list that completes each sentence.

crack, self-image, drug, controlled substance, physical, drug abuse, overdose, withdrawal, over-the-counter drugs, cocaine, fitness, addiction, psychological, alcoholic

Physical ___(1)___ improves the functions of body systems. If you have a positive ___(2)___, you feel good about yourself. A substance that is taken into the body and affects it in some way is a ___(3)___. Aspirin and cough syrup are examples of ___(4)___. A drug that requires a prescription or is illegal is a ___(5)___. The improper use of drugs is ___(6)___. When a drug abuser cannot function normally without a drug, the person has developed an ___(7)___. This condition results from a ___(8)___ dependency, in which the body develops a tolerance for a drug. ___(9)___ dependency is an emotional need for a drug. Drug addicts who stop using a drug may experience physical symptoms called ___(10)___. A drug ___(11)___ occurs when a person takes too much of a drug. A stimulant that comes in powdered form and is inhaled is ___(12)___. A very dangerous form of this drug, called ___(13)___, is on the rise

CHAPTER REVIEW

among adolescents today. A person with a drinking problem is called a(an) ___(14)___.

SUMMARIZING

If the sentence is true, write *true*. If the sentence is false, change the *italicized* term to make the statement true.

1. A drug that can be purchased without a prescription is *a controlled* drug.
2. Heroin is an example of a *hallucinogen*.
3. The *heart* absorbs more alcohol than any other organ.
4. Alcohol is a *stimulant*.
5. *Al-Anon* is an organization that helps teenagers with alcoholic parents.

INTERPRETING INFORMATION

Use the information on the label shown in Figure 19-18 to answer the following questions.

1. What is the proper dosage for a two-year-old who weighs 26 pounds?
2. If this child took a dosage at 10 a.m., when should the next dosage be given?
3. If a child is under two years of age, what must be done before giving the child a dosage?

THINK AND DISCUSS

Use the section number in parentheses to help you find each answer. Write your answer in complete sentences.

1. Describe a good physical fitness program. (19-1)
2. Why do some young people become addicted to drugs? (19-2)
3. Why is drinking excessive amounts of alcohol considered to be a form of drug abuse? (19-3)

Figure 19-18 Label on Drug Bottle

CHILDREN'S CHEWABLE TABLETS
ACETAMINOPHEN
FOR PAIN AND FEVER RELIEF

USAGE: for temporary relief of fever and discomfort due to colds and 'flu', and of simple pain and discomfort due to teething, immunizations, and tonsillectomy.
DOSAGE: all dosages may be repeated every four hours, but not more than 5 times daily.

AGE (yr)	Under 2	2-3	4-5	6-8	9-10	11
WEIGHT (lb)	Under 24	24-35	36-47	48-59	60-71	72-95
TABLETS	Consult physician	2	3	4	5	6

CHAPTER REVIEW

GOING FURTHER

1. Design several posters to discourage teen alcohol and drug use.
2. Find out how programs in your area help recovering drug addicts and alcoholics.

COMPETENCY REVIEW

1. The best way to improve your self-image is to
   a. eat nutritious meals.
   b. try to improve in small ways.
   c. try to improve in one large way.
   d. not think about self-image.
2. The improper use of drugs is called
   a. drug tolerance.   b. drug abuse.
   c. withdrawal.   d. cirrhosis.
3. A drug that can be purchased without a prescription is
   a. a controlled substance.
   b. a tranquilizer.
   c. a narcotic.
   d. an over-the-counter drug.
4. Which of the following is true about alcohol?
   a. It is a stimulant.
   b. It is a good source of energy.
   c. It is a depressant.
   d. It is broken down in the digestive system.
5. A drug that is used to calm the nerves is
   a. an antibiotic.   b. a hallucinogen.
   c. a stimulant   d. a tranquilizer.
6. Angel dust is an example of a
   a. narcotic.   b. depressant.
   c. hallucinogen.   d. stimulant.

7. The organization that counsels adolescents whose parents have drinking problems is called
   a. Alcoholics Anonymous.
   b. Al-Anon.
   c. Alateen.
   d. National Council on Alcoholism.

Questions 8-10 are based on Figure 19-19.

Figure 19-19 Substance Abuse among 18–25 Year Olds, 1985

Substance	Percent polled who used at least once
Alcohol	92.8
Cigarettes	76.0
Marijuana	60.5
Cocaine	25.2

8. What percent of those surveyed used marijuana?
   a. 92.8   b. 76.0
   c. 60.5   d. 25.2
9. Which substance was used least often?
   a. alcohol   b. cigarettes
   c. marijuana   d. cocaine
10. What percent of 18- to 25-year-olds surveyed used alcohol?
    a. 92.8   b. 76.0
    c. 60.5   d. 25.2

CHAPTER 20

HUMAN REPRODUCTION

Look at some photographs taken of you over the years. Compare the way you looked as a baby and as a small child with the way you look today. Think about the things you do now that you could not do when you were younger. Make a list of some of the ways in which you have changed.

You have gone through many changes from the time of your birth through childhood, to your present age. You even went through changes before you were born, just like the developing unborn child shown in Figure 20-1. Your physical appearance changed before you were born as well as after your birth. You also have continued to develop not only physically, but in interests and abilities. Moreover, you will continue to change throughout the rest your life.

Where did you come from? How did you grow and develop? What changes will take place as you grow older? People develop from a single cell into a complete human being. That cell is created through reproduction. Males and females are adapted for reproducing new generations. The organs that produce reproductive cells and enable a new person to form make up the **reproductive system.**

20-1 Human Reproductive Organs

■ *Objectives*

☐ *Name the parts of the human male and human female reproductive systems.*

☐ *Compare the structure of the sperm and egg cell.*

☐ *Describe the process of fertilization in the human female.*

☐ *Describe the four stages of the menstrual cycle.*

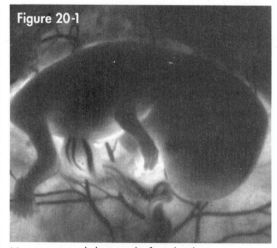

Figure 20-1

Human growth begins before birth.

You came about by means of sexual reproduction, the process that provides for the continuation of life. During sexual reproduction, a sperm cell from your father combined with an egg cell from your mother. This process of combining is called fertilization. Recall from Chapter 4 that both the sperm and egg are produced during a type of cell division called meiosis. As a result of fertilization, the first living cell, the zygote, formed. The zygote developed into a complete human being.

Sperm and Egg Cells

What does a human sperm look like? The sperm is so tiny it can only be seen through a microscope. Find the head, midpiece, and tail of the sperm shown in Figure 20-2. The head contains the nucleus. Inside the nucleus are 23 chromosomes. These chromosomes contain the genes inherited from the male. The midpiece contains many mitochondria. Mitochondria release the energy the sperm uses to move about. The tail helps the sperm move.

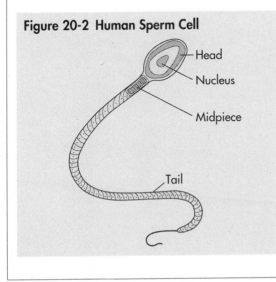

Figure 20-2 Human Sperm Cell

Head

Nucleus

Midpiece

Tail

Compare the sperm cell with the human egg cell shown in Figure 20-3. An egg cell is round and is much larger than a sperm cell. The egg cell is large because it contains a large amount of stored food. This food nourishes a fertilized egg during the very early stages of development. Find the nucleus. Like the nucleus of the sperm, the nucleus of the egg contains 23 chromosomes.

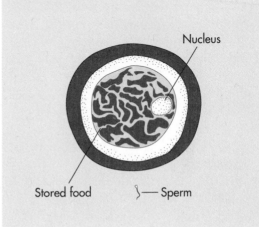

Figure 20-3 Human Egg Cell

Nucleus

Stored food

Sperm

During fertilization, the nucleus of the human sperm and the human egg combine. As a result, the 23 chromosomes from each nucleus form 23 pairs, or a complete set, of chromosomes. Thus, the newly formed zygote has a complete set of 46 chromosomes.

Male Reproductive System

Sperm are produced in two testes. Sperm cells form under the influence of hormones from the pituitary gland. These hormones travel from the pituitary gland to the testes through the bloodstream. Find the testes in the male reproductive system shown in Figure 20-4. Each testis is found in a pocket of skin called the **scrotum** (SKROHT-um). The scrotum is attached to the outside of the body.

Figure 20-4

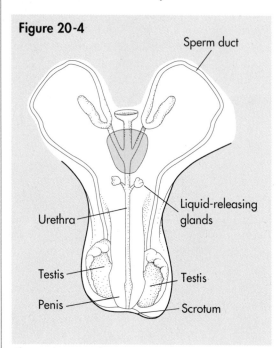

The male reproductive system

The temperature in the scrotum is one or two degrees cooler than the temperature in the rest of the body. The cooler temperature inside the testes is ideal for sperm production. Sperm can survive for only a short time at body temperature.

Find the tube called the sperm duct that extends from each testis. The sperm duct carries sperm cells from the testes into the body cavity of the male. Glands located near the testes release a liquid into the sperm ducts. This liquid provides a medium within which sperm cells can use their

tails to swim. The mixture of sperm and liquid from the glands is called **semen**.

Semen passes from the sperm ducts into a tube called the **urethra** (yuh-REE-thruh). The urethra is located inside the **penis**. When the penis becomes stiff or erect a process called **ejaculation** may take place. During ejaculation, semen passes out of the male's body through the opening in the penis.

Female Reproductive System

Figure 20-5 shows the female reproductive system. Find the ovaries located in the female's abdomen. Each female has two ovaries, which produce the female sex cells, or egg cells. An ovary releases one egg cell during the process of **ovulation.** Ovulation takes place about every 28 days.

Figure 20-5 Human Female Reproductive System

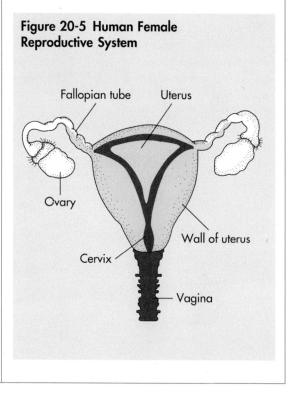

A tube called an oviduct extends from each ovary. In human females, the oviducts are called **fallopian** (fuh-LOH-pee-un) **tubes**. After ovulation, the egg cell travels from the ovary through the fallopian tube. The fallopian tubes lead to a hollow muscular organ called the **uterus**. If the egg is fertilized, it will remain in the uterus, where it will develop into a baby. If the egg is not fertilized, it will pass out of the female's body.

Find the narrow neck of the uterus called the **cervix**. The cervix opens to a muscular tube called the vagina. Sperm cells enter the body of the female when a male places the penis into the vagina. The vagina also functions as the birth canal. When a baby is ready to be born, it leaves the body of the mother through the vagina.

Menstrual Cycle

Females generally begin to ovulate between the ages of 10 and 14. At this time the **menstrual cycle** begins. The menstrual cycle is a series of events that prepares the uterus for the arrival of a fertilized egg.

The menstrual cycle averages about 28 days in length. The length of the cycle varies from female to female, however. The menstrual cycle consists of four stages. Use Figure 20-6 to follow the stages of the menstrual cycle.

During the first stage, hormones produced by the pituitary gland cause the ripening of an egg. Also the uterine wall begins to thicken and fill with blood vessels. The first stage lasts about 14 days.

During the second stage, an egg is released from the ovary. This stage, called ovulation, occurs on or about the fourteenth day of an average 28 day cycle. After ovulation the egg starts to move through the fallopian tube to the uterus.

In the third stage, the uterine wall continues to thicken and becomes filled with blood vessels. This process prepares the uterus for the arrival of an embryo if an egg has been fertilized. The third stage lasts about 14 days.

The fourth stage of the menstrual cycle begins if the egg is not fertilized. This stage of the cycle is called **menstruation**. Tissue, blood, and mucus from the thick lining of the uterus flow out of the body. The flow usually lasts three to five days. During menstruation, another egg starts

Figure 20-6

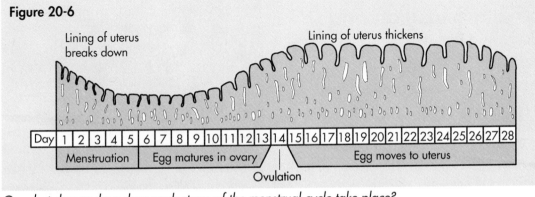

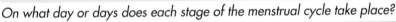

On what day or days does each stage of the menstrual cycle take place?

to mature in the ovary, beginning the menstrual cycle once more.

▰▰▰ Section 20-1 Review ▰▰▰

Write the definitions of the following terms in your own words.

1. **reproductive system**
2. **semen**
3. **penis**
4. **ovulation**
5. **menstruation**

Answer these questions.

6. Compare the structure of a sperm and an egg cell.
7. Why are the testes located in a pocket of skin attached to the body?
8. What two materials make up semen? Why is each necessary?
9. Trace the path of an egg cell through the female reproductive system.
10. Describe the four stages of the menstrual cycle.

20-2 Fertilization and Development

■ *Objectives*

☐ *Describe the process of the fertilization of a human egg cell.*

☐ *List and describe the main stages in the development of a fertilized egg.*

☐ *Explain how the developing embryo and fetus are nourished during pregnancy.*

☐ *Describe the changes that take place in a pregnant female.*

If a sperm and an egg unite during fertilization, a new human will develop. Upon ejaculation millions of sperm cells enter the vagina and swim into the uterus. A few hundred of these sperm cells may travel into the upper fallopian tube. These sperm cells may live for as long as five days.

Fertilization usually takes place in the upper fallopian tube. Look at the electron micrograph of a human egg cell in Figure 20-7. Hundreds of sperm cells surround the egg. Only one sperm cell can enter an egg cell, however. Once a sperm enters, the egg forms a membrane that prevents other sperm cells from entering.

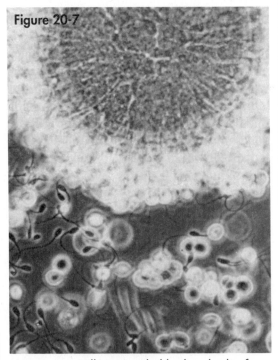

Figure 20-7

Human egg cell surrounded by hundreds of sperm cells

If fertilization takes place, the female will become **pregnant**. Pregnancy is the time between fertilization and the birth of a baby. This is the time in which a baby develops. Pregnancy usually lasts about nine months.

Development

After fertilization, the fertilized egg, or zygote, travels down the fallopian tube into the uterus. As it travels toward the uterus, the zygote divides rapidly by mitosis into two daughter cells. These two daughter cells rapidly divide into four cells. The four cells divide into eight cells and so on. Once the zygote has divided, the embryo stage of human development has begun.

This rapid cell division by mitosis is called **cleavage**. The result of cleavage is the formation of a hollow ball of cells. Figure 20-8 reviews the steps in cleavage.

About 10 days pass from the time fertilization occurs until the embryo develops into the hollow ball of cells. Then the hollow ball of cells attaches to the lining of the uterus. The embryo stage continues through the second month of pregnancy.

The hollow ball of cells becomes deeply buried in the lining of the uterus. Then one side of the hollow ball pushes inward, forming a two-layered structure. Soon a third layer forms between the first two layers. Figure 20-9 shows an early human embryo. Find the three cell layers in the embryo.

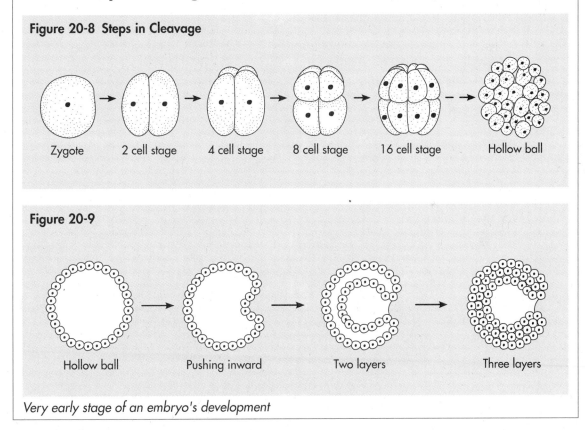

Figure 20-8 Steps in Cleavage

Zygote · 2 cell stage · 4 cell stage · 8 cell stage · 16 cell stage · Hollow ball

Figure 20-9

Hollow ball · Pushing inward · Two layers · Three layers

Very early stage of an embryo's development

As Figure 20-10 shows, each layer of cells will form different tissues and organs in the developing human. The outer cell layer forms the skin and nervous system. The middle cell layer forms the skeletal, circulatory, and reproductive systems. The innermost cell layer forms the digestive and respiratory systems.

During the embryo stage, fingerlike projections called villi form around the embryo. The villi become filled with blood vessels, forming a structure called the placenta. The placenta holds the embryo tightly in the lining of the uterus. Find the placenta in Figure 20-11.

As the figure shows, the placenta is made of tissue from both the mother and the embryo. The placenta contains two separate bloodstreams — the mother's and the embryo's. At the placenta, materials are exchanged by diffusion between mother and embryo. The blood of the mother and embryo never mix, however.

Figure 20-10

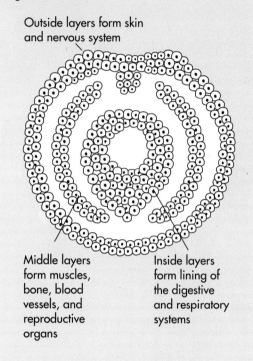

Outside layers form skin and nervous system

Middle layers form muscles, bone, blood vessels, and reproductive organs

Inside layers form lining of the digestive and respiratory systems

Which systems form from which layers?

Figure 20-11

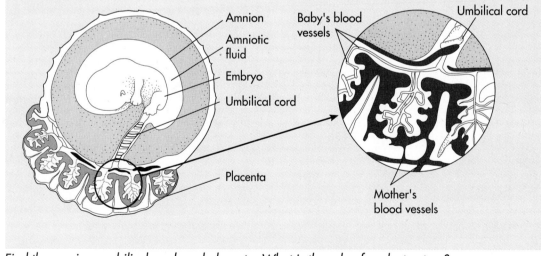

Amnion

Amniotic fluid

Embryo

Umbilical cord

Placenta

Baby's blood vessels

Umbilical cord

Mother's blood vessels

Find the amnion, umbilical cord, and placenta. What is the role of each structure?

A ropelike structure called the umbilical cord connects the embryo with the placenta. Blood vessels in the umbilical cord carry food and oxygen provided by the mother from the placenta to the embryo. Blood vessels in the umbilical cord also carry excretory wastes such as carbon dioxide away from the embryo to the placenta. In the placenta, these wastes diffuse from the embryo's blood into the mother's blood. The mother excretes the embryo's excretory wastes along with her own.

SKILL BUILDER

Constructing a Bar Graph

During pregnancy, a woman should gain about 14 kilograms. Figure 20-12 shows average breakdowns of how this weight is gained. Study the figure and answer the questions that follow.

Figure 20-12 Weight Gain During Pregnancy	
Distribution	**Kilograms**
Baby	4 (A)
Placenta	1 (B)
Amniotic fluid	1 (C)
Uterus	1 (D)
Breasts	1 (E)
Additional blood	2 (F)
Extra body fluids	1.5 (G)
Mother's stored nutrients	2.5 (H)
Total	14 (I)

1. What accounts for the greatest portion of the weight gained during pregnancy?
2. What accounts for the second and third greatest portions of weight gain? Why do you think this is so?
3. On a separate sheet of paper, make a bar graph of the data shown in Figure 20-12. Use Figure 20-13 as a guide. Match each item in Figure 20-12 with the appropriate letter in parentheses. Then list the weights below your graph. B has been done for you.

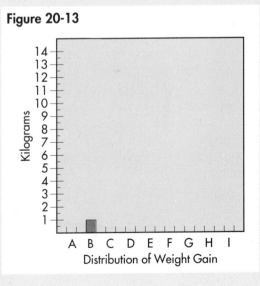

Figure 20-13

Find the **amnion** (AM-nee-an) in Figure 20-11. The amnion is a clear membrane that surrounds the embryo. A fluid that fills the amnion keeps the embryo moist. This fluid is called the amniotic fluid. The amnion also cushions the embryo, protecting it from shock.

Many changes take place as the embryo continues to develop. During the third month, the embryo begins to look human and is now called a **fetus**. The major organ systems develop during the fetal period. Arms and legs form. The heart begins to beat. The brain, eyes, and ears develop.

Many changes also take place in the female's body during pregnancy. The uterus expands as the fetus grows. The lower abdomen becomes larger and rounder. The breasts enlarge, preparing to produce milk for the newborn baby. The mother may feel nauseous and tired, especially during the early months of pregnancy.

As soon as a woman learns that she is pregnant, she should see a doctor. Proper **prenatal** care, or care before birth, will help ensure the birth of a healthy baby. Good prenatal care includes seeing a doctor regularly throughout pregnancy. A pregnant woman should eat a well-balanced diet, exercise, and get enough rest. She should not smoke cigarettes, take drugs, or drink alcohol. Nicotine from cigarette smoke, and chemicals from drugs or alcohol can harm her baby.

S K I L L   B U I L D E R

Interpreting Information

In most pregnancies, only one embryo develops. Sometimes, however, two embryos develop during the same pregnancy. Then the mother gives birth to twins. Do you know any twins? Do they look almost exactly alike? If so, they are identical twins. Other twins, including brother and sister pairs, do not look as much alike and are called fraternal twins. Figure 20-14 shows how twins form. Study the figure, then answer the questions.

1. Will twins A be identical or fraternal? Explain your answer. What about twins B?
2. Sometimes three or four babies, triplets or quadruplets, are born. Draw diagrams like those in Figure 20-14 to show how identical and fraternal triplets and quadruplets form.

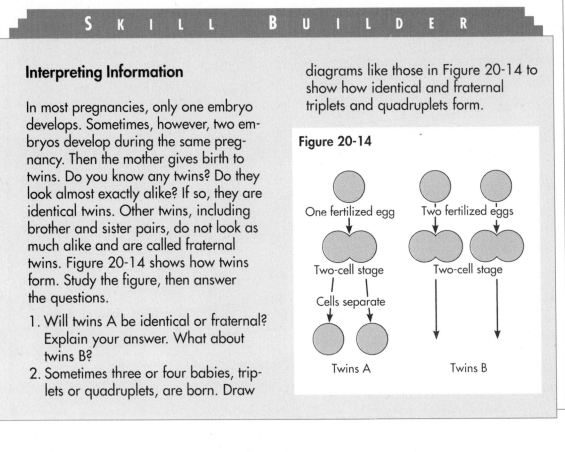

Figure 20-14

One fertilized egg   Two fertilized eggs

Two-cell stage   Two-cell stage

Cells separate

Twins A   Twins B

▰▰ Section 20-2 Review ▰▰

Write the definitions for the following terms in your own words.

1. **pregnant**
2. **cleavage**
3. **fetus**
4. **amnion**

Answer these questions.

5. How does a human sperm reach and fertilize an egg?
6. Distinguish between an embryo and a fetus.
7. How does the embryo receive food and oxygen? How does it eliminate wastes?
8. Summarize the events that take place during early embryonic development.
9. What would happen if the placenta separated from the uterus?

20-3 Birth and Human Development

■ *Objectives*

☐ *Describe the events involved in birth.*

☐ *Describe the characteristics of each stage of human development.*

The fetus in Figure 20-15 is nine months old and is ready to be born. Notice that the head of the fetus is pointing down toward the cervix. Usually the fetus assumes this position just before it is born. The head of the baby is born first, preventing the umbilical cord from wrapping around the baby's neck. Because its head appears first, the baby is also able to breathe more quickly.

Figure 20-15

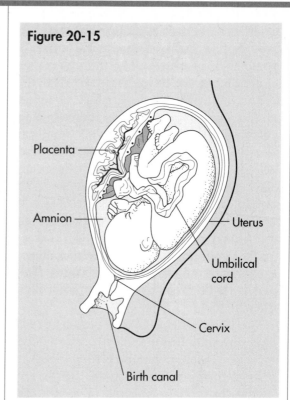

This baby is ready to be born. Describe the position of the baby.

How does the mother know when her baby is ready to be born? Sometimes the amnion bursts, releasing amniotic fluid through the vagina. The muscles in her uterus contract, or tighten, and then relax. Repeated contraction and relaxation of the uterine muscles is called **labor**.

During the early stages of labor, the contractions are weak. They occur regularly but are widely spaced. As labor continues, the contractions become stronger and more frequent.

During labor, the cervix stretches open to a diameter of about ten centimeters. This opening is wide enough for the baby's head to pass through as you can see from Figure 20-16. The muscle contractions push the baby out of the uterus, into the vagina, and out of the mother's body.

The umbilical cord remains attached to the newborn baby. The person who helps deliver the baby ties the umbilical cord and cuts it. The small piece of cord left on the baby will eventually fall off, leaving a scar called the **navel,** or belly button.

After the baby is born, the muscles in the uterus continue to contract. These contractions push the placenta and the remains of the amnion out of the mother's body. The discharged placenta and amnion are called the afterbirth.

The newborn baby no longer gets food through the umbilical cord. Therefore, it must get food from another source. Hormones in the mother cause her breasts to produce milk. Most babies can get milk from their mother's breasts soon after birth.

Stages of Human Development

During their lifetimes, human beings pass through a series of changes called stages. These stages make up the human life cycle. Certain characteristics and events define each stage.

Infancy   A newborn baby, or infant, cannot survive on its own. The infant must be held, fed, and kept clean and healthy. Although infants are helpless, they can let people know when they are uncomfortable. They can cry, grasp, suck, and swallow.

An infant's brain doubles in mass during the first year after birth. During the first year, infants gradually develop control of their muscles. They learn to sit up and crawl. Walking begins in later infancy. Many infants can walk by the age of one.

Figure 20-16

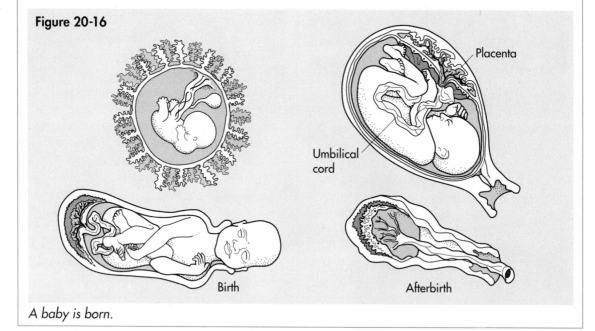

Placenta

Umbilical cord

Birth

Afterbirth

A baby is born.

What are the Characteristics of Infants and Children?

Process Skills observing, organizing information

Materials paper, pencil, people to observe

Procedure
1. Find a relative, friend, or neighbor who has an infant between the ages of six months and two years. Ask for permission to observe the infant for about 20 minutes.
2. Write down the following.
   - The age of the infant
   - Verbal abilities such as crying or speaking
   - Motor skills such as crawling or walking
   - Any other physical characteristics or mental abilities that you observe.
3. Repeat steps 1 and 2. This time, however, observe a child between the ages of three and five.

Conclusions
4. What differences did you observe between the infant and the child? Compare your findings with those of your classmates.
5. Construct a data table like the one shown in Figure 20-17. Use the table to organize the information you obtained from your observations.

Figure 20-17 Characteristics of Infants and Young Children

Characteristics	Infant	Child
Age		
Physical Characteristics		
Mental Abilities		

Childhood Infancy is followed by childhood. Childhood lasts from about age 2 to age 10 or 12. During this stage, children learn to speak. Increased muscle control enables children to feed themselves, dress themselves, and play. Children also learn to read and write. They grow taller and gain weight. The first set of teeth is replaced by a permanent set.

Adolescence The stage following childhood is called **adolescence.** Adolescence begins at **puberty,** the time when secondary sex characteristics develop. Puberty usually begins between ages 10 and 12 and lasts about two years. During puberty, the pituitary gland increases its secretion of hormones. Under the influence of these hormones, the testes in the male and the ovaries in the female develop. The male produces sperm cells and the female releases egg cells. Both males and females experience a period of rapid growth.

Hormones also cause the development of secondary sex characteristics. In boys, hormones from the testes cause the voice to deepen. Body hair begins to appear, and the muscles become stronger. In girls, hormones from the ovaries cause the breasts to develop and the hips to broaden.

S K I L L   B U I L D E R

Interpreting Information

You have learned that humans grow during the first three stages of human development: infancy, childhood, and adolescence.

Figure 20-18 shows the average height in centimeters for males and females from birth through age 18. Use this information to answer the questions that follow.

1. When does the greatest increase in height occur for boys and girls?
2. When is the average height for girls greater than the average height for boys?
3. When does the increase in height begin to slow down?
4. Between the ages of 14 and 18, do boys grow more quickly than girls or do girls grow more quickly than boys?
5. During infancy and childhood, are the average growth rates of boys and girls similar or very different?
6. What factors do you think affect human growth?

Figure 20-18 Average Growth in Humans

Age (years)	Height	
	Girls (cm)	Boys (cm)
Birth	51	52
2	86	88
4	102	103
6	116	118
8	125	126
10	137	137
12	150	148
14	159	161
16	163	172
18	163	176

Adulthood Adulthood begins between the ages of 18 and 21, when the body is fully grown. At adulthood, a person reaches maturity. Both the body and the brain are fully developed. During adulthood people become more independent. They begin to develop career and family goals, and to assume bigger challenges and responsibilities. Most people leave home and begin to earn their own living. Some people start their own family.

Older Age As people grow older, aging occurs. Starting at about age 30, tissues and organs gradually begin to weaken. Eyesight and hearing begin to worsen. Muscle tone and physical strength often decrease.

Between the ages of 45 and 55 women enter a stage called **menopause**. At menopause, women no longer ovulate and therefore can no longer have children. As men grow older, they produce fewer sperm cells.

Today greater numbers of people live well into their seventies and eighties. Figure 20-19 shows two examples of how life expectancy has increased in the United States since 1930. Longer life expectancy is due in part to the fact that doctors can offer better advice about diet and nutrition. In addition, medication can control high blood pressure, heart disease, and other disorders. As a result, many older people stay healthy and productive.

■ Section 20-3 Review ■

Write the definitions for the following terms in your own words.

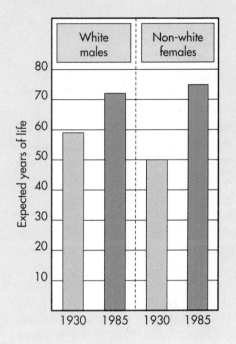

Figure 20-19 Sample Life Expectancies in the United States

1. **labor**
2. **navel**
3. **adolescence**
4. **puberty**
5. **menopause**

Answer these questions.

6. Describe what happens when a baby is born.
7. What is the afterbirth? Why is it no longer needed by the mother?
8. Why are more people today living longer, healthier lives?
9. Briefly describe the stages of human development.

SCIENCE, TECHNOLOGY, & SOCIETY

Testing for the Health of a Fetus

All parents hope their children will be born strong and healthy. Some unborn children, however, are at risk of inheriting a genetic disease. A genetic disease is passed from parents to offspring through the chromosomes. Doctors can perform tests to determine whether a developing fetus has a genetic disease or other disorder.

In a test called amniocentesis, a long needle is used to withdraw a small amount of amniotic fluid from the amnion. Figure 20-20 shows this procedure. Amniocentesis is performed between the sixteenth and twentieth week of pregnancy.

At this stage of pregnancy, the amniotic fluid contains cells from the fetus. These cells are analyzed for errors in the chromosomes or missing enzymes. Through amniocentesis, scientists can determine whether or not the fetus has any of several genetic diseases.

A newer procedure called chorionic villi sampling involves snipping tissue from the developing fetal sac. The cells of this tissue are analyzed for chromosome errors or for missing enzymes. Chorionic villi sampling provides the same information as amniocentesis. Chorionic villi sampling, however, can be done earlier in the pregnancy. Researchers hope to develop a test that can reveal abnormalities even before the embryo becomes implanted in the uterus.

Researchers are also developing ways to treat fetuses that have a genetic disease. They hope to be able to remove abnormal genes from an embryo and replace them with normal genes. This procedure could be performed on an embryo as early as the 4-to-16 cell stage. The baby would then be normal at birth. For now, however, amniocentesis and chorionic villi sampling can only detect disorders in the fetus.

Follow-up Activity
Research some other advances in fetal care, such as ultrasound and fetal surgery.

Figure 20-20 Amniocentesis

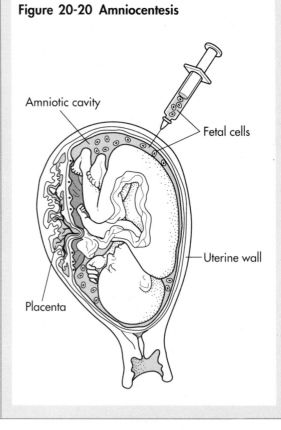

Amniotic cavity

Fetal cells

Uterine wall

Placenta

Section 20-1 Human Reproductive Organs

1. Sexual reproduction provides for the continuation of life by producing new human offspring.
2. The male reproductive system consists of testes, sperm ducts, and the penis.
3. The female reproductive system consists of the ovaries, fallopian tubes, uterus, and vagina.

Section 20-2 Fertilization and Development

1. Fertilization occurs in the upper fallopian tube. Only one sperm can fertilize an egg.
2. Cleavage occurs immediately after fertilization. A hollow ball of cells forms and attaches to the lining of the uterus.
3. Food, oxygen, and wastes are exchanged between mother and embryo at the placenta. The umbilical cord connects the embryo to the placenta.

Section 20-3 Birth and Human Development

1. When a baby is ready to be born, the cervix widens and the muscles of the uterus begin to contract. The baby is usually born head first.
2. Humans pass through a series of stages called a life cycle. These stages include infancy, childhood, adolescence, adulthood, and older age.

BUILDING VOCABULARY

Write the term from the list that matches each description.

menstrual cycle, scrotum, ejaculation, fetus, semen, ovulation, umbilical cord, ovary, urethra, labor

1. the organ that produces egg cells
2. the process in which an egg cell is released
3. structure that connects the embryo to the placenta
4. the pocket of skin where the testes are located
5. substance containing sperm cells and liquid
6. the passing of semen through the penis
7. series of contractions of the uterus
8. a 28-day cycle in which the uterus lining thickens in preparation for the arrival of a fertilized egg
9. stage of human development from third month of pregnancy to birth
10. tube through which semen leaves the body

Explain the difference between the terms in each pair.

11. ovulation, menstruation
12. oviduct, fallopian tube
13. uterus, cervix
14. embryo, fetus
15. labor, birth

SUMMARIZING

Write the missing term for each sentence.

1. Sperm cells are carried from the testes to the urethra by the ___ .

2. The ___ carries the egg cell from the ovary to the uterus.
3. At birth, a baby leaves the mother's body through the ___.
4. The organ that produces egg cells is the ___.
5. Fertilization usually takes place in the upper part of the ___.
6. The egg is released on or about the fourteenth day of the ___ cycle.
7. A human in the first month of development is called a (an) ___.
8. The exchange of materials between mother and embryo takes place in the ___.
9. The ___ stretches to about ten centimeters wide when a baby is born.

INTERPRETING INFORMATION

Use Figure 20-21 and your knowledge of life science to answer these questions.

1. In what organ does fertilization take place?
2. What is taking place at point A?

3. When does the embryo attach to the lining of the uterus?

THINK AND DISCUSS

Use the section number in parentheses to help you find each answer. Write your answers in complete sentences.

1. Compare the functions of the male and female reproductive systems. (20-1)
2. Why is the menstrual cycle necessary to human reproduction? (20-1)
3. How is the uterus adapted for supporting and nourishing a developing fetus? (20-2)
4. Explain why it is an advantage for a baby to be born head first. (20-3)
5. During which stage of the life cycle do you think the most changes occur? Explain your answer. (20-3)

GOING FURTHER

1. Research how the use of alcohol and drugs during pregnancy can harm an

Figure 20-21 Stages in Early Development of a Human Embryo

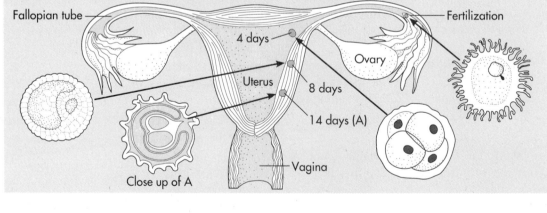

unborn child. Discuss your findings with your classmates.

2. Some mothers nurse their baby. Others do not. Research the advantages and disadvantages of nursing.

3. Do library research or talk to a doctor or nurse about the risks involved in pregnancy. Find out why the medical risks of pregnancy are greater for teenagers than for adults.

COMPETENCY REVIEW

1. Which statement is true?
   a. A fertilized egg usually leaves the female's body.
   b. A fertilized egg usually develops in the uterus.
   c. An egg is fertilized by many sperm cells.
   d. An egg has enough stored food for the first five months of development.

2. An egg is released from the ovary during a process called
   a. menstruation.   b. regeneration.
   c. regulation.   d. ovulation.

3. A baby leaves the mother's body through the
   a. oviduct.   b. fallopian tube.
   c. vagina.   d. urethra.

4. At five months of pregnancy, a developing individual is called a (an)
   a. embryo.   b. zygote.
   c. baby.   d. fetus.

5. The structure that connects the placenta to the embryo is called the
   a. ovary.   b. oviduct.
   c. sperm duct.   d. umbilical cord.

6. The stage when a female no longer menstruates is called
   a. puberty.   b. adolescence.
   c. menopause.   d. adulthood.

7. The structure that protects the embryo from shock is the
   a. umbilical cord.   b. amnion.
   c. placenta.   d. navel.

8. Which stage of embryo development takes place first?
   a. formation of umbilical cord and placenta
   b. attachment to the uterine wall
   c. cleavage
   d. development of the nervous system

9. The contraction of the muscles of the uterus is called
   a. ovulation.   b. pregnancy.
   c. labor.   d. fertilization.

10. In Figure 20-22, food and wastes are exchanged between mother and embryo in
    a. A.   b. B.
    c. C.   d. D.

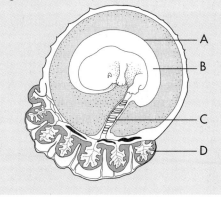

Figure 20-22

CHAPTER 21

INHERITING TRAITS

Has anyone ever told you that you are a "chip off the old block"? This expression means that you look like one or both of your parents. Compare your features with those of your parents. In what ways do you look like them? In what ways are you different? Now look at the mother and daughter in Figure 21-1. How are these two members of a family similar to one another? How are they different?

People inherit, or receive, characteristics such as eye color and hair color from their parents. Recall from Chapter 4 that inherited characteristics are called traits. Make a list of some human traits that are inherited. Your list will probably include height, hair color, eye color, hair texture, and many more.

Overall, you and your parents share the same general physical characteristics. Like them, you have two eyes, a nose, mouth, arms, and legs, as well as the same kinds of internal organs. You will, however, notice many differences as well.

How are traits passed on from generation to generation? Scientists who study **genetics** attempt to answer these questions. Genetics is the study of heredity, or the passing of traits from parents to offspring.

21-1 Experiments of Gregor Mendel

■ *Objectives*

☐ *State that the inheritance of some traits can be predicted.*

☐ *Explain how Mendel's experiments led to his theories of inheritance.*

☐ *Discuss the role of genes and chromosomes in the inheritance of traits.*

Gregor Mendel was an Austrian monk who lived in the mid-1800s. While tending

Figure 21-1

What traits do this mother and daughter share?

his garden, Mendel wondered how traits were passed from one generation of plants to the next. To answer this question, Mendel decided to study pea plants. He chose them because pea plants mature quickly and produce seeds in only two months.

Mendel studied many generations of plants. He noticed the variety of traits among pea plants. Notice in Figure 21-2 that the flowers and seeds have different colors. The peas may be smooth or wrinkled seeds. Some plants are tall and others are short. Mendel identified patterns in the way these traits are passed from one generation to the next. The knowledge Mendel gained from his experiments led him to form the basis of genetics.

Crossing Pea Plants

Pea plants are self-pollinating. Pollen travels from the stamen to the pistil in the same flower. The petals of the pea flower completely cover the stamen and pistil, preventing pollen from reaching other flowers.

Because pea plants are self-pollinating, Mendel was able to grow separate groups of pea plants for each trait. For example, he grew one group of plants that always produced short plants. He grew a separate group of plants that always produced tall plants. Mendel called the plants that always reproduced the same traits in their offspring **purebred** plants. When Mendel had a large number of purebred plants, he began his experiments.

Mendel wondered what would happen if he cross-pollinated purebred pea plants from the first group with purebred plants from the second group. In one experiment he brushed off pollen from a purebred tall plant and dusted it onto the pistils of a purebred short plant.

The new plants matured and produced seeds. Mendel planted the new seeds and waited for them to grow into new pea

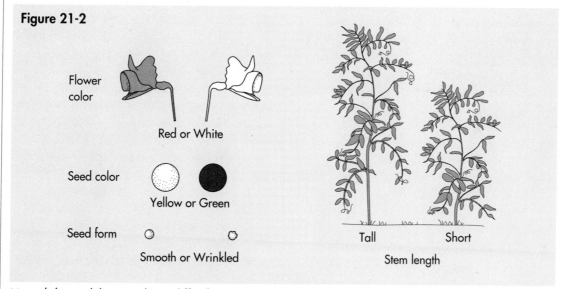

Figure 21-2

Flower color

Red or White

Seed color

Yellow or Green

Seed form

Smooth or Wrinkled

Tall   Short

Stem length

How did Mendel's pea plants differ from one another?

plants. Figure 21-3 shows the results of this cross-pollination. Mendel was surprised to see that all the offspring were tall. Mendel crossed, or cross-pollinated, purebred tall plants with purebred short plants over and over again. Each time, all plants of the next generation were tall.

Mendel also crossed purebred plants that produce yellow seeds with purebred plants that produce green seeds. All of the offspring produced yellow seeds. In fact each time Mendel crossed two groups of purebred plants, the offspring were all purebred for one of the traits.

Consider the cross between purebred tall plants and purebred short plants. Since all of the offspring were tall, Mendel concluded that the tallness trait somehow masked the shortness trait. Mendel referred to the trait that appears in the offspring as **dominant**. He referred to the trait that was hidden or masked by the dominant trait as **recessive**.

Law of Dominance

Mendel hypothesized that every plant inherits two factors, one from each parent, for each of its traits. Mendel used letters to represent these factors, a capital for the factor that produces the dominant trait and a small letter for the factor that produces the recessive trait. For example, in pea plants, T stands for tall stem and t stands for short stem. A purebred tall plant inherits two factors for tall stems, TT. A purebred short plant inherits two factors for shortness, tt.

Suppose a TT plant were crossed with a tt plant. The tall plant could pass on only a factor for tallness, T. The pure short plant can pass on only a factor for shortness, t. The offspring would inherit a factor from each purebred parent plant, making it Tt. Because the tall factor, T, is dominant, the offspring will be tall. Offspring that have both a dominant and a recessive factor are called **hybrids**.

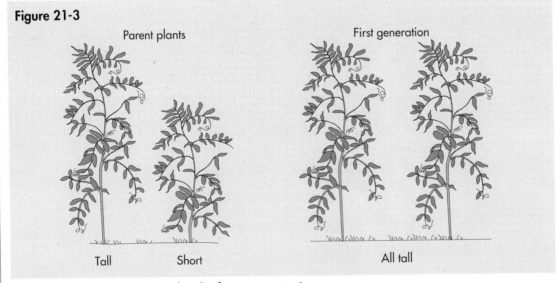

Figure 21-3

Parent plants

First generation

Tall   Short

All tall

What types of plants appeared in the first generation?

Mendel summarized these findings in the **Law of Dominance**. This law states that when organisms having purebred but opposite traits are crossed, the offspring will resemble only one parent, the one with the dominant trait. The recessive trait does not appear in the offspring.

Hundreds of traits, including some human traits, are either dominant or recessive. For example, brown or black eyes are dominant over blue eyes. Dark hair color is dominant over light hair. Dark skin color is dominant over light skin.

Law of Segregation

Mendel next wanted to find out what happens when two hybrid plants are crossed. He crossed Tt hybrid tall pea plants with each other. He then planted the new seeds and waited for the offspring to grow. Look at the results of this cross in Figure 21-4. Three out of four offspring in the next generation were tall. One in four offspring was short. Note that the small *x* in the figure means a cross between the two plants.

Mendel repeated these hybrid crosses over and over again. He also crossed hybrid plants for many other traits. His results were always the same. The dominant trait appeared about three fourths of the time. The hidden recessive trait always appeared about one fourth of the time. Thus, in a hybrid cross, the offspring have a 75-percent chance of inheriting the dominant trait. They have a 25-percent chance of inheriting the recessive trait.

Look at Figure 21-5 to understand how this ratio occurs. Each hybrid tall plant has one factor for tallness and one factor

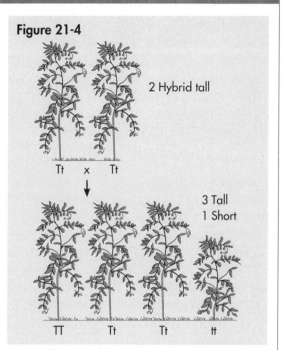

Figure 21-4

2 Hybrid tall

Tt × Tt

3 Tall
1 Short

TT   Tt   Tt   tt

Why will there be three times as many tall plants as short?

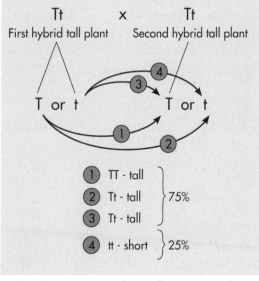

Figure 21-5

Tt   ×   Tt
First hybrid tall plant   Second hybrid tall plant

T or t   T or t

1 TT - tall
2 Tt - tall   } 75%
3 Tt - tall
4 tt - short   } 25%

Why will 75 percent of the offspring be tall?

What Role Does Probability Play in Inheritance of Traits?

Process Skills modeling, calculating

Materials two pennies, paper, pencil

Probability is a measure of the likelihood that an event will occur. In this activity you will determine the probability of whether a penny will come up heads or tails. Probability is also a factor in determining which traits an organism inherits. Therefore, probability in coin tosses can be used as a model for the inheritance of traits.

Procedure

1. Toss a penny into the air and let it fall onto your desk. Was the result a head or a tail? What is the probability of obtaining a head or a tail in a coin toss?
2. Toss the penny 100 times. Keep a record of the results. About what fraction of the time did a head appear? About what fraction of the time did a tail appear?
3. Toss two pennies into the air at the same time. Let them fall onto your desk. The results may be both heads, both tails, or one head and one tail. Repeat this two-coin toss 100 times. Record the results in a table similar to Figure 21-6.

Conclusions

4. Use your results from the two-coin toss as a model for a cross between two hybrid tall pea plants. Which coin combination, heads-heads, heads-tails, or tails-tails, represents a hybrid tall pea plant, Tt? Which combinations represent a pure tall plant, TT, and a pure short plant, tt?
5. Compare the ratios for coin tosses to the ratios of offspring likely to occur in a hybrid cross.
6. What role does probability play in the inheritance of traits?

Figure 21-6 Results of Two-Coin Toss

Coin combination	Number of tosses	Fraction
Heads-Heads		
Heads-Tails		
Tails-Tails		
Total Tosses:	100	

for shortness, Tt. Each plant passes on either a tall factor, T, or a short factor, t. As the figure shows, four different combinations of offspring may result.

One combination is a purebred tall plant, TT. Another combination is Tt, a hybrid tall plant. A third combination is tT, another hybrid. The fourth combination, tt, produces purebred short offspring. Therefore, when two hybrid tall plants are crossed, the offspring have a 75-percent chance of being tall and a 25-percent chance of being short.

As a result of crossing hybrid tall pea plants, Mendel stated the **Law of Segregation**. This law states that when hybrids are crossed, the hidden recessive trait separates out and may appear in about $1/4$ of the offspring. Mendel's laws also hold true for other organisms. Guinea pigs may be crossed to produce animals that are hybrid for black fur, Bb. What happens when the hybrids are crossed? Look at Figure 21-7 for the results.

The Discovery of Genes and Chromosomes

Gregor Mendel stated that a pair of factors determines a hereditary trait. He stated three hypotheses about these factors. First, each organism has two factors for each trait. Second, some factors are dominant and others are recessive. Third, an organism receives one factor from each parent for each trait.

Mendel never knew exactly what these factors were. The first clues about how traits are inherited were discovered in the early 1900s. At this time scientists first observed rod-shaped structures found in

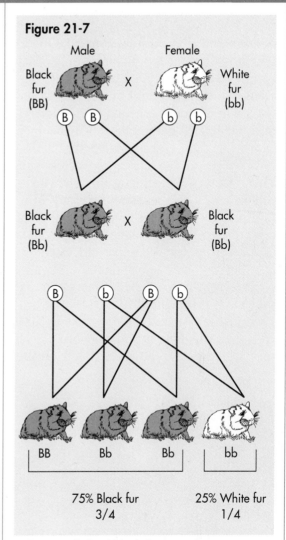

Figure 21-7

75% Black fur
3/4

25% White fur
1/4

When two hybrid black fur guinea pigs are crossed, 25 percent of the offspring will have white fur.

the nuclei of cells. These structures were chromosomes. Chromosomes always occur in pairs. Each kind of organism has a certain number of chromosome pairs. The same number of pairs of chromosomes is contained in each cell in an organism.

Look at Figure 21-8, which shows a micrograph of chromosomes from a body cell of the girl in the picture. Notice that the girl's cell, like those of all other humans, contains 23 pairs of chromosomes. Each chromosome contains many of Mendel's factors. Together the chromosomes shown in Figure 21-8 contain the factors for all of the girl's physical characteristics. These factors are actually tiny structures called genes. Genes she received from her parents control the development of her inherited traits. Since chromosomes she received from her parents occur in pairs, genes occur in pairs, too.

How are genes, the determiners of traits, passed on from parent to offspring? Chromosomes are found in the nuclei of all cells, including sperm and egg cells. Recall from Chapter 4, however, that during meiosis each sperm and egg cell receives only one of each pair of chromosomes. As the chromosome pairs separate during meiosis, so do the genes located on these chromosomes. Therefore each sperm or egg contains only a single gene for each trait. During fertilization chromosomes and genes are paired once again. As a result, the offspring inherit one gene for a trait from each parent.

Figure 21-9 shows the results of crossing hybrid tall pea plants, Tt. One parent plant provides sperm and the other parent provides egg cells. Notice that one half of the sperm have the T gene and the other half have the t gene. Likewise, one half of the eggs have the T gene and the other half have the t gene. At fertilization, several different gene combinations could result. About one fourth of the

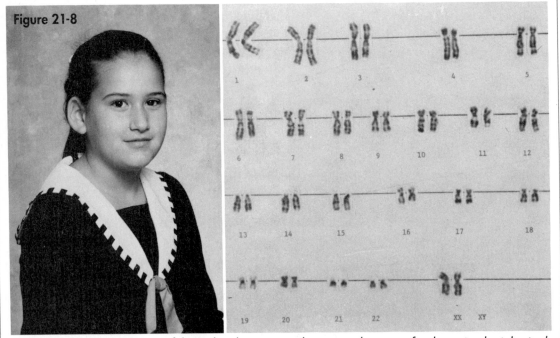

Figure 21-8

These are the chromosomes of the girl in the picture. They carry the genes for the traits she inherited.

Figure 21-9

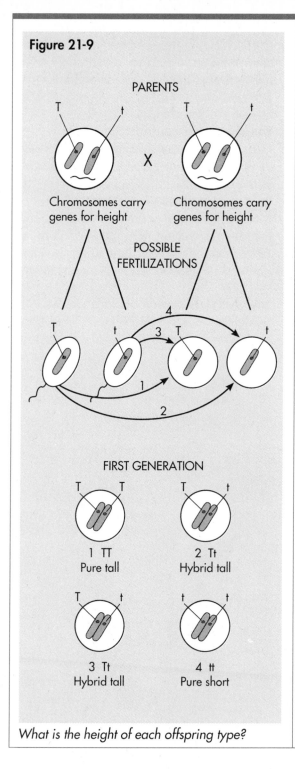

PARENTS

Chromosomes carry genes for height   X   Chromosomes carry genes for height

POSSIBLE FERTILIZATIONS

FIRST GENERATION

1 TT
Pure tall

2 Tt
Hybrid tall

3 Tt
Hybrid tall

4 tt
Pure short

What is the height of each offspring type?

offspring would be pure tall, TT, about one half would be hybrid tall, Tt, and about one fourth would be pure short, tt.

The genetic makeup, or combination of genes an organism inherits, is called its **genotype** (JEE-nuh-typ). For example, genotype of a purebred tall pea plant is TT. The genotype of a hybrid tall plant is Tt. Both plants, however, are tall. The outward appearance of an organism is called its **phenotype** (FEE-nuh-typ). The TT and Tt plants have the same phenotype. What is the genotype for a short pea plant?

SKILL BUILDER

Performing Calculations

Suppose a scientist crossed a hybrid tall pea plant, Tt, with a purebred short pea plant, tt. In a labeled diagram, show the cross and the results. Use Figure 21-9 as a model.

1. What is the probability that the offspring will be short?
2. What is the probability that the offspring will be tall purebreds?
3. What is the probability that the offspring will be tall hybrids?

Suppose a scientist crossed a hybrid tall pea plant, Tt, with a purebred tall pea plant, TT. In a labeled diagram show the cross and the results.

4. What is the probability that tall offspring will appear?
5. What is the probability that short offspring will appear?

Section 21-1 Review

Write the definitions for the following terms in your own words.

1. **genetics**
2. **purebred**
3. **dominant**
4. **recessive**
5. **hybrid**

Answer these questions.

6. What is the difference between a purebred and a hybrid organism?
7. What were Mendel's results when he crossed two hybrid pea plants?
8. Summarize Mendel's three hypotheses of genetics.
9. What role do genes and chromosomes play in the inheritance of traits?
10. Suppose a gardener crosses a plant with purple flowers with a plant with white flowers. The results are all plants with purple flowers. What will happen when the new generation of plants with purple flowers is crossed?

21-2 Your Inherited Traits

■ *Objectives*

☐ *State that a trait may be determined by a single pair of genes or several pairs of genes.*

☐ *Describe incomplete dominance.*

☐ *Describe how the sex of an organism is determined.*

☐ *Define sex-linked trait.*

A boy has blue eyes. Both of his parents have brown eyes. How could two brown-eyed parents have a blue-eyed child?

Inheriting Your Traits

You know that you inherit genes for traits from your parents. You inherited the color of your eyes, the color of your hair, your sex, and many other traits. How do the laws of genetics apply to humans?

Suppose a purebred brown-eyed man marries a purebred blue-eyed woman. What color eyes will their children have? Figure 21-10 shows the expected results.

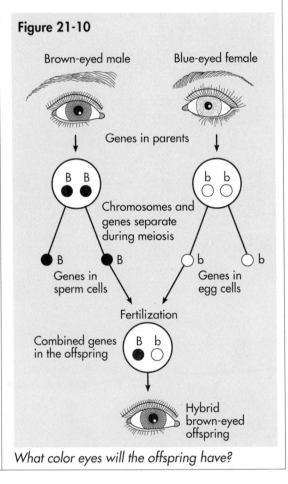

Figure 21-10

Brown-eyed male   Blue-eyed female

Genes in parents

Chromosomes and genes separate during meiosis

Genes in sperm cells   Genes in egg cells

Fertilization

Combined genes in the offspring

Hybrid brown-eyed offspring

What color eyes will the offspring have?

The brown-eyed man has a pair of genes for brown eyes, BB, and the blue-eyed woman has a pair of genes for blue eyes, bb. Their children will inherit one gene from each parent. Each child will get a gene for brown eyes, B, from the father and a gene for blue eyes, b, from the mother. Thus all of their children will have the genotype, Bb.

The gene for brown eyes is dominant over the gene for blue eyes. Only the effect of the gene for brown eyes is visible. The children, therefore, will all have brown eyes.

How could two brown-eyed parents have had a blue-eyed boy? Since the gene for blue eyes is recessive, the boy's genotype must be, bb. Thus in order for the son to have blue eyes, he must inherit a gene for blue eyes from each parent. Both parents, therefore, had to be hybrid with phenotype brown eyes.

Figure 21-11 shows how two hybrid parents could produce a blue-eyed boy. Notice that the offspring have only a one-in-four chance of inheriting two recessive genes. The chances are three out of four that the offspring will have the dominant trait, in this case brown eyes.

Incomplete Dominance

In the traits you have studied so far, one gene shows complete dominance over another. For example, the gene for tallness, T, in pea plants is dominant over the gene for shortness, t. In the inheritance of some other traits, however, genes do not show complete dominance.

Figure 21-11

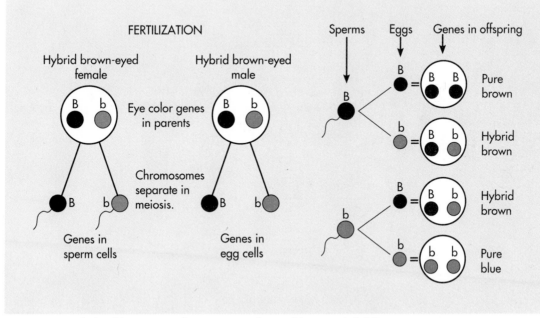

How can two hybrid brown-eyed parents produce a blue-eyed child?

One example of such a trait is the color of some horses. Look at Figure 21-12. The two purebred forms of this animal are either brown, BB, or white, WW. If a brown stallion, BB, and a white mare, WW, mate, all of their offspring are hybrid, BW. The hybrids are neither brown nor white, but golden. Neither the B nor the W gene is dominant. Instead, both contribute to the appearance of the offspring. This type of inheritance is called **incomplete dominance.**

Certain kinds of chickens inherit color in the same way. Purebred forms of these chickens have either black feathers, B, or white feathers, W. Neither trait is dominant. When pure black and pure white chickens are mated, all of the offspring are hybrid, or BW. These hybrids have neither black nor white feathers. Instead, the hybrids have blue-gray feathers.

You have learned that in humans the gene for brown eyes is dominant and the gene for blue eyes is recessive. Look around you. You will see people with brown eyes, hazel eyes, dark blue eyes, light blue eyes, and so on. It would appear that incomplete dominance is the cause. However, if only two genes determined eye color, and if one were always dominant over the other, people could only have brown or blue eyes. Scientists now know that eye color is determined not by one pair of genes, but by several pairs. Other human traits determined by several gene pairs include hair color and skin color.

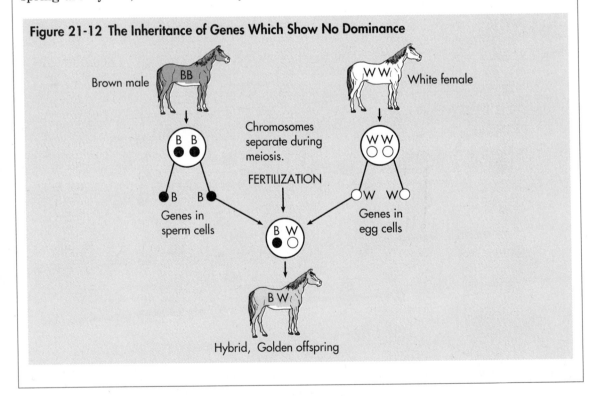

Figure 21-12 The Inheritance of Genes Which Show No Dominance

Brown male

White female

Chromosomes separate during meiosis.

FERTILIZATION

Genes in sperm cells

Genes in egg cells

Hybrid, Golden offspring

Inheritance of Sex

You have probably noticed that males and females are about equal in number. Why is this the case? Figure 21-13 compares the chromosomes of a human female and the chromosomes of a human male. The first 22 pairs of chromosomes look alike in both sexes. The chromosomes of the twenty-third pair, however, differ. This pair contains the **sex chromosomes**, the chromosomes that determine the sex of the individual. Females have two identical sex chromosomes called X chromosomes. Males have one X chromosome and one Y chromosome.

The sex of an individual is determined the moment a sperm fertilizes an egg. Recall that during meiosis each sperm cell receives only one chromosome from each chromosome pair. Half of the sperm cells carry the X chromosome, and half carry the Y chromosome. During meiosis each egg cell also receives only one chromosome from each chromosome pair. The sex chromosome each egg receives is always an X chromosome, however.

Look at Figure 21-14, which shows the possible combinations of sex chromosomes. If a sperm carrying a Y chromosome fertilizes an egg, the resulting offspring will be male (XY). If a sperm carrying an X chromosome fertilizes an egg, the resulting offspring will be female (XX). The sex of the offspring always depends on which type of sperm, X or Y, fertilizes an egg. Because equal numbers of sperm carry X and Y chromosomes, offspring have an equal chance of being male or female.

Sex-Linked Traits

Have you ever heard of a disease called **hemophilia** (hee-muh-FIL-ee-uh)? When people with hemophilia are cut or wounded, their blood does not clot. For this reason, even a minor injury can be life threatening to a person with hemophilia.

Most people who have hemophilia are male. This is true because hemophilia is a **sex-linked trait**. The gene that determines a sex-linked trait is recessive and is carried on the X chromosome. The Y

Figure 21-13

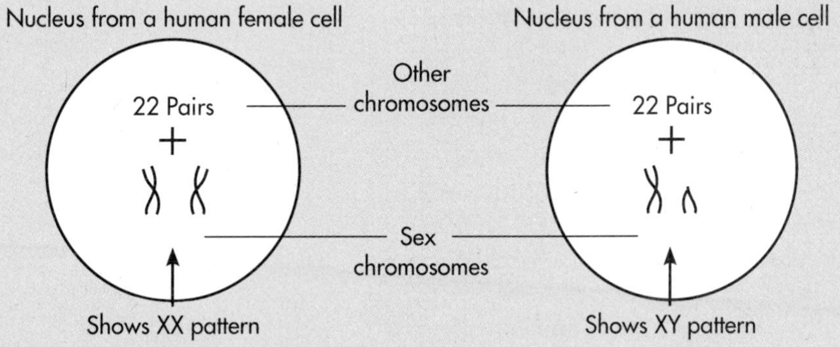

Nucleus from a human female cell   Nucleus from a human male cell

22 Pairs   Other chromosomes   22 Pairs

Sex chromosomes

Shows XX pattern   Shows XY pattern

The X and Y chromosomes determine the sex of an individual.

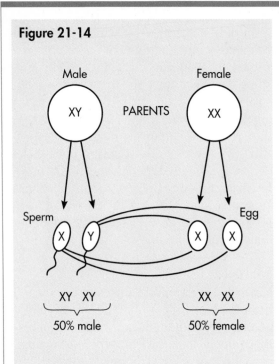

Figure 21-14

Male   Female

XY   PARENTS   XX

Sperm   Egg

X   Y   X   X

XY   XY   XX   XX

50% male   50% female

Why are the numbers of males and females about the same?

chromosome has no corresponding gene for this trait. The recessive gene for hemophilia and genes for other sex-linked traits, such as color blindness, are carried on the X chromosome.

Suppose a female has one X chromosome with a gene for hemophilia and one normal X chromosome. She does not have hemophilia, but she is a **carrier** for the disease. A carrier is a person who has a recessive abnormal gene but who shows the dominant normal trait. Hemophilia is recessive, so both X chromosomes must carry the recessive gene for a female to have hemophilia.

On the other hand, a male inherits only one X chromosome. If his X chromosome has the gene for hemophilia, he will have the disease. If his X chromosome does not have the gene for hemophilia, he will be normal.

Genetic Diseases

Inherited diseases are not always sex-linked. For example, **sickle-cell disease** is a genetic blood disease that, in the United States, mainly affects African Americans. About one out of nine African Americans in the United States carries the sickle-cell gene.

People who have sickle-cell disease are unable to make normal hemoglobin. The abnormal hemoglobin gives the red blood cells a sickle shape. Figure 21-15 compares normal cells and sickle cells. The sickle cells cannot carry enough oxygen to the body. As a result, people with sickle-cell disease suffer severe pain, organ damage, and even death.

Figure 21-15 Normal and Sickle-Shaped Red Blood Cells

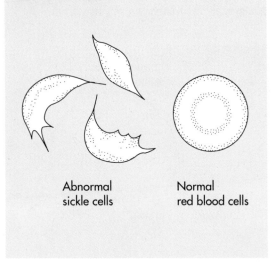

Abnormal   Normal
sickle cells   red blood cells

Neither the gene for normal cells, N, nor the gene for sickle cells, S, is dominant. People who are hybrid for this trait, NS, have both normal and sickle cells, and are considered carriers. Carriers, however, may suffer minor symptoms of the disease. Suppose a hybrid male and a hybrid female have children. Their offspring could be either NN, NS, or SS. Each child would have a 25 percent chance of inheriting sickle-cell disease, a 50 percent chance of being a carrier, and a 25 percent chance of being normal.

Another human genetic disease is **Cooley's anemia.** It is caused by the inheritance of a pair of recessive genes. This is a blood disease that affects people whose ancestors came from Italy, Greece, or other Mediterranean countries. About one out of 25 Italian-Americans carries a recessive gene for this disease. Jews of Eastern European descent are another group affected by a genetic disease called **Tay-Sachs** (TAY-SAKS) **disease**. Tay-Sachs disease, which causes breakdown of the nervous system and eventual death, is also controlled by a recessive gene. A small number of Jews living in the United States carry this recessive gene.

■■■ Section 21-2 Review ■■■

Write the definitions for the following terms in your own words.

1. **sex chromosomes**
2. **hemophilia**
3. **carrier**
4. **sex-linked trait**
5. **sickle-cell disease**

Answer these questions.

6. Suppose a hybrid brown-eyed man marries a purebred brown-eyed woman. Explain why this couple cannot produce a blue-eyed child.
7. Name two traits controlled by genes that show incomplete dominance.
8. Explain why the number of males and females is about equal.
9. Suppose a woman who carries the gene for hemophilia is married to a normal man. Could their daughter inherit this disease? Why or why not?

21-3 DNA and Genes

■ *Objectives*
☐ *Explain the structure and function of DNA.*
☐ *Relate DNA to the inheritance of traits.*
☐ *Explain how genetic engineering has been used to benefit humans.*

You learned that pairs of genes are responsible for hereditary traits. How do genes actually determine whether an individual will have blue or brown eyes? How do genes determine whether a pea plant will be tall or short? The answers to these questions are found in the complex chemicals that make up genes.

The Structure of DNA
Genes are made of molecules of a chemical called **DNA**. DNA stands for **deoxyribonucleic** (dee-AHK-si-ry-boh-new-klee-ik)

acid. It is these DNA molecules that determine your traits.

In 1953 two scientists, James Watson and Francis Crick, discovered the structure of DNA. As Figure 21-16 shows, the Watson-Crick DNA model looks like a twisted ladder. This twisted ladder is known as a double helix.

Figure 21-16 The Double-Helix Structure of DNA

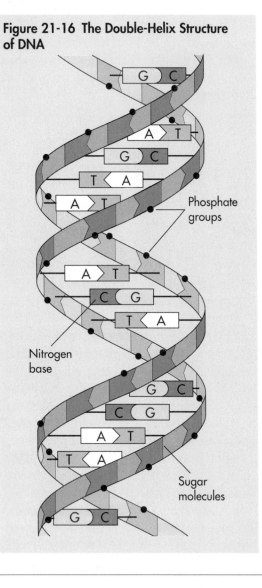

Phosphate groups

Nitrogen base

Sugar molecules

Notice that the sides of the double helix consist of long chains of alternating sugar and phosphate molecules. The "steps" of the ladder consist of substances called **nitrogen bases**. Notice that a nitrogen base is attached to each sugar molecule. Four different types of nitrogen bases are found in DNA molecules. These bases always appear in pairs. Adenine is always paired with thymine, A-T. Guanine is always paired with cytosine, G-C. Very weak chemical bonds hold these nitrogen base pairs together. Thousands of DNA molecules make up a gene. In turn, thousands of genes make up one chromosome.

The DNA Code How do DNA molecules determine human traits? The nitrogen bases that make up the steps of the double helix appear in a certain sequence, or order. The sequence of nitrogen bases forms a special code.

Different base sequences are codes for the production of different enzymes. The kinds of enzymes a cell produces control which chemical processes occur there. The products of these processes lead to genetic traits. For example, the genes for eye color contain codes for certain enzymes. These enzymes in turn stimulate the production of proteins called pigments. If you have brown eyes, your genes have the code for the production of brown pigment in your irises.

DNA does not leave the chromosomes. How, then, do the instructions contained in the DNA code reach the cells? A chemical called **RNA** aids the production of enzymes and proteins. RNA stands for ribonucleic acid. RNA works with DNA to produce the enzymes and proteins that determine your traits. Locate the DNA and RNA in Figure 21-17.

RNA takes the information stored in the base sequence of the DNA. The RNA then carries this information to organelles called ribosomes. The ribosomes interpret the information and use this information to make enzymes. The kinds of enzymes produced decide which proteins will be produced in that cell.

DNA Replication Traits are passed on to the next generation when offspring receive chromosomes from their parents. Before a cell can reproduce, it must first make a copy of each chromosome. The genes that make up the chromosomes are made of DNA. Therefore, to make more genes and chromosomes, you must first make more DNA.

Figure 21-18 shows how a DNA molecule replicates, or makes a copy of itself. First the DNA molecule unwinds and then "unzips." The two halves of the DNA molecule separate between the weakly bonded base pairs. Each DNA molecule now acts as a mold upon which a new half will form.

Where does the cell get more sugars, phosphates, and bases? Your cells get more of these compounds from the nutrients carried through the bloodstream. Notice how individual bases made in the cells fit together like locks and keys. In this way two new identical molecules form from one DNA molecule. As a result of DNA replication, a new set of genes and chromosomes is made, making cell reproduction possible.

Sometimes a sudden change occurs in the DNA code. A change in the order of bases in the DNA molecule or an error in DNA replication may occur. Changes like these are called mutations. Changes in the structure of chromosomes or in the numbers of chromosomes are also mutations. Mutations may be caused by a pollutant or some radioactive substance. Most mutations are harmful to organisms, even causing death. Some mutations, however, produce a trait that benefits

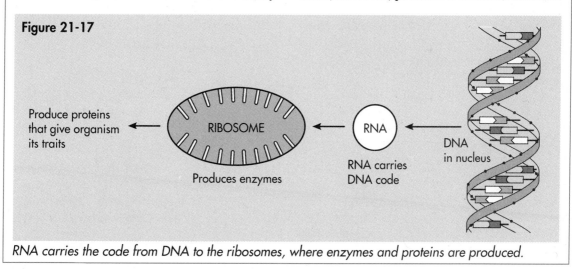

Figure 21-17

Produce proteins that give organism its traits

RIBOSOME

Produces enzymes

RNA

RNA carries DNA code

DNA in nucleus

RNA carries the code from DNA to the ribosomes, where enzymes and proteins are produced.

Figure 21-18

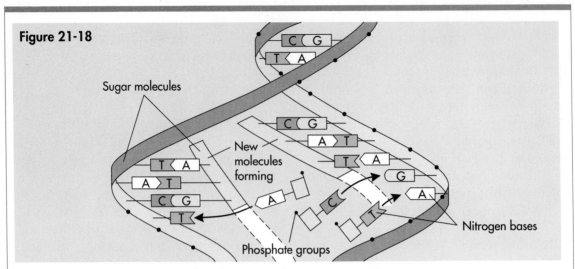

During replication, DNA unwinds and unzips to form two new molecules.

an organism. If this trait makes the organism better adapted to its environment, the trait will be passed on to future generations. In this way, natural selection will work toward increasing the number of organisms with this trait. Thus, evolution of species occurs as a result of beneficial mutations.

Genetic Engineering

Knowledge of genetics has enabled scientists to develop the field of **genetic engineering.** Genetic engineering is the use of genetic principles to develop processes and products useful to people. For example, certain bacteria can be programmed to produce chemicals that can clean up oil spills in the ocean. You read in Chapter 17 that bacteria are programmed to produce human insulin and other hormones.

Figure 21-19 shows how the process of **gene splicing** is used to program bacteria. In the gene-splicing process, DNA from one organism is placed into the DNA of

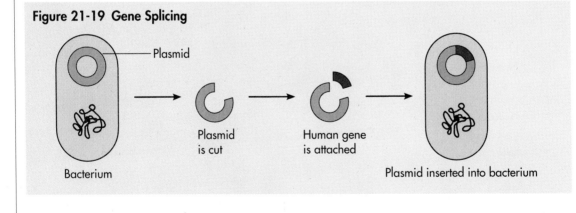

Figure 21-19 Gene Splicing

Plasmid

Bacterium

Plasmid is cut

Human gene is attached

Plasmid inserted into bacterium

another organism. First a ring of DNA called a **plasmid** is taken from a cell of a bacterium. Next an enzyme is used to remove a small section of DNA from the plasmid. Then a gene taken from a human cell is attached to the plasmid. Finally, the plasmid is closed and returned to the cell of the bacterium.

When the cell of the bacterium divides, it passes on the plasmid containing the human gene to its offspring. Soon thousands of bacteria containing the human gene are produced. The human gene spliced onto the plasmid directs the bacterium to make a human protein, such as insulin.

Scientists have also used gene splicing in bacteria to produce **interferon**. Interferon is a human protein that fights infections caused by viruses. Genetic engineers can splice the human gene that directs the production of interferon into the plasmids of bacteria. The bacteria and their offspring are then able to make interferon. The manufactured interferon is given to people to help fight diseases caused by viruses.

Another process used in genetic engineering is called cloning. In cloning, organisms are developed with identical chromosomes and genes. A clone is an organism which is identical to its parents in every way.

One scientist cloned a frog by removing a nucleus from the egg cell of frog A. The scientist replaced this nucleus with a nucleus taken from an intestinal cell of frog B. The egg cell containing its new nucleus developed into a frog that was genetically identical to frog B. Using a similar technique, scientists have been successful in cloning offspring of rabbits and mice.

One day scientists may be able to remove a gene from one human and put it into a human embryo. What effect will this have on the new individual? The individual would receive a trait of that human from which the gene was taken. These scientific techniques may open up many questions about how far science should go in the interest of improving human life.

■ Section 21-3 Review ■

Write the definitions of the following terms in your own words.

1. **DNA**
2. **nitrogen base**
3. **RNA**
4. **genetic engineering**
5. **gene splicing**

Answer these questions.

6. Describe the structure of the DNA molecule.
7. What role does the DNA base sequence play in determining a trait? Give one example.
8. Imagine a cell that has no nitrogen bases. Would DNA be able to replicate? Why or why not?
9. What is a mutation? What are some causes of mutations?
10. What are some products and processes that genetic engineers have developed?

SCIENCE, TECHNOLOGY, & SOCIETY

Genetic Engineering

You know that human genes can be spliced into genes of bacteria. Did you know that human genes can also be inserted into plants? This kind of genetic engineering can turn plants into miniature factories that produce large quantities of human protein. For example, tobacco plants have been engineered to produce human antibodies. Scientists hope that some day soon plants will be able to make human growth hormones and human enzymes.

Some human genes have even been inserted into animals. As Figure 21-20 shows, human genes for blood proteins have been inserted into fertilized mouse eggs. The resulting embryos containing these genes are placed into the uterus of a female mouse and left to develop. When these mice are born they will be able to produce human blood proteins in their cells. If the mice carrying these human genes are female, the milk which they give to their young may also contain human blood protein.

Scientists may one day be able to remove defective genes from a human embryo and replace them with normal genes. This procedure may help cure genetic diseases such as sickle-cell disease and cystic fibrosis. This type of genetic engineering would certainly improve human lives.

Some people are concerned about possible consequences of genetic engineering.

They think that genetic research must be closely monitored so that no new and deadly organisms are created. Suppose bacteria spliced with DNA from a cancer-causing virus escapes into the air. What would happen if the bacteria carrying the cancer-causing DNA reproduced, spread, and infected humans? The possibility that such an event could occur concerns some people.

Follow-up Activity
Hold a class discussion in which you express your opinions about the benefits and risks of genetic engineering.

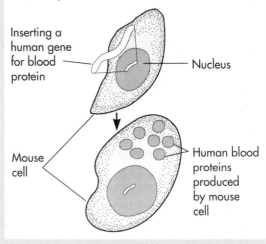

Figure 21-20

Inserting a human gene for blood protein

Nucleus

Mouse cell

Human blood proteins produced by mouse cell

Mouse cells may be genetically engineered to produce human blood proteins.

KEEPING TRACK

Section 21-1 Experiments of Gregor Mendel

1. Mendel's experiments showed that the inheritance of some traits can be predicted.
2. According to Mendel, traits are controlled by at least two factors. If the factors are the same, the organism is purebred. If the factors are different, the organism is hybrid.
3. The trait that appears in a hybrid organism is dominant. The trait that does not appear in a hybrid organism is recessive.
4. Genotype refers to the genetic makeup or gene combinations of an organism. Phenotype refers to the appearance of the organism or the expression of genes as traits.

Section 21-2 Your Inherited Traits

1. If a hybrid organism shows a different phenotype from either of its purebred parents, the genes for that trait show incomplete dominance.
2. Sex is determined by the X and Y chromosomes. A male has an X chromosome and a Y chromosome. A female has two X chromosomes.
3. Genes for sex-linked traits such as hemophilia are located on the X chromosome.
4. Genetic diseases include sickle-cell disease, Cooley's anemia, and Tay-Sachs disease.

Section 21-3 DNA and Genes

1. Genes are made of chemicals called DNA. Watson and Crick discovered that the structure of DNA is a double helix.
2. DNA contains codes for the production of enzymes. These enzymes direct the production of proteins that determine the traits of an organism.
3. Genetic engineering uses the principles of genetics to develop processes and products useful to people.
4. Through gene splicing, genes can be removed from one organism and inserted into another.

BUILDING VOCABULARY

Write the term from the list that best completes each sentence.

interferon, Mendel, phenotype, Cooley's anemia, plasmid, genotype, recessive, dominant, DNA, Tay-Sachs disease

___1___ stated that each trait is controlled by at least two factors. In a hybrid organism, the trait that appears is ___2___. The trait that does not appear is ___3___. An organism's ___4___ is its genetic makeup. An organism's ___5___ is its visible traits. ___6___ is a genetic blood disease that mainly affects people of Mediterranean descent. ___7___ is a genetic disease that mainly affects Jews of Eastern European descent. Genes and chromosomes are made of molecules called ___8___. In gene splicing, a human gene may be inserted into a ring of bacterial DNA called a ___9___. Genetic engineering has been used to make ___10___, a protein that fights viral infections.

If the sentence is true, write *true.* If the sentence is false, change the *italicized* term to make the statement true.

1. Inherited characteristics are called *traits.*
2. Gregor Mendel studied genetics by raising *mice.*
3. When individuals that have different but purebred traits are crossed, the trait that does not appear in the offspring is the *dominant* trait.
4. When two hybrid organisms are crossed, the offspring have a *50 percent* chance of inheriting the recessive trait.
5. *Phenotype* refers to the genetic makeup of an organism.
6. A female who has only one gene for hemophilia is called a *carrier.*
7. A genetic disease that mainly affects African Americans is *Tay-Sachs disease.*
8. A chromosome contains many *genes.*
9. Genes are made of molecules called *ATP.*
10. *Genetic engineering* is the use of genetic principles to develop processes and products useful to people.

INTERPRETING INFORMATION

Figure 21-21 shows a cross between two carriers for sickle-cell disease. Use the figure to answer the following questions.

1. What are the three possible gene combinations in the offspring?
2. What is the likelihood that each of these genotypes will occur?

Figure 21-21 Sickle-cell Disease

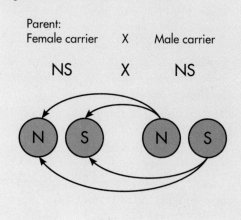

Parent:
Female carrier   X   Male carrier

NS   X   NS

3. What percentage of the offspring will be carriers?
4. Which genotype is often deadly?

THINK AND DISCUSS

Use the section numbers in parentheses to help you find each answer. Write your answers in complete sentences.

1. Why did Gregor Mendel use the pea plant and not humans for his genetic studies? (21-1)
2. Use diagrams to show the cross of a pea plant hybrid for yellow seeds with a plant purebred for green seeds. What is the chance that the offspring will have green seeds? Yellow seeds? (21-1)
3. Explain why more males than females inherit hemophilia (21-2)
4. Why is it important that DNA is able to replicate? (21-3)

5. What is gene splicing? What are some benefits of gene spicing? What are some burdens? (21-3)

1. Do library research to learn about cloning and answer the following questions. Do you think scientists will one day be able to clone human beings? Do you think that they should be allowed to do so? Why or why not? Present your views to the class.
2. Do library research to find out how mutations in bacteria have made some antibiotics less effective than they were originally.

1. Mendel's discovery that traits are inherited by factors passed on from generation to generation resulted from his
   a. examination of chromosomes under a microscope.
   b. dissection of pea flowers.
   c. mating experiments with pea plants.
   d. mating experiments with mice.
2. What is the chance that a purebred blue-eyed female and a hybrid brown-eyed male will have blue-eyed offspring?
   a. 25 percent   b. 50 percent
   c. 75 percent   d. 15 percent
3. If purebred tall pea plants are crossed with purebred short pea plants, the offspring will be
   a. all Tt.
   b. all TT.
   c. all tt.
   d. half TT and half tt.

4. In guinea pigs black coat color is dominant over white coat color. If two hybrid black guinea pigs are mated, which ratio is likely to appear in the offspring?
   a. two black to two white
   b. one black to three white
   c. three black to one white
   d. four black and no white
5. In humans, sex is determined by
   a. the sex chromosome in the egg cell.
   b. the sex chromosome in the sperm cell.
   c. the number of chromosomes inherited.
   d. the number of genes inherited.
6. A sudden change in a chromosome or gene is known as a
   a. mutation.
   b. recession.
   c. replication.
   d. generation.
7. Chromosomes and genes are made of a chemical substance called
   a. glucose.   b. enzyme.
   c. DNA.   d. ATP.
8. One example of a sex-linked disease is
   a. sickle-cell disease.
   b. Tay-Sachs disease.
   c. hemophilia.
   d. tuberculosis.
9. The structure of DNA was discovered by
   a. Darwin.   b. Mendel.
   c. Hooke.   d. Watson and Crick.
10. The technique of placing a piece of human DNA into a bacterial plasmid is called
   a. amniocentesis.   b. cloning.
   c. gene splicing.   d. replication.

CHAPTER 22

HUMAN EVOLUTION

Right now you are doing something that no other species but a human being can do. You are reading a book. You are able to read because, like other humans, you have a highly developed brain. You use your brain to read and interpret the words on this page. The well-developed brain is just one characteristic that sets humans apart from other forms of life. Another characteristic that sets humans apart is that they always walk upright with two feet firmly on the ground.

How did these characteristics develop in humans? Where did human beings come from? To find out how humans evolved, scientists study fossils of early humans. They study human chromosomes and compare them with those of closely related species, such as chimpanzees and gorillas. By such efforts, scientists infer a great deal about the evolution of humans.

As you read this chapter, keep in mind that the story of human evolution is not yet complete. Scientists like the one shown in Figure 22-1 continue to hunt for and study human fossils and other evidence of evolution. These scientists, called **paleontologists** (pay-lee-an-TAL-uh-justs), use evidence they find to complete the story of human evolution.

22-1 Classifying Human Beings

■ *Objectives*

☐ *Identify the kingdom, phylum, class, order, family, genus, and species to which humans belong.*

☐ *List the characteristics of primates.*

☐ *Explain why humans are classified as primates.*

In Chapter 5 you learned that human beings are members of the animal kingdom

Figure 22-1

A paleontologist looks at fossil remains.

and the chordate phylum. Humans are classified as chordates because the early human embryo has a rod of cartilage called a notocord. In the fully formed individual, the notocord becomes the backbone. Because human beings have hair on their bodies and produce milk for their young, they belong to the mammal class. Humans are further classified into an order of mammals known as **primates**. Other primates include tree shrews, lemurs, tarsiers, monkeys, and apes.

Primates

The earliest primates probably lived on Earth over 65 million years ago. Scientists think the early primates resembled the mammal shown in Figure 22-2. The fossil record suggests that these early primates were probably the ancestors of

Figure 22-2

The common ancestor of all primates may have looked like this mammal.

later primates, including monkeys, apes, and humans.

All primates have certain characteristics in common. The first primates were adapted to living in trees. Most modern primates are tree dwellers too. All primates have fingers and toes with joints that can flex, or bend. Most primates also have an **opposable thumb**. An opposable thumb is one that can touch all the other fingers.

Figure 22-3 shows the opposable thumb of a human and an ape. The opposable thumb enables primates to grasp objects. Some primates also have an opposable big toe, which is also used for grasping. Lift your book up from your desk. Notice the position of your thumb as you grasp the object. If not for your opposable thumb, you would not be able to lift and handle many objects.

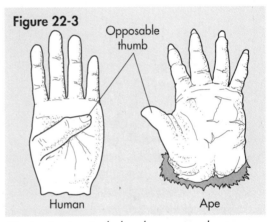

Figure 22-3

Opposable thumb

Human   Ape

Most primates, including humans and apes, have an opposable thumb.

As you know, the top surface of your fingers and toes has a nail near the tip. The presence of nails and not claws on the top surfaces of fingers and toes is a characteristic of all primates. Nails leave the bottom surfaces of the fingers and toes free to touch and explore objects.

Look at the faces of the primates in Figure 22-4. Notice that the eyes of all of these species, including humans, are located in the front of their head. This position gives all primates **frontal vision**. Frontal vision enables primates to look straight ahead at an object with both eyes at the same time. Primates also have **stereoscopic** (ster-ee-uh-SKAP-ik) **vision**. Stereoscopic vision is the ability to see depth.

Figure 22-4

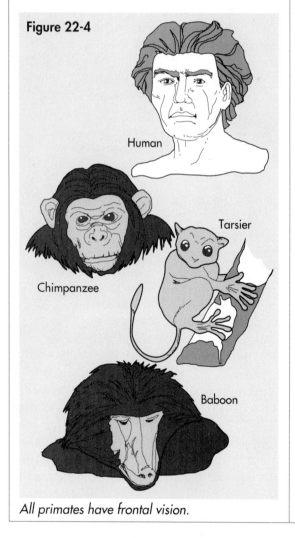

Human

Chimpanzee

Tarsier

Baboon

All primates have frontal vision.

Hominids

The primate order is further divided into families. Humans belong to a family called **hominids** (HAM-uh-nuds). Hominids have characteristics that other primates do not have. For example, hominids are **bipedal**, meaning they can stand upright and walk on two legs. Other primates walk on all fours. Figure 22-5 compares the way the two types of primates walk.

Another trait that sets hominids apart from other primates is a larger and more highly developed brain. The highly developed brain enables them to use language to communicate. All humans living today are members of the genus *Homo* and the species *sapiens*.

Figure 22-5

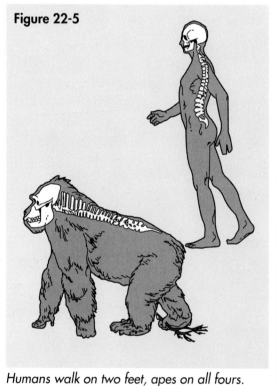

Humans walk on two feet, apes on all fours.

What Are Some Adaptations of Humans?

Process Skill determining relationships

Materials paper and pencil, adhesive tape, spoon

One characteristic that sets human beings apart from all other species is the ability to use the brain to think, reason, imagine, and create. In this exercise you will use your imagination to learn how some other human traits are adaptations for survival.

Procedure

1. Imagine that you are unable to stand upright and walk on two legs. Use both your hands and feet for support as you walk around your classroom.
2. Imagine that your thumb is attached to your index finger and that you cannot move it. Ask a classmate to tape your thumb to your index finger so that you are unable to move it. Now, without the use of your thumb, pick up a pencil from your desk and use it to write your name. Pick up a spoon and pretend to use it to feed yourself.
3. Imagine you do not have stereoscopic vision and therefore cannot see depth. Imagine being unable to judge how far away from you objects are.

Conclusions

4. What are some things that you would be unable to do if you had to move about on all fours?
5. What are some advantages of having an opposable thumb?
6. How would the lack of stereoscopic vision affect your activities?

Section 22-1 Review

Write the definitions for the following terms in your own words.

1. **paleontologist**
2. **primate**
3. **opposable thumb**
4. **stereoscopic vision**
5. **hominid**

Answer these questions.

6. What evidence might have led scientists to hypothesize that the ancestor of modern primates resembled the mammal shown in Figure 22-2?
7. Identify the kingdom, phylum, class, order, family, genus, and species to which you belong.
8. What are some of the characteristics of primates?
9. Why are humans classified as primates?
10. How are humans different from other primates?

22-2 Origin of the First Humans

■ *Objectives*

☐ *Describe the evidence used by scientists to construct a tree of life that illustrates hominid evolution.*

☐ *Name four species of Australopithecus.*

☐ *Compare the characteristics of Australopithecus afarensis and Australopithecus africanus.*

☐ *Explain the relationship of Australopithecus species to each other and to later human species.*

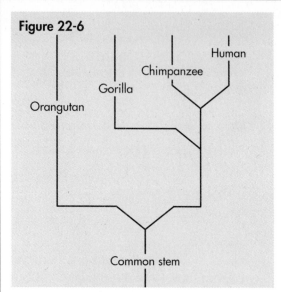

Figure 22-6

Many scientists believe that an animal resembling the orangutan may represent the common stem from which humans and apes evolved.

Scientists hypothesize that the first hominids appeared on the earth about 20 million years ago. Hominids evolved as certain primates developed the ability to stand and walk upright. Primates with this ability were able to leave the trees and live on the ground.

Scientists have carefully studied both fossil primates and living primates to determine how they might be related. Look at Figure 22-6, which shows a possible family tree of apes and humans. Evidence shows that humans did not evolve from apes. Rather, humans share a common ancestor with a variety of apes, including orangutans, gorillas, and chimpanzees. The common stem at the base of the tree represents the ancestor from which apes and humans may have evolved.

Biochemical evidence also supports the theory that humans and apes evolved from a common ancestor. For example, the structure of DNA in apes and humans

is similar. Humans and apes also have an identical blood protein called cytochrome c. The presence of identical proteins is further evidence that humans and apes share a common ancestor.

Australopithecus

The earliest known hominids belong to the genus *Australopithecus* (aw-stray-loh-PITH-uh-kus). Scientists have discovered the fossils of several *Australopithecus* species. In 1974 a group of paleontologists went to northeastern Africa to hunt for fossils in Ethiopia. One member of the group, Donald Johanson, discovered the fossil remains of an organism unlike anything ever seen before. Johanson found the remains of an adult female. He nicknamed her Lucy. Judging from her remains, scientists believe that Lucy weighed about 30 kilograms and was 1.1 meters tall.

Scientists estimated that Lucy lived about 3.5 million years ago. What made the discovery of Lucy so exciting is that she is the oldest known hominid. Johanson gave Lucy the scientific name *Australopithecus afarensis,* or *A. afarensis.*

The fossil remains show that Lucy walked in an upright position. Scientists used this evidence to classify Lucy as a hominid. Lucy had a curved jaw that stuck out from her face. She had a low forehead with large ridges over her eyebrows, as seen in Figure 22-7.

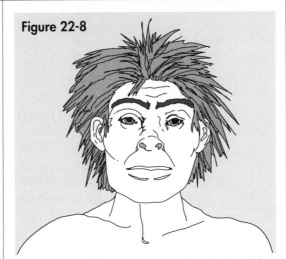

Figure 22-8

Artist's view of what Lucy may have looked like.

Figure 22-7

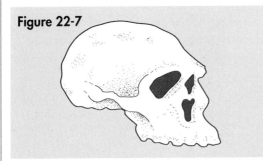

A. afarensis *had ridges over the eyebrows and a low forehead.*

Lucy's braincase was larger than that of apes but less than half the size of a modern human's braincase. From her remains, scientists have formed conclusions about Lucy's appearance. She probably looked somewhat like the drawing in Figure 22-8. Many scientists think that the ancestors of modern humans evolved from *A. afarensis.*

Before the discovery of Lucy, the oldest known hominid species was *Australopithecus africanus.* Scientists discovered the first *A. africanus* fossil in South Africa in 1924. Nicknamed the Taung child, the fossil had a round skull and jaw, a relatively large brain, and an erect posture. Figure 22-9 shows two fossil skulls of *A. africanus.* Compare these skulls with that of *A. afarensis* in Figure 22-7.

Figure 22-9

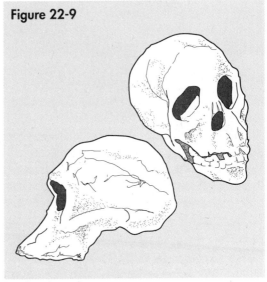

Skulls of A. africanus

Scientists have also found the fossil remains of two other more recent *Australopithecus* species. Scientists named these species *A. robustus* and *A. boisei*. Scientists believe that both probably evolved later than *A. africanus,* over 1.5 million years ago. Look at the fossil remains of these species in Figure 22-10. All *Australopithecus* species are now extinct. The genus *Homo,* however, which includes humans, is believed to have evolved from *Australopithecus.*

Figure 22-10 Some Fossil Remains of A. robustus and A. boisei

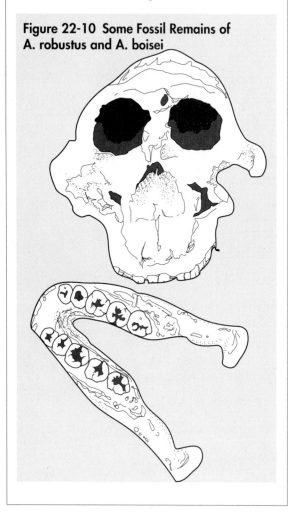

■ Section 22-2 Review ■

Write the definition for the following term in your own words.

1. *Australopithecus*

Answer these questions.

2. What information has helped scientists construct a model of hominid evolution?
3. Imagine that you are identifying the fossil remains of an *Australopithecus* species. The braincase is less than half the size of that of a modern human. The forehead is low and the jaw curved. What species is it?
4. How is *Australopithecus* important to the study of evolution?

22-3 Evolution of Modern Humans

■ *Objectives*

☐ *Compare the characteristics of* Homo habilis, Homo erectus, *and* Homo sapiens.

☐ *Describe the characteristics of Neanderthal.*

☐ *Draw an evolutionary tree for hominids.*

The first known members of the genus *Homo* lived about 1.8 million years ago. In 1959 paleontologists Mary and Louis Leakey discovered these earliest *Homo* fossils in East Africa. They used radioactive dating to determine the age of their fossils. The Leakeys named this hominid *Homo habilis* (HOH-moh HAB-il-is), meaning "skillful human." A *Homo habilis* skull is shown in Figure 22-11.

Figure 22-11

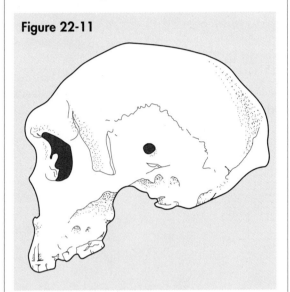

The skull of H. habilis *looks more like a modern human skull than that of* A. africanus.

Homo habilis looked more like a modern human than did the *Australopithecus* species. It had a larger and more highly developed brain than its ancestors. It stood erect, and its teeth were more humanlike than those of its ancestors.

Simple stone tools have been found alongside *H. habilis* fossils, so scientists concluded that *H. habilis* was a maker of tools. *H. habilis* used stone to make simple tools such as knives and scrapers and used the tools to hunt and remove the meat from animals.

Many scientists think that *H. habilis* evolved from *A. afarensis*. Scientists think that *H. habilis* was better adapted for

survival than *A. afarensis*. Because of a more highly developed brain, *H. habilis* could make hunting tools. *H. habilis* may have lived in groups and may have had more control over its surroundings than did *A. afarensis*. As a result, it may have been able to protect itself, which helped it survive.

Homo erectus

The hominid species most closely related to modern humans was *Homo erectus* (HOH-moh uh-REK-tus), or "upright human." The first *H. erectus* skull was found along a river in Java in 1891. It is shown in Figure 22-12. Another *H. erectus* skull was uncovered in a cave near Peking, China, in 1929. During the 1970s and 1980s, Richard Leakey uncovered hundreds of fossil remains of *H. erectus* in a lake in the eastern African nation of Kenya. Fossils of *H. erectus* have also been found in Europe and Asia. Scientists think that some groups of *H. erectus* first lived in Africa and migrated to other places.

Figure 22-12 Skull of H. erectus

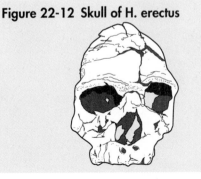

Using radioactive dating, scientists learned that *Homo erectus* probably lived about 1.6 to 0.5 million years ago. Many scientists think that *H. erectus* evolved from *H. habilis* and that *H. habilis* then became extinct. *H. erectus* had many characteristics that made members of this species better adapted for survival than members of *H. habilis*. Their brain was more complex, enabling them to do more things. They may have developed more advanced speech. They were the first hominids to use fire to cook and to keep warm. They established homes in caves.

H. erectus made fine stone tools, which were used to hunt food.

Scientists do not know why some groups of *H. erectus* left Africa. Perhaps overpopulation forced them to move. Perhaps they needed to find new sources of food. They may even have been curious about unknown areas.

Figure 22-13 shows a model of human evolution. Scientists still disagree about the exact relationships among hominid

Figure 22-13

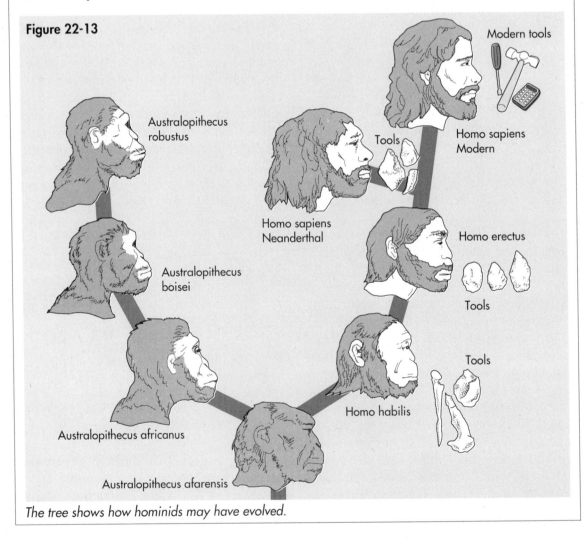

The tree shows how hominids may have evolved.

species. This evolutionary tree, however, reflects the views of many scientists.

Path to Modern Humans

Modern humans belong to the species *Homo sapiens,* meaning "wise human." The fossil record shows that *Homo sapiens* evolved in Africa from *Homo erectus* about 500,000 years ago. The first fossils of *Homo sapiens* were uncovered in 1856 in the Neander Valley in Germany. Other similar fossils were found in other parts of Europe. These fossils were named **Neanderthal** (nee-AN-dur-thal). A Neanderthal skull is shown in Figure 22-14.

Figure 22-14 Skull of Neanderthal

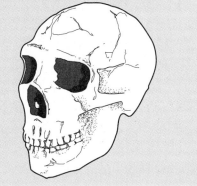

Neanderthals lived 130,000 to 35,000 years ago. They were shorter than humans of today, but they were also much stronger. They walked erect. They had large heads with flat, sloping foreheads and ridges at the eyebrows. Their jaws stuck out and they had receding chins. Their brains were as large as those of humans of today and probably as highly developed.

Neanderthals lived during the Ice Age. Their intelligence enabled them to adapt to the very cold climate of that time. They built and lived in caves and rock shelters. They used fire to keep warm. They also made fine tools.

Neanderthals were the first humans known to bury their dead. Often tools and animals were buried with the dead person. Some scientists have inferred from this evidence that Neanderthals were religious and believed in life after death. Perhaps they buried animals and tools with their dead, thinking that the dead would be able to use both animals and tools in an afterlife.

What happened to the Neanderthals? The fossil record indicates that the Neanderthals disappeared quickly, about 30,000 years ago. Scientists do not know why they disappeared so rapidly.

Look back at Figure 22-13 and find the position of Neanderthal. Notice how its branch comes to a dead end. Neanderthals became extinct without evolving into a new species. However, because the behavior and appearance of Neanderthals were so much like those of modern humans, most scientists consider Neanderthals an early kind of *Homo sapiens.*

Cro-Magnons

The first fossil skulls of modern *Homo sapiens* were uncovered by railway workers in southern France in 1868. Other fossils of early modern humans were found in Germany, England, and Spain. These fossil skulls looked very much like the skulls of humans of today. Like today's humans, they had a high forehead, a chin, and reduced brow ridges. Radioactive dating showed these fossil skulls to be about 35,000 years old. Scientists call the early modern humans **Cro-Magnons** (kroh-MAG-nuns).

Cro-Magnons lived in caves and were skilled hunters. They made fine tools, including spear throwers, blades, and bows and arrows. They used these tools to hunt large animals such as bison, mammoth, and reindeer.

Scientists have uncovered evidence that the Cro-Magnons developed a rich culture. They engraved bones and created cave paintings like that shown in Figure 22-15. Cro-Magnons buried their dead and lived in social groups.

Many scientists think that Cro-Magnons evolved from *Homo erectus* in Africa. From Africa, *Cro-Magnons* migrated westward into Europe and north to parts of Asia. Cro-Magnons are believed to be the immediate ancestors of the humans of today.

Scientists think that Cro-Magnons first reached North America over 12,000 years ago. During the last ice age, some Cro-Magnons crossed the Bering land bridge, shown in Figure 22-16, to enter North America. The Bering land bridge is underwater today.

Humans in a Technological Society

Humans have come a long way since their early origins over 3 million years

Figure 22-15 Cro-Magnon Cave Painting

S K I L L   B U I L D E R

Making Inferences

When you infer, you state a conclusion based on facts and information, rather than on direct observation. For example, scientists cannot directly observe how early hominids lived. Scientists can, however, make inferences about the way of life of hominids by studying fossils. What might scientists infer from the following findings?

1. Tools and bones of animals are often found next to the fossil remains of a Neanderthal.
2. Beautiful paintings of animals are often found on the walls of caves where early *Homo sapiens* lived.
3. Neanderthals disappeared from the fossil record about 30,000 years ago.

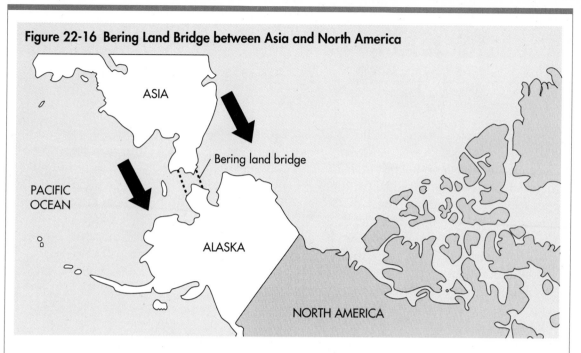

Figure 22-16 Bering Land Bridge between Asia and North America

ASIA

Bering land bridge

PACIFIC
OCEAN

ALASKA

NORTH AMERICA

ago. They have used their hands and their brains to make complicated tools from stone, metal, and, more recently, from synthetic materials such as plastics. People use these tools for hunting, farming, home building, and many other purposes.

Today people live in a highly technological society. Jet planes enable people to fly. Rocket ships carry them to the moon and perhaps one day to other planets. Computers have made doing many tasks easier and more efficient. Communications and weather satellites keep people in better touch with their surroundings.

Will people use their wisdom to build a better world? Or will they use technology to pollute or even destroy their own planet? The future of human society rests in your hands.

Section 22-3 Review

Write the definitions for the following terms in your own words.

1. **Homo habilis**   2. **Homo erectus**
3. **Homo sapiens**   4. **Neanderthal**
5. **Cro-Magnon**

Answer these questions.

6. In what ways might members of *H. habilis* have been better adapted for survival than *A. afarensis*?
7. In what ways might *H. erectus* been better adapted for survival than *H. habilis*?
8. Why do scientists believe that Cro-Magnons were the direct ancestors of modern humans?

SCIENCE, TECHNOLOGY, & SOCIETY

Fossil Dating

Discoveries of fossil bones from humans who lived long ago have added more pieces to the puzzle of human evolution. To state that a human fossil is a certain age, scientists must be able to back up their claims. For example, how did scientists conclude that Lucy lived millions of years ago? There is no way of knowing for certain. However, scientists used several techniques to give dates for when Lucy might have lived.

Radioactive dating is one technique scientists used. You learned about this technique in Chapter 6. To date fossils that are several million years old, scientists use the radioactive element potassium. Radioactive potassium decays into a gas called argon at a constant rate. By finding how much argon gas is given off from a fossil, its age can be calculated. However, finding enough potassium in fossil bones is difficult. Instead, scientists took samples of volcanic rock that came from near Lucy's bones. These samples were placed in a chamber like the one shown in Figure 22-17, in which all the air was taken out. Then the samples were heated, causing them to give off tiny traces of argon gas. From the amount of argon given off, scientists calculated the age of the rock. From that they drew a conclusion about the age of the fossils.

Another technique used for dating is by examining rocks crystals near the hominid fossils. When certain crystals are carefully examined under a microscope, tiny scratches can be detected. These scratches indicate that millions of years have passed. The age of the crystals helps date the age of nearby fossils. The scientists used all the information from these and other techniques to come up with an approximate time in which the fossil hominid must have lived.

Follow-up Activity
Imagine that you have found a fossil bone that could have come from a human being. Why would you need several tests in order to claim that it is was a very old fossil?

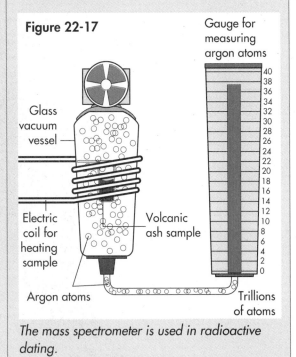

Figure 22-17

Gauge for measuring argon atoms

40 38 36 34 32 30 28 26 24 22 20 18 16 14 12 10 8 6 4 2 0

Glass vacuum vessel

Electric coil for heating sample

Volcanic ash sample

Argon atoms

Trillions of atoms

The mass spectrometer is used in radioactive dating.

Section 22-1 Classifying Human Beings

1. Humans belong to the animal kingdom, the phylum chordate, the class mammal, the order primate, the family hominid, the genus *Homo*, and the species *sapiens*.
2. Primates have opposable thumbs, frontal and stereoscopic vision, and nails on the top surface of their fingers and toes.
3. The ability to walk upright on two legs and to use their highly developed brains to communicate using language sets humans apart from all other species.

Section 22-2 Origin of the First Humans

1. Evidence suggests that humans and apes evolved from a common ancestor.
2. *Australopithecus afarensis* is believed to be the earliest hominid.

Section 22-3 Evolution of Modern Humans

1. The hominid ancestors of modern humans may have evolved from *A. afarensis*.
2. *Homo habilis* may have evolved from *A. afarensis*. *H. habilis* was a skilled tool maker.
3. *Homo erectus* evolved from *H. habilis*. *H. erectus* was the first species to use fire for cooking and for heat. *H. erectus* was the first hominid to migrate from Africa to other parts of the world.
4. Neanderthal was an early form of *Homo sapiens*. Neanderthals are believed to have evolved from *H. erectus*. Neanderthals lived in caves, built rock shelters, used fire, and buried their dead.

5. Cro-Magnons are the immediate ancestors of modern humans. They had a rich culture, as indicated by bone carvings and cave paintings. During the last ice age, some Cro-Magnons migrated to North America.

Write the term from the list below that best matches each description.

Neanderthal, Cro-Magnon, primate, *Homo sapiens,* **bipedal, hominid**

1. an early human from which modern humans evolved
2. an early human who became extinct without evolving into a new species
3. family in which all prehistoric and modern humans are classified
4. genus and species name for modern humans
5. order of organisms that have an opposable thumb
6. type of organism that walks on two feet

Explain the difference between the terms in each pair.

7. *Australopithecus afarensis*, Lucy
8. primate, hominid
9. *Homo sapiens*, Cro-Magnon
10. frontal vision, stereoscopic vision
11. *Homo habilis, Homo erectus*

Write the missing term that completes each sentence.

1. The ability to look straight ahead at an object with both eyes is known as ___ vision.
2. *Australopithecus* ___ is the oldest known hominid.
3. All species of *Australopithecus* have become ___.
4. The name *Homo habilis* means ___.
5. Many scientists believe that *Homo erectus* evolved from *Homo* ___.
6. All modern humans belong to the species ___.
7. The early humans known for their bone carvings and cave paintings are ___.
8. All hominids belong to the ___ order.

■■■ INTERPRETING INFORMATION ■■■

Use Figure 22-18 to answer the following questions.

1. Name the earliest hominid to appear on Earth. About how long ago did this hominid first appear?
2. Name two hominid species that lived about 2 million years ago.
3. Which hominid species inhabited the earth for the longest period of time? When did this species first appear on the earth? When did it become extinct?

■■■ THINK AND DISCUSS ■■■

Use the section number in parentheses to help you find each answer. Write your answers in complete sentences.

1. Early primates were all tree-dwelling organisms. Why does this fact add to the difficulty of tracing human evolution? (22-1)

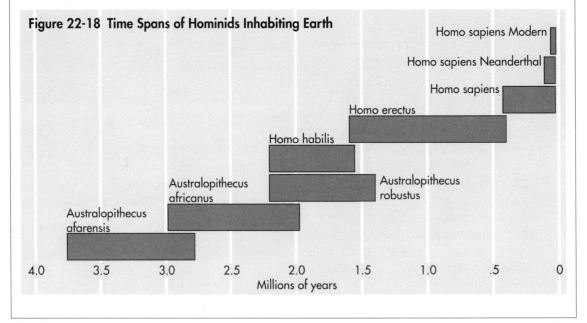

Figure 22-18 Time Spans of Hominids Inhabiting Earth

Homo sapiens Modern
Homo sapiens Neanderthal
Homo sapiens
Homo erectus
Homo habilis
Australopithecus africanus
Australopithecus robustus
Australopithecus afarensis

4.0   3.5   3.0   2.5   2.0   1.5   1.0   .5   0
Millions of years

2. Suppose you found a hominid fossil that was about 4 million years old. How would you decide whether this hominid belonged to *A. afarensis* or a new hominid species? (22-2)
3. What have scientists inferred about *Homo erectus* after finding their fossils in Africa, China, Europe, and Asia? (22-3)
4. Why is *Homo sapiens* an appropriate name for modern humans? (22-3)

GOING FURTHER

1. Visit a museum to find information about the history of humans. Write a report on the evolution of humans.
2. Look at pictures of the skulls of early humans in books or observe the fossil skulls in a museum. Describe how the appearance of human faces and heads has changed over time.

COMPETENCY REVIEW

1. To which order of mammals do humans belong?
   a. carnivore   b. rodent
   c. primate   d. amphibian
2. Which of the following is a trait found in apes?
   a. an opposable thumb
   b. claws on the fingers
   c. scales covering the body
   d. the ability to draw
3. Which characteristic is common to all primates?
   a. ability to make complicated tools
   b. ability to paint drawings on the walls of caves

   c. frontal vision
   d. the presence of a tail
4. Which of the following organisms is a hominid?
   a. chimpanzee   b. human
   c. ape   d. gorilla
5. The earliest hominid to inhabit the earth was
   a. *Homo erectus.*
   b. *Homo sapiens.*
   c. *Australopithecus afarensis.*
   d. Neanderthal.
6. "Wise human" is the meaning of
   a. *Australopithecus africanus.*
   b. *Australopithecus robustus.*
   c. *Homo habilis.*
   d. *Homo sapiens.*
7. A scientist who uncovered early hominid fossil remains was
   a. Lamarck.   b. Darwin.
   c. Mendel.   d. Leakey.
8. The most recent ancestor of modern humans is
   a. the ape.   b. Neanderthal.
   c. Lucy.   d. Cro-Magnon.
9. Which statement about Neanderthals is true?
   a. They did not use tools.
   b. They became extinct.
   c. They live on the earth today.
   d. They were probably weaker than modern humans.
10. Modern humans have lived in North America for over
    a. 2 million years.   b. 12,000 years.
    c. 100,000 years.   d. 1 million years.

CHAPTER 23

THE MICROBIAL WORLD

Have you ever had strep throat? If so, then you had a disease caused by bacteria. Bacteria cause a number of other diseases as well, including tuberculosis and some forms of pneumonia.

Most kinds of bacteria, however, do not cause disease. In fact, many kinds of bacteria are quite useful to people. People depend on bacteria for many food products. Yogurt and cheese are produced by the action of bacteria on milk. Sour pickles and sauerkraut are produced by the action of bacteria on cucumbers and cabbage.

More importantly, bacteria are essential in maintaining the balance in the ecosystem. They break down wastes and dead organisms in soil and water. This process recycles materials needed for living things.

Bacteria are one type of **microbe**. A microbe is an organism too small to be seen with the naked eye. In addition to bacteria, microbes include viruses, protists, and some fungi and algae. The microbe shown in Figure 23-1 has been magnified many times.

Hundreds of thousands of microbe species are known to exist. In fact, the greatest number and variety of all living things are microbes. In this chapter you will learn about these tiny organisms and how they influence human lives.

23-1 Characteristics of Microbes

■ *Objectives*

☐ *Describe the structure of viruses and bacteria.*

☐ *Explain how bacteria are classified.*

☐ *Describe the characteristics of protozoa and algae.*

☐ *Explain how microbes affect people.*

The inventions of the compound micro-scope and the electron microscope have

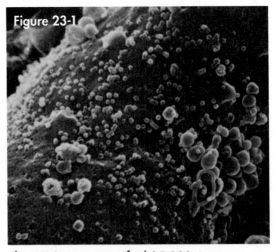

Figure 23-1

The AIDS virus magnified 25,000 times.

enabled scientists to study microbes carefully. Using these microscopes, scientists have discovered and identified a great variety of microbes. This variety is so great, in fact, that scientists have classified microbes into several groups including viruses, bacteria, protists, and fungi.

Viruses

Viruses are the smallest microbes, ranging in size from 0.08 to 0.3 microns. They are so small that scientists must use an electron microscope to see them. Despite their small size, viruses have many different shapes. Some viruses look soft and fluffy. Other viruses look like long, thin rods. Still others look like many-sided crystals. Figure 23-2 shows several kinds of viruses.

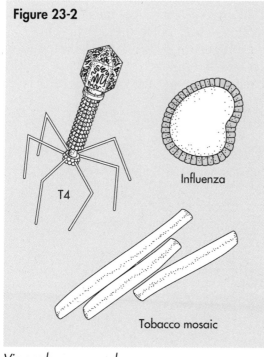

Figure 23-2

Influenza

T4

Tobacco mosaic

Viruses have many shapes.

In Chapter 5 you learned that viruses do not fit into any of the five kingdoms of living things. Many scientists even think that viruses are not living things at all. Viruses are not made of cells. They consist only of DNA surrounded by a protein coat. They can reproduce only when they are inside other living cells. When outside a cell, viruses can do nothing.

Viruses cause many diseases in animals. Microbes that cause disease are called **pathogens**. A pathogenic virus infects a cell by reproducing inside it. When a virus infects a cell, the cell becomes very weak and may even die. In the meantime, the newly formed viruses move on to other cells. As this cycle repeats over and over again, the entire organism may be weakened or harmed. In animals, the immune system fights the virus infection.

Viruses infect different kinds of living cells. Some viruses infect bacteria. Other viruses infect plant or animal cells. Some viruses infect human cells. These viruses cause such diseases as colds, measles, chicken pox, flu, polio, and AIDS. Evidence also indicates that some forms of cancer are caused by viruses.

Bacteria

The first forms of life on Earth were probably bacteria. Today bacteria are among the simplest and most plentiful living things. As you learned in Chapter 5, bacteria are one-celled organisms. They range in size from 0.3 microns to 40 microns. The smallest bacteria must be viewed with an electron microscope. The larger bacteria, however, may be seen through a compound microscope.

Bacteria have a tough cell wall. They lack a true nucleus surrounded by a nuclear membrane. Most bacteria cannot make their own food and therefore must get food from other living things. Although most cannot move, bacteria are well adapted for survival.

Scientists classify bacteria according to their shape. The **cocci** are ball shaped. Another group, the **bacilli** (buh-SIL-eye), are rod shaped. A third group of bacteria, the **spirilla** (spy-RIL-uh), are coiled into a spiral shape. Use Figure 23-3 to compare the three groups.

Some bacteria exist in groups. These groups may take the form of pairs, chains, or clusters. Cocci that live in pairs are called diplococci. One kind of diplococcus causes pneumonia. Cocci that form chains are called streptococci. Streptococci include the bacteria that cause throat infections and blood poisoning. Cocci that form clusters are called staphylococci. Some kinds of staphylococci can cause boils and pimples.

Bacteria are found almost everywhere. They live in air, water, food, and even inside your body. Bacteria are found in places where no other organism can survive. Scientists have found bacteria in the atmosphere 20 kilometers above the earth's surface. Other bacteria survive in the ocean's greatest depths or buried in ice at the North and South Poles. Some bacteria, called **anaerobic** (an-uh-ROH-bik) bacteria, do not even use oxygen. Bacteria that do need oxygen to survive are called **aerobic** bacteria.

What makes bacteria so hardy? When the conditions for growing are unfavorable, bacteria form spores and enter a resting stage. As spores, bacteria can survive a very long time until conditions improve. Then bacteria come out of their spores and begin to grow and reproduce.

Many bacteria live inside your body. In the warm, moist, dark environment of your digestive system, some bacteria live off partly digested food. Many of the bacteria that normally live in your body

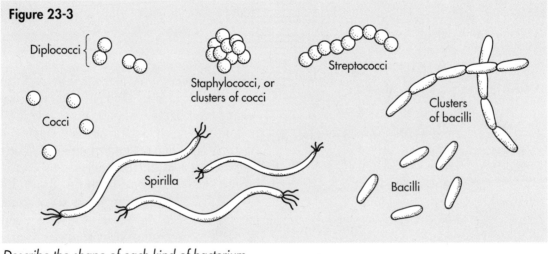

Figure 23-3

Diplococci

Staphylococci, or clusters of cocci

Streptococci

Cocci

Clusters of bacilli

Spirilla

Bacilli

Describe the shape of each kind of bacterium.

are helpful to you. For instance, one kind of bacterium that lives in your mouth produces enzymes that fight tooth decay. Another kind of bacterium that lives in your intestine makes vitamin B_{12} and vitamin K.

Some bacteria cause disease, however. These bacteria may enter your body from air, water, or food. Once inside your body, they may multiply rapidly. Your body is able to fight off and destroy many of these bacteria. Some kinds of bacteria, however, produce poisons that can damage your tissues and organs. Diseases caused by bacteria include tuberculosis, some kinds of pneumonia, strep throat, and diphtheria.

Protists

Among the largest and most complex microbes are the protists. In Chapter 5 you learned that most protists are one-celled organisms. Unlike bacteria, protists have a true nucleus surrounded by a nuclear membrane. Protists contain cell organelles such as mitochondria, which are not found in bacteria.

Algae are plantlike protists containing chloroplasts. Some algae are unicellular. Others live together in groups, forming chains or colonies. The algae that live in chains or colonies can be seen in oceans, lakes, and ponds. These algae are an important source of food for fish and other aquatic animals.

Protozoa are microscopic, animal-like protists. Protozoa cannot make their own food because they have no chloroplasts. Therefore, protozoa depend on other living things for food.

Most protozoa, such as *Paramecium*, are not harmful to humans. Other protozoa are pathogenic, such as the protozoan that causes malaria. Figure 23-4 shows how this organism harms the body's red blood cells.

Fungi

Some organisms from the fungi kingdom are classified as microbes. These fungi include yeasts and molds. Both yeasts and molds are organisms that reproduce by means of spores.

Fungi have cell walls but lack chloroplasts. They therefore depend on other organisms for food. Fungi often live on the source of their food. For example, bread mold produces enzymes that digest the starch in the bread into glucose. The bread mold then absorbs the glucose and uses it for energy. The mold that causes athlete's foot lives between the toes. This mold uses the chemicals in human cells for food.

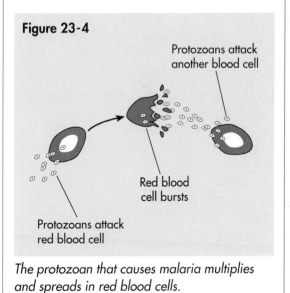

Figure 23-4

Protozoans attack another blood cell

Red blood cell bursts

Protozoans attack red blood cell

The protozoan that causes malaria multiplies and spreads in red blood cells.

Where Are Microbes Found?

Process Skill making observations

Materials three clear plastic food containers with covers, dried peas or beans, bread from the bakery, decaying fruit, forceps, microscope, slides and cover slips, medicine dropper

Bacteria and other microbes are found nearly everywhere. When provided with the materials and conditions needed for growth, each microbe may multiply until it forms a mass called a colony. A colony is usually large enough to be seen with the unaided eye.

Procedure

1. Add dried peas or beans with a little water to one food container. Moisten a piece of bread and put it into the second food container. Place a piece of decaying fruit into the third container.

2. Cover all three containers and place them in a warm place away from direct sunlight. Carefully observe the containers each day for five days. Record any changes.

3. Your teacher will remove bits of each of the colonies growing on the foods and make a wet mount slide for each. **Warning** Students allergic to molds should be excused from participating in this activity.

4. Observe each specimen under a microscope. Make drawings in your notebook of each.

Conclusions

5. How many different kinds of microbes did you see on the food samples?

6. What kinds of microbes are growing on the food samples? What enabled you to identify each microbe?

▬ Section 23-1 Review ▬

Write the definitions for the following terms in your own words.

1. **microbe**
2. **pathogen**
3. **anaerobic**
4. **aerobic**

Answer these questions.

5. What are the four types of microbes?
6. Why have scientists only recently begun to study viruses?
7. Describe some ways in which microbes are helpful to people.
8. How may some microbes be harmful to people?
9. A student accidentally leaves a sandwich in a locker for a week. What kind of microbes might be found on it?

23-2 Isolating and Culturing Microbes

■ *Objectives*

☐ *Explain how viruses grow and reproduce in nature and in the laboratory.*

☐ *Describe the conditions necessary for bacterial growth.*

☐ *Describe the techniques scientists use to isolate and culture bacteria.*

☐ *Explain how aseptic techniques are used when culturing bacteria.*

Although microbes are found almost everywhere, they are too small to be seen with the unaided eye. Scientists study them with a microscope. In order to study microbes, however, scientists must first isolate, or separate, them.

Growing Viruses

You learned in Chapter 5 that viruses can only grow inside living cells. Therefore, viruses cannot be grown on a nutrient medium inside a test tube. To grow new viruses, scientists must first place them in the cells of another organism.

Figure 23-5 shows how viruses grow inside bacteria. The virus becomes active when it comes into contact with the bacterium. First it attaches itself to the bacterium. The virus then injects its DNA into the bacterium. Once inside the bacterium, viral DNA directs the cell to reproduce new viruses. After many new viruses are made, the cell breaks open and dies, releasing the new viruses. The new viruses go on to infect more cells.

Some viruses infect cells of bacteria. Other viruses infect cells of plants or animals. Scientists often use fertilized eggs to culture or grow viruses. A virus is injected into a fertilized egg. The egg undergoes cell division, forming many cells. The virus invades the cells of the developing embryo and reproduces thousands of new viruses.

Culturing Bacteria

Bacteria reproduce asexually by binary fission. During fission, the DNA in the

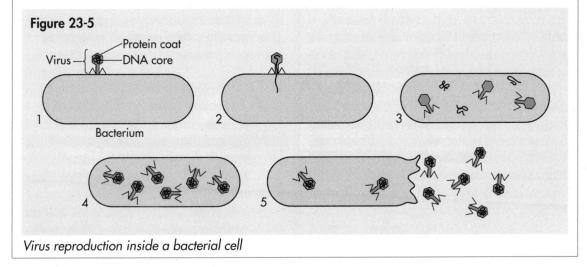

Figure 23-5

Virus reproduction inside a bacterial cell

bacterial cell replicates. Then the cell wall and cell membrane pinch inward, forming two daughter cells. Each daughter cell receives identical DNA, as shown in Figure 23-6.

Because bacteria reproduce quickly, scientists can easily grow bacteria in the laboratory. Bacteria grown in the laboratory are called **cultures**. To culture bacteria, scientists must provide the proper temperature and the proper amount of light, moisture, oxygen, and food. Under these conditions, some bacteria will divide as fast as once every 20 minutes. At this rate, after only three hours, a single bacterium will produce over 100,000 offspring.

In one day a single bacterium may produce millions of cells. This mass, large enough to be seen with the naked eye, is called a **colony**. A colony, like the ones shown in Figure 23-7, consists of large numbers of one kind of bacterium.

Conditions Required for Growing Bacteria

How do scientists provide bacteria with the proper conditions for growth? First they must supply the bacteria with food and moisture. Most bacteria do not carry on photosynthesis and cannot produce

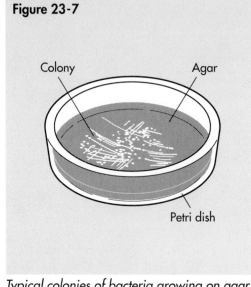

Figure 23-7

Colony　　　　Agar

Petri dish

Typical colonies of bacteria growing on agar in a petri dish

their own food. In nature, some bacteria feed on living plants and animals. Others get food from dead organisms. Most bacteria, however, can live on a large variety of foods.

In the laboratory, bacteria are cultured in a **petri dish**, a shallow covered dish made of plastic or glass. Bacteria may also be grown in test tubes, as shown in Figure 23-8. Bacteria are grown in either a solid

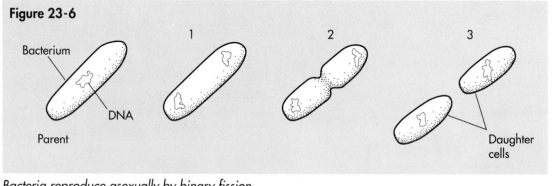

Figure 23-6

Bacterium

DNA

Parent

1

2

3

Daughter cells

Bacteria reproduce asexually by binary fission.

Figure 23-8

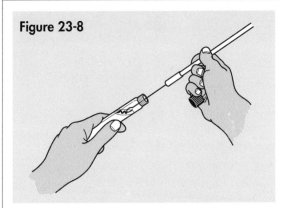

Bacteria growing on agar in a test tube

or liquid substance called a **culture medium**. A commonly used solid medium is **agar**. Agar is a gelatinlike substance obtained from seaweed. Beef extract is added to the agar to create an ideal culture medium for bacteria. Bacteria may also be grown in broth, which is a liquid medium. Beef extract broth is a common liquid-culture medium.

Most bacteria grow best between 25° and 40°C. To maintain the proper temperature for growth, petri dishes containing bacteria are placed in an **incubator**. An incubator is a temperature-controlled chamber.

A few species of bacteria require light in order to grow. Most bacteria, however, grow best in darkness. Since an incubator is dark, it is a good place for growing most bacteria.

Techniques for Culturing Bacteria When growing bacteria, scientists must make sure that other microbes do not contaminate their bacterial culture. If the scientists are working with pathogenic bacteria, they must also make sure that

these organisms do not escape into the environment. Scientists follow special procedures to ensure that all microbes other than the bacteria being studied are killed. These procedures are called **aseptic techniques**. Aseptic techniques protect the scientists, the environment, and the bacterial cultures from contamination. Figure 23-9 describes several important aseptic techniques.

Figure 23-9 Aseptic Techniques

Treat all microbes as though they are pathogens.

Do not eat or drink in the laboratory. Keep fingers and pencils out of the mouth.

Wear a lab coat to protect clothing from contamination.

Clean the work area with a disinfectant, a chemical that kills microbes.

Immediately wipe up all spills with a disinfectant.

Wash hands with a hand disinfectant before and after every procedure.

Use an autoclave to sterilize all equipment, including needles, petri dishes, and tubes, before and after use.

Carefully dispose of all plastic petri dishes. Do not reuse them.

How Do You Transfer Bacteria from a Test Tube to a Petri Dish?

Process Skills *performing lab techniques, using lab equipment*

Materials test tube culture of nonpathogenic bacteria, Bunsen burner, inoculating loop, petri dish, medium, disinfectants

Warning Do this activity only under the strict supervision of your teacher and after reading the procedure carefully.

Procedure

1. Put on a pair of goggles and your laboratory coat. Wash your hands.
2. Use a Bunsen burner to sterilize an inoculating loop, as in Figure 23-10.
3. Remove the cotton plug or cap. Use the loop to draw some culture from the tube. Flame the top of the tube to sterilize it. Replace the plug.
4. Raise the lid of the petri dish just high enough to insert the wire loop.
5. With the lid raised, quickly streak the inoculating loop across the petri dish, as shown in Figure 23-11. Do not break the surface of the agar. Replace the lid on the petri dish.

Figure 23-11

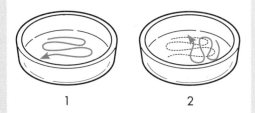

1   2

6. Sterilize the used loop in the flame.
7. Incubate the petri dish for several days at 37° C.
8. Wash your lab station with a disinfectant and your hands with a hand disinfectant.
9. After several days, observe the petri dish. Describe the size, shape, and color of each bacterial colony.

Figure 23-10

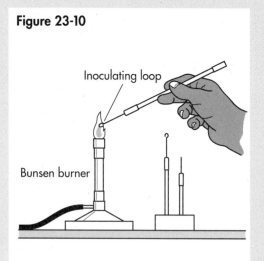

Inoculating loop

Bunsen burner

Conclusions

10. Why must aseptic techniques be used ?
11. Explain the pattern of growth of the colonies of bacteria.
12. Why should the lid of the petri dish be raised only briefly?

The process of destroying microbes on laboratory equipment is called sterilization. Scientists use a pressure cooker called an **autoclave** shown in Figure 23-12. An autoclave sterilizes equipment. Water at the bottom of the autoclave is changed to steam. Because the steam cannot escape, it increases pressure within the autoclave. As a result, the temperature increases, killing any microbes that might be growing on the equipment.

Figure 23-12 Autoclave

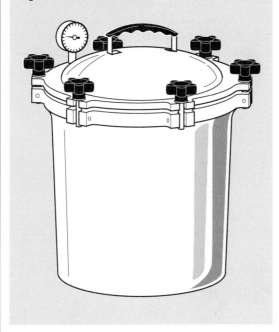

Scientists often obtain a culture of one species of bacterium from a supply house. Cultures of bacteria are shipped to the laboratory in test tubes. Once the samples arrive, scientists usually transfer some of the bacteria to petri dishes containing culture medium. If the bacteria are left in the test tubes, they will soon use up their food supply and die.

Using a Microscope to Observe Bacteria
Individual bacteria can be seen only with the aid of a powerful microscope. Usually a compound called a **stain** is used to color the bacterial cells so that they can be seen more clearly. Staining outlines the boundary of a cell and the organelles within it. Scientists identify bacteria by looking at their size and shape under the microscope. Scientists also identify bacteria by the appearance of the colonies they form.

◼ Section 23-2 Review ◼

Write the definitions for the following terms in your own words.

1. **culture**
2. **colony**
3. **culture medium**
4. **aseptic technique**
5. **stain**

Answer these questions.

6. Why are aseptic techniques used when working with bacteria?
7. What are two kinds of culture media?
8. How does a colony of bacteria form?
9. What would happen if a petri dish containing nutrient medium were left uncovered for several hours?
10. How do scientists identify unknown bacteria?

How Can You Make a Slide of Bacteria?

Process Skills *performing lab techniques, making observations*

Materials inoculating loop, test tube containing nonpathogenic bacteria, glass slide, medicine dropper, methylene blue stain, Bunsen burner, tongs, microscope, goggles, disinfectants

Procedure

1. Put on a pair of goggles and a laboratory coat. Wash your hands.
2. Sterilize an inoculating loop by following the procedure on page 428. Open the test tube of bacteria and pass the mouth of the tube briefly through the flame.
3. Use the loop to remove a small amount of bacteria. Place the bacteria on a glass slide.
4. Mix the bacteria and water.
5. Flame the inoculating loop and the mouth of the test tube. Plug the tube.
6. Air dry the slide. Holding the slide with tongs, pass it through the flame, as shown in Figure 23-13.
7. Apply a few drops of stain to the slide. Wait two or three minutes; then carefully rinse off the extra stain.
8. Observe the bacteria under the microscope, using low power and then high power.
9. Dispose of materials properly. Then wash your lab station with a disinfectant and your hands with a hand disinfectant.

Conclusions

10. List the steps of this activity in which you used aseptic techniques.
11. Draw some bacteria as seen under high power. Describe the shape of each.

Figure 23-13

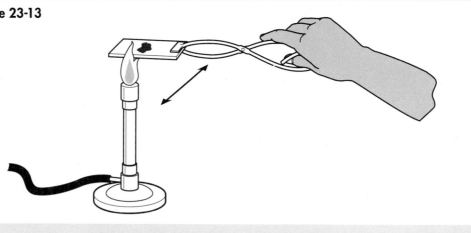

23-3 Helpful Microbes

■ *Objectives*

☐ *Explain why microbes living in soil are important for maintaining balance in an ecosystem.*

☐ *Name two ecological cycles that depend on the activities of microbes in the soil.*

☐ *Explain what happens to sewage in a sewage treatment plant.*

☐ *List some foods whose flavors are obtained from cultures of microbes.*

Although people tend to think of microbes as the cause of disease, only about five percent of microbes are pathogens. Most microbes play an important role in ecology. For example, bacteria that live in the soil decompose, or break down, dead organisms. Bacteria that live in the human intestine are necessary for normal digestion. Still other bacteria give flavor to many foods.

Microbes in the Soil

Microbes that live in the soil include bacteria, molds, algae, protozoa, and some yeasts. These microbes play a necessary role in maintaining the balance in the ecosystem. In Chapter 8 you learned about the nitrogen cycle, in which nitrogen compounds circulate from the soil to organisms and back to the soil. During the nitrogen cycle, bacteria called decomposers break down proteins in the cells of dead organisms into inorganic molecules. Some of these bacteria release ammonia into the soil. Other bacteria in the soil change the ammonia into nitrates.

How Can You Demonstrate the Presence of Microbes in Soil?

Process Skills observing, using laboratory equipment

Materials petri dish containing nutrient agar, sterile jar with a lid, inoculating loop, soil sample, incubator, Bunsen burner

Procedure

1. Collect a soil sample and place it in a sterile covered jar.
2. Place an inoculating loop in the flame of a Bunsen burner to sterilize it.
3. Use the inoculating loop to transfer some soil from the jar to the petri dish. Carefully dot the dish very lightly with the soil.
4. Incubate the soil sample for 24 to 48 hours.
5. Without opening the dish, count the number of colonies that formed on each dish.
6. Dispose of the unopened dish properly.

Conclusions

7. Describe the color and shape of each colony. Estimate its size. Why do the colonies look different from each other?
8. Why are bacteria found in the soil important to all living things?
9. How might excessive use of pesticides be hazardous to all living things?

The roots of plants absorb these nitrates from the soil and use them to manufacture proteins.

Soil bacteria are also important in an ecological cycle called the **sulfur cycle**. In the sulfur cycle, bacteria break down proteins in the cells of dead organisms into inorganic compounds called sulfates. As with nitrates, plants absorb sulfates from the soil and use them to manufacture proteins.

All living things eventually die and decay into material used in the growth of other living things. Human activities, however, often upset the ecological cycles just described. For example, farmers use large quantities of pesticides to protect their crops. Unfortunately, these pesticides often kill helpful decomposers as well as insect pests. When people build roads or parking lots, they pave over large areas of soil. These activities destroy the homes of many organisms living within the soil.

Microbes in Sewage Treatment

Have you seen signs on beaches warning "No swimming – polluted water"? Such signs have become common sights in areas where the water has become polluted. Many coastal cities such as New York City and Boston have a large human population. The high population has contributed to the water pollution problems in these areas. Each day, vast amounts of human waste are produced and flushed into pipes from millions of homes, apartments, schools, and businesses. These human wastes make up sewage.

Unfortunately, sewage is often discharged into the ocean surrounding large cities. Many inland cities also have high levels of water pollution. Lakes, ponds, rivers, and streams in highly populated areas may be polluted with sewage.

Sewage is 99 percent water. The other 1 percent includes urea, proteins, carbohydrates, and fats. Sewage contains pathogenic as well as nonpathogenic microbes. Sewage must be treated in a sewage treatment plant before being discharged into bodies of water. Treatment of sewage speeds up the process of decay.

Bacteria play an important role in the treatment of sewage. In one kind of sewage treatment plant, raw sewage enters aeration tanks. There the sewage is churned and mixed with oxygen. Aerobic bacteria begin to decompose the sewage.

Heavy solid matter from the sewage settles to the bottom of the tank. This solid material is pumped into a pipe that carries it into a separate tank. Here the solid material is further decomposed by anaerobic bacteria.

This decomposition changes the solid material into methane gas. The methane gas is burned off. The solid material that remains is called **sludge**. The sludge may be burned or it may be dumped in the sea, hundreds of miles from land. If it is burned, the powdered residue or ash that remains is recovered and used as fertilizer for crops.

What happens to the sewage in the liquid that does not settle to the bottom of the tank? The liquid sewage is pumped into another tank called a trickling filter tank. The trickling filter tank contains rocks on which bacteria and algae grow.

The liquid runs down through these rocks. Algae and bacteria feed on the sewage in the liquid, breaking it down even further. The feeding action of the algae and bacteria partly clean the liquid. This less polluted liquid travels to another tank called a settling tank. Gravity carries any additional solid material to the bottom of the settling tank. This solid is then added to the sludge-containing tank. Figure 23-14 shows how the parts of a treatment plant work together.

Figure 23-14

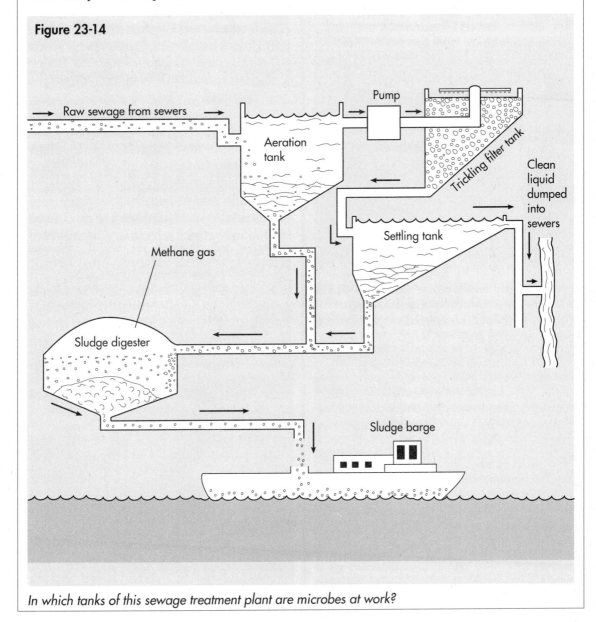

Raw sewage from sewers

Pump

Aeration tank

Trickling filter tank

Clean liquid dumped into sewers

Settling tank

Methane gas

Sludge digester

Sludge barge

In which tanks of this sewage treatment plant are microbes at work?

Interpreting Data

You have learned that microbes play an important role in producing many of the foods you eat. The menu shown in Figure 23-15 includes several of these foods.

1. Determine which of the foods in the menu were partially made by the action of microbes.
2. Explain the role of microbes in forming each one.

Figure 23-15

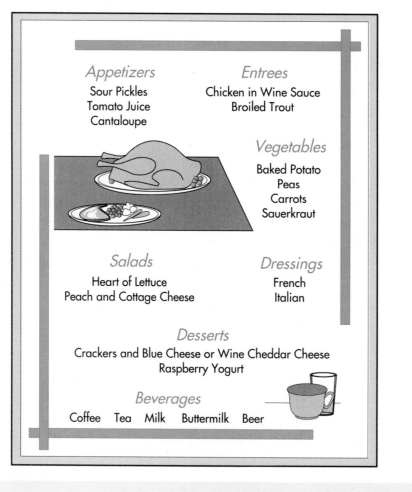

Appetizers
Sour Pickles
Tomato Juice
Cantaloupe

Entrees
Chicken in Wine Sauce
Broiled Trout

Vegetables
Baked Potato
Peas
Carrots
Sauerkraut

Salads
Heart of Lettuce
Peach and Cottage Cheese

Dressings
French
Italian

Desserts
Crackers and Blue Cheese or Wine Cheddar Cheese
Raspberry Yogurt

Beverages
Coffee   Tea   Milk   Buttermilk   Beer

Microbes and Foods

Many foods, such as breads, cheeses, and wines, get their special flavors from cultures of microbes. For example, yeast and bacteria are used to break down sugars under anaerobic conditions to produce alcohol. This process is called **fermentation**. Wine is made from fruit juices that have been fermented by bacteria or yeasts.

Yeasts are added to bread dough to make bread rise. Yeasts ferment starch and sugar in the dough, producing carbon dioxide. The carbon dioxide expands when heated, causing the bread to rise.

Molds and bacteria are used to make many foods. Molds are used in the production of various cheeses. Blue cheeses are produced by adding molds to the cheese curd. Many other foods, including those shown in Figure 23-16, are prepared with the assistance of bacteria.

Bacteria are also used to make food for farm animals. Silage, a food for cattle, is prepared by placing finely chopped plants in silos. The silage forms when bacteria ferment the sugar in these plants. Cattle feed on this silage throughout the winter.

▬ Section 23-3 Review ▬

Write the definitions for the following terms in your own words.

1. **sulfur cycle**　　2. **sludge**
3. **fermentation**

Answer these questions.

4. How do microbes in the soil help maintain balance in an ecosystem?
5. What would happen to the ecosystem if all bacteria in the soil were destroyed?
6. What is a sewage treatment plant?
7. What foods are partially made by the action of microbes?

Figure 23-16

Cultures of bacteria are added during the preparation of these dairy products.

SCIENCE, TECHNOLOGY, & SOCIETY

Tiny Microbes Attack a Huge Problem

What happens to the nearly 600 million tons of hazardous waste that are produced by Americans each year? In many places, such wastes are being cleaned up by very specialized bacteria and fungi. These microbes can actually digest some of the most poisonous wastes produced by industry.

Over 1000 species of bacteria and fungi are being used to digest oil, gasoline, plastics, and other harmful chemicals. For example, in some places where wood products are treated, harmful wood preservative chemicals were leaking from storage tanks into nearby water supplies. To clean up the mess, bacteria like those in Figure 23-17 were used. They broke down the chemicals into carbon dioxide, water, and harmless chloride chemicals. Within one year, the bacteria had managed to break down over two thirds of a pile of waste weighing several hundred tons.

Another place where poison-eating microbes are used is in the areas around filling stations. Sometimes gasoline leaks out of underground storage tanks around filling pumps. To clean up the gasoline, several strains of bacteria are used at the same time. One kind of bacteria breaks down gasoline into benzene. Then another type breaks benzene down into another product.

Some of these microbes develop through natural selection. One microbe in a population may have a natural resistance to a harmful chemical, even if the rest of the population is poisoned by it. If the resistant microbe reproduces, its offspring will produce a more resistant population than the original one.

There are many advantages to the technology of using microbes for chemical clean up. Poisonous wastes do not have to be moved or trucked to another location. The bacteria used cost less than trucking wastes elsewhere. There also are disadvantages. The bacteria do not always work in certain soils, such as clay. Also, bacteria may work more slowly than some other methods.

Follow-up Activity

Suppose you owned a factory and found that poisonous chemicals were leaking out of storage containers. Would you use microbes to aid your clean-up? Explain.

Figure 23-17

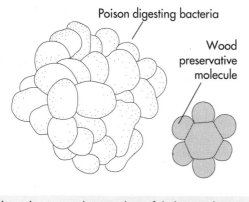

Poison digesting bacteria

Wood preservative molecule

These bacteria digest a harmful chemical. How do they help the environment?

KEEPING TRACK

Section 23-1 Characteristics of Microbes

1. Microbes make up the greatest number and variety of living things. Microbes include viruses, bacteria, protozoa, and fungi.
2. Viruses live and reproduce only when they are in living cells. They cause diseases such as chicken pox, measles, colds, flu, polio, and AIDS.
3. Bacteria are classified by shape. They may be rod shaped, round, or spiral shaped.
4. Some bacteria, protozoa, and fungi cause disease. These organisms are called pathogens.

Section 23-2 Isolating and Culturing Microbes

1. In order to grow, bacteria need the proper temperature and proper amount of light, moisture, oxygen, and food.
2. In the laboratory, bacteria are cultured in petri dishes or test tubes containing culture medium.
3. To prevent contamination, aseptic techniques should always be used when handling bacteria.

Section 23-3 Helpful Microbes

1. Some bacteria and molds act as decomposers. They break down organic molecules in dead organisms to inorganic molecules and return them to the soil. Plants use these inorganic substances to manufacture proteins.
2. Aerobic and anaerobic bacteria are used to treat sewage. These bacteria speed up the process of decay, changing sewage into compounds such as methane gas, which can be burned.
3. Some bacteria, yeast, and molds are used in the production of foods and drinks such as bread, wines, and cheeses.

BUILDING VOCABULARY

Write the term from the list that best completes each sentence.

spirilla, aseptic technique, agar, incubator, cocci, microbes, petri dish, autoclave, bacilli, culture medium

Microscopic organisms such as bacteria and viruses are called ___1___. Ball-shaped bacteria are called ___2___. Rod-shaped bacteria are called ___3___. Spiral-shaped bacteria are called ___4___. Bacteria may be grown in a test tube or in a ___5___. Scientists place bacteria in a ___6___, which provides food and moisture. An example is ___7___, a gelatinlike substance made from seaweed. Bacteria grow well in a(an) ___8___, which provides a warm, dark environment. Using ___9___ when working with bacteria prevents contamination of equipment. Equipment can be sterilized in a(an) ___10___.

SUMMARIZING

If the sentence is true, write *true*. If the sentence is false, change the *italicized* word to make the statement true.

1. Viruses are *larger* than bacteria.
2. *Viruses* are used in sewage treatment.
3. Rod-shaped bacteria are called *cocci*.

4. Bacteria that cause disease are called *pathogens*.
5. A large number of bacteria cells of the same kind growing together on a petri dish form a *tissue*.
6. *Producers* are bacteria that break down proteins in the cells of dead organisms into inorganic molecules.
7. The solid material that remains after bacteria break down sewage is called *sludge*.
8. During fermentation, yeast produces a gas called *methane*.

INTERPRETING INFORMATION

Figure 23-18 shows a protozoan as seen under low power of a compound microscope. Use the figure to answer these questions.

Figure 23-18 Protozoan

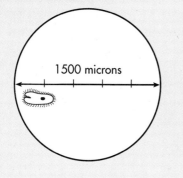

1500 microns

1. Estimate the length of the protozoan in microns and in millimeters. Explain how you got your answer.
2. The largest viruses are about 0.3 microns. About how many times larger is this protozoan than a virus?

THINK AND DISCUSS

Use the section numbers in parentheses to help you find each answer. Write your answers in complete sentences.

1. Name four types of microbes. For each type, give one example of its effect on human lives. (23-1)
2. Design an experiment to test the effects of temperature on the growth rate of a certain kind of bacterium. (23-2)
3. Tuberculosis is a disease caused by bacteria that infect the lungs. Are these bacteria aerobic or anaerobic? How do you know? (23-2)
4. What is the role of bacteria in a sewage treatment plant? (23-3)
5. Imagine that you and two friends each bake a loaf of bread from the same recipe. One of you forgets to add yeast. Could you tell which loaf lacked yeast just by looking? Why? (23-3)
6. A farmer stopped using pesticides and the soil improved. Why? (23-3)

GOING FURTHER

1. Chlorination and fluoridation are methods of destroying pathogenic microbes found in public water supplies. Research the advantages and disadvantages of treating drinking water with chlorides and fluorides.
2. Most plastics are nonbiodegradable solid wastes. Do research to learn what this means. Find out what steps are being taken to reduce the amount of plastics in solid wastes.

CHAPTER REVIEW

1. Some microbes are harmful to people because they
   a. decompose sewage.
   b. decompose dead organisms.
   c. prevent digestion of food in the small intestine.
   d. cause disease.

2. Look at Figure 23-19. How does temperature affect the growth rate of bacteria?
   a. Temperature has no effect.
   b. High temperature increases growth rate.
   c. Low temperature increases growth rate.
   d. No conclusion can be drawn from the information given.

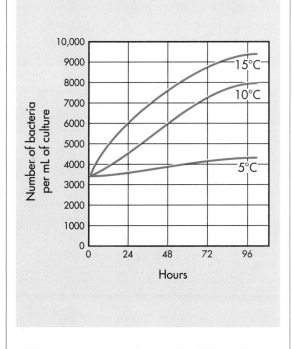

Figure 23-19 Growth Rate of Bacteria

This information applies to questions 3 and 4. Equal amounts of bread and bread mold were placed in test tubes A through D. Test tubes B, C, and D received increasing amounts of chemical X. The test tubes were then incubated for 14 days.

3. Which test tube was the control?
   a. A   b. B
   c. C   d. D

4. What was the variable?
   a. type of mold
   b. amount of mold
   c. amount of chemical X
   d. incubation time

5. A group of bacteria growing together is called a
   a. tissue.   b. colony.
   c. cluster.   d. tumor.

6. Which food obtains its flavor from cultures of bacteria?
   a. yogurt.
   b. bread.
   c. blue cheese.
   d. eggs.

7. Which group of microbes is ordered from smallest to largest?
   a. mold, protozoan, bacterium, virus
   b. bacterium, protozoan, virus, mold
   c. virus, bacterium, protozoan, mold
   d. protozoan, mold, bacterium, virus

8. Microbes not made of cells are called
   a. bacteria.
   b. viruses.
   c. fungi.
   d. protozoa.

CHAPTER 24

DISEASE

Have you ever felt fine one day and felt sick the next? Perhaps you caught a cold or the flu. Colds and flu are caused by microscopic organisms called pathogens that spread from one individual to another. Other diseases that are spread by pathogens include measles, mumps, smallpox, and diphtheria. The pathogen that causes tuberculosis, a type of bacteria, is shown in Figure 24-1.

Other diseases, such as heart disease and cancer, are not caused by pathogens. You cannot catch these diseases. Some other diseases not caused by pathogens include vitamin deficiencies and disorders caused by glands that do not function properly.

Until recent years, most people died from diseases caused by pathogens. Today, however, many of these diseases are under control. Smallpox, for example, has been eliminated from the world. Tuberculosis, a deadly lung disease, is now rare in most places. The discovery of cures for these diseases has enabled more people to live to old age. In this chapter, you will read about several types of diseases. You also will learn about their causes and prevention and the search for their cures.

24-1 Infectious Diseases

■ *Objectives*

☐ *Explain how infectious diseases are transmitted.*

☐ *Discuss the nature of some infectious diseases, including AIDS.*

☐ *Explain how the body defends itself against infectious diseases.*

☐ *Distinguish between active, passive, and natural immunity.*

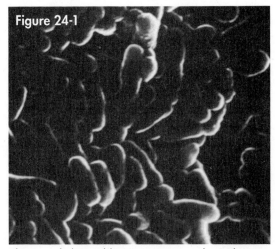

Figure 24-1

These rod-shaped bacteria cause tuberculosis.

Diseases that can be passed from one individual to another are called **infectious diseases**. Infectious diseases were once leading causes of death. However, as scientists began discovering which pathogens cause infectious diseases, they also began learning how to control them.

A German doctor named Robert Koch first determined that microbes cause infectious diseases. Koch began his studies in the 1870s, when an outbreak of tuberculosis killed thousands of people. Koch examined blood from people with and without the disease. He discovered that the blood of tuberculosis (TB) patients contained a type of bacterial cell not found in healthy people.

Koch hypothesized that these bacteria caused tuberculosis. To test his hypothesis, Koch conducted experiments with laboratory mice. Figure 24-2 summarizes his experiments. Koch's results led him to conclude that bacteria caused tuberculosis.

Diseases Caused by Bacteria

Once inside the human body, bacteria may cause an infection. An infection is the entrance, growth, and reproduction of bacteria in the body, which results in disease. People infected with bacteria may transfer them to other people. Your body's natural defenses, however, can usually keep harmful bacteria under control.

Your First Line of Defense Your skin is part of your first line of defense against invasion by bacteria. Skin cells cover the surface of your body and keep bacteria from reaching internal organs. Your skin

Figure 24-2

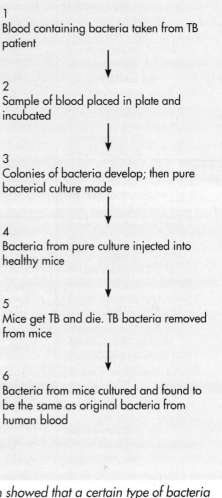

1
Blood containing bacteria taken from TB patient

2
Sample of blood placed in plate and incubated

3
Colonies of bacteria develop; then pure bacterial culture made

4
Bacteria from pure culture injected into healthy mice

5
Mice get TB and die. TB bacteria removed from mice

6
Bacteria from mice cultured and found to be the same as original bacteria from human blood

Koch showed that a certain type of bacteria cause tuberculosis.

cannot completely keep bacteria out of your body, however. Bacteria enter your nose and mouth when you breathe. The mucus that lines the inside of your nose and throat traps many of these bacteria. Mucus also lines parts of your digestive and respiratory systems.

Your respiratory system is also lined with tiny cilia, as seen in Figure 24-3. These cilia push bacteria out of the body. Together, mucus and cilia prevent bacteria from entering other parts of your body.

Bacteria also enter your digestive system when you swallow them with food. In Chapter 12, you learned that your stomach makes hydrochloric acid. This acid kills many bacteria.

Figure 24-3

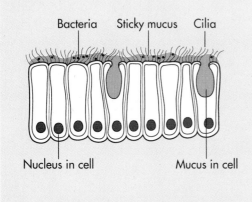

Bacteria   Sticky mucus   Cilia

Nucleus in cell   Mucus in cell

How do cells that line the throat keep bacteria out?

Your Second Line of Defense Sometimes bacteria get past the first line of defense. They may enter your blood through a break in your skin or through your digestive system. These bacteria may begin to grow and reproduce. Then your second line of defense acts on them.

Your white blood cells are your body's second line of defense. They attack and destroy bacteria that enter your blood. White blood cells called **phagocytes** (FAG-uh-syts) rush to the body part

where bacteria have entered. There they surround and ingest the bacteria.

Perhaps you have had a pimple or wound that became infected. You probably noticed that a whitish fluid called pus formed around the infection. Pus is made of large numbers of dead bacteria and phagocytes. Figure 24-4 shows how pus is formed.

Sometimes, however, bacteria reproduce faster than white blood cells can kill them. Bacteria may also produce chemicals that kill white blood cells. Fortunately, your body has a third line of defense.

Your Third Line of Defense The presence of certain pathogens causes your body to produce proteins called **antibodies**. Your blood contains many kinds of antibodies. Each antibody fights **antigens** (ANT-i-juns), substances the body recognizes as

Figure 24-4

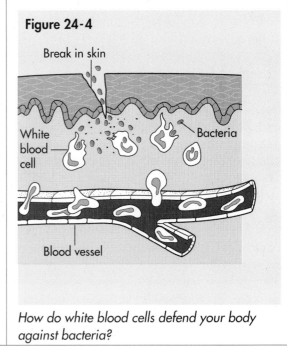

Break in skin

White blood cell

Bacteria

Blood vessel

How do white blood cells defend your body against bacteria?

foreign. The body recognizes bacteria, for example, as foreign proteins.

Antibodies act against antigens in several ways. Some antibodies clump bacteria together so that phagocytes can easily ingest and kill them. Other antibodies destroy bacteria by dissolving them. Still others neutralize poisons called toxins made by bacteria.

Antibodies continue to circulate in your blood long after you have had a disease. Should more of the bacteria that cause the disease enter your body, your antibodies destroy them immediately.

Some infectious diseases can now be prevented by a process called **vaccination**. When you were an infant, you were vaccinated against a disease called diphtheria. Weakened diphtheria bacteria were injected into your blood. Your blood, in turn, made antibodies to destroy the pathogens that cause diphtheria.

Fighting Disease

A vaccine gives you **immunity** against a disease. Immunity is the ability to resist a disease. Some people have a **natural immunity** to a disease. A natural immunity is an inborn, inherited resistance to a disease. When your body produces antibodies to fight bacteria, it develops **active immunity**. Active immunity occurs whether you actually have the disease or are vaccinated against it.

Your body may also develop **passive immunity** to an infectious disease. Passive immunity occurs when you receive antibodies produced by another organism. These antibodies temporarily protect the person from the disease.

Doctors may prescribe an **antibiotic** such as penicillin to a person who has a bacterial disease. An antibiotic is a substance produced by microbes such as fungi, that kills bacteria. Antibiotics work along with your body's own defenses to fight against disease.

Diseases Caused by Viruses

You wake up with a sore throat. By evening you have a high fever, aching muscles, and a cough. Your doctor tells you that you have a flu caused by a virus. Viruses cause more than 50 diseases that infect humans.

The flu and the common cold are highly infectious viral diseases. You can catch these diseases by shaking hands or sharing a drinking glass with an infected person. You can also breathe in the virus from the air. As Figure 24-5 shows, a cough or sneeze sends a spray of water droplets containing viruses into the air.

Figure 24-5

How are colds passed from one individual to another?

How Can You Conduct a Survey about Diseases?

Process Skills *organizing information, analyzing*

Materials 100 classmates and one parent of each, paper and pencil

In this activity, you will conduct a survey to learn how many people in two generations had diseases caused by viruses.

Procedure

1. Ask 100 classmates whether they have had any of the diseases listed in Figure 24-6. Record the answers.
2. Have each of the students surveyed ask one of their parents the same questions.
3. Record in a data table the number of students and parents who have had each disease.

Conclusions

4. Which diseases appeared more often among the parents than among your classmates?

Figure 24-6

Disease	Number of people with disease	
	Younger generation	Older generation
Measles		
Mumps		
Chicken pox		
Flu		

5. Which diseases appeared about as frequently among your classmates and their parents?
6. Why might certain diseases appear less frequently among your classmates than among their parents?

AIDS One of the most deadly viral diseases is **AIDS**. AIDS stands for Acquired Immune Deficiency Syndrome. Neither a cure nor a vaccine for AIDS has yet been developed. AIDS affects the ability of the body to fight infection. The AIDS virus, called HIV, destroys white blood cells that protect the body from infection. As white blood cells are destroyed, the body loses its ability to fight pathogens. As a result, a pathogen that would normally be controlled by the body's immune system may cause serious illness.

Symptoms of AIDS may not appear until several years after infection occurs. People with AIDS often develop certain types of pneumonia and skin cancer. As the disease progresses, these patients may

Analyzing

AIDS is one of the fastest-spreading diseases of the century. In New York City, AIDS is now the third leading cause of death, next only to heart disease and cancer. Study Figure 24-7, which shows leading causes of death for different groups of people in New York City in 1988. Then answer the following questions.

1. Based on the data table, which of the following statements is true?

a. Only adult males can get AIDS.
b. Only male children can get AIDS.
c. Men, women, and children can get AIDS.
2. Which disease caused the most deaths among men and women ages 25 to 34?
3. How many males between the ages of 1 and 14 died of AIDS?
4. What was the leading cause of death among females aged 1 to 14?
5. How many men and women aged 25 to 34 died of AIDS?

Figure 24-7 Top Five Causes of Death in New York City in 1988

Men, aged 25-34	Women, aged 25-34	Children, aged 1-14	
		Male	Female
1. AIDS 982*	1. AIDS 288	1. Accidents 69	1. Accidents 45
2. Homicide 541	2. Drug dependence 102	2. Cancer 38	2. Cancer 28
3. Drug dependence 275	3. Cancer 97	3. Birth defects 28	3. AIDS 24
4. Accidents 138	4. Homicide 92	4. Homicide 26	4. Birth defects 18
5. Cancer 120	5. Liver disease 39	5. AIDS 25	5. Homicide 14

*Indicates number of deaths

experience seizures, trembling, and loss of memory. Figure 24-8 shows how the HIV causes these symptoms after first attacking white blood cells.

The AIDS virus is spread by exchange of blood and other body fluids. The HIV has been found in blood, breast milk, saliva, and semen. During sexual contact, a person infected with the AIDS virus may pass it on to another person through semen. AIDS is also spread when a drug user shares a needle with someone who has AIDS. AIDS is not spread through casual contact, through the air, or in food. You cannot get AIDS by touching, kissing, or talking with someone who has the AIDS virus.

Body Defenses against Viruses Your body defends itself against viruses in the the same way that it fights bacteria. Skin, white blood cells, and antibodies all work to protect the body from viral diseases. In addition, vaccines have almost eliminated viral diseases such as smallpox, mumps, measles, and polio.

Antibiotics have no effect against viruses. Interferon, however, prevents the growth and reproduction of viruses. Interferon is a protein produced when viruses enter your cells.

▬ Section 24-1 Review ▬

Write the definitions for the following terms in your own words.

1. **infectious disease**   2. **antibody**
3. **antigen**   4. **antibiotic**
5. **immunity**

Answer these questions.

6. How did Robert Koch use the scientific method to determine the cause of tuberculosis?
7. In Mary's school, there was an outbreak of an infectious disease. Mary was vaccinated against the disease and remained healthy. What kind of immunity did she develop? How do you know?

Figure 24-8

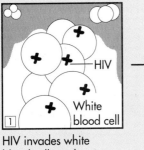
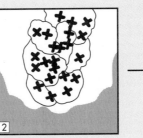

HIV invades white blood cells and reproduces

White blood cells are killed and resistance to disease decreases

A person with AIDS may become seriously ill from an illness normally controlled by the immune system

How does the AIDS virus weaken the body?

8. How does the AIDS virus attack the immune system?
9. Why has the number of infectious diseases in the United States declined?

24-2 Controlling Undesirable Microbes

■ *Objectives*

□ *Recognize that to prevent infection, contamination, and spoilage, microbes must be destroyed.*

□ *Note that microbes are responsible for food spoilage.*

□ *List the methods used to control the growth of microbes.*

Microbes not only cause disease. They can also destroy food and livestock. People have developed many ways of preventing infection, spoilage, and contamination by microbes. These processes may remove, kill, or slow their growth.

Sterilization

The processes by which all living microbes are destroyed are types of **sterilization**. Sterile, or aseptic, conditions are important wherever people might come in contact with harmful microbes. Canned foods must be sterilized to prevent the growth of bacteria that could cause spoilage. Laboratory equipment must be sterile to protect researchers. Doctors and dentists sterilize their instruments to protect themselves and their patients against disease.

Disinfection

A process used to destroy all pathogenic organisms is called disinfection. Chemicals called **germicides** are used to disinfect an area. A germicide is any agent that kills pathogens. Disinfection may or may not result in sterilization.

Germicides are used in the laboratory to disinfect equipment and hands. Doctors like the one shown in Figure 24-9 use germicides to disinfect body surfaces before surgery. These germicides destroy pathogenic bacteria. Other germicides are

Figure 24-9

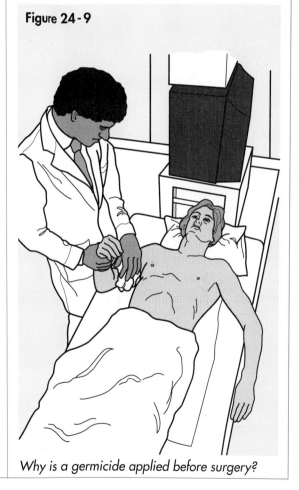

Why is a germicide applied before surgery?

used around swimming pools to destroy the fungus that causes athlete's foot. Although germicides kill pathogens, they are not harmful to people when used properly.

Preserving Foods

If food is not prepared and stored carefully, harmful microbes may contaminate it. The spread of microbes in foods must therefore be controlled. Food manufacturers use a variety of processes to preserve different types of foods.

Pasteurization Harmful microbes in milk and fruit juices are killed by a process called **pasteurization** (pas-chuh-ruh-ZAY-shun). Pasteurization is the use of heat to kill microbes. Pasteurized milk, for example, is heated to about 62°C for about 30 minutes. This treatment kills all harmful bacteria found in milk. The foods shown in Figure 24-10 are also pasteurized.

Canning Many foods, especially fruits and vegetables, can be preserved by canning. Canning can be done at home, although most canning is done commercially. The food is first sealed in an airtight can and then sterilized. The can is heated to about 121°C for 20 to 30 minutes. This amount of heat will kill even highly resistant bacterial spores.

On rare occasions, canned food may become contaminated with a poisonous type of anaerobic bacterium. This bacterium can cause a serious intestinal disease called **botulism** (BACH-uh-liz-um). Swelling is often the sign that a food can is contaminated. For this reason, you should never eat food from a swollen can.

Drying and Curing When foods are dried, moisture is removed. Since microbes cannot grow without moisture, these foods will last for a long time without spoiling. Perhaps you have bought packages of dried foods such as soups, herbs, and beans. Before you eat these foods, you must add water or other liquid to them.

Some foods are preserved by pickling. Pickling is the treating of foods with acids such as vinegar. Other foods, such as meat and fish, may be preserved by salt curing or smoking. Salt curing is the adding of large amounts of salt to foods. Smoking is the treating of food with smoke from burning wood.

Ultraviolet Light Sunlight has been used to destroy microbes. Ultraviolet rays, a form of radiation in sunlight, can kill many spore-forming bacteria not destroyed by

Figure 24-10

Why are foods pasteurized?

cells in your liver make cholesterol from saturated fats, such as animal fats, whole milk, butter, coconut oil, and palm oil. Saturated fats are those that are solid or nearly solid at room temperature.

Your body needs some cholesterol to stay healthy. However, when the blood contains too much cholesterol, the excess cholesterol may collect on the artery walls. Notice in Figure 24-13 how these fatty cholesterol deposits thicken the artery walls. These deposits eventually harden and clog the arteries as calcium and other materials mix with the cholesterol. This condition is called hardening of the arteries, or **arteriosclerosis**.

Because the arteries become narrower, less blood can flow through them. As a result, less food and oxygen reach the body cells. Arteriosclerosis may start early in life and may not produce symptoms for many years.

If the arteriosclerosis progresses, blood flow to the heart becomes inadequate. A **heart attack** may result. A heart attack

is a condition during which the heart stops pumping and blood stops circulating through the body. The attack usually begins with pain in the chest or muscles. A lack of oxygen may cause permanent damage to the heart muscle. Without immediate medical treatment, a heart attack victim may die.

Extensive artery damage may cause a decrease in blood flow to the brain. Then a **stroke** may occur. A stroke is a condition during which the brain does not receive enough oxygen. As a result, brain cells die. The effects of a stroke depend on which part of the brain is damaged. A mild stroke might result in muscle weakness or forgetfulness. A severe stroke may cause paralysis or even death.

High Blood Pressure Arteriosclerosis reduces the amount of blood that can flow through the arteries. As a result, the heart must pump harder and faster to push enough blood through the arteries. This condition is known as high blood pressure.

Blood pressure is a measure of the force or pressure of the blood as it flows through the arteries. A normal blood pressure reading for a young healthy adult is about 120/80. The first number is the blood pressure when the heart pumps. The second number is the blood pressure when the heart is at rest. A blood pressure reading above 140/90 signals high blood pressure.

High blood pressure may not produce symptoms for many years. Eventually, however, high blood pressure may cause kidney failure or heart attacks. For this

Figure 24-13

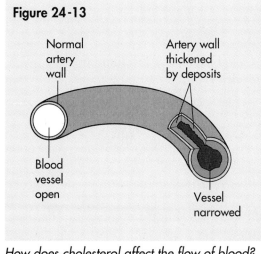

Normal artery wall

Artery wall thickened by deposits

Blood vessel open

Vessel narrowed

How does cholesterol affect the flow of blood?

reason, people should have their blood pressure checked regularly.

Preventing Heart Disease Will you suffer from heart disease? No one can predict for sure who will develop heart disease and who will not. You can reduce your risk of getting heart disease, however, by following these guidelines.

- Watch your diet. Eat foods that are low in saturated fat and cholesterol. These foods include lean meats, fish, grains, fruits, and vegetables.
- Watch your weight. Overweight people often have high levels of blood cholesterol. In addition, extra weight places stress on your heart.
- Exercise regularly. Regular exercise helps you control your weight and lower your blood pressure and blood cholesterol. Exercise also strengthens your heart and circulatory system.
- Do not smoke. Smokers have a greater risk of heart disease than nonsmokers.
- Visit your doctor at least once a year. A doctor can identify poor health habits and early signs of heart disease before they become serious.

Following these guidelines will not guarantee that you will not get heart disease. Evidence suggests that heredity helps determine who will get heart disease. If your grandparents or parents have heart disease your chances of having heart disease are increased. In addition, males are more likely to develop heart disease than are females. The more you reduce the risk of heart disease by following sensible health guidelines, however, the better your chances of living a long, healthful life.

Cancer

Next to heart disease, cancer is the second leading cause of death in the United States. Cancer is a group of diseases caused by the uncontrolled growth of abnormal cells. Figure 24-14 compares normal cells and cancer cells. Uncontrolled growth of cells can take place in any organ of the body. Cancer strikes people of all ages.

When abnormal cells reproduce at a very fast rate, they form lumps called

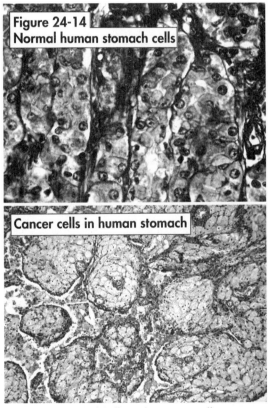

Figure 24-14
Normal human stomach cells

Cancer cells in human stomach

Compare normal cells with cancer cells.

tumors. Some tumors, called **benign** (bi-NYN) **tumors**, do not harm the body. Other tumors, called **malignant tumors**, are dangerous. The cells of a malignant tumor may break off and travel through the blood to other parts of the body. In this way, cancer is spread throughout the body.

Causes of Cancer Scientists do not know for sure how cancer develops. Researchers have identified certain substances that cause cancer, however. Some of these substances, called **carcinogens**, are listed in Figure 24-15.

Forms of Cancer Cancer can occur anywhere in the human body. Once it begins

Figure 24-15 Types of Carcinogens

Pesticides

Wastes from plastics manufacturing

Wastes from coal and oil burning

Motor vehicle exhaust

Cigarette smoke

Some food preservatives

Ultraviolet light

X rays

Some viruses

in one organ, cancer cells may travel throughout the body. Lung cancer is one of the most common and deadly kinds of cancer. It strikes both men and women. People who smoke cigarettes are more likely to develop lung cancer than people who do not smoke. Cancer of the large intestine and the rectum also causes many deaths in the United States each year. Research, however, shows that eating a high-fiber, low-fat diet reduces the risk of getting these types of cancer.

Breast cancer is a leading form of cancer in women. It begins as a lump, or thickening, in the breast. If it is discovered early enough, breast cancer can be controlled.

A type of blood cancer called **leukemia** (lew-KEE-mee-uh) may strike people of all ages, including children. A person with leukemia produces millions of abnormal white blood cells in the bone marrow. These white blood cells interfere with normal blood functions. Many scientists think that a virus may cause leukemia.

Protecting Yourself against Cancer You can take several steps to reduce your risk of getting cancer. Eat a low-fat, high-fiber diet. Do not smoke. If you must spend long periods of time in the sun, use a protective sunscreen.

Perhaps your best protection against cancer is early detection. Although no cure for cancer has been found, most cancers can be treated or removed if discovered early. Your doctor will be able to help you get the care needed to make sure that the body functions normally and that you or a member of your family stay healthy.

Figure 24-16 lists seven warning signs that may indicate the start of cancer. If you or a member of your family has any of these warning signals, you should see your doctor.

▬ Section 24-3 Review ▬

Write the definitions for the following terms in your own words.

1. **noninfectious disease**
2. **cholesterol**
3. **arteriosclerosis**
4. **heart attack**
5. **tumor**

Answer these questions.

6. What are some causes of noninfectious diseases?
7. Name two reasons why more people are developing noninfectious diseases today than ever before.
8. What is the relationship between cholesterol and arteriosclerosis?
9. Doctors sometimes refer to high blood pressure as the "silent killer?" Why do you think this is so?
10. Distinguish between a benign tumor and a malignant tumor.

Figure 24-16 The Warning Signs of Cancer

Warning sign	Possible location of cancer
1. Lump in the body	Part of the body where lump is found
2. Sore that does not heal	Skin
3. Blood in the urine or in the feces	Excretory or digestive system
4. Change in the appearance of a wart or mole	Skin
5. Nagging cough, sore throat, or hoarseness	Lung; throat
6. Change in frequency of elimination or in consistency of solid wastes	Large intestine, rectum, or urinary bladder
7. Constant, long-lasting indigestion; difficulty swallowing	Stomach; throat

Analyzing

Study the data table in Figure 24-17. Then answer the following questions.

1. What were the three leading causes of death in 1900 and in 1980? Are these infectious or noninfectious diseases?

2. Which leading diseases from 1900 did not appear on the 1980 list? Which diseases on the 1980 list did not appear in the 1900 list?

3. Suggest reasons for the decline in infectious diseases and the increase in noninfectious diseases between 1900 and 1980.

Figure 24-17 Leading Causes of Death

Ten leading causes of death in the United States in 1900		Ten leading causes of death in the United States in 1980	
Cause	Deaths per 100,000 population	Cause	Deaths per 100,000 population
1. Pneumonia and influenza	215	1. Heart disease	340
2. Tuberculosis	185	2. Cancer	185
3. Diarrhea	140	3. Accidents	95
4. Heart disease	130	4. Stroke	85
5. Stroke	110	5. Pneumonia and influenza	40
6. Kidney disease	85	6. Diabetes	35
7. Accidents	75	7. Liver disease	30
8. Cancer	65	8. Artery disease	25
9. Senility	55	9. Suicide	20
10. Diphtheria	40	10. Homicide	15

SCIENCE, TECHNOLOGY, & SOCIETY

Finding and Treating Cancer

The earlier that cancer is detected, the greater a person's chance of survival. Early detection is important because malignant tumors can grow and spread rapidly. Once the cancer is located, treatment can begin to stop its spread.

A type of X ray called a mammogram is used to detect breast cancer. Small, safe amounts of X rays are passed through the breast. Doctors study the image that forms to see if any tumors have started to grow.

Cancer of the cervix, uterus, or ovaries is detected by a procedure called a pap smear. A small instrument is used to scrape a few cells from the wall of a woman's cervix. Doctors then examine these cells for signs of cancer.

A substance called barium is used to detect tumors in the large intestine and rectum. A series of X rays is taken while the barium is held in the large intestine. If tumors are present, the barium will make them visible in the X rays. Brain tumors may be detected with a CAT scan or magnetic resonance imaging, two techniques you learned about in Chapter 18.

Once cancer is detected, three types of treatment may be possible. A doctor may perform surgery to remove a tumor from an organ. Radiation is the treatment of cancer by radioactivity. Radiation therapy, such as that shown in Figure 24-18, destroys cancer cells and may prevent them from spreading. Chemotherapy uses

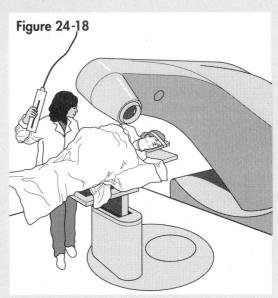

Figure 24-18

Radiation therapy is often used to treat cancer.

medication to control cancer. The medication kills cancer cells. It may be taken by mouth or by injection.

The disadvantage of radiation and chemotherapy is that they may kill normal cells as well. Side effects such as hair loss, fatigue, nausea, and vomiting are common. The possibility of living a long, productive life usually outweighs the discomforts of the treatments, however.

Follow-up Activity

Sometimes bone marrow transplants are used to treat leukemia patients. Do research to learn more about this technique. Report your findings to the class.

Section 24-1 Infectious Diseases

1. Infectious diseases are caused by pathogens that can be spread from one individual to another.
2. The body's defense against infectious disease includes the skin, secretions of mucus and hydrochloric acid, and phagocytes and antibodies in the blood.
3. Immunity is the ability to resist disease.
4. Antibodies are proteins that attack foreign proteins, called antigens. Antibiotics are chemicals that stop the growth of bacteria.

Section 24-2 Controlling Undesirable Microbes

1. Some microbes are responsible for food spoilage and disease.
2. To prevent infection, contamination, and spoilage, microbes must be killed or their growth must be slowed.

Section 24-3 Noninfectious Diseases

1. Noninfectious diseases are caused by such factors as deficiencies in diet, organs that do not function properly, and environmental pollutants.
2. Noninfectious diseases such as heart disease and cancer are on the rise.

Write the term from the list that best completes each description.

stroke, carcinogen, AIDS, leukemia, tuberculosis, heart disease, natural immunity, phagocyte, antibiotic, vaccination

1. group of diseases that affect the heart and blood vessels
2. type of cancer that affects white blood cells
3. type of white blood cell that attacks and ingests pathogens
4. an inherited ability to resist disease
5. bacterial disease that was studied by Robert Koch
6. disease that occurs when brain cells do not get enough blood
7. substance that causes cancer
8. disease caused by a virus that affects the ability to fight infections
9. an injection of a dead or weakened pathogen to protect against disease
10. chemical produced by living things that stops the growth of pathogens

Explain the difference between the terms in each pair.

11. infectious disease, noninfectious disease
12. sterilization, disinfection
13. antibody, antigen
14. passive immunity, active immunity
15. benign, malignant

Write the missing term for each sentence.

1. Disease-producing organisms are called ___.

2. The skin and mucus secretions are part of the body's ___ line of defense against disease.
3. Proteins that defend the body against foreign substances are called ___.
4. The ability to resist disease is called ___.
5. A drug used to stop the growth of bacteria in the body is a (an) ___.
6. The process used to kill pathogenic organisms in milk is ___.
7. A chemical that kills microbes on the body surface is called a ___.
8. Treating foods with an acid such as vinegar is a process called ___.
9. The ___ rays in sunlight are used to kill microbes.
10. A viral disease that affects the body's ability to fight pathogens is ___.

INTERPRETING INFORMATION

Lyme disease is a bacterial infection spread by the painless bite of an infected deer tick. Lyme disease begins with a rash and flulike symptoms. If untreated, it may damage the nervous and circulatory systems. The infected ticks, found in woods and meadows, have spread through many counties of New York State as shown in Figure 24-19.

1. In which counties were infected ticks first found?
2. Which counties were the last to be infested with these ticks?
3. Do you think that infected ticks will spread over larger areas in the future? If so, what will be the cause?

Figure 24-19 Spread of Lyme Disease in New York State

Year first seen	County
1984	Nassau, Putnam, Suffolk, Westchester
1986	Ulster
1987	Dutchess, Queens, Rockland
1988	Orange
1989	Albany, Columbia, Greene, Rensselaer, Sullivan

THINK AND DISCUSS

Use the section number in parentheses to help you find each answer. Write your answers in complete sentences.

1. How does placing a bandage over a wound help protect your body from pathogens? (24-1)
2. Design an experiment to test the effectiveness of a germicide. (24-2)
3. Why does a milk carton have an expiration date stamped on it but a box of pasta does not? (24-2)
4. What are some steps you can take to lower your risk of developing heart disease? Why

should you take these steps when you are young? (24-3)

GOING FURTHER

Do some research to find out what causes AIDS and how close scientists are to finding a cure. Why is AIDS an example of an infectious disease?

COMPETENCY REVIEW

1. Which is not a cause of noninfectious diseases?
   a. vitamin deficiency
   b. pollutants in the environment
   c. a damaged organ
   d. pathogenic bacteria

Use Figure 24-20 to answer questions 2 and 3.

2. Which statement best describes the relationship between cholesterol level and age?

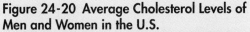

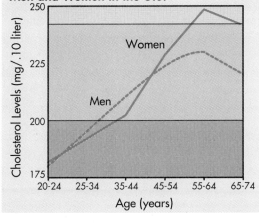

Figure 24-20 Average Cholesterol Levels of Men and Women in the U.S.

a. Cholesterol levels increase steadily until about age 55.
   b. Cholesterol levels increase steadily from age 55 to age 74.
   c. Cholesterol levels are higher for women than men between ages 25 and 45.
   d. Cholesterol levels for men and women are the same at all ages.

3. The average cholesterol level for 45-year-old men is about
   a. 200 mg/.10 liter.   b. 175 mg/.10 liter.
   c. 250 mg/.10 liter.   d. 225 mg/.10 liter.

4. When milk is pasteurized,
   a. all microbes are destroyed.
   b. all harmful bacteria are destroyed.
   c. its taste is improved.
   d. its fat content is lowered.

5. Which statement about infectious diseases is true?
   a. They are caused by microbes.
   b. They are caused by chemicals.
   c. They cannot spread from individual to individual.
   d. They are caused by hormones.

6. Before doctors perform surgery, instruments must first be
   a. pasteurized.   b. frozen.
   c. cured.   d. sterilized.

7. Penicillin is an example of a (an)
   a. antibody.   b. antibiotic.
   c. antigen.   d. infection.

8. Which is not a warning sign of cancer?
   a. blood in urine or feces
   b. nagging cough or hoarseness
   c. pain in the chest and muscles
   d. a sore that does not heal

CAREERS IN LIFE SCIENCE

Many people become interested in careers related to life science because of courses they take in school or from experiences in their lives. A career related to life science may be for you if you are curious and enjoy solving challenging problems. To get a better idea of what careers are related to life science, read the following descriptions. Perhaps you will one day join the ranks of those who work in the life sciences.

Careers in Health

Registered Nurse A nurse works in hospitals, at homes for the aged, and in people's houses caring for the sick. Nurses promote good health and teach people how to prevent illness. To become a nurse, you need a bachelor's degree from an accredited college, including courses in natural and social science.

Physician or Doctor A doctor works with a wide variety of people, including nurses, medical laboratory technicians, paramedics, and others to help comfort and cure people who are sick. Some doctors have a general practice whereas others, such as eye doctors and heart surgeons, specialize in one organ or organ system. To become a doctor, you must go to an undergraduate college for four years and to a medical school for another four years. Then you must do an internship and a residency in a hospital. At college, you must take courses in human development, anatomy, physiology, and in identifying and treating diseases.

Dentist A dentist takes care of diseases of the teeth and the gums. A dentist graduates from a four-year college with a degree in science and then goes to dental school for four more years. In dental school, a dentist learns about the anatomy of the teeth and gums, the nature of saliva, and diseases of the mouth.

Physician's Assistant The job of physician's assistant is to help a doctor. The assistant takes the patients' histories, performs routine physical examinations (like taking pulse and blood pressure), takes electrocardiograms, draws blood for testing, and does urine analysis. The assistant may also give injections and put casts on broken limbs. To become a physician's assistant, you need two years of college which include courses like biology and chemistry, as well as a supervised internship.

Medical Technologist A medical technologist performs tests on tissues, blood, and other body fluids. Training to become a medical technologist includes attending an accredited four-year college where courses in science and practical training are taken.

Pharmacist A pharmacist works in a pharmacy or hospital filling prescriptions ordered by doctors for their patients. Four years of college in an accredited school of pharmacy are required.

Other careers in health that you may want to learn more about include chiropractor, speech therapist, optometrist, audiologist, public and environmental health specialist, coroner, health care administrator, medical librarian, exercise physiologist, specialist in sports medicine, veterinarian, X-ray technician, medical secretary, emergency medical trainer, and dietitian.

Life Scientists

Life scientists may work in the laboratory or in the field to answer questions about living things. These scientists usually specialize in one area of life science. For example, an ecologist might travel to a rain forest to study the relationships between plants and animals there. A geneticist might work in a laboratory to study how traits are inherited.

Other careers that you may want to learn more about include pathologist, marine biologist, bacteriologist, pharmacologist, paleontologist, bioengineer, herpetologist, and botanist, among others. To become a life scientist, at least four years of college and often a doctorate in the field of study are required. For more information, write to the American Institute of Biological Sciences, 3900 Wisconsin Avenue NW, Washington, DC 20016 and to the Office of Opportunities in Sciences, American Association for the Advancement of Science, 1776 Massachusetts Avenue NW, Washington, DC 20036.

Science Teacher

A science teacher may work in an elementary, junior high, or high school, a community college, a four-year college, or a university. A science teacher attends at least four years of college and majors in biology, chemistry, physics, or geology. Sometimes a science teacher also obtains a minor in education. College science teachers usually have a PhD in one of the four sciences. To learn more, write to the National Association of Biology Teachers, 11250 Roger Bacon Drive, Reston, VA 22090.

Science Writer

A science writer may write for wildlife organizations, environmental groups, drug companies, or associations like the American Lung Association. Science writers may write books as well as articles for magazines and newspapers. In addition to college-level work in science, they take courses in journalism and communications. To obtain more information, write to the National Association of Science Writers and Editors, PO Box 294, Greenlawn, NY 11740.

Life Science Careers in Agriculture

Many life science careers are related to agriculture. These careers require a four-year college degree and/or related experience in the field. For example, a horticulturist may work in a nursery, greenhouse, florist shop, or orchard growing plants to be sold commercially. A fish and game manager works out in the field enforcing laws to protect wildlife or supervising at a wildlife preserve. For additional information, write to the American Society of Farm Managers, 950 S. Cherry Street, Suite 106, Denver, CO 80222 and the U.S. Department of Interior, Fish and Wildlife Service, Division of Personnel Management, Room 3458, Washington, DC 20240.

Pronunciation Key

When difficult terms appear, they are respelled to aid pronunciation. A syllable in CAPITAL LETTERS receives the most stress. The key lists the letters used for respelling. It includes examples of words using each sound and shows how the words would be respelled.

Symbol	Example	Respelling
ah	hypothesis	(hy-PAHTH-uh-sis)
aw	chlorophyll	(KLAWR-uh-fil)
ay	deceleration	(de-sel-uh-RAY-shun)
e	cryogenics	(kry-uh-JEN-iks)
ee	variable	(VER-ee-uh-bul)
ew	nucleic	(new-KLEE-ik)
f	chlorophyll	(KLAWR-uh-fil)
ih	electromagnet	(ih-lek-troh-MAG-net)
j	energy	(EN-uhr-gee)
k	aerodynamic	(ar-oh-dy-NAM-ik)
ks	mixture	(MIKS-ohur)
oh	thermodynamics	(thur-moh-dy-NAM-iks)
oo	supersonic	(soo-puhr-SAHN-ik)
or	thesaurus	(thuh-SOR-us)
oy	colloid	(kahl-OYD)
uh	ion	(EYE-un)
y	science	(SY-uns)
yoo	formula	(FOR-myoo-lah)
z	dissolve	(diz-AHLV)
zh	measure	(MEZH-ur)

absorption: process by which soluble end products of digestion enter bloodstream (p. 236)

accessory organ: organ that does not directly digest food, but produces chemicals used in digestion (p. 230)

acquired characteristic: trait that develops in an organism for its survival (p. 128)

adaptation (ad-ap-TAY-shun): any characteristic of an organism that helps it survive and live successfully in its environment (p. 37)

addiction: state in which a person can no longer function normally without a particular drug (p. 348)

adolescence: human stage of development that follows childhood (p. 375)

ADP: molecule into which ATP is changed when energy is released to do work in the body (p. 270)

adrenal glands: endocrine glands located on top of each kidney (p. 314)

adrenaline (uh-DREN-el-un): hormone produced during stress that provides extra energy (p. 310)

aerobic bacteria (uh-ROH-bik): bacteria that use oxygen (p. 422)

agar: gelatinlike substance obtained from seaweed used as a culture medium for bacteria (p. 427)

AIDS: acquired immune deficiency syndrome, a deadly viral disease that affects ability of the body to fight infection (p. 444)

alga (plural—algae): plant-like protist that may be unicellular or multicellular (p. 98)

alveolus (plural—alveoli): microscopic air sac within lung (p. 264)

amnion (AM-nee-an): clear membrane that surrounds an embryo (p. 372)

anaerobic bacteria (an-uh-ROH-bik): bacteria that do not use oxygen (p. 422)

analyze: to look for patterns and relationships (p. 17)

antibiotic: drug that fights bacterial disease (p. 443)

antibody: protein produced by the body to fight certain pathogens (p. 442)

antigen: substance that the body recognizes as foreign (p. 442)

aorta (ay-ORT-uh): largest artery in the body (p. 248)

artery: blood vessel that carries blood away from heart (p. 250)

arteriole (are-TEER-ee-ohl): small branch of an artery (p. 251)

arteriosclerosis: hardening of arteries caused by deposits on artery walls (p. 451)

arthropod: invertebrate animal characterized by an exoskeleton and jointed legs (p. 106)

aseptic techniques: procedures used to culture bacteria that prevent contamination (p. 427)

atom: basic unit of matter (p. 29)

ATP: large molecule in which energy from cellular respiration is stored (p. 270)

atrium (AY-tree-um) (plural—atria): one of two upper chambers of heart (p. 248)

Australopithecus (aw-stray-loh-PITH-uh-kus): genus of earliest known hominids (p. 408)

autoclave: oven used to sterilize equipment used to culture bacteria (p. 429)

autonomic nervous system: part of peripheral nervous system made up of nerves that lead to and from internal organs (p. 304)

axon: long fiber that carries impulses away from a nerve cell body (p. 297)

bacteriophage (bak-TIR-ee-uh-fayj): virus that attacks bacteria (p. 97)

behavior: any response of an organism to a stimulus from the environment (p. 326)

binary fission: asexual reproduction during which a parent cell divides in two (p. 72)

biochemistry: study of atoms and molecules found in cells of organisms (p. 127)

biological succession: orderly sequence of events over a long period of time that changes one living community into a different one (p. 168)

biologist: person who studies life science (p. 9)

biome: large area of the earth that has a particular climate (p. 163)

biosphere (BY-uh-sfiur): all parts of the earth where life exists (p. 156)

bipedal: term used to describe an animal that can walk on two legs (p. 406)

blood: liquid of circulatory system that carries food, oxgyen, and wastes as well as chemicals that fight disease and heal wounds (p. 254)

botulism (BACH-uh-liz-um): serious intestinal disease caused by anaerobic bacteria (p. 448)

brain: organ that is control center of the body (p. 298)

bronchitis: inflammation of bronchial tubes of lung (p. 272)

bryophyte (BRY-uh-fyt): nonvascular plant such as moss (p. 102)

budding: form of asexual reproduction in which division of nuclear material is equal, but division of cytoplasm is unequal (p. 73)

Calorie: 1000 calories (p. 209)

cancer: disease characterized by the uncontrollable spread of abnormal cells and growth of tumors (p. 272)

capillary (KAP-uh-ler-ee): microscopic blood vessel (p. 251)

carbohydrate (kar-boh-HY-drayt): organic compound made of carbon, hydrogen, and oxygen such as starch or sugar (p. 32)

carcinogen (kar-SIN-uh-jun): substance that causes cancer (p. 272)

cardiac muscle: involuntary muscle found in heart (p. 202)

carrier: person who has a recessive abnormal gene but who shows dominant normal trait (p. 394)

cartilage (KART-ul-ij): soft material that acts as a cushion where bones come together (p. 196)

cell: basic structure of all organisms (p. 34)

cell division: process by which cells produce new cells (p. 70)

cell membrane: membrane that surrounds and protects a cell and controls the passage of materials into and out of it (p. 58)

cell theory: theory which states that all living things are made of cells, that life processes take place in cells, and that all cells come from other cells of the same type (p. 51)

cellular respiration: combining of oxygen and food molecules to release energy and produce carbon dioxide and water as waste products (p. 41)

Celsius (SEL-see-us): scale used to measure temperature in metric system (p. 14)

central nervous system: system made of brain and spinal cord (p. 302)

cerebellum (ser-uh-BEL-um): part of the brain that coordinates movements of skeletal muscles (p. 303)

cerebrum (suh-REE-brum): largest part of the brain and center of thought, learning, reasoning, and memory (p. 302)

chemical digestion: digestion during which nutrients in foods are changed into smaller molecules (p. 230)

cholesterol: fatty substance found in blood (p. 258)

chordate: animal, such as a vertebrate, that has a solid rod of bonelike material and a hollow nerve cord along back (p. 108)

chromatin (KROH-mut-in): loose, uncoiled chromosome material of a cell that is not undergoing mitosis (p. 71)

chromosome (KRO-muh-sohm): threadlike structure in a cell nucleus made of genes that control cell activities (p. 58)

circulatory system (SUR-kyuh-luh-tohr-ee): organ system that works to transport important materials throughout the body (p. 243)

cirrhosis (suh-ROH-sus): liver disease caused by drinking too much alcohol (p. 356)

classification: organization of living things according to their similarities (p. 93)

cleavage: formation of hollow ball of embryonic cells that follows rapid cell division after fertilization (p. 369)

climate: average yearly rainfall and temperature of an area calculated over a long period of time (p. 163)

climax community: final stage of biological succession (p. 168)

cochlea (KOH-klee-uh): coiled, snail-shaped structure in inner ear that picks up sound vibrations (p. 292)

colony: mass of bacteria large enough to be seen with naked eye (p. 426)

community: all populations living in the same area (p. 155)

complex reflex: reflex in which action is triggered by an impulse from brain (p. 300)

compound: substance made up of two or more different elements (p. 30)

compound microscope: light microscope made of two or more lenses (p. 52)

conclusion: one or more statements that tell whether or not results of an experiment support hypothesis (p. 11)

conditioning: learning that occurs when an organism responds to a replacement stimulus the way it responded to an original stimulus (p. 329)

conifer: plant that has needlelike leaves and developed from a seed inside a cone (p. 103)

conservation: wise and careful use of natural resources (p. 178)

controlled substances: substances such as prescription drugs and illegal drugs (p. 348)

cornea: transparent layer that covers pupil and iris of eye (p. 291)

crack: highly concentrated, highly addictive form of cocaine often smoked in a glass pipe (p. 350)

culture medium: solid or liquid substance on which bacteria are grown (p. 427)

cutting: piece of a stem and leaves from a plant which will develop into a new plant (p. 77)

cytoplasm (SYT-oh-plaz-um): fluid that fills inside of cells (p. 58)

dark reaction: part of photosynthesis during which glucose is formed that can take place whether or not light is present (p. 143)

data: facts obtained during an experiment (p. 11)

daughter cells: two new cells identical to parent cell produced by cell division (p. 70)

deciduous forest: biome characterized by moderate climate and many species of deciduous trees (p. 164)

decomposer: organism that breaks down dead organisms and returns nutrients to soil (p. 158)

dendrite: fiber that extends from a nerve cell body to pick up nerve impulses (p. 297)

deoxygenated blood: oxygen-poor blood (p. 251)

depressant: drug that slows down body systems (p. 351)

development: changes that take place in an organism over its lifetime (p. 43)

diabetes: disease characterized by inability to produce insulin needed to control blood sugar level (p. 314)

diaphragm (DY-uh-fram): thick sheet of muscle under lungs (p. 266)

diffusion (dif-YOO-zhun): movement of molecules from an area containing many molecules to an area containing few molecules (p. 244)

digestive system: organ system that breaks food down into useful nutrients (p. 230)

DNA: deoxyribonucleic (dee-AHK-si-ry-boh-new-klee-ic) acid: molecule that makes up genes and determines traits (p. 395)

dominant: term used to describe a trait that appears in offspring (p. 384)

drug abuse: improper use of drugs (p. 347)

dwarfism: condition that results from too little pituitary growth hormone produced during childhood (p. 319)

eardrum: thin sheet of tissue that stretches across inside of outer ear that vibrates when sound waves strike (p. 292)

ecosystem: combination of biotic and abiotic factors in an environment (p. 156)

egg: female gamete (p. 78)

electron microscope: most powerful microscope used by scientists (p. 56)

element: substance made up of only one kind of atom (p. 30)

emphysema: disease that causes breakdown of alveoli walls (p. 272)

emulsify (ee-MUHL-si-fy): break apart large pieces of fat into tiny particles (p. 235)

endangered species: species in danger of becoming extinct (p. 184)

endocrine glands: ductless glands that produce hormones (p. 311)

endocrine system: organ system that produces hormones (p. 310)

environment (in-VY-run-munt): everything in an organism's surroundings (p. 35)

era: span of time millions of years in length (p. 123)

erosion: loss of topsoil due to blowing wind or running water (p. 179)

erythrocyte (ih-RITH-ruh-syt): red blood cell (p. 254)

esophagus: food tube that connects mouth with stomach (p. 232)

estimate: make an intelligent guess about a quantity (p. 16)

estrogen: female sex hormone that influences production of egg cells and appearance of secondary sex characteristics (p. 315)

evaluate: to think about meaning or importance of something (p. 21)

evolution: process by which species change over time (p. 118)

excretion: life process of removing wastes from cells (p. 43)

exhale: breathe out (p. 266)

exoskeleton (ek-soh-SKEL-ut-n): supporting frame on outside of the body (p. 106)

experiment: procedure scientists use to test a hypothesis (p. 10)

extinct: no longer exists (p. 120)

fat: nutrient, such as oil, which can provide energy (p. 211)

fatty acid: product of fat digestion used by the body to build cell membranes (p. 213)

fecal material: solid waste material formed in large intestine which passes out of the body through anus (p. 237)

fermentation: process by which yeast and bacteria break down sugars to produce alcohol (p. 435)

fertilization: process by which a sperm unites with an egg cell during sexual reproduction (p. 78)

fetus: a human embryo from third month of development until birth (p. 372)

flower: reproductive structure of flowering plants (p. 104)

food additive: chemical added to food to improve it in some way (p. 218)

food web: combination of several overlapping food chains (p. 159)

fossil: imprint or remains of an organism that lived in the past (p. 119)

fossil fuel: energy resource such as oil, coal, and gas that formed from remains of animals and plants that lived millions of years ago (p. 186)

fruit: structure which covers and protects seeds of a flowering plant (p. 104)

fungus (FUN-gus) (plural—fungi): organism with cell walls but no chloroplasts (p. 100)

gall bladder: small organ in which bile produced by liver is stored (p. 235)

gamete (GAM-eet): specialized sex cell produced by each parent during sexual reproduction (p. 78)

gene splicing: process in which DNA from one organism is placed into DNA of another (p. 398)

genetic engineering: use of genetic principles to develop useful processes and products (p. 398)

genetics: study of heredity, the passing of traits from parents to offspring (p. 382)

genotype (JEE-nuh-typ): combination of genes an organism inherits (p. 389)

germicide: agent that kills pathogens (p. 447)

germinate (JUR-muh-nayt): to grow as a plant embryo grows after its seed coat splits open (p. 149)

giantism: condition that results from too much pituitary growth hormone produced during childhood (p. 320)

gill: thin flap of tissue in fish which filters dissolved oxygen from water (p. 108)

gill slit: structure in all chordates which develops into gills in fish and disappears in other chordates during embryo development (p. 108)

global warming: rise in average temperature of the earth

(p. 24)

glucagon: hormone produced by pancreas that causes starch from liver to change into glucose (p. 314)

glucose: simple sugar (p. 32)

glycerol (GLIS-uh-rawl): product of fat digestion used by the body to build cell membranes (p. 213)

goiter: enlargement of thyroid gland as a result of a lack of dietary iodine (p. 313)

gonad: gland that produces reproductive cells (p. 315)

graduated cylinder: instrument used to measure volume of a liquid (p. 13)

habit: chain of learned responses that becomes automatic as a result of repetition (p. 330)

habitat: certain place in an ecosystem occupied by each organism (p. 157)

half-life: time required for half of amount of radioactive element in an object to decay (p. 122)

hallucinogens (huh-LOOS-un-uh-juns): drugs that affect nervous system causing illusions and hallucinations (p. 349)

heart: muscular pump that sends blood through blood vessels to all body cells (p. 247)

heart attack: condition during which the heart stops pumping, sometimes caused by inadequate blood flow to heart (p. 451)

hemoglobin: protein molecule found in red blood cells on which oxygen is carried (p. 254)

hemophilia (hee-muh-FIL-ee-uh): genetic disease in which blood does not clot properly (p. 393)

hermaphrodite (hur-MAF-ruh-dyt): organism that produces both sperm and egg (p. 81)

hibernate: remain inactive during cold weather (p. 41)

hominids (HAM-uh-nuds): primate family in which humans belong (p. 406)

Homo erectus (HOH-moh uh-REK-tus): "upright human," hominid species most closely related to modern humans (p. 411)

Homo habilis (HOH-moh HAB-il-is): "skillful human," first human ancestor to use tools (p. 411)

homologous (hoh-MAHL-uh-gus) structures: body parts with similar bone structures (p. 126)

Homo sapiens: "wise human," species name of modern humans (p. 413)

hormone: chemical messengers that regulate many body processes (p. 310)

hybrid: offspring that has both a dominant and a recessive gene for a trait (p. 385)

hypothalamus: gland that links nervous and endocrine systems to control life processes (p. 321)

hypothesis (hy-PAHTH-uh-sus): suggested solution to a problem (p. 10)

immunity: ability to resist a disease (p. 443)

impulse: message carried by nervous system (p. 296)

indigestible food: food such as roughage that cannot be digested and absorbed (p. 237)

infectious disease: disease that can be passed from one individual to another (p. 441)

inferior vena cava: vein that returns blood from lower part of the body to right atrium (p. 249)

ingestion: process of taking in food (p. 42)

inhale: breathe in (p. 266)

insulin: hormone produced by pancreas that causes glucose to leave blood (p. 314)

instinct: complex pattern of inborn behavior (p. 327)

interferon: human protein that fights infections caused by viruses (p. 399)

invertebrate: animal without a backbone (p. 105)

involuntary muscle: muscle not under a person's control (p. 202)

joint: place in skeleton where bones are connected to each other (p. 198)

kidneys: paired, bean-shaped organs located in middle of the back in which wastes are removed from blood (p. 283)

kilogram (kg): basic unit for measuring mass (p. 14)

kinetic energy (kuh-NET-ik): energy of moving molecules (p. 243)

kingdom: large group used to classify organisms (p. 93)

labor: repeated contraction and relaxation of uterine muscles that occur before birth (p. 373)

large intestine: organ in which water from undigested foods is absorbed (p. 237)

larva (plural—larvae): wormlike stage in an insect's life cycle which develops from an egg (p. 86)

lens: part of eye that bends light (p. 291)

leucocyte (LOO-kuh-syt): white blood cell (p. 255)

leukemia (lew-KEE-mee-uh): blood cancer (p. 454)

life cycle: series of changes or stages through which a developing organism passes during its lifetime (p. 86)

life science: study of living things (p. 9)

ligament: strong band of connective tissue that holds bones together (p. 200)

light reaction: that part of photosynthesis in which chlorophyll traps light energy from sun; water splits into hydrogen and oxygen (p. 143)

lipid: organic compound such as fat, oil, or wax (p. 32)

liter: basic unit of liquid volume equal to 1000 mL (p. 13)

liver: accessory organ of digestion that produces bile; organ of excretion that removes worn red blood cells from blood (pp. 235, 285)

lung: spongy organ of respiration (p. 262)

magnification (mag-nuh-fuh-KAY-shun): power of a microscope lens, often marked with an X (p. 52)

mammary gland: gland in which mammals produce milk for their offspring (p. 84)

marijuana: drug derived from hemp plant that causes psychological dependence (p. 352)

marrow: soft, spongy tissue in center of bone (p. 198)

mass: amount of material an object contains (p. 14)

matter: anything that has mass and takes up space (p. 28)

meiosis (my-OH-sus): kind of cell division which results in gametes that have only half the chromosome number found in body cells (p. 79)

meniscus (muh-NIS-kus): curved surface of a liquid held in a container (p. 14)

menopause: stage in human development that occurs when a woman no longer ovulates (p. 377)

menstruation: time during menstrual cycle when blood and mucus from lining of uterus flows out of the body (p. 367)

meter: basic unit of length (p. 12)

microbe: organism too small to be seen with naked eye (p. 420)

micron: 1/1000 millimeter (p. 55)

migrate: to travel long distances as seasons change (p. 41)

mineral: natural, nonliving material that people take from the earth for various uses; material, such as calcium, needed for growth and repair of body cells (pp. 185, 214)

mitochondrion (myt-uh-KAN-dree-on) (plural— mitochondria): organelle within which digested food and oxygen combine during cellular respiration (p. 58)

mitosis: duplication of chromosomes in nucleus during cell division (p. 70)

model: diagram or object that helps explain a thing or event that cannot be observed (p. 18)

mold: fungus which consists of masses of tiny threadlike structures; fossil formed from hard parts of an organism (pp. 101, 119)

molecule: smallest possible piece of a substance that has properties of that substance (p. 30)

molt: to shed an outer covering such as an exoskeleton (p. 107)

moneran: simple organism such as a bacterium that lacks a nuclear membrane (p. 97)

motor neuron: nerve cell that carries messages to muscles (p. 298)

mucus: moist, sticky substance that lines nasal passages (p. 263)

mutation (myoo-TAY-shun): sudden change in a gene or chromosome (p. 132)

mutualism: relationship in which both organisms benefit (p. 162)

narcotics: drugs such as heroin, opium, morphine, or codeine, which dull nervous system and can cause physical dependence (p. 348)

natural resource: material from the earth, such as air, water, minerals, or fuel, used by people (p. 178)

natural selection: process of survival by those organisms best suited to their environment (p. 131)

negative feedback system: system in which a change in one part shuts off another part (p. 317)

nerve cord: hollow cord along backbone of a chordate (p. 108)

nervous system: organ system which helps the body respond to changes in the environment (p. 290)

neuron: nerve cell (p. 296)

niche: needs and activities of a species in its habitat

(p. 157)

nicotine: dangerous substance in cigarette smoke which, in large amounts, can kill a person (p. 273)

nitrogen bases: paired compounds that make up steps of DNA ladder (p. 396)

nitrogenous waste: waste, such as urea, that contains the element nitrogen (p. 281)

noninfectious disease: disease that is not passed from one individual to another (p. 450)

nonrenewable resource: resource that cannot be replaced or recycled (p. 178)

nucleic acid: organic compound that stores and carries information that controls cells and determines heredity (p. 34)

nucleus (plural—nuclei): center of the atom; control center of the cell (pp. 29, 58)

nutrient: useful substance from food needed for growth or energy (p. 42)

nutrition: life process during which nutrients for energy and growth are obtained; study of food and how it affects health (pp. 42, 209)

observe: to use the five senses to gather information about surroundings (p. 15)

opposable thumb: thumb that can touch all other fingers (p. 405)

optic nerve: nerve that carries messages from eye to brain (p. 292)

organ: group of tissues that work together to do a certain job (p. 62)

organelle: part of a cell (p. 58)

organic compound: compound that contains carbon atoms (p. 32)

organism: living thing (p. 34)

organ system: group of organs that work together to carry on a certain life process (p. 195)

osmosis (ahs-MOH-sus): diffusion of water across a cell membrane (p. 246)

ovary (OHV-uh-ree) (plural—ovaries): structure in females in which egg cells are produced (p. 81)

overpopulation: condition which exists when an ecosystem has more members of a species than it can support (p. 176)

over-the-counter drugs: drugs that can be bought in a store without a doctor's prescription (p. 347)

ovulation: release of a female egg cell that occurs about every 28 days (p. 366)

oxidation: process by which a compound combines with oxygen and releases energy (p. 211)

oxygenated blood (AHK-sih-juh-nayt-ed): oxygen-rich blood (p. 250)

ozone layer: layer of gas in the atmosphere that screens out harmful ultraviolet rays from the sun (p. 176)

paleontologist (pay-lee-an-TAL-uh-jist): scientist that uses fossil evidence to study evolution (p. 404)

pancreas: accessory organ of digestion that produces pancreatic juice; endocrine gland that produces insulin and glucagon (pp. 235, 314)

parathyroid glands: four small glands that produce hormones that control levels of calcium and phosphorus in blood (p. 313)

pasteurization (pas-chuh-ruh-ZAY-shun): use of heat to kill microbes (p. 448)

pathogen: microbe that causes disease (p. 421)

penis: male reproductive organ from which sperm is released (p. 366)

peripheral nervous system: all nerves that are not part of central nervous system (p. 304)

peristalsis (per-uh-STAHL-sus): series of rhythmic muscular actions that move food along digestive system (p. 232)

petri dish: shallow, covered dish made of plastic or glass in which bacteria are cultured (p. 426)

phagocytes (FAG-uh-syts): white blood cells that surround and ingest bacteria (p. 442)

phenotype (FEE-nuh-typ): outward appearance of an organism (p. 389)

phloem (FLOH-em): plant cells which carry food produced in leaves or stored in roots to all parts of plant (p. 140)

photosynthesis: process by which plants use sunlight, carbon dioxide, and water to make food (p. 41)

phylum (FY-lum) (plural—phyla): division of a kingdom used to classify organisms (p. 93)

physical dependency: condition in which a drug abuser's body develops a tolerance for a drug (p. 348)

physical digestion: digestion during which food is broken into smaller pieces (p. 228)

physical fitness: ability to do all normal daily activities, with energy left over to handle emergencies (p. 345)

pistil: female reproductive organ of a flower (p. 148)

pituitary gland (puh-TOO-uh-ter-ee): endocrine gland that regulates activities of other endocrine glands (p. 317)

plasma: liquid part of blood (p. 256)

plasmid: ring of DNA from bacteria (p. 399)

platelets: parts of blood that clot blood (p. 256)

pleura: double membrane that covers and protects lungs (p. 264)

pollutant: harmful material added to a natural resource by humans (p. 181)

population: group of organisms of same species that live in same area (p. 155)

pore: tiny opening in skin through which perspiration is released (p. 282)

predator: animal that hunts and kills other animals for food (p. 158)

predict: to state in advance that something will take place (p. 19)

preservative: food additive that keeps food from spoiling (p. 219)

primary consumer: animal that feeds directly on plants (p. 158)

primary succession: biological succession that occurs whenever areas without life begin to support life (p. 168)

primates: order of mammals that includes shrews, lemurs, tarsiers, monkeys, apes, and humans (p. 405)

progesterone: female sex hormone that thickens the uterine wall in preparation for the arrival of an embryo (p. 315)

protein: very large organic molecules made up of amino acids; nutrient needed to repair and replace cells (pp. 32, 213)

protist: kingdom which includes both simple unicellular and multicellular organisms such as protozoa and algae (p. 98)

protozoan (proht-uh-ZOH-un) (plural—protozoa): animal-like protist which is usually unicellular (p. 98)

psychological dependency: condition that occurs when a person has a strong emotional need for a drug (p. 348)

puberty: time when secondary sex characteristics develop (p. 378)

pulmonary circulation: circulation of blood from heart to lungs and back to heart (p. 248)

pulse: surge of blood felt as heart pumps blood through blood vessels (p. 247)

pupa (plural—pupae): developmental stage in which an insect forms a covering such as a cocoon (p. 86)

purebred: organisms that always produce the same traits in their offspring (p. 383)

pus: yellow fluid that forms around a wound which consists of white blood cells, blood plasma, and bacteria (p. 256)

reasoning: power to think in an orderly and sensible way (p. 338)

receptor: special nerve cell from a sense organ (p. 291)

recessive: term used to describe a trait that is hidden or masked by a dominant trait (p. 384)

reforestation: planting of seedlings to replace trees that have been cut down (p. 182)

regeneration: process by which body parts of animals grow into new organisms (p. 76)

regulation: life process that keeps internal balance of an organism constant (p. 43)

renewable resource: natural resource that can be replaced or recycled (p. 178)

reproduction: process by which organisms produce new generations (p. 38)

respiration: life process in which organisms obtain energy from food, usually by combining with oxygen (p. 42)

respond: react (p. 35)

retina: inner lining of eye where pictures of light are projected (p. 291)

rib cage: structure made of ribs which surrounds and protects heart and lungs (p. 197)

ribosome (RY-buh-sohm): cell structure in which amino acids form proteins necessary for life processes (p. 58)

RNA: ribonucleic (ry-boh-new-KLEE-ik) acid: chemical that works with DNA to produce enzymes and proteins that determine traits (p. 396)

root: underground structure that holds a plant firmly in soil (p. 139)

root hair: extension of root cells that enables a plant to absorb water and minerals quickly (p. 139)

roughage: indigestible food such as tough fibers of

vegetables (p. 237)

saliva: mixture of juices produced by salivary glands which begin digestion in mouth (p. 231)

salivary glands: glands near mouth that produce saliva (p. 231)

scavenger: animal that does not hunt, but eats dead animals (p. 158)

science: existing knowledge of natural world and process of gathering this knowledge (p. 8)

science process skill: skill involving using scientific method (p. 15)

scientific method: an organized and logical way to solve a problem (p. 9)

secondary consumer: animal that eats primary consumers (p. 158)

secondary succession: biological succession that occurs when natural events or human activities destroy or change an existing community (p. 168)

secrete: release of a chemical substance (p. 311)

sedimentary rock: rock formed from particles deposited in layers at bottom of lakes or oceans in which fossils are found (p. 119)

seed: tiny plant embryo surrounded by food (p. 149)

self-image: idea a person has about himself or herself (p. 345)

semen: mixture of sperm and a liquid from glands which helps sperm to swim (p. 366)

semicircular canals: loop-shaped tubes in the inner ear that help maintain balance (p. 293)

sense organ: structures such as eyes, ears, mouth, nose, and skin, that help keep a human in touch with the environment (p. 291)

sepal: outermost leaf in a flower (p. 147)

sewage: waste material that flows from toilets, drains, and sewers (p. 181)

sex chromosomes: chromosomes, such as X and Y, that determine sex of individual (p. 393)

sex-linked trait: trait determined by a gene carried on the X chromosomes (p. 393)

sickle-cell disease: a genetic blood disease (p. 394)

simple reflex: reaction that does not have to be learned, such as a knee jerk (p. 298)

skeletal muscle: long, slender muscle cells which move bones (p. 202)

skull: thick, hard bones that protect brain (p. 197)

slime mold: fungus-like protist (p. 100)

sludge: solid material that remains after sewage is treated (p. 432)

small intestine: long, coiled organ in which digestion is completed (p. 235)

smooth muscle: short, slender, involuntary muscle cells found inside organs (p. 202)

solvent: substance in which chemicals dissolve (p. 41)

species: smallest classification group in which members look alike and can reproduce among themselves (p. 93)

sperm: male gamete (p. 78)

spinal column: backbone made of vertebrae

spongy layer: layer of loosely-arranged cells in which photosynthesis in leaves occurs (p. 141)

spontaneous generation: idea of life from nonlife (p. 69)

spore: tiny structure formed asexually that can grow into a new organism (p. 73)

spore case: round structure which contains thousands of asexual spores (p. 74)

stain: compound used to color cells so that they can be seen more clearly (p. 429)

stamen: male reproductive organ of a flower (p. 148)

stereoscopic vision: ability to see depth (p. 406)

sterilization: process by which all living microbes are destroyed (p. 447)

stimulants: drugs that speed up heartbeat, raise blood pressure, prevent sleep, and reduce appetite (p. 350)

stimulus (STIM-yuh-lus): change in the environment that causes an organism to react (p. 35)

stomach: pouchlike organ of digestion (p. 232)

stomate (STOH-mayt): tiny opening on the lower epidermis of a leaf (p. 141)

stroke: condition during which brain does not receive enough oxygen (p. 451)

superior vena cava: vein that returns blood from upper part of the body to right atrium (p. 249)

sweat glands: glands near surface of skin that excrete salts, urea, and water from blood (p. 282)

synapse (SIN-aps): space between two neighboring neurons (p. 297)

tadpole: larva stage of a frog (p. 86)

taiga (TY-guh): biome south of the tundra in which conifers are dominant plant life (p. 163)

tar: yellow, sticky substance in cigarette smoke that has been linked to lung cancer (p. 274)

taste bud: nerve ending in tongue that responds to bitter, sour, salty, or sweet tastes (p. 294)

technology: use of science to develop products and processes that improve quality of life (p. 21)

testosterone (teh-STAS-tuh-rohn): male hormone that results in production of sperm and appearance of secondary sex characteristics (p. 315)

thyroid gland: endocrine gland in neck (p. 312)

tissue: groups of cells that look the same and do the same job (p. 62)

trachea (TRAY-kee-uh): windpipe (p. 263)

tracheophyte (TRAY-kee-uh-fyt): plant that has vascular tissue (p. 103)

trait: characteristic of an organism (p. 128)

transport: life process by which nutrients and oxygen are carried through an organism (p. 42)

trial and error: learning by trying possible solutions until correct one is found (p. 336)

triple beam balance: instrument scientists use to measure mass (p. 14)

tumor: lump of cells which may be benign (harmless) or malignant (dangerous) (p. 452)

tundra: biome characterized by long winters and short summers (p. 163)

umbilical cord (um-BIL-i-kul): structure containing blood vessels that connects a mammal embryo with placenta (p. 85)

urea: nitrogenous waste product that comes from oxidation of amino acids (p. 281)

urine: waste made of water, salts, and urea (p. 285)

urinary bladder: sac in which urine is held until it is passed from the body (p. 285)

uterus: large, muscular organ in female mammals in which a developing embryo implants (p. 85)

valve: flap of tissue in heart and blood vessels that keeps blood flowing in one direction (p. 250)

vascular tissue: system of tubes which conducts food and water to all parts of a plant (p. 102)

vegetative propagation (VEJ-uh-tayt-iv prap-uh-GAY-shun): process by which a complete plant may develop from part of a plant (p. 76)

vein: vascular tissue located within leaves of plants; blood vessels that carry blood to heart (pp. 142, 250)

ventricle (VEN-trih-kul): one of two lower chambers of heart (p. 248)

venules: tiny veins that combine to form a vein leading back to heart (p. 253)

vertebrate: animal that has a backbone (p. 105)

vestigial structure (ve-STIG-ee-ul): structure that is reduced in size and has no function (p. 126)

villus (plural—villi): microscopic, fingerlike bump found on small intestine wall through which food is absorbed by blood (p. 236)

virus: microscopic particles which have characteristics of both living and nonliving things, some of which cause disease (p. 96)

vitamin: chemical found in small quantities in certain foods that has proven importance to the body (p. 215)

vitamin deficiency (di-FISH-un-see): disease suffered by people who do not get enough of certain vitamins (p. 216)

voluntary muscle: muscle under a person's control (p. 202)

voluntary nervous system: part of nervous system that includes nerves from sense organs and voluntary muscles (p. 304)

warm-blooded animal: animal whose body temperature remains constant regardless of outside temperature (p. 111)

xylem (ZY-lum): plant cells which carry water and minerals from roots to all parts of plant (p. 140)

yeast: one-celled fungus often used in baking bread (p. 101)

zygote (ZY-goht): fertilized egg (p. 78)

INDEX

Page numbers printed in **bold** type have illustrations or tables.

A

abiotic factors, 156
absorption, 236, 243
accessory organs, 230
acid rain, 44, **183**
acquired characteristics, 128, **129**
Acquired Immune Deficiency Syndrome (AIDS), 349, 444-46, **446**
active immunity, 443
adaptation, **37**, 37-38, **38**, **39**, 133, 407
addiction, 348, 351
additives, food, 217-20, **218**, **219**
adolescence, 375-376
ADP molecules, 270, **271**
adrenal glands, 314
adrenaline, 310, 314
aerobic bacteria, 422
agar, **426**, **427**, 427
AIDS, 349, 444-46, **446**
air pollution, 182-83, **183**, 271-72, **272**, 276
air resources, 182-83, **183**
Al-Anon, 359
Alateen, 357, 359, **359**
alcohol/alcohol abuse, **353**, 353-59, **354**, 360, 435
alcoholics, helping, 357-59, **359**
Alcoholics Anonymous (AA), 357
algae, 98-99, **99**, 423
alveoli, 264, **265**, **269**, 272
American elm tree, 150, **150**
amino acids, 32, 214, **214**
amniocentesis, 378, **378**
amnion, **370**, 372
amoeba, **70**, 70, **98**, 98
amphetamines, 350
amphibians, 82-84, **83**, **84**, 110
anaerobic bacteria, 422
analyzing, 17-18, **18**
anemia, Cooley's, 395
animal cells, 57-59, **59**, **60**
animals, **94**, 94, 105-8, 404

as consumers, 147
endangered species, 114, **184**, 184
invertebrates, 105, **106**, 106
reproduction in, 81-85
vertebrates, 105, 108-13
anther, 148
antibiotics, 443, 446
antibodies, 442-43
antigens, 442-43
aorta, **248**, 248-49
arteries, 250-54, **251**, **253**
hardening of, 450-51
pulmonary, **248**, 248, 269
arterioles, **251**, 251
arteriosclerosis, 451
arthropods, 106-7, **107**
artificial kidneys, 286
asbestos, 276
aseptic techniques, **427**, 427, 447
asexual reproduction, 72-78, 425-26
associative neurons, **298**, 298
atoms, **29**, 29-30, **30**
ATP molecules, 270, **271**
atrium, **248**, 248
Australopithecus, 408-10, **409**, **410**
autoclave, 429, **429**
autonomic nervous system, 304-5
axon, **296**, 297

B

Bacilli, 422
bacteria, 34-35, 97, 420, 421-23, **422**
anaerobic vs. aerobic, 422
controlling undesirable, 447-49
cultures, 425-29
diseases caused by, 423, **440**, 440, 441-43
helpful, 322, 423, 432-33, 435, **435**, **436**, 436
making slide of, **430**, 430
nitrifying, 160
nitrogen-fixing, 160
shapes, **34**, **422**, 422
bacteriophage, **96**, 97

ball-and-socket joint, **199**, 199
behavior, 326-43
inborn, 326-28
learned, 328-35
methods of learning, 335-39
benign tumors, 452-53
biceps, **201**, 201
bile, 235
binary fission, 72-73, 425-26, **426**
biological succession, 167-69
biologists, 9
biomes, 163-67
biosphere, 156
biotic factors, 156
bipedal, 406
birds, **111**, 111
birth, 373-74, **374**
blood, **194**, 250, 251, 254-57
blood plasma, 256
blood pressure, high, 451-52
blood vessels, 250-54, **251**, **253**
blue-green bacteria, 97
bones, 197-98, **201**, 201
botulism, 448
brain, 298, 300, **302**, 302-4, **303**, 340, 354-55, 404, 406
breastbone, **196**, 197
breast cancer, 453, 456
breathing rate, 305
breath test, **360**, 360
bronchi, 264
bronchitis, 272, 275
bryophytes, **102**, 102-3
budding, **73**, 73
buds, 76, **77**
bulb, **76**, 76

C

caffeine, 350
calcium, 198, 214
calculating, 16-17, 56, 389
Calorie (kilogram-calorie), 209, 210
calories, 33, 209, 210
cancer, 272, 274, 276, 452-54, **452**, **453**, **454**, 456